T0353436

Implementing Computational Intelligence Techniques for Security Systems Design

Yousif Abdullatif Albastaki
Ahlia University, Bahrain

Wasan Awad
Ahlia University, Bahrain

A volume in the Advances in
Computational Intelligence and
Robotics (ACIR) Book Series

Published in the United States of America by
   IGI Global
   Information Science Reference (an imprint of IGI Global)
   701 E. Chocolate Avenue
   Hershey PA, USA 17033
   Tel: 717-533-8845
   Fax: 717-533-8661
   E-mail: cust@igi-global.com
   Web site: http://www.igi-global.com

Library of Congress Cataloging-in-Publication Data

Names: Albastaki, Yousif, 1962- editor. | Awad, Wasan, 1969- editor.
Title: Implementing computational intelligence techniques for security
   systems design / Yousif Abdullatif Albastaki, Wasan Awad, editors.
Description: Hershey, PA : Information Science Reference, 2020. | Includes
   bibliographical references. | Summary: "This book explores the
   applications of computational intelligence and other advanced techniques
   in information security"-- Provided by publisher.
Identifiers: LCCN 2019039269 (print) | LCCN 2019039270 (ebook) | ISBN
   9781799824183 (h/c) | ISBN 9781799824190 (s/c) | ISBN 9781799824206
   (eISBN)
Subjects: LCSH: Computer networks--Security measures. | Data protection. |
   Security systems--Design and construction. | Computational intelligence.
Classification: LCC TK5105.59 .I437 2020 (print) | LCC TK5105.59 (ebook)
   | DDC 006.3--dc23
LC record available at https://lccn.loc.gov/2019039269
LC ebook record available at https://lccn.loc.gov/2019039270

This book is published in the IGI Global book series Advances in Computational Intelligence and
Robotics (ACIR) (ISSN: 2327-0411; eISSN: 2327-042X)

British Cataloguing in Publication Data
A Cataloguing in Publication record for this book is available from the British Library.

All work contributed to this book is new, previously-unpublished material.
The views expressed in this book are those of the authors, but not necessarily of the publisher.

For electronic access to this publication, please contact: eresources@igi-global.com.

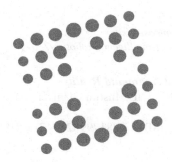

Advances in Computational Intelligence and Robotics (ACIR) Book Series

ISSN:2327-0411
EISSN:2327-042X

Editor-in-Chief: Ivan Giannoccaro, University of Salento, Italy

MISSION

While intelligence is traditionally a term applied to humans and human cognition, technology has progressed in such a way to allow for the development of intelligent systems able to simulate many human traits. With this new era of simulated and artificial intelligence, much research is needed in order to continue to advance the field and also to evaluate the ethical and societal concerns of the existence of artificial life and machine learning.

The **Advances in Computational Intelligence and Robotics (ACIR) Book Series** encourages scholarly discourse on all topics pertaining to evolutionary computing, artificial life, computational intelligence, machine learning, and robotics. ACIR presents the latest research being conducted on diverse topics in intelligence technologies with the goal of advancing knowledge and applications in this rapidly evolving field.

COVERAGE

- Adaptive and Complex Systems
- Artificial Life
- Cognitive Informatics
- Heuristics
- Computational Intelligence
- Computer Vision
- Pattern Recognition
- Brain Simulation
- Algorithmic Learning
- Computational Logic

IGI Global is currently accepting manuscripts for publication within this series. To submit a proposal for a volume in this series, please contact our Acquisition Editors at Acquisitions@igi-global.com or visit: http://www.igi-global.com/publish/.

Titles in this Series

For a list of additional titles in this series, please visit:
https://www.igi-global.com/book-series/advances-computational-intelligence-robotics/73674

Managerial Challenges and Social Impacts of Virtual and Augmentd Reality
Sandra Maria Correia Loureiro (Business Research Unit (BRU-IUL), Instituto Universitário de Lisboa (ISCTE-IUL), Lisboa, Portugal)
Engineering Science Reference • © 2020 • 318pp • H/C (ISBN: 9781799828747) • US $195.00

Innovations, Algorithms, and Applications in Cognitive Informatics and Natural Intelligence
Kwok Tai Chui (The Open University of Hong Kong, Hong Kong) Miltiadis D. Lytras (The American College of Greece, Greece) Ryan Wen Liu (Wuhan University of Technology, China) and Mingbo Zhao (Donghua University, China)
Engineering Science Reference • © 2020 • 403pp • H/C (ISBN: 9781799830382) • US $235.00

Avatar-Based Control, Estimation, Communications, and Development of Neuron Multi-Functional Technology Platforms
Vardan Mkrttchian (HHH University, Australia) Ekaterina Aleshina (Penza State University, Russia) and Leyla Gamidullaeva (Penza State University, Russia)
Engineering Science Reference • © 2020 • 355pp • H/C (ISBN: 9781799815815) • US $245.00

Handbook of Research on Fireworks Algorithms and Swarm Intelligence
Ying Tan (Peking University, China)
Engineering Science Reference • © 2020 • 400pp • H/C (ISBN: 9781799816591) • US $295.00

Handbook of Research on Emerging Trends and Applications of Machine Learning
Arun Solanki (Gautam Buddha University, India) Sandeep Kumar (Amity University, Jaipur, India) and Anand Nayyar (Duy Tan University, Da Nang, Vietnam)
Engineering Science Reference • © 2020 • 674pp • H/C (ISBN: 9781522596431) • US $375.00

For an entire list of titles in this series, please visit:
https://www.igi-global.com/book-series/advances-computational-intelligence-robotics/73674

701 East Chocolate Avenue, Hershey, PA 17033, USA
Tel: 717-533-8845 x100 • Fax: 717-533-8661
E-Mail: cust@igi-global.com • www.igi-global.com

Editorial Advisory Board

Table of Contents

Preface.. xvi

Acknowledgment xxiii

Chapter 1
Applications of Computational Intelligence in Computing Security: A Review...1
    Yousif Abdullatif Albastaki, Ahlia University, Bahrain

Chapter 2
A Hybrid Connectionist/ Substitution Approach for Data Encryption 23
    Raed Abu Zitar, Ajman University, UAE
    Muhammed Jassem Al-Muhammed, American University of Madaba,
        Jordan

Chapter 3
Improving Spam Email Filtering Systems Using Data Mining Techniques........43
    Wasan Shaker Awad, Ahlia University, Bahrain
    Wafa M. Rafiq, Ahlia University, Bahrain

Chapter 4
Odor Sensing Techniques: A Biometric Person Authentication Approach 73
    Yousif A. Albastaki, Ahlia University, Bahrain

Chapter 5
Agent-Based Intrusion Detection in Wireless Networks 97
    Leila Mechtri, Badji Mokhtar University, Algeria
    Fatiha Tolba Djemili, Badji Mokhtar University, Algeria
    Salim Ghanemi, Badji Mokhtar University, Algeria

Chapter 6
Using an Artificial Neural Network to Improve Email Security 131
    Mohamed Abdulhussain Ali Madan Maki, Ahlia University, Bahrain
    Suresh Subramanian, Ahlia University, Bahrain

Chapter 7
A Review of Machine Learning Techniques for Anomaly Detection in Static
Graphs 146
    Hesham M. Al-Ammal, University of Bahrain, Bahrain

Chapter 8
Composite Discrete Logarithm Problem and a Reconstituted ElGamal
Cryptosystem Based on the Problem: New ElGamal Cryptosystems With
Some Special Sequences and Composite ElGamal Cryptosystem 163
    Çağla Özyılmaz, Ondokuz Mayıs University, Turkey
    Ayşe Nallı, Karabuk University, Turkey

Chapter 9
Characteristic Analysis of Side Channel Attacks and Various Power Analysis
Attack Techniques 182
    Shaminder Kaur, Chitkara University, Punjab, India
    Balwinder Singh, C-DAC Mohali, India
    Harsimran Jit Kaur, Institute of Engineering and Technology, Chitkara
        University, Punjab, India

Chapter 10
Bahrain Government Information Security Framework: CyberTrust Program . 196
    Yusuf Mohammed Mothanna, Information and eGovernment Authority,
        Bahrain
    Yousif Abdullatif Albastaki, Ahlia University, Bahrain
    Talal Mohamed Delaim, Information and eGovernment Authority,
        Bahrain

Chapter 11
Critical Cybersecurity Threats: Frontline Issues Faced by Bahraini
Organizations 210
    Adel Ismail Al-Alawi, University of Bahrain, Bahrain
    Sara Abdulrahman Al-Bassam, The Social Development Office of His
        Highness the Prime Minister's Diwan, Kuwait
    Arpita A. Mehrotra, Royal University for Women, Bahrain

Chapter 12
Building New Relationships: Social Media Trustworthiness in Gulf
Cooperation Countries 230
    Afaf Mubarak Bugawa, Arabian Gulf University, Bahrain
    Noora Abdulla Janahi, Arabian Gulf University, Bahrain

Chapter 13
Cybersecurity: Cybercrime Prevention in Higher Learning Institutions 255
    Adel Ismail Al-Alawi, University of Bahrain, Bahrain
    Arpita A. Mehrotra, Royal University for Women, Bahrain
    Sara Abdulrahman Al-Bassam, The Social Development Office of His
        Highness the Kuwait Prime Minister's Diwan, Kuwait

Chapter 14
Cyber Security, IT Governance, and Performance: A Review of the Current
Literature 275
    Abdalmuttaleb M. A. Musleh Al-Sartawi, Ahlia University, Bahrain
    Anjum Razzaque, Ahlia University, Bahrain

Compilation of References 289

About the Contributors 323

Index 330

Detailed Table of Contents

Preface... xvi

Acknowledgment... xxiii

Chapter 1
Applications of Computational Intelligence in Computing Security: A Review...1
Yousif Abdullatif Albastaki, Ahlia University, Bahrain

This chapter is an introductory chapter that attempts to highlight the concept of computational intelligence and its application in the field of computing security; it starts with a brief description of the underlying principles of artificial intelligence and discusses the role of computational intelligence in overcoming conventional artificial intelligence limitations. The chapter then briefly introduces various tools or components of computational intelligence such as neural networks, evolutionary computing, swarm intelligence, artificial immune systems, and fuzzy systems. The application of each component in the field of computing security is highlighted.

Chapter 2
A Hybrid Connectionist/ Substitution Approach for Data Encryption................23
Raed Abu Zitar, Ajman University, UAE
Muhammed Jassem Al-Muhammed, American University of Madaba,
Jordan

The authors believe that the hybridization of two different approaches results in more complex encryption outcomes. The proposed method combines a symbolic approach, which is a table substitution method, with another paradigm that models real-life neurons (connectionist approach). This hybrid model is compact, nonlinear, and parallel. The neural network approach focuses on generating keys (weights) based on a feedforward neural network architecture that works as a mirror. The weights are used as an input for the substitution method. The hybrid model is verified and validated as a successful encryption method.

Chapter 3

Improving Spam Email Filtering Systems Using Data Mining Techniques 43

Wasan Shaker Awad, Ahlia University, Bahrain
Wafa M. Rafiq, Ahlia University, Bahrain

Email is the most popular choice of communication due to its low-cost and easy accessibility, which makes email spam a major issue. Emails can be incorrectly marked by a spam filter and legitimate emails can get lost in the spam folder or the spam emails can deluge the users' inboxes. Therefore, various methods based on statistics and machine learning have been developed to classify emails accurately. In this chapter, the existing spam filtering methods were studied comprehensively, and a spam email classifier based on the genetic algorithm was proposed. The proposed algorithm was successful in achieving high accuracy by reducing the rate of false positives, but at the same time, it also maintained an acceptable rate of false negatives. The proposed algorithm was tested on 2000 emails from the two popular spam datasets, Enron and LingSpam, and the accuracy was found to be nearly 90%. The results showed that the genetic algorithm is an effective method for spam classification and with further enhancements that will provide a more robust spam filter.

Chapter 4

Odor Sensing Techniques: A Biometric Person Authentication Approach 73

Yousif A. Albastaki, Ahlia University, Bahrain

With advances in technology and the never-ending goal of making life simpler for humans, it is obvious that odor sensing could lead to a better tomorrow. This chapter addressed the multiple cases in which odor sensing could be used and applied specially when identifying individuals. Various research has been carried out in this field using multiple other methods to assist create this field of studies. Most of research has been specifically focused on a single industry or field of application of odor sensing techniques. The work focused on and developed a system using artificial neural network with odor sensing techniques and laid the foundation for a general-purpose system that can be used for authentication and identification of individuals.

Chapter 5

Agent-Based Intrusion Detection in Wireless Networks 97

Leila Mechtri, Badji Mokhtar University, Algeria
Fatiha Tolba Djemili, Badji Mokhtar University, Algeria
Salim Ghanemi, Badji Mokhtar University, Algeria

The need for effective, optimal, and adaptive intrusion detection systems that fit wireless networks' requirements caused agent-based intrusion detection systems to prevail though the complexity and challenges entailed by their deployment. This chapter presents the recent achievements in terms of the proposed frameworks, architectures, and implementations for the application of agent technology to intrusion detection in wireless networks. The chapter highlights their main features, strengths, and limitations. It also discusses the main issues that most existing works do not address like IDS security and proposes solutions to cope with some of the presented problems.

Chapter 6

Using an Artificial Neural Network to Improve Email Security.......................131
    Mohamed Abdulhussain Ali Madan Maki, Ahlia University, Bahrain
    Suresh Subramanian, Ahlia University, Bahrain

Email is one of the most widely used features of internet, and it is the most convenient method of transferring messages electronically. However, email productivity has been decreased due to phishing attacks, spam emails, and viruses. Recently, filtering the email flow is a challenging task for researchers due to techniques that spammers used to avoid spam detection. This research proposes an email spam filtering system that filters the spam emails using artificial back propagation neural network (BPNN) technique. Enron1 dataset was used, and after the preprocessing, TF-IDF algorithm was used to extract features and convert them into frequency. To select best features, mutual information technique has been applied. Performance of classifiers were measured using BoW, n-gram, and chi-squared methods. BPNN model was compared with Naïve Bayes and support vector machine based on accuracy, precision, recall, and f1-score. The results show that the proposed email spam system achieved 98.6% accuracy with cross-validation.

Chapter 7

A Review of Machine Learning Techniques for Anomaly Detection in Static
Graphs 146
    Hesham M. Al-Ammal, University of Bahrain, Bahrain

Detection of anomalies in a given data set is a vital step in several applications in cybersecurity; including intrusion detection, fraud, and social network analysis. Many of these techniques detect anomalies by examining graph-based data. Analyzing graphs makes it possible to capture relationships, communities, as well as anomalies. The advantage of using graphs is that many real-life situations can be easily modeled by a graph that captures their structure and inter-dependencies. Although anomaly detection in graphs dates back to the 1990s, recent advances in research utilized machine learning methods for anomaly detection over graphs. This chapter will concentrate on static graphs (both labeled and unlabeled), and the chapter summarizes some of these recent studies in machine learning for anomaly detection in graphs. This includes methods such as support vector machines, neural networks, generative neural networks, and deep learning methods. The chapter will reflect the success and challenges of using these methods in the context of graph-based anomaly detection.

Chapter 8

Composite Discrete Logarithm Problem and a Reconstituted ElGamal
Cryptosystem Based on the Problem: New ElGamal Cryptosystems With
Some Special Sequences and Composite ElGamal Cryptosystem 163

Çağla Özyılmaz, Ondokuz Mayıs University, Turkey
Ayşe Nallı, Karabuk University, Turkey

In this chapter, the authors have defined a new ElGamal cryptosystem by using the power Fibonacci sequence module m. Then they have defined a new sequence module m and the other ElGamal cryptosystem by using the new sequence. In addition, they have compared that the new ElGamal cryptosystems and ElGamal cryptosystem in terms of cryptography. Then the authors have defined the third ElGamal cryptosystem. They have, particularly, called the new system as composite ElGamal cryptosystem. The authors made an application of composite ElGamal cryptosystem. Finally, the authors have compared that composite ElGamal cryptosystem and ElGamal cryptosystem in terms of cryptography and they have obtained that composite ElGamal cryptosystem is more advantageous than ElGamal cryptosystem.

Chapter 9

Characteristic Analysis of Side Channel Attacks and Various Power Analysis
Attack Techniques 182

Shaminder Kaur, Chitkara University, Punjab, India
Balwinder Singh, C-DAC Mohali, India
Harsimran Jit Kaur, Institute of Engineering and Technology, Chitkara
    University, Punjab, India

Embedded systems have a plethora of security solutions and encryption protocols that can protect them against a multitude of attacks. Hardware engineers infuse lot of time and effort in implementing cryptographic algorithms, keeping the analysis of design constraints into rumination. When it comes to designs in potential hostile environment, engineers face a challenge for building resistance-free embedded systems against attacks called side channel attacks. Therefore, there is a strong need to address issues related to side channel attacks. This chapter will provide an insight into the field of hardware security, and will provide a deep investigation of various types of side channel attacks and better understanding of various power analysis tools, which will further give researchers a vision to build efficient and secure systems in order to thwart attacks. This chapter mainly focuses on passive attacks as compared to active attacks since passive attacks are easy to perform and lot of research is going on these attacks.

Chapter 10
Bahrain Government Information Security Framework: CyberTrust Program .196
  Yusuf Mohammed Mothanna, Information and eGovernment Authority,
    Bahrain
  Yousif Abdullatif Albastaki, Ahlia University, Bahrain
  Talal Mohamed Delaim, Information and eGovernment Authority,
    Bahrain

Information technology is perceived as an important enabler for government entities to accomplish their goals. The proliferation of electronic government services that can provide value for citizens and residents have pushed governments all over the world to adopt and deploy these services. However, governments have realized that it is critical to build proper defense to protect the information. Implementing information security by using international or national information security frameworks helps organizations to ensure the safeguard of information assets. This chapter reviews useful information security frameworks. Also, this chapter provides a proposed information security framework implemented in the Government of Bahrain, which is called CyberTrust Program. This framework was developed based on best practices and local resources and culture.

Chapter 11
Critical Cybersecurity Threats: Frontline Issues Faced by Bahraini
Organizations 210
  Adel Ismail Al-Alawi, University of Bahrain, Bahrain
  Sara Abdulrahman Al-Bassam, The Social Development Office of His
    Highness the Prime Minister's Diwan, Kuwait
  Arpita A. Mehrotra, Royal University for Women, Bahrain

One common reason for cybercrime is the goal of damaging a business by hacking or destroying important information. Another such reason is the criminal's goal of gaining financially from the hack. This chapter analyzes Bahraini organizations' vulnerability to digital security threats. It has used qualitative research to analyze industry performance. Moreover, with the support of secondary research, it has also explored cybersecurity threats faced by such organizations. The discussion based on secondary data analysis has explored two major aspects of Bahraini organizations and the cybersecurity threats they face. Firstly, the data and finances of both sectors are at huge risk in Bahraini organizations. Secondly, one important aspect of exploration has been to identify the most frequently encountered forms of cybercrime. Its analysis reveals that the kind of cybersecurity threat that a business is most likely to face is cyberwarfare. This may affect two rival businesses while they are competing with each other. Competitors' data may be destroyed or hacked—leading to long-term losses.

Chapter 12

Building New Relationships: Social Media Trustworthiness in Gulf
Cooperation Countries 230

    Afaf Mubarak Bugawa, Arabian Gulf University, Bahrain

    Noora Abdulla Janahi, Arabian Gulf University, Bahrain

Given the current widespread popularity of social media, such as Twitter, Instagram, Snapchat, and many other applications, understanding users' attitudes and usage behavior of social media applications becomes a necessity in order to develop future placements of such technologies and increase the level of trust among the users. Therefore, the aim of this chapter is to shed light on the impact of trustworthiness of social media on the intention to use it. Data is gathered through a quantitative method, in which a questionnaire is used as a primary data. A convenient sampling is applied, in which the most easily accessible managers and employees in Ministry of Interior in Bahrain are chosen. The results demonstrate that there is a significant positive relationship between trustworthiness and intention to use social media. The study recommends future works to study the impact of security awareness on the usage of social media in public sector in Bahrain.

Chapter 13

Cybersecurity: Cybercrime Prevention in Higher Learning Institutions 255

    Adel Ismail Al-Alawi, University of Bahrain, Bahrain

    Arpita A. Mehrotra, Royal University for Women, Bahrain

    Sara Abdulrahman Al-Bassam, The Social Development Office of His

        Highness the Kuwait Prime Minister's Diwan, Kuwait

The internet has revolutionized the way people communicate, how they manage their business, and even how they conduct their studies. Organizations can conduct meetings virtually and store all their data online. With this convenience, however, comes the risk of cybercrime (CC). Some of the world's most renowned organizations have found themselves having to incur huge recovery costs after falling prey to CC. Higher learning institutions' databases are increasingly falling victim to CCs, owing to the vast amounts of personal and research data they harbor. Despite this, the area of CCs in learning institutions remains understudied. This chapter seeks to identify how CC is manifested in such institutions and the specific cybersecurity measures that stakeholders could use to minimize their exposure to the same. The qualitative case study was designed to explore the research questions, and collected data through semistructured interviews. The findings showed hacking, phishing, and spoofing as the most common manifestations of cybercrime in higher learning institutions.

Chapter 14
Cyber Security, IT Governance, and Performance: A Review of the Current
Literature..275
Abdalmuttaleb M. A. Musleh Al-Sartawi, Ahlia University, Bahrain
Anjum Razzaque, Ahlia University, Bahrain

Cybersecurity is an emerging field with a growing body of literature and publications.
It is fundamentally based in computer science and computer engineering but has
recently gained popularity in business management. Despite the explosion of
cybersecurity, there is a scarcity of literature on the definition of the term 'Cybers
Security' and how it is situated within different contexts. Henceforth, this chapter
presents a review of the work related to cybersecurity, within different contexts,
mainly IT governance and firm performance context. The work reviewed is separated
into four main categories: the importance of cybersecurity and how it is measured,
corporate governance and IT governance, IT governance mechanisms, and financial
performance measures.

Compilation of References 289

About the Contributors 323

Index 330

Preface

The explosive growth of computer systems and their network-based interconnections has increased organizations' dependence on the information stored and communicated through these systems. This, in turn, has led to increased awareness of the need for data protection. Therefore, in information security and cryptology, a lot of work has been done.

The design of algorithmic models to solve increasingly complicated issues is a significant thrust in algorithmic growth. By modelling biological and natural intelligence, enormous accomplishments have been gained, leading in so-called Computational Intelligence. These Computational Intelligence Algorithms (CIAs) include artificial neural networks, evolutionary computation, swarm intelligence, artificial immune systems, and fuzzy systems. CIAs and information security have become an agenda issue in various academic and professional research works. It has become recognized as a significant source of competitive advantage by many authors and researchers.

In latest years, there has been a hype about Artificial Intelligence (AI) and its related technologies that enhance industry and academia in academia research and business. AI which encapsulates Machine learning (ML), Deep leaning (DNN) and computational Intelligence (CI) show up in countless articles out of the technology motivated ones. Computational Intelligence has the potential of estimating both continuous and discrete function

Computational intelligence includes ideas, paradigms, algorithms and implementations for practical adaptation and self-organization that allow or promote suitable actions (smart conduct) in complicated and evolving settings. Although the applications of CI (and other advanced techniques) in information security has been widely discussed by many academicians and practitioners, there is no specific book to discuss and provide information on how we can apply the CI techniques to solve the problems of information security.

IEEE Computational Intelligence Society describes as the theory, design, application and development of biologically and linguistically motivated computational paradigms. Neural Networks, Fuzzy Systems and Evolutionary Computation have historically been the three main pillars of CI. However, many computer paradigms inspired by nature have evolved over time. CI is therefore an evolving field and currently includes computing paradigms such as ambient intelligence, artificial life, cultural learning, artificial endocrine networks, social reasoning, and artificial hormone networks in addition to the three main constituents.

Computational Intelligence plays an important role in the development of successful smart systems, including computing security in general and cyber security. Therefore, this book has a goal of providing the opportunity for industry and academic and related researchers belonging to the different, vast communities of Computational Intelligence and Information Security to contribute in enhancing this field of study by sharing their work and experience in the field.

This book is an attempt to increase information security awareness in organizations by providing a clear direction for the effective implementation of information security and computational intelligence, which could improve organizational learning and performance excellence. The book covers the most important concepts and key issues which relate CI to information security and cover emerging practices in information security.

The book presents the most important achievements in solving security problems using CI techniques such as GA and genetic programming are presented. The aim is to show the applicability of these techniques in solving problems, in addition to provide interested researchers with an overview of the new methodologies and new directions in information security.

The book is divided into two parts, part one encompasses chapter one to chapter eight which focuses on the utilization of computing intelligence in solving computing security related issues. Part two of the book encompasses chapter nine to chapter 14 which covers supporting security and cyber security issues to be considered when tackling computational intelligence systems.

Chapter 1 is an introductory chapter which describes and to highlights the concept of computational intelligence and its application in the field of computing security. The chapter begins with a brief description of the underlying artificial intelligence concepts and addresses the role of machine intelligence in overcoming the shortcomings of traditional artificial intelligence. Then the chapter briefly discusses various computational intelligence techniques or modules such as Neural Networks, Evolutionary Computing, Swarm Intelligence, Artificial Immune Systems, and Fuzzy Systems. This chapter focused on evaluating several computer intelligence algorithms with an emphasis on applications of computer security and cyber security issues. As a conclusion, this chapter attempts to demonstrate that CI systems can recreate behaviours contained in learning sequences, create inference rules and generalize knowledge in situations where assumptions are expected to be made or classified based on previously established categories.

Chapter 2 claims that the hybridization of two different approaches results in more complex encryption outcomes. Therefore, this chapter proposes a method which combined a symbolic approach based on a table substitution method with a paradigm that models real-life neurons. The overall research idea presented in this chapter adapts a nonlinear and parallel compact hybrid model with a neural network approach which focuses on generating weights based on a feedforward neural architecture that works ass a mirror. The author(s) claim that different layers of encryption /decryption and neural mapping will make it extremely difficult for hackers to decode the encrypted text. Finally, that chapter concludes that with an appropriate selection of architecture and training parameters and with the availability of reasonable hardware, blocks of text or input data can be efficiently encrypted in a manner very competent to traditional methods.

Chapter 3 demonstrates how increasing the accuracy of spam filters using genetic algorithms might result in improving classification rate of emails, consequently decreasing the high email traffic accounted to spam and eventually reducing load taken by mail servers. The chapter starts by claiming that emails can be incorrectly marked by a spam filter and as a result legitimate emails can get lost in the spam folder or the spam emails can deluge the users' inbox. Therefore, this chapter described some existing spam filtering methods and proposed a spam email classifier based on the Genetic algorithm to reduce marking legitimate emails as spams. The proposed algorithm demonstrated successfully in achieving high accuracy by reducing the rate of false positives but at the same time it also maintained an acceptable rate of false negatives. Finally, the chapter describes how the proposed algorithm was tested on 2000 emails from the two popular spam datasets, Enron and LingSpam, and the accuracy was found to be nearly 90%. As a conclusion this chapter claims that the results showed that the employing Genetic algorithm is an effective method for spam classification and with further enhancements that will provide a more robust spam filter.

Chapter 4 describes how to design a machine-learning -based system for detecting human body odor to identify individuals. The proposed system is capable to be trained on many body odors using different types of sensors. The research work in this chapter adapts artificial neural network as its machine learning algorithm together with OMX-GR semiconductor sensor for collecting body odors. The scheme established in this chapter manged to distinguish between different kinds of odors with a precision of between 93-100 percent. The chapter claims that using Artificial Neural Networks can demonstrate a very effective results with smell sensors to detect multiple odors owing to the big quantity of information engaged in the nature of the issue and ANN's ability to learn and train further as more information is supplied, thereby improving its accuracy. The chapter then described some limitations and constraints affecting of this research study such as the smell sensor used in this study is an OMX-GR sensor that was old. Because of this, the technique of information collection had to be adjusted to the restriction of the sensor. Finally, the chapter concludes that the proposed system was trained and tested with two different types of body odors collected from two individuals with a very encouraging and promising result.

Chapter 5 presents recent developments in the proposed systems, architectures and implementations for the use of agent software in wireless network intrusion detection through highlighting their main features, strengths and limitations. It also discusses the main issues that most existing related works did not address like IDS security and proposes solutions to cope with some of the presented problems. The chapter then describes key notions related to the field of intrusion detection in wireless networks and presents a literature review highlighting the recent achievements in the field of the study by identifying static agent based IDSs, mobile agent based IDSs, and hybrid agent based IDSs as key points finding of the review process. The chapter concludes that the scalability, performance and fault tolerance can be improved using agents to perform intrusion detection tasks. In addition, agents proved their utility in overcoming some MANET/WSN related problems such as the constrained resources and the heterogeneity of platforms. Finally, the chapter shows that the use of agents and mainly mobile agents might bring new vulnerabilities to the network.

Chapter 6 focuses on how email productivity has been decreased due to security issues such as phishing attack, spam emails and virus; with a highlight is spotted on how filtering the email flow is demonstrating a challenging task to researchers due to techniques that spammers used to avoid spam detection. The chapter proposes an email spam filtering system that filters the spam emails using Artificial Back Propagation Neural Network (BPNN) technique by utilizing Enron1 dataset to extract features and transform them into frequency after the pre-processing TF-IDF algorithm. The chapter then applied mutual information technique to choose best feature to allow measuring performance of classifiers using BoW, n-gram and chi-squared methods. The chapter then contrasted BPNN with Naïve Bayes and Support Vector Machine based on accuracy, precision, recall and f1-score. Finally, the chapter concluded with demonstrating how the proposed emails spam system achieved 98.6% accuracy with cross-validation.

Chapter 7 presents the detection of anomalies in data sets with an emphasis on how vital it is many cybersecurity applications such as intrusion detection, fraud, and social network analysis. The chapter then describes many of these techniques and how it detects anomalies by examining graph-based data explaining that analysing graphs makes it possible to capture relationships, communities, as well as anomalies. The advantage of using graphs technique is identified by that many real-life situations can be easily modelled by a graph that captures their structure and inter-dependencies. The chapter then claims that even anomaly detection in graphs dates to the 1990s, recent advances in research utilized machine learning methods for anomaly detection over graphs. The chapter focuses on static graphs (both labelled and unlabelled), with the summary of recent studies in machine learning for anomaly detection in graphs by including different techniques such as Support Vector Machines, Neural Networks, Generative Neural Networks, and Deep Learning Methods. The chapter then concludes that there has been a surge of recent activity in community-based anomaly detection in graphs and how this research work demonstrated a great promise for new results and better algorithms even that recent advances in high performance computing and big data have also not been fully utilized.

Chapter 8 focuses on asymmetric cryptography and how it cited that discrete logarithm problem which is one of the mathematical difficult problems that are used in asymmetric cryptography and ElGamal cryptosystem based on the discrete logarithm problem. The chapter proposes a new discrete logarithm problem and new ElGamal cryptosystem with new applications. The chapter defined new ElGamal cryptosystem using the power Fibonacci sequence module m by defining a new sequence module m and the other ElGamal cryptosystem by utalizing the new sequence. In addition, chapter compared the new ElGamal cryptosystems and ElGamal cryptosystem in terms of cryptography and defined the third ElGamal cryptosystem called composite ElGamal cryptosystem. Finally, the chapter presented an application of composite ElGamal cryptosystem and compared that composite ElGamal cryptosystem and ElGamal cryptosystem in terms of cryptography and concluded that composite ElGamal cryptosystem is more advantageous than ElGamal cryptosystem.

Chapter 9 describes an in-depth investigation of different types of side channel attacks and provides a better understanding of various power analysis tools, which will further give researchers a vision to build efficient and secure systems in order to thwart attacks. This chapter mainly focuses on passive attacks as compared to active attacks since passive attacks are claimed to be easy to perform as so many research works are tackling these types of attacks. The chapter claims that although many mathematical models and different encryption algorithms, countless embedded devices are becoming victim to side channel attacks every day and malicious attackers have become smart enough to impose threats on them and to build an attack resistant free embedded device, a hardware engineer has to understand their threats. The chapter then attempts to describe and analyse the properties of side channel attacks viz power attacks in detail that aim to break the security of embedded systems. Different types. Various types of power analysis techniques are also discussed in this chapter with some countermeasures to power attack are also briefly discussed. The chapter concludes that in era of IOT and embedded systems, hardware and software developers both needs to join hands and put additional efforts in tranquillizing the effects of attacks on embedded devices

Chapter 10 aims at reviewing and evaluating different information security frameworks such as COBIT and Critical Security Controls (CSC). The chapter then investigates the needs of the government of the Kingdom Bahrain supported with the findings from the review process, proposes an information security framework named CyberTrusts program to be implemented in the Government of Bahrain, this framework was developed based on best practices and local resources and culture. The chapter mainly focuses on and describing the Bahraini government initiatives and developed a CyberTrust Program that helps to enhance the level of information security in government entities. Finally, the chapter concludes with a set of recommendations to improve and enhance this framework.

Chapter 11 aims to explore cybersecurity issues and to suggest techniques of securing and improving the existing security problems in Bahraini organizations. The chapter starts by addressing various holes in which the cybersecurity of Bahraini organizations can be breached and are currently being breached through analyzing these organizations' vulnerability to digital security threats. The chapter adopts a qualitative research methodology to analyze industry performance with the support of secondary research, it has also explored cybersecurity threats faced by such organizations. The chapter then identifies two major aspects of Bahraini organizations and the cybersecurity threats they face, firstly, the data and finances of both sectors are at huge risk in Bahraini organizations and secondly, one important aspect of exploration has been to identify the most frequently encountered forms of cybercrime. Finally, the chapter concludes by showing the results of its analysis which reveals that the kind of cybersecurity threat that a business is most likely to face is cyberwarfare which may affect two rival businesses while they are competing with each other which may results on competitors' data may be destroyed or hacked—leading to long-term losses.

Chapter 12 aims to discuss the current widespread popularity of social media, such as Twitter, Instagram, Snapchat, and many other applications, with a focus on understanding users' attitude and usage behavior of social media applications and how it is becoming a necessity in order to develop future placements of such technologies and increase the level of trust among the users. After evaluating Web 2.0 technologies and social media technologies, the chapter, proposes a framework for users' trust and shows how it is built to study the impact of trustworthiness of social media on the intention to use it among users. The chapter then describes the case of Ministry of Interior in the Kingdom of Bahrain to link the conceptual framework developed to practice. The chapter also describes how data is gathered through a quantitative research method, in which a questionnaire is used as a primary data and a convenient sampling is applied, in which the most easily accessible managers and employees in Ministry of Interior in Bahrain are chosen. Finally, the chapter concludes by showing how the results demonstrate that there is a significant positive relationship between trustworthiness and intention to use social media with a recommendation for future works to study the impact of security awareness on the usage of social media in public sector in Bahrain.

Chapter 13 focuses on cybercrime within higher learning institutions and it provides insight into the factors that predispose such institutions to cybercrime, the ways in which the same is manifested, and the measures that could be used to minimize the risk of exposure. The chapter then argues that many of the world's most renowned organizations have found themselves having to incur huge recovery costs after falling prey to cybercrime, additionally, many higher learning institutions' databases are increasingly falling victim to cybercrimes, owing to the vast amounts of personal and research data they harbour. The chapter then explores how cybercrime is manifested in such institutions and the specific cybersecurity measures that stakeholders could use to minimize their exposure to the same. The chapter concludes its findings by showing how hacking, phishing, and spoofing as the most common manifestations of cybercrime in higher learning institutions.

Chapter 14 is a review chapter which describes the work related to cyber security, within different contexts, mainly IT governance and firm performance context. The work reviewed is classified in four main categories: the importance of cybersecurity and how it is measured, corporate governance and IT governance, IT governance mechanisms, and financial performance measures. The chapter focused on the lack of collaboration across disciplines such as computer science and business management and identified the need for more comprehensive standard terminology for both cyber security and broader cyber research. The chapter then argues that to guarantee that different firms are working efficiently with improved financial performance level, they must first understand the term and scope of cyber security system, since it provides a higher stage of security for both users and workers. The chapter finally, recommends that training employees is most important aspects that increase their knowledge about day to day enhancement.

Acknowledgment

The authors wish to express their sincere thanks for all people who participated in the development and evaluation of the work in this book. The authors re especially grateful to IGI Global publishing and their representatives for administering and monitoring the process of the development of the manuscript and for exercising such care and skill to see the work of this book through to publication. Thanks also goes to all who participated in the review process of the chapters of the book.

Authors would also like to thank Adam Leeman for communicating, correcting errors and careful reading of the various materials during the process of developing the book. Thanks also go to Thabet Albastaki for his reading and administering the material in this book and for communicating with various parties during the process of Finalizing of the material covered by the book.

Yousif Abdullatif Albastaki
Ahlia University, Bahrain

Wasan Awad
Ahlia University, Bahrain

Chapter 1
Applications of Computational Intelligence in Computing Security:
A Review

Yousif Abdullatif Albastaki
https://orcid.org/0000-0002-6866-2268
Ahlia University, Bahrain

ABSTRACT

This chapter is an introductory chapter that attempts to highlight the concept of computational intelligence and its application in the field of computing security; it starts with a brief description of the underlying principles of artificial intelligence and discusses the role of computational intelligence in overcoming conventional artificial intelligence limitations. The chapter then briefly introduces various tools or components of computational intelligence such as neural networks, evolutionary computing, swarm intelligence, artificial immune systems, and fuzzy systems. The application of each component in the field of computing security is highlighted.

INTRODUCTION

The aim of artificial intelligence (AI) is to simulate human intelligence on machines so that they can act and think like humans. AI is regarded as a wide field of knowledge that involves reasoning, machine learning, planning, intelligent search and building perception. Reasoning aims to reach a predetermined objective of a problem using a set of facts supplied and a predefined base of information or what we call a

DOI: 10.4018/978-1-7998-2418-3.ch001

knowledge base. The knowledge base consists of a compilation of IF-THEN rules or a conceptual graphic structure reflecting the knowledge of the professional in a specialized field. On the other hand, learning can be described as a process of encoding the situation-action pairs at memory so that the memory can remember the correct action. The learning process is carried out on machines either by training the machine with established situation-action pairs or by enabling the machine to adjust the parameters of the specified learning rule in a trial sense. Whereas preparation is about the sequence of steps to solve a problem. To be more precise, provided a knowledge base and a set of facts, preparation calls for the sequencing of the rule firing phase, so that there is at least one such target lading sequence.

Therefore, AI's main goals are to develop methods and systems for solving problems that are normally solved by human intellectual activity, such as image recognition, language and speech processing, preparation and forecasting, thereby enhancing computer information systems; and to develop models that simulate living organisms and, in general, the human brain, thereby improving our understanding. There is a large AI literature (Jain and Lazzerini, 199), (Jain, 1999) and (Mitchell, 1997) that covers various techniques of representation of information, reasoning (Shapiro, 2010) and (Rashmi & Neha, 2017)., machine learning (Shai & Shai, 2014) and (Yu-Wei, 2015), image and language understanding (Mishra, 2018) and (Rastgarpour & Shanbehzadeh, 2011), planning, smart search and realization of knowledge. A detailed discussion on these issues goes beyond this chapter's reach.

It is clearly reported by a number of researchers that AI was incompetent to meet the growing demand for search, optimization and machine learning in information systems with broad biological and commercial databases and factory automation for the steel, aerospace, energy and pharmaceutical industries claims Konar (2005). These pitfalls of traditional AI can be summarised as follows:

- Traditional problem-solving approaches in AI are primarily concerned with the representation of problem states by symbols and the construction of a set of rules to define transitions in problem states.
- In general AI is a tool with the capability to handle inductive and analogy-based learning, but is inefficient for supervised
- Traditionally, AI is utilized functionally in search algorithm, but conventional AI is not very qualified to deal with real world optimization problems.

The shortcoming of this classical AI has opened up new opportunities for non-classical models in different intelligent based applications. Such computational analytical tools and techniques have led to a new field called computational intelligence.

Computational Intelligence (CI) is a set of computational models and techniques that incorporate components of learning, adjustment, or potentially heuristic advancement. It is utilized to help study issues that are hard to unravel utilizing regular computational calculations and algorithms. The three main pillars of CI are neural networks, evolutionary computing, and fuzzy systems. In recent years, the scope of computational intelligence technologies has been applied to emerging areas such as swarm intelligence, artificial immune systems (AIS), supporting vector machines, rough collections or sets, chaotic structures or systems, and others. Figure 1 illustrates the main pillars for CI.

This chapter is and interlocutory chapter to describe CI techniques and models. It starts with a number of CI definitions to build the foundation for this emerging

Figure 1. Computational intelligence pillars

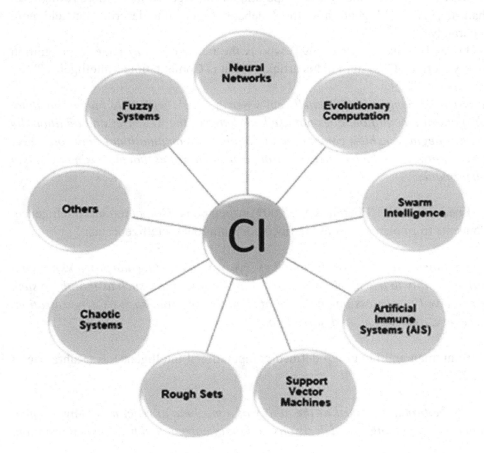

paradigm. Different pillars and new emerging components of CI such as neural networks, evolutionary computing, fuzzy systems, swarm intelligence and artificial immune systems (AIS) will be tackled in the remaining sections of this chapter.

COMPUTATIONAL INTELLIGENCE DEFINED

To have a better understanding of computational Intelligence and its scope as a new field of research and study, we begin looking at different definition of CI.

The term computational intelligence if first coined in 1983 as reported by Bezdek when explained his personal email communication about the IJCI journal with **Nick Cercone (Bezdek, 1994)** "Back in 1983 my colleague Gordon McCalla and I were the executives for the *Canadian Society for Computational Studies of Intelligence* (CSCSI), ... We decided that Computational Intelligence was a more fitting term than Artificial Intelligence after much debate; it seemed to describe our field more accurately."

James Bezdek (Bezdek, 1994) who is the father of fuzzy pattern recognition theory, defined CI system in his article "What is Computational Intelligence?"

A system is computational intelligent when it: deals with only numerical data, has pattern recognition, does not use knowledge in the AI sense; and additionally when it begin to exhibit computational adaptivity, computational fault tolerance, speed approaching human-like turnaround and error rates that approximate human performance

Eberhart and Shi (Eberhar & Shi, 2007) in their book "Computational Intelligence: Concepts to Implementations" defined computational intelligence as:

Computing Intelligence is a methodology involving computing that provides a system with an ability to learn and/or to deal with new situations, such as that the system is perceived to possess one or more attributes of reason, such as generalization, discovery, association, and abstraction.

Kahraman and his group defined computational intelligence as (Kahraman et al., 2010):

CI can be broadly defined as the ability of a machine to react to an environment in new ways, making useful decisions in light of current and previous information.

One of the most concise and comprehensive definition of computation intelligence is provided by IEEE Computational Intelligence Society as follows (IEEE CIS, 2019):

Computational Intelligence (CI) is the theory, design, application and development of biologically and linguistically motivated computational paradigms. Traditionally the three main pillars of CI have been Neural Networks, Fuzzy Systems and Evolutionary Computation.

Having presented the basic definitions of CI, next this chapter will review the theory and technology foundations of computational intelligence tools and component methodologies.

NEURAL NETWORKS

The concept of the neural network, more accurately referred to as the 'Artificial' Neural Network (ANN), was given by the inventor of one of the first neuro-computers, Robert Hecht-Nielsen (Hecht-Nielsen, 1987). The neural network is defined as:

...a computing system made up of a number of simple, highly interconnected processing elements, which process information by their dynamic state response to external inputs.

Neural Networks suggests machines that are something like brains and it can be viewed as an interconnected assembly of basic processing components, units or nodes, the design of which is loosely based on an animal neuron. The processing power of the network shall be stored in the inter-unit relation strengths or weights obtained by the method of adaptation to, or learning from, a set of training patterns. Just as the brain uses a network of interconnected cells called neurons to create a massive parallel processor, ANN uses a network of artificial neurons or nodes to solve learning difficulties.

The human brain is made up of about 100 billion nerve or neurons which are connected with approximately 10^{15} interneuron connections mediated by electrochemical junctions called **synapses**, allowing a complicated network with a capability of representing a large amount of knowledge. Every neuron usually receives several thousands of contacts from other neurons and is therefore continuously receiving a multitude of incoming signals that eventually reach the cell body. Figure 2 illustrates biological neuron (left) and an ANN mathematical model (right).

Neural networks are mainly applied to perform statistical analysis and data modelling (Hsieh & Tang, 1998), where their function is viewed as an alternative

Figure 2: Biological neuron (left) and a common ANN mathematical model (right)

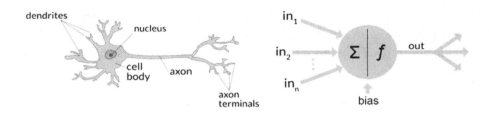

to traditional nonlinear regression or cluster analysis techniques. As a consequence, they are usually used in problems that may arise in terms of classification or forecasting. Examples here might include image and speech recognition, textual character recognition, and areas of human experience such as medical diagnostics, oil geological surveys, and financial market forecasting indicators.

Neural Networks Security Applications: Securing digital assets and intellectual property is becoming a concern for organizations. Recent studies have identified internal hacking as the primary cause of data loss in the corporate sector. Organizations are working hard to take appropriate measures to protect their data from destruction or leakage. Many researches work in the field of intrusion detection systems utilizes neural network power to design, implement and enhance security monitoring system. The following paragraphs describe some of the research work in this field.

Parveen's article (Parveen, 2017) "Neural Networks in Cyber Security" is a good example for utilizing neural network in designing an intrusion detection system to protect a network from external cyber threats. This research work starts by describing the challenges faced by IT leaders with respect to Internet Security now a days. These threats are related to how to protect organizations, customers, citizens and data, while upsetting attacks from cyber criminals. As a result of these threats, the author proposes an Intrusion Detection System (IDS) to protect the network from cyber criminals and cyber threats by employing neural networks to detect and classify network activity based on minimal, incomplete and non-linear network security data sources. The article concludes that by combining advanced techniques such as Artificial Intelligence and Neural Networks can play a significant role in achieving one of highest detection rates in the industry of cyber security.

Igor and his team in their article (Igor et al., 2013) "Application of Neural Networks in Computer Security", focused on ensuring data communication system control that neural network technologies in connection with traditional methods used in expert systems. They proposed a solution which specifies an innovative method to identifying data elements in transmission networks, addresses the transformation of their parameters for neural network input and determines the type and design of an effective neural network. Igor and his team began by analysing the security of communication of control systems and then analysed the possible use of neural networks by validating the data transfer and selected an appropriate type of neural network. As a result, they developed a practical security system design and implemented the communication network security model system using appropriate tools. Finally, this research work suggests using a much broader neural network for future development that would be able to separate incoming packets into more groups. The research can also be used to expand the model with other neural networks to look for other anomalies in the data stream.

EVOLUTIONARY COMPUTING

Evolutionary Computing (EC) is a computer science research area. It is, as the name suggests, a special computing flavour that draws inspiration from the natural evolution process (Eiben and Smith, 2015). It is claimed by Fogel that the notion of applying Darwinian concepts to automatic problem-solving dates to the 1940s, long before the software revolution (Fogel,1998). Eiben and Smith claimed that Turing proposed "genetic or evolutionary search" as early as 1948, and Bremermann carried out computer experiments on "optimization through evolution and recombination" as early as 1962. Three different basic concept implementations were developed in different places during the 1960s (Eiben and Smith, 2015). Fogel, Owens, and Walsh (Fogel et al., 1966) implemented evolutionary programming in the United States, while Holland named his method a genetic algorithm (Holland, 1973) and in Germany, production techniques were discovered by Schwefel (Schwefel, 1995).

Eiben and Schoenauer (Eiben& Schoenauer, 2002) in their article "Evolutionary computing" showed that Evolutionary Computing consists of constructing, implementing and learning algorithms based on Darwin's natural selection principles. Oduguwa and his research team claimed that: Genetic algorithms (GA), evolutionary programming (EP), evolutionary strategies (ES) and genetic programming (GP) are the core Evolutionary Computing methodologies (Oduguwa et al., 2004). Figure 3 illustrates this concept.

Evolutionary Computing and Security Applications: Evolutionary computation (genetic algorithms and genetic programming), are becoming increasingly present in the area of computer security, both in the area of network host security and in the very challenging area of cryptology. The computer security community is

Figure 3. Components of evolutionary computing

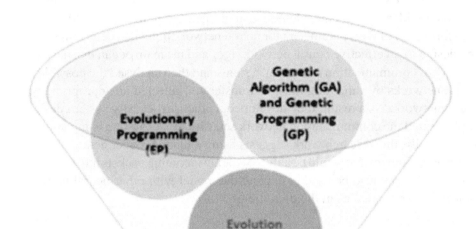

increasingly interested in evolutionary computing techniques as a result of successes implementations, but there are still a range of open issues to be addressed in the field. One of these open issues is describe by Cesar (Cesar, 2004) in the field of cryptanalysis is how to define fitness functions for the various heuristic methods (say genetic algorithms, simulated annealing, etc.) which avoid the problem of the landscape of deceptive fitness. The following paragraphs describe some of the research work in employing evolutionary computing in solving security issues.

Amro and his research group (Amro et al., 2012) in their work "Evolutionary Computation in Computer Security and Forensics: An Overview claimed that evolutionary computation is an appropriate technique to find an optimal solution to a problem and evolutionary computing can provide an effective way to solve those related to computer security and forensics among these problems. Their work looked at the methods provided by evolutionary computation to find an optimal solution to a problem and it explored evolutionary computing can be applied in various computer security and forensics scenarios. In summary Amro et al., research work shows how Evolutionary computation (EC) is inspired by the natural evolution process and expresses its rules in algorithms that can be used to search for the most suitable solutions to solve a problem. Evolutionary computation thus mimics natural evolution, but on a computer, through a series or sequence of optimization algorithms that typically rely on a set of rules and the optimization process improves the quality of solutions iteratively until a better one is reached. As result, evolutionary computation does not derive its ideas from human intelligence, but rather from the transition of species from one generation to the next.

Lugo, in his work "Coevolutionary Genetic Algorithms for Proactive Computer Network Defences" (Lugo, 2017) investigates the use of coevolutionary genetic algorithms as tools to build proactive defences in the computer network and implemented rIPCA, a new coevolutionary algorithm based on speed and performance. This research work refers to the threat of disruption posed by adaptive attackers in computer networks and the aim was to strengthen network defences by modelling the actions of adaptive attackers and anticipating threats so it can protect against them proactively. o counter this, we are launching RIVALS, a new cybersecurity project designed by using coevolutionary algorithms to better defend against adaptive agents. As a contribution, this research work described the current suite of coevolutionary algorithms built by RIVALS and how they explore archiving to sustain progressive discovery. The proposed model in this work enables us to investigate a network's connectivity under an adversarial risk model. The work then conducted a generic coevolutionary test (Compare-on - one) and RIVALS simulations on 3 different network topologies to evaluate the efficacy of the package and the experiments showed that current algorithms either compromise the speed of execution or give up maintaining consistent results.

SAWRM INTELLIGENCE

A swarm can be viewed as a relatively large group of homogeneous, simple agents that communicate locally with each other and their environment, without central control to allow an interesting global behaviour. Biologists and natural scientists researched social insect behaviours because of the incredible efficiency of these natural swarm systems. Ahmad and Glasgow reported that in the late 1980s, computer scientists proposed to the field of artificial intelligence the scientific insights of these natural swarm systems (Ahmed and Glasgow, 2012). Beni and Wang first introduced the term "Swarm Intelligence" as a set of algorithms for controlling robotic swarm in the global optimization framework (Beni and Wang, 1989). Dorigo introduced Ant Colony Optimization in 1992 as a novel meta-heuristic inspired by nature to solve difficult combinatorial optimization problems (Dorigo, 1992). In 1995, Kennedy and Eberhar introduced Particle Swarm Optimization and it was first intended to simulate the social behaviour of the bird flocking (Kennedy and Eberhart, 1995). It is reported by Beni and Wang that by the late 1990s, both Ant Colony Optimization and Particle Swarm Optimization are considered to be the most successful swarm intelligence algorithms started to go beyond pure scientific interest and enter the domain of applications in the real world. In 2005, Karabago proposed the Artificial Bee Colony Algorithm as a new member of the swarm intelligence algorithms family (Karabago, 2005). Figure 4 illustrates Swarm Intelligence Algorithms.

Swarm Intelligence and Security Application: Swarm-based algorithms have recently emerged as a family of population-based, nature-inspired algorithms capable of producing low-cost, rapid and robust solutions to several complex problems such as Intrusion Detections (ID). When an intrusion occurs, the security of a computer system or network is compromised. An intrusion can be characterized as any set of actions that attempt to compromise a resource's credibility, privacy or availability. Techniques such as firewalls, access control and authentication for intrusion prevention have failed to fully secure networks and systems against rising attacks and malware. Therefore, Intrusion Detection System has become a key component of the security infrastructure to detect and monitor these threats. As these Intrusion Detection Systems must have a high Detection Rate of Attack, at the same time having a low False Alarm Rate, building such a system is a challenging task. A promising solution for such a problem was swarm intelligence techniques and it is utilized by many researchers for improving the performance of Intrusion Detection Model. The following paragraphs describe some of the research work in employing swarm intelligence algorithms in solving security issues.

Amudha and Abdulrauf in their article (Amudha and Abdulrauf, 2012) "A Study on Swarm Intelligence Techniques in Intrusion Detection" provided an overview of the research progress in swarm intelligence techniques to assist tackling the problem of intrusion detection. The review mainly aimed to use the capabilities of swarm intelligence techniques for improving the performance of intrusion detection model. This work started by reviewing the theory behind Intrusion Detection with an emphasis on the needs for a technique such as Swarm Intelligence Algorithms Model as an aid in solving network intrusion issues. This research work identified two most common performance evaluation metrics in designing Intrusion Detection Systems to be Detection Rate (DR), which is defined as the ratio of the number of correctly detected attacks to the total number of attacks, and False Alarm Rate

Figure 4. Swarm intelligence algorithms

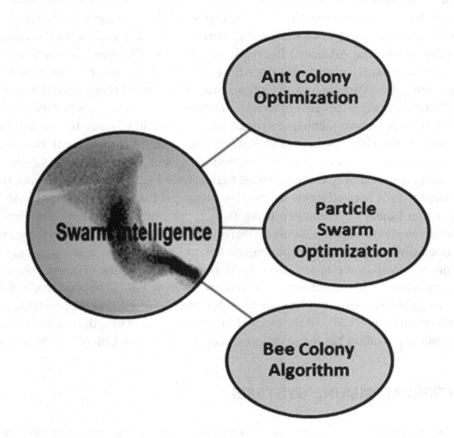

(FAR), or False Positive Rate (FPR), which is the ratio of the number of normal connections misclassified as attacks to the total number of normal connections. Different swarm intelligence techniques used by researchers in evaluating intrusion detection template quality were examined in this research work and as a conclusion from the empirical study carried out, this work found that its application to the field of intrusion detection, which is still to be explored, is constrained.

Jeswani and Kale in their article (Jeswani & Kale, 2015) "The Particle Swarm Optimization Based Linear Cryptanalysis of Advanced Encryption Standard Algorithm" applied the swarm Optimization technique in enhancing network security. Cryptography algorithms are the main component and the key factor in data storage and uninterrupted network transmission protection mechanisms and the data security depends purely on the cryptography algorithm and therefore the cryptography keys must be handled in an appropriate manner. Therefore, mechanisms of security are established when a security threat is identified. This research work describes the implementation of computational intelligence-based approach for the known cryptanalysis of the Advanced Encryption Standard (AES) algorithm is to define the security risk associated with the AES algorithm. The Authors of this research work utilized the Particle Swarm Optimization (PSO) based cryptanalysis which is used much now a days because of its fast convergence rate, they implemented a PSO-oriented cryptanalysis technique to crack the key used in advance by the standard encryption algorithm. Jeswani and Kale claimed that this technique is known as a text-only cipher attack for an AES encryption system, where the key is deduced in a minimum search space as opposed to the Brute Force Attack. In general, this research work it applied a new method for Advanced Encryption Standards (AES) Algorithm Linear Cryptanalysis using Particle Swarm Optimization. The fitness function used in this approach ensures that the solution is efficient, and this technique successfully identifies the Cryptographic key bits using cipher text attack only to ensure minimal search space allowing less overhead and time-efficient solution. As a conclusion this research work demonstrated how PSO is applied to the AES allowing the key length 128 bits where 76 bits are identified, and the percentage of result obtained is 59.37 and the elapsed time is 17.3 sec. Thus, the use of Particle Swarm Optimization has led to the good reduction factor in Linear Cryptanalysis.

ARTIFICIAL IMMUNE SYSTEMS

An Artificial Immune System (AIS) is a system that uses some of the biological immune system technology to construct algorithms or technologies that tackle systemic objectives, and this may include the computational and computer simulation of immune systems, or the integration into algorithms of certain concepts related to immunology. Reviewing literature suggested four main AIS algorithms were based on the development of various AIS applications. Daudi classifies these four AIS algorithms as: Negative Selection Based Algorithms, Clonal Selection Based Algorithms, Artificial Immune Networks (AINs) and Danger Theory and Dendritic Cell Algorithms (Daudi, 2015). Figure 5 describes the major AIS algorithms. The following paragraphs will briefly highlight on each AIS algorithm.

Negative Selection Based Algorithm: Inspired by the selection processes that occur in the thymus during cell maturation. Delona's research team reported that negative selection refers to the recognition and elimination (apoptosis) of self-reacting cells, which are T cells that can pick and invade tissues of their own (Delona et al., 2017). This algorithm is used for problem domains of classification and pattern recognition. For example, the algorithm prepares a collection of exemplary pattern detectors trained on ordinary (non-anomalous) patterns that model and detect unseen or anomalous patterns in the case of an anomaly detection domain. Delona also reported that the NSA was motivated by the negative process of selection in the natural immune system. In thymus, if a T-cell detects any self-cell, it is removed, and immune functionality is then performed in a process of T-cell maturation.

Clonal Selection Based Algorithms: The theory of clonal selection in an immune system is used to explain the adaptive immune system's basic response to an antigenic stimulus. Burnet described the theory of Clonal Selection Based Algorithm as an idea that relies on the concept of proliferating only cells capable of recognizing an antigen (Burnet, 1959).

Artificial Immune Networks: A successful implementation models of Artificial Immune Systems are Artificial Immune Networks. Framer's research team proposed their immune network model (Farmer et al., 1986) which became the fundamental for various Artificial Immune Systems algorithm and hence based on this the first immune network algorithm was proposed by Ishida (Ishida, 1990). Subsequently, The Artificial Immune Network algorithm sets the foundation and the extension for optimization problems known as the Optimization Artificial Immune Network algorithm. The algorithm of the Artificial Immune Network is inspired by the theory of the immune system acquired. The principle of clonal immunity selection accounts for the immune system's adaptive actions, including the ongoing selection and proliferation of cells choosing potentially harmful (and usually foreign) material in the body. A clonal selection theory's problem is that it presumes that the reactive cell repertoire stays idle when there is no pathogen to respond to. Jerne suggested an Immune Network Theory (Idiotypic Networks) in which immune cells do not rest in the absence of pathogen but identify and respond to each other's antibodies and immune cells.

Artificial Immune Systems Security Applications: Organizations should defend their networks from interference and attacks on computer from unintended or unauthorized access, change, or destruction and these securities should detect anomalous patterns by taking advantage of recognized signatures when tracking normal computer programs and abnormality network use. Computer security is facing huge challenges with network development. Until causing widespread harm, such as virus attacks and Intrusion Detection have become an indispensable element for detecting unusual behaviours to solve this problem. Computer science has a great tradition of learning nature's good ideas. The brain has inspired the model of the neural network, the basis of many attempts to develop artificial intelligence. The application of theoretical immunology and immune functions to solve security issues slowly became a research field based on applying Artificial Immune Systems (AIS) techniques to aids in solving these security issues. Researchers made significant

Figure 5. Artificial immune systems (AIS)

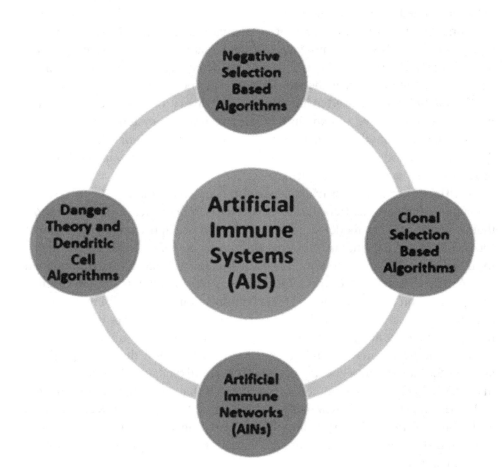

contributions to AIS production. Many AISs have been developed for a wide range of applications, such as fraud detection, optimization, machine learning, robotics, and computer security. The following paragraphs describe some of the research work in employing Artificial Immune Systems algorithms in solving security issues.

Harmer's research team in their article (Harmer et al., 2002) "An Artificial Immune System Architecture for Computer Security Applications" describe how the task of detecting and classifying new viral stains and intrusion patterns could overwhelm existing antivirus and network intrusion detection (ID) solutions. Within a hierarchical layered architecture, a self-adaptive decentralized agent-based immune system based on biological strategies is proposed by Harmer's team. An interactive software system is designed, implemented and tested in Java. The findings validate the use of a biological-system distributed-agent approach to computer-safe virus elimination and ID problems. The experimental implementation of this research work is based on the prototypes and it provides an effective solution for detecting, recognizing and removing malicious code and bad packets. The efficacy level of this implementation can be adjusted by selecting the number of antibodies, the length of the antibody, and the threshold for detection. These must be selected on the basis of known self-content and with an understanding of their ramifications on negative selection time, scanning time, and coverage of non-self-space.

Yang's research group in their research work (Yang et al., 2014) "A Survey of Artificial Immune System Based Intrusion Detection" reported that there is a lot of literature about Intrusion Detection Systems, their study only surveys the approaches based on Artificial Immune System (AIS) and the use of AIS in ID is an attractive term in today's techniques. Yang's research work discussese AIS-based ID approaches from a new perspective; a model for AIS-based ID Systems (IDSs) development is also proposed and based on three core aspects, this model is evaluated and discussed: antibody / antigen encoding, generation algorithm and mode of evolution. This research work collates into the proposed system the widely used algorithms, their implementation features, and the design of IDSs. Finally, it also highlights some of the future challenges in this field.

FUZZY SYSTEMS

Zadeh introduced fuzzy sets as a way of representing and manipulating information that was not reliable but rather confusing (Zadeh, 1965). The main inspiration behind the introduction of the theory of fuzzy sets was the need to model phenomena of the real world, which are inherently vague and ambiguous. Utilizing the imprecise terms of natural language, human knowledge about complex issues can be successfully represented through implementing fuzzy sets theories and fuzzy logic which can offer formal methods for numerical representation and efficient data processing. Fuzzy Logic FL is a reasoning system which is like human reasoning. FL's approach imitates the way human decision-making includes all intermediate possibilities between YES and NO virtual values. The standard logic blocks a machine can understand takes correct input and generates a definite output such as TRUE or FALSE that is like the YES or NO of humans. Mendel defined a fuzzy logic system (FLS) as the non-linear mapping of a set of input data to a scalar output (Mendel, 1995). A FLS consists of four main parts: fuzzifier, rule base, engine of inference, and defuzzier. Figure 6 shows these elements and the overall structure of an FLS.

Fuzzy logic has always been one of the key areas of research in the field of informatics, as it helps to cope with vagueness and ambiguity in the real world. A

Figure 6. Components of fuzzy logic system

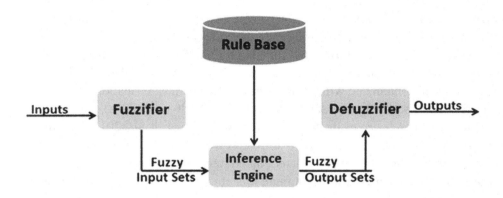

variant of fuzzy logic systems has gained enormous popularity for research purposes in recent years, Type-2 Fuzzy Logic. An overview of the study trends of Type-2 Fuzzy logic is given in this paper.

Fuzzy Systems Security Applications: The value of protecting computer systems and networks from attack cannot be underestimated due to the growing reliance of corporations and government agencies on their systems and networks. A single malicious invasion of a computer network can cause an organization a lot of damage. Therefore, computer security tackles the protection of information and property from misuse by unauthorized people. Digital forensics offers strategies for storing, gathering, validating, recognizing, evaluating, describing, recording and presenting digital evidence from digital sources to recreate criminal activity or breach policy. Fuzzy logic can be used properly to help address issues related to computer security and computer forensics. The following paragraphs describe some of the research work in employing fuzzy logic systems in solving security issues.

Javed and Pandey in their article "Advance Cyber Security System using fuzzy logic" (Javed & Pandey, 2014)reported that increasingly, critical infrastructure sites and software facilities rely on integrated physical and cyber-based real-time control systems and the existence of these omnipresent and sometimes unrestrained communications interconnections results in a growing cyber security risk. Cyber security is not a single issue, but a group of very different issues involving different sets of threats. On the other hand, an advanced cyber security system using fuzzy logic is a system consisting of a depository of rules and a mechanism to access and execute the rules. Javed and Pandey tried to use fuzzy logic in their work to develop an integrated cyber security platform and their study suggested a cyber security program using fuzzy logic that alerts system administrators about cyber threats anticipated. The also assumed that the system works well if the cyber threat scenario is applied. The model developed was not intended to protect a system but to warn the system administrator of expected threats. When tested the developed system showed its superiority in the areas of development flexibility and fast response for cyber threats.

Al-Ali and AlMogren in their research work (Al-Ali & AlMogren, 2017) "Fuzzy logic methodology for cyber security risk mitigation approach" described the impacts of criminal activity based on the nature of the crime, the victim, and the context of cybercrime impacts (whether short-term or long-term. They showed how the Kingdom of Saudi Arabia faces various cyber threats, including malware, spam and phishing email attacks. While recent findings highlight the poor state of the information security system in Saudi Arabia, it is within the current premise that a special cyber security risk assessment should be established claimed Al-Ali and AlMogren and using the concept of Fuzzy Logic (FL), they proposed a Fuzzy Inference System (FIS) to generate risk mitigation and attempt to solve these problems for proposed entities. The researchers in this work reported that technological advancement and its association with digital wellness can be described as a two-edged metaphoric sword, one providing new insight into the vulnerabilities of the global cyber network, and another seeking a way to rectify the possibilities of successive cyber-attacks and there are numerous attempts, both at local and global level, to counter cybercrime and reduce the risk of cyber-attacks in both the private and public spheres. As a result of this conceptualization of the hiring of additional cyber security experts is unavoidable as the main strategy for eliminating cyber vulnerabilities from the top three security threats. Applying Fuzzy logic, however, may give organizations a vision abroad to quantify risk and evaluate risk factors, and may end up assessing the most important security steps.

THE FUTURE OF CI

Achieving the full potential of Computational Intelligence technologies and models poses research challenges that involve a radical transformation of the CI research market, driven by significant and sustained investment in different applications especially in the field of computing security and cyber security. These are the key findings of a recent study conducted by researchers in the field.

When we understand that intelligence is not limited to a single brain, we may expect a more promising future; it also exists in communities such as insect colonies, organisations and human societies markets, to name a few. In all these instances, large numbers of agents able to perform specific tasks that can be viewed as computations participate in collective behaviour that effectively solves a number of problems that exceed a single individual's ability to solve. And they do so often without global controls, while sharing incomplete and sometimes delayed data.

Many of the features that underlie distributed intelligence can be found in our planet's computer networks. Processes are produced or "made" within these systems, migrate across networks and spawn other processes on remote computers. And as they do, we solve complex problems - think about what it takes to make a movie on your computer - when vying for assets like bandwidth and CPU that are threatened by other system.

Ironically, we understand distributed intelligence quality, both natural and artificial, much better than individual minds ' functions. This is partly due to the ease with which the interactions between individuals and programs can be observed and measured when navigating complex information spaces. Compare this with the complexity of studying comprehensive cognitive processes in the human brain. And we know from this wide range of knowledge that while the overall performance of a distributed system is determined by the ability of many agents to exchange partial results that are not always optimal, success is determined by the few who make the most progress per unit time.

CONCLUSION

This chapter analysed several computational intelligence algorithms based on computing security and cyber security problems applications. Considering the rapidly changing and increasingly complex nature of global security, we continue to see a remarkable interest in novel, flexible and resilient strategies in computing security, cyber security and network security environments that can cope with the challenging issues that arise in this area. Such problems arise not only because of the vast amount of data collected by a multitude of sensing and tracking modalities, but also because of the advent of creative groups of decentralized, mass-scale communication protocols and networking structures, and the advancement in Computational Intelligence techniques such as Neural Networks, Evolutionary Computing, Swarm Intelligence, Artificial Immune Systems and Fuzzy Systems.

Inspired by imitative aspects of living systems, CI systems common feature is that data is processed by symbolic knowledge representation. CI systems are capable of reconstructing behaviours found in learning sequences, creating inference rules, and generalizing information in circumstances where assumptions are expected to be made or predicted categorized based on categories previously observed. The CI literature contains research articles and research works that show promising potential practical applications in the field of computing security.

REFERENCES

Ahmed, H., & Glasgow, J. (2012). *Swarm Intelligence: Concepts, Models and Applications*. Technical Report 585. School of Computing. Queen's University Kingston, Ontario, Canada.

Al-Ali, M., & AlMogren, A., (2017). Fuzzy logic methodology for cyber security risk mitigation approach. *Journal of Networking Technology, 8*(3).

Amro, S., Elizondo, D., Solanas, A., & Martinez-Balleste, A. (2012). Evolutionary Computation in Computer Security and Forensics: An Overview. In Computational Intelligence for Privacy and Security, SCI 394, (pp. 25–34). Springer-Verlag Berlin Heidelberg.

Amudha, P., & Abdulrauf, H. (2012). *A Study on Swarm Intelligence Techniques in Intrusion Detection. IJCA*.

Beni, G., & Wang, J. (1989). *Swarm intelligence in cellular robotic systems*. NATO.

Bezdek, J. (1994). *What is Computational Intelligence? Computational Intelligence Imitating Life*. IEEE Press.

Burnet, F. M. (1959). *The clonal selection theory of acquired immunity*. Cambridge University Press.

Cesar, J. (2004). Evolutionary Computation in Computer Security and Cryptography. *New Generation Computing, 23*, 193–199.

Daudi, J. (2015). An Overview of Application of Artificial Immune System in Swarm Robotic Systems. Automation. *Control and Intelligent Systems, 3*(2), 11–18. doi:10.11648/j.acis.20150302.11

Delona, C., J., Haripriya, P., V., & Anju, J., S. (2017). Negative Selection Algorithm: A Survey. *International Journal of Science, Engineering and Technology Research, 6*(4).

Dorigo, M. (1992). *Optimization, learning and natural algorithms* (Ph.D. Thesis). Dipartimento diElettronica, Politecnico di Milano, Italy.

Eberhart, R., & Shi, Y. (2007). *Computational Intelligence: Concepts to Implementations*. Elsevier. doi:10.1016/B978-155860759-0/50002-0

Eiben, A. E., & Schoenauer, M. (2002). Evolutionary computing. *Information Processing Letters, 82*(1), 1–6. doi:10.1016/S0020-0190(02)00204-1

Eiben, A. E., & Smith, J. E. (2015). *Introduction to Evolutionary Computing* (2nd ed.). Springer-Verlag Berlin Heidelberg. doi:10.1007/978-3-662-44874-8

Farmer, J. D., Packard, N. H., & Perelson, A. S. (1986). The immune system, adaptation, and machine learning. *Physica, 22*, 187–204.

Fogel, B. (Ed.). (1998). *Evolutionary Computation: The Fossil Record*. Piscataway, NJ: IEEE Press. doi:10.1109/9780470544600

Fogel, L., Owens, A., & Walsh, M. (1966). *Artificial Intelligence through Simulated Evolution*. Chichester, UK: Wiley.

Harmer, P., Williams, P., Gunsch, G., & Lamont, G. (2002). An Artificial Immune System Architecture for Computer Security Applications. *Transactions on Evolutionary Computation, 6*(6).

Hecht-Nielsen, R. (1987). *Kolmogorov's Mapping Neural Network Existence Theorem*. Hecht-Nielsen Neurocomputer Corporation.

Holland, J. (1973). Genetic algorithms and the optimal allocation of trials. *SIAM Journal on Computing, 2*, 88–105.

Hsieh, W., & Tang, B. (1998). Applying Neural Network Models to Prediction and Data Analysis in Meteorology and Oceanography. *Bulletin of the American Meteorological Society, 79*(9), 1855–1870. doi:10.1175/1520-0477(1998)079<1855:ANNMTP>2.0.CO;2

IEEE CIS. (2019). *What is Computational Intelligence?* Retrieved from: https://cis.ieee.org/about/what-is-ci

Igor, H., Bohuslava, J., Martin, J., & Martin, N. (2013). Application of Neural Networks in Computer Security. In *24th DAAAM International Symposium on Intelligent Manufacturing and Automation*. Elsevier Ltd.

Ishida, Y. (1990). Fully distributed diagnosis by PDP learning algorithm: towards immune network PDP model. *IEEE International Joint Conference on Neural Networks*. 10.1109/IJCNN.1990.137663

Jain, C. (Ed.). (1999). *Intelligent Biometric Techniques in Fingerprint and Face Recognition*. Boca Raton, FL: CRC Press.

Jain, C., & Lazzerini, B. (Eds.). (1999). *Knowledge-Based Intelligent Techniques in Character Recognition*. Boca Raton, FL: CRC Press.

Javed, A., & Pandey, M. K., (2014). Advance Cyber Security System using fuzzy logic. *Journal of Management and IT, 10*(1).

Jeswani, D., & Kale, S. (2015). The Particle Swarm Optimization Based Linear Cryptanalysis of Advanced Encryption Standard Algorithm. *International Journal on Recent and Innovation Trends in Computing and Communication, 3*(4).

Kahraman, C., Ihsan Kaya, I., & Didem, C. (2010). Computational Intelligence: Past, Today, and Future. In D. Ruan (Ed.), *Computational Intelligence in Complex Decision Systems*. doi:10.2991/978-94-91216-29-9_1

Karaboga, D. (2005). *An Idea Based On Honey Bee Swarm for Numerical Optimization*. Academic Press.

Kennedy, J., & Eberhart, R. (1995). Particle Swarm Optimization. *Proceedings of IEEE International Conference on Neural Networks*, 1942–1948.

Konar, A. (2005). *Computational Intelligence-Principles, techniques and Applications*. Springer-Verlag Berlin.

Lugo, A. (2017). *Coevolutionary Genetic Algorithms for Proactive Computer Network Defences* (Master's thesis). MIT.

Mendel, J. (1995). Fuzzy logic systems for engineering: A tutorial. *Proceedings of the IEEE, 83*(3), 345–377. doi:10.1109/5.364485

Mishra, S. (Ed.). (2018). *Artificial Intelligence and Natural Language Processing*. Newcastle upon Tyne, UK: Cambridge Scholars Publishing.

Mitchell, M. (1997). *Machine Learning*. New York: McGraw-Hill.

Oduguwa, V., Tiwari, A., & Roy, R. (2004). Evolutionary computing in manufacturing industry: An overview of recent applications. *Applied Soft Computing, 5*(3), 281–299. doi:10.1016/j.asoc.2004.08.003

Parveen J., R., (2017). Neural Networks in Cyber Security. *International Research Journal of Computer Science, 9*(4).

Rashmi, S., & Neha, S. (2017). Knowledge Representation in Artificial Intelligence using Domain Knowledge and Reasoning Mechanism. *International Journal of Scientific Engineering and Research, 5*(3), 17–20.

Rastgarpour, M., & Shanbehzadeh, J. (2011). Application of AI Techniques in Medical Image Segmentation and Novel Categorization of Available Methods and Tools. *Proceeding of the International Multi Conference of Engineers and Computer Scientists*.

Schwefel, H. (1995). *Evolution and Optimum Seeking*. New York: Wiley.

Shai, S., & Shai, B. (2014). *Understanding Machine Learning: From Theory to Algorithms*. New York: Cambridge University Press.

Shapiro, S. (2010). Knowledge Representation and Reasoning Logics for Artificial Intelligence. University at Buffalo, The State University of New York Buffalo.

Sonakshi V., Amita, J., Devendra, T., & Oscar, C. (2018). An Analytical Insight to Investigate the Research Patterns in the Realm of Type-2 Fuzzy Logic. *Journal of Automation, Mobile Robotics & Intelligent Systems, 12*(2).

Yang, H., Li, T., Hu, X., Wang, F., & Zou, Y. (2014). A Survey of Artificial Immune System Based Intrusion Detection. The Scientific World Journal. doi:10.1155/2014/156790

Yu-Wei, C. (2015). *Machine Learning with R Cookbook*. Birmingham, UK: Packt Publishing Ltd.

Zadeh, L. A. (1965). Fuzzy Sets. *Information and Control, 8*(3), 338–353. doi:10.1016/S0019-9958(65)90241-X

Chapter 2
A Hybrid Connectionist/ Substitution Approach for Data Encryption

Raed Abu Zitar
iD https://orcid.org/0000-0003-2693-2132
Ajman University, UAE

Muhammed Jassem Al-Muhammed
iD https://orcid.org/0000-0002-1845-4364
American University of Madaba, Jordan

ABSTRACT

The authors believe that the hybridization of two different approaches results in more complex encryption outcomes. The proposed method combines a symbolic approach, which is a table substitution method, with another paradigm that models real-life neurons (connectionist approach). This hybrid model is compact, nonlinear, and parallel. The neural network approach focuses on generating keys (weights) based on a feedforward neural network architecture that works as a mirror. The weights are used as an input for the substitution method. The hybrid model is verified and validated as a successful encryption method.

INTRODUCTION

Securing a network for digitally stored or transmitted data is an ultimate need for all organizations in the world. There is everlasting need to keep enhancing encryption and protection. Many encryption techniques have been proposed in the literature

DOI: 10.4018/978-1-7998-2418-3.ch002

(Al-Muhammed et al, 2017; Bogdanov et al, 2014; Kunden et al, 2015; Mathur et al, 2016; Daemen et al, 2002; Nie et al, 2009; Al-Muhammed, Abuzitar et al, 2017; Patil et al, 2016; "TDEA", 2012; Bogdanov, Mendel et al, 2014; Stallings et al, 2016; Anderson et al, 2018; Burwick et al, 1999; Isenburg et al, 2003; Soto et al, 2018; Rukhin et al, 2001; Soto et al, 1999). They use different models that implement different processing techniques as stream based or block based models. Different key based diffusion and confusion operations were proposed. Mesh-based technique and directive operators are also used in (Al-Muhammed, 2017). However, these methods lack the needed confusion due to its quasi-linear nature and might be exploited by hackers. The mapping can be more deceptive if it was nonlinear. On the other hand, the proposed diffusion in this paper has connectionist nonlinear and complex nature that makes it even difficult for predicting the nature of the encryption even if the keys were known. Additional information at both ends should be shared regarding the architecture of the NN and the nature of the activation functions used to complete the process. All parts of the key (i.e. weights) work collectively and in parallel in generating the encrypted/decrypted data. Neural networks with Jordan training method were used in generating keys for encryption (Komal et al, 2015). A neural network was trained as sequential machine for encoding process. However, sequential machines have a problem of delay, especially for long input sequences. Other researchers used the neural network to generate encryption keys and they repeated the training process at the receiving end to generate the decryption keys (Zitar et al, 2005). In that sense, they did not take advantage of the compactness and the mirroring capabilities of the neural networks.

To apply our hybrid method, we will use the weights in a substitution heuristic that uses a look-up table to provide new mapping framework. The outcome of this substitution method is based on a pre-set table known at both sides of the transmitter and receiver. This table should be updated occasionally with coordination between both sides at the two ends. At the receiving end and using the weights sent by the transmitter, the substitution is reversed and the "neurally" encrypted data is recovered. Now we move to step 10 where the "neurally" encrypted data is, in return, recovered through processing it with the output layer using the sent weights.

In summary the chapter offers the following contributions:

1. More effective hybrid nonlinear mapping technique is used to overcome any embedded exploitable linearity in the mappings followed by traditional look-up table substitution that can be occasionally updated.
2. More complexity is generated with the parallel computational method used.
3. The cipher text has more confusion since efficient processing with "real type" data is used (such as multiplication and addition of real numbers). No more straight text manipulation is used with neural networks.

4.   It uses a block-based cipher rather than stream based one and keys are re-generated for every block.

5.   Keys used for encoding are different than keys used for decryption and that adds another security feature.

6.   The relatively time-consuming training is done once, and during transmission the created keys are used in generating the encrypted signal and recovering the original data at the receiving end with very low cost of calculations (single loop for every neuron only using single layer at both ends).

7.   The added layer of substitution (table look-up) adds more complexity and still it does not manipulate original the plain text itself. It deals with data encrypted by the hidden layer of the neural network.

The contributions of the paper are summarized as follows:

1.   Section 2 describes the encryption/decryption model being proposed.
2.   Section 3 discusses the weights and inputs/outputs.
3.   Section 4 presents the encryption/decryption process.
4.   Section 5 Substitution using table look-up method (encryption/decryption)
5.   Section 6 is discussions.
6.   Section 7 is conclusions and future work

The paper presents detailed description for the steps of the algorithm with examples. The different layers of encryption /decryption and neural mapping will make it extremely difficult for hackers to decode the encrypted text. The paper presents decryption of the encrypted plain text that is retrieved 100% at the receiver end.

ENCRYPTION/DECRYPTION MODEL DETAILS

A two-layer feedforward neural network (NN) (8X8) is trained to function as a mirror. Every input vector fed to the NN gives an identical output vector. The output of the trained NN should be an equal vector to its input binary values. This is done for all possible 256 binary input values. The idea here is to train this NN on 256 possible 8-bit binary vectors using a gradient descent learning algorithm. After training is complete with almost zero accumulated error, the hidden layer of the trained NN is used to encode (encrypt) input vectors from the input plain text (that is already converted to binary). The binary values from input stream are grouped into strings of eight bits and fed to the hidden layer. During this stage of encryption the binary input vector of 8 bits coming from the original block is replace by the 8-bit output of the hidden-layer neurons. The output of this layer should have no correlations whatsoever with the input vectors. Only, the weights of the output layer are sent as a key to the receiving end. At the receiving end, those weights are used in a single layer NN to function in a similar way to the output layer in the original trained NN. The encrypted values in this case will be the inputs to this single layer and the outputs of this layer will be similar to the original input vectors that were used as inputs for the hidden layer at the transmitter end. This process of encryption/decryption is done for every group of 8 bits streaming to the hidden layer NN at the transmitting end and the decryption is done at a similar stage at the receiving end as explained earlier. Please see Fig 1, which depicts the process of encryption/decryption.

The training for the two-layer NN is done one time. After training is complete, the network is separated into two parts. The hidden layer is used in encrypting 8-bit groups from the input stream, and the output layer is used in decryption at the receiving end. The training for the two-layer NN could be repeated with new initialization for the weights whenever there is need for that. The encryption/decryption processes are not time consuming at all. The training only takes almost one second if it is done on a multipurpose dual core computer. Of course, the identical input/target vector pairs that are used in the training are the same 256 possible binary inputs/targets used every time. This will finish the stage of training. The average CPU time for this is 1.0313 seconds using Matlab 14 on Core i5 7th generation computer with 8GB RAM. That could be minimized using more efficient hardware and using assembly language instead of Mat lab 14 since we are dealing with binary values (future work). For every new block of data being transmitted (10k bits), a new training phase could be invoked and a new set of weights (for the output layer) can be generated and sent along with the encrypted data. The weights for the output layer are sent with the encoded data at the beginning of the encrypted block. The whole process will be repeated as long as there is data transmission. More details regarding the NN properties are below:

Network Properties

Training Algorithm used here is Bayesian regularization backpropagation, please see Figure 2 and Figure 3. In Figure. 3, both curves for "Train" and "Test" totally match.

Network training updates the weight and the bias values according to Levenberg-Marquardt optimization. It minimizes a combination of squared errors and weights, and then determines the correct combination so as to produce a network that generalizes outputs similar to targets. This training process is called Bayesian regularization. In our network, the training stops when the performance gradient falls below minimum gradient error value. In Fig 2, mu is the control parameter for the algorithm used to train the neural network. Gamk is the effective number of parameters. ssX – is the

Figure 1. The mirror two-layered NN used for encryption/decryption

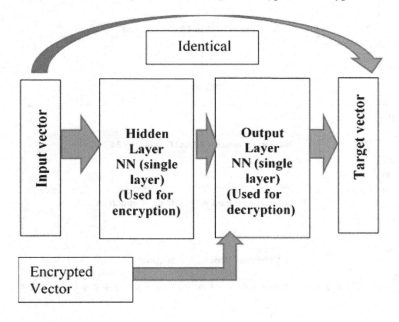

Table 1.

Number of Layers=2
Inputs= 8
One Hidden layer
Number of neurons in hidden is 8
Transfer function is TANSIG
Number of neurons in Output layer is 8.
Network type: Feed-forward backpropagation.
Training function: Levenberg-Marquardt backpropagation Algorithm (Trainlm)
Adaption learning function: Gradient descent with momentum weight and bias learning function (Learngdm)
Performance function: Mean Squared Error.
Training Ratio: 0.7
Validation Ratio: 0.15
Test Ratio: 0.15

Figure 2. Training and validation parameters

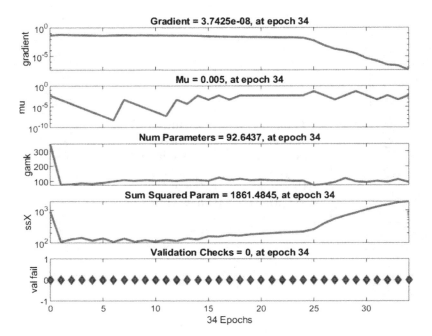

Sum squared Parameter. Valfail- is number of failures in validation checks which was zero for all epochs (Burwick et al, 1999).

BINARY WEIGHTS & INPUT/OUTPUT

Maximum value for weight found was less than 23, so it requires only 5 bit as exponent. Precision values are limited to 6 bits weights, the key can be represented as a 12 bit vector as follows:

The Appendix (Tables 4-6) shows the weights of both layers as a training outcome example. All the encrypted values are associated with weights and biases shown in those tables. At each new phases of training, new sets of weights (new keys) will be generated.

Table 2.

Sign Exponent Precision											
+/-	1	2	3	4	5	1	2	3	4	5	6

Figure 3. Training error versus epochs (an epoch is a whole batch of input vectors)

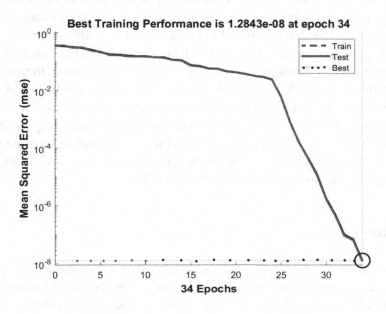

Figure 4. Correlation of a sample between input values and encrypted values

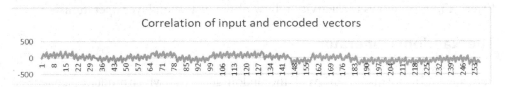

The Encryption/Decryption Process

Training is completed using a whole set of binary values from 0 to 255 as inputs and identical targets (mirroring). This would cover all possible binary values of characters that could be generated with 8 bits. The weights in the hidden layer are used as a key to encrypt the inputs and the weights in the output layer are used as a different key for decrypting the encrypted inputs. When a block is packed for transmission it is accompanied with the binary values of the output layer weights to be used as the decryption key. Those weights consist of 8x8 = 64 values. If each weight is encoded with 12 bits, as mentioned above, then the total decryption key has 8x8x12 = 768 bits. With proper compression for the binary values of the key, the key length can be reduced by 1:11 ratio (Isenburg et al, 2003). On average, the key length will be around 70 bits and that is acceptable if a block of data with length 10K bits is processed. For more security and confusion in the sent data, the whole process is repeated for every 100 blocks of data being transmitted. A new decryption key will be generated and accompanied with the next 100 blocks of encrypted data. All will be packed and sent in a similar way to the previous phase. In this case we guarantee that the same key will not be used for more than 100 blocks of data. If the transmission rate is 1M bits per second (10k X 100) and the total time needed to transmit the 100 blocks is 1 second, then in this 1 second (assuming we are using our Matlab 14 and the 5i dual core computer) will be enough to generate another key. The new encrypted block will be pipelined with the previous block. Other processing times are negligible and can be discarded.

Distortion Layer

The output of the NN layer will be further confused using our distortion layer. The distortion layer manipulates the symbols (output of the NN layer) using a set of operations whose main objective to is to greatly weaken the correlation between the plaintext and resulting text (ciphered-text). The distortion layer processes its input in two stages working synergistically to produce highly confused output. The distortion layer declares two major manipulating methods: Substitution and the Key Effect. Figure 5 shows the activity follow of the distortion layer operations.

The Random Generator

Fundamental to our distortion layer is the random generator, which produces sequences of random numbers that provide inputs for some of the distortion layer operations. The choice of the random generator is extremely important since the quality of the distortion directly relies on the quality of the sequences of random numbers. A random generator must have fundamental properties to be acceptable in encryption. First, it must have very large period (i.e. can generate really long sequences without

Figure 5. The distortion layer operations

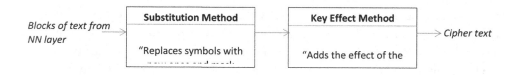

repeating the same sequence). This is important property because otherwise the generator will repeat the same sequences again over again causing similar patterns to appear in different encrypted blocks. Second, the generated sequences must pass important randomness tests; otherwise the sequences of random numbers may show patterns (recurred sub-sequences) that can be exploited by information hackers. Third, sequences that are generated using different seeds (encryption keys) should show no correlation between them. Fourth, the generator must be efficient: high speed with minimal memory requirements.

With these properties in mind, we found the random generator described in (Al-Muhammed, 2019) satisfies all the above requirements. The proposed random number generator in (Al-Muhammed, 2019) uses the encryption key (the weights) to generate sequences of random numbers with high quality. In fact, this generator possesses in addition to the four requirements another fundamental property that makes it highly effective in the security field: it has a high sensitivity to the changes of the key regardless whether the change is in a single bit or more. Table 3 shows the pseudo-code for the random generator as described in (Al-Muhammed, 2019).

In step 1, the generator extends the key to 64 symbols so that the period of the generator increases. The key expansion method extends encryption keys to any arbitrary length. The method uses two operations: Substitute operation and Manipulate operation. These two operations as described in (Al-Muhammed, 2019) can take any sequence and extend it into arbitrary length. (The technical details of the substitution and manipulation operations can be found elsewhere (Al-Muhammed, 2019).) The steps (2)–(7) define the major functionality of the generator. Step (2) uses the Substitute method. The substitution method as described in (Al-Muhammed, 2019) takes a sequence of n symbols, substitute each symbol using S-BOX (basically a table that contains all the combinations of the byte), and returns a sequence of n symbols. The main objective of this method is to propagate the changes in any bit of the key to the other symbols–this ensures that a small change results in highly different seed. The manipulation operation introduces deep changes to the block,

Table 3.

Input: **Key**
Output**: sequence of key-based numbers with an arbitrary length.**
1. Extend the key to 64 symbols to get the Seed.
2. Seed = Substitute (Seed)
3. Seed = Flip^R (Seed, n, m) /*flip the right n bits in the symbol Seed[m]*/
4. Seed = Shift^L(Seed, k) /* circular left shift symbols of Seed k positions*/
5. **For** i=1 to |Seed| /*|Seed| is the length of Seed*/
6. SUM += 256$^{|Seed|-i}$ × (INT) Seed[i] /*Seed[i] is the symbol at index i*/
7. RAND = SUM mod P /*mod is module operation and P is the range of the numbers*/
8. **If** More numbers needed, **GO TO 2**

yielding highly different sequence. Step (3) declares the operation Flip^R, which flips the right n bits of the symbol at index m. The values of n and m are respectively the integer values for the seed symbol at index 0 and the seed symbol at index 1 (i.e. n = (INT) Seed [0] and m= (INT) Seed [1]). Step (4) declares the operation Shift^L, which circularly left shifts the symbols of the resulting Seed by k positions. The value of k is the integer value for Seed [2]. Clearly the operations (3) and (4) change the Seed, allowing the Substitute operation (2) to more effectively change the Seed. Steps (5) and (6) sum up the symbols of the resulting Seed by multiplying the integer value of the Seed symbol at index i with the power of 256. The reason for taking the power of 256 is that radix for the symbols 0 to 255 is 256. Therefore, this summation never yields the same Sum value for different Seeds. See Table 3. please.

The Substitution Method

The substitution method used a 16 × 16 table that contains all the combination of the byte (8 bits). We call this table SUB-TAB. These combinations of the byte are organized as in AES encryption method. In addition, the method also utilizes two other arrays. The first array is 4 × 4 table, which contains directives that instruct the substitution method to move toward particular direction with the SUB-TAB. We call this array DIR-TAB. The content of DIR-TAB's cells is four directions with respect to some reference cell (within SUB-TAB). These directions are U (Up), D (Down), L (Left), and R (Right). The second array is also 4 × 4 table, called MOV-TAB. Each of the 16 cells of MOV-TAB contains the numbers from 0 to 15, which represent the possible amounts of movement with the SUB-TAB. In order to increase the effectiveness of the substitution method, we randomly shuffle the content of DIR-TAB and MOV-TAB; each is independently shuffled using a different sequence of random numbers obtained from our random generator. The shuffling for the contents of each of the two arrays (DIR-TAB and MOV-TAB) is straightforward: swap the content of the cell (i) with the content of the cell (r_i), where r_i is a random number. The substitution method declares an innovative model for replacing symbols with new ones using the table SUB-TAB. This replacement is augmented with a random-noise insertion technique that intelligently adds random effects to the outcome of the replacement. Thus, we can describe the substitution method as follows. Let $x_1 x_2 ... x_n$ be the symbols to be substituted. Suppose that each symbol is represented by 8 bits.[1] Each symbol x_i is first substituted using the left four bits (say k) of the symbol as an index to the rows of SUB-TAB and the right four bits (say l) as an index to columns. This initial index (k, l) is highly masked with a random effect, which is computed as follows. Let r_i be a random number obtained from our random generator. The left four bits of r_i, say c, are used to index one of the move direction directives (DIR-TAB). Basically, we use the left two bits of c to index one of the rows of DIR-TAB and the right two bits to index one of its columns. The right four bits of r_i, say z, is used to index one of the move amounts (MOV-TAB) in exactly the same way in which the table DIR-TAB is indexed. The outcome of the random effect operation is a pair (M, V), where M is a move direction directive and V is the amount of the move. Therefore, the substitution method moves from the initial index (k, l) a number of positions equal to V along the direction M. The symbol at the reached cell, say (u, t), is retrieved as a replacement to the original symbol.

For instance, the random noise operation returns the pair is $(U, 8)$ and the initial index is $(3, 4)$, this instructs the substitution method to move up (U) for eight (8) positions within the SUB-TAB. The substitution method then moves starting from the cell $(3, 4)$ up for 8 positions (wrapping down if the upper boundary if SUB-TAB reached). The symbol at newly reached cell $(11, 4)$ within SUB-TAB is retrieved as replacement for the symbol x_i. The output of the substitution method receives additional masking using the mutation operation. The mutation operation declares 14 different flipping actions summarized in Table. (Note, we assume that each symbol is represented in 8 bits. Once again, this assumption is never restrictive since the idea of flipping is working regardless of the number of bits representing a symbol.)

These 14 actions are placed in a 4×4 table. We call this table F-TAB (see Table 3). Since, the table has 16 entries and we have only 14 actions, two entries will contain a dummy action (does nothing). The content of the array are randomly shuffled using random numbers obtained from our random generator. Given these flipping actions, the substituted block is further masked as follows. Suppose that $y_1 y_2 ... y_n$ is the substituted block and $w_1 w_2 .... w_n$ is the sequence of random numbers that was used in the random effect stage. The middle half bits of each wi is used to index one of the actions of F-TAB. For instance, if the w_i is represented by "01110010", then bits "1100" are used as an index. If the indexed action is a dummy one, no processing is performed on the current input symbol y_i. If the indexed action is, however, not dummy, the action is executed on the current symbol y_i yielding a new symbol z_i. As a result, the substitution operation produces the highly confused block $z_1 z_2 ... z_n$.

Observe that because of the random jumping within the SUB-TAB (i.e. adding the random effect), the substitution becomes highly non-linear. This substitution actually depends not only on the symbol to be mapped, but also on the random effect that is produced from the random number generator. Moreover, the flipping actions ensure a high degree of confusion because their impact is random.

The Key Effect

In order to even more secure the encrypted text, we seal this text with the key effect. We do not, however, use directly the key to avoid leaking any clues that may give useful hints that can be exploited by information hackers. To effectively avoid the

Table 4. The F-TAB table

Flipping Actions	Functionality
Fi $(i=1,2,...,8)$	*This action flips the ith bit of the input symbol. For instance, F3 flips the third bit from the left.*
$F^{L/2}$	*This action flips the left half bits of the input symbol.*
$F^{R/2}$	*This action flips the right half bits of the input symbol.*
$F^{L/4}$	*This action flips the left quarter bits of the input symbol. For instance, if the symbol is represented using 8 bits, this operation flips the leftmost 2 bits.*
$F^{S/4}$	*This action flips the second quarter bits of the input symbol. For instance, if the symbol is represented using 8 bits, this operation flips the third and fourth bits (from the left).*
$F^{T/4}$	*This action flips the third quarter bits of the input symbol.*
$F^{R/4}$	*This action flips the rightmost quarter bits of the input symbol. For instance, if the symbol is represented using 8 bits, this operation flips the last 2 bits (from right).*

direct use of the key, we use a sequence of random numbers, which is generated using our random generator, to seal the encrypted text. We simply add the effect of the key by XORing each symbol of the encrypted text with the corresponding random number.

THE INVERSE DISTORTION LAYER

The inverse distortion layer cancels the effect of the distortion layer and thus restores the original block from the encrypted one. To restore the original block, we first use the same key as a seed for the random generator to generate a sequence of random numbers. First and before the decryption process can start, the arrays DIR-TAB, MOV-TAB, and F-TAB must be initialized. In other words, we must randomly shuffle the content of these three arrays so that have the same state they had during the encryption: the order of their contents is identical to that used during the encryption process. When these three tables are fully initialized, the decryption process can start. To decrypt a block of ciphered-text, we first obtain a sequence of random numbers whose length equals to the length of the sequence that was used during the encryption. The decryption process follows the same steps as the encryption except that we execute the Key Effect method first followed by the substitution method. In addition, some other small modifications must apply specifically in the way we use the sequence of random numbers.

First, the decryption process uses the sequence of random numbers backwards. Therefore, the rightmost n numbers are used to inverse the effect of the key. Removing the effect of the key is done by XORing each symbol of the encrypted text with the corresponding random number. The next step in the decryption process is to re-map the symbols to restore the original ones. Suppose that the current input symbol is y_i and the random number is r_i. The middle half of r_i's bits are used to index one of the mutation actions. Because the random number ri is the one that was used to index the mutation action during encrypting the symbol y_i, the indexed operation is the same one that was used to encrypt y_i. Thus, when we apply this action to y_i, it will restore the flipped bits to their original state yielding the new symbol, say z_i. Eventually, we re-substitute the resulting symbol using SUB-TAB as follows. The left half bits of the random number r_i is used to index one of the move directions (by accessing DIR-TAB). The right half bits are used to index the mount of move (by accessing MOV-TAB). The symbol z_i is looked up from SUB-TAB and the indexes (i, j) at which the symbol z_i is located are used to retrieve the original symbol. To do so, we use the retrieved move direction and the amount of move. However, instead of using the move direction itself, we use its inverse. That is, if the retrieved direction is U, then we use the move direction D and move down the current index (i, j) a number of positions equal to the amount of move to reach the new index (k, l). The symbol at this index "(k, l)" is retrieved, which is the original symbol.

DISCUSSIONS

The high non-linearity and the unpredictability of resulting weights of the NN result in highly elusive encrypted codes and unpredictable keys. The keys, however, are modified every 100 blocks of data transmitted. This is done with no waste of time as transmission process and new training of the NN will be going on in parallel. The standard deviation of randomly selected blocks of data is around 100. This an acceptable value knowing that the decimal values of transmitted data (encoded/ encrypted) varies from 1 to 256 (8 bits). Random test for data correlation gives values of -0.3 based on the decimal values of the encoded data. Figure 4 shows the relation between the decimal values of text (binary) and the encoded (encrypted) data. The decimal input values of the 256 possible characters show no correlation /relation at all with the associated encrypted values. The high nonlinearity and no-association pattern makes it difficult for any hacker to break the encryption. The correlation factor at different segments (every 10 characters) showed different values between [-1] and [+1]. In general, the approach is compact and very simple, the ability to re-generate new keys and their highly nonlinear implementation by the neural network is the reason of producing very illusive encrypted data. They key used for encryption is different than the key used for decryption. The key used for decryption is used at the receiver end only. This approach is direct comparing to other existing methods that use boxes, meshes, and tables for different mappings. No exhausting shuffling is used. Shuffling, mapping, and encoding are implemented implicitly and in parallel by the hidden layer of the NN. The output layer of the NN is reversing what the hidden layer has done. The 8 bits input is processed in parallel due to the parallel nature of the NN. This implies more efficiency and collectivity in generating the encoded data. Fig2 and Fig 3 summarize the training process. The validation has zero failures and the NN was acting like a mirror perfectly. More efficient training techniques could be used to minimize training time. In this method, no keys are directly generated based on random numbers generators. Expanded keys used in many methods are also indirectly based on those random number generators. Those generators are pseudo in nature and their output behaviors are cyclic and predictable. Although the weights in the NN are initially generated randomly, the encoded data do not depend directly on those keys. All weights are incrementally updated during the training (learning) process. Moreover, their output is passed through a highly nonlinear activation function with variable characteristics. The Encrypted data cannot be reversed even if the encryption key is known unless the second half of the NN is used.

The overall process of hybridization of the two methods briefly goes as follows; the hidden layer of the NN provides encrypted data, the weights of this layer are utilized also as keys in the second stage of encryption done by the substitution/ distortion method described above. At the receiving end, the substitution/distortion is reversed using the existing NN hidden layer key (weights) providing first stage of decrypted data. This data is passed to the output layer to be further decrypted by the weights of the output layer. This would result in the original plain text that was input to the hidden layer. This is what we call mirroring. It is done by the two layers of the NN. The substitution/distortion method was in between the layers of the NN. Please see Figure 7 that summarizes the whole process.

The distortion layer provides a highly effective guard against potential known attacks such as Differential Cryptanalysis (Biham et al, 1991) and Linear Cryptanalysis (Al-Muhammed et al, 2019). This layer takes the output of the NN layer to different space, causing any relationships to the original text (the input to the NN layer) to greatly melt. Specifically, as proven elsewhere (Al-Muhammed et al, 2019). the substitution operation defined herein can effectively cancel any correlation between the original text and the cipher text (the output of the distortion layer). This distortion layer defined in this chapter, adds a significant masking that eliminate any remaining tiny traces of correlation. That is because, when the result of the substitution method is exposed to random effects using the mutation operation, some of the bits of the symbols may flip causing an extra masking to be introduced to the cipher text. The key effect adds more diffusion to the cipher text and makes this cipher text greatly

Figure 6. The chart summarizing the process

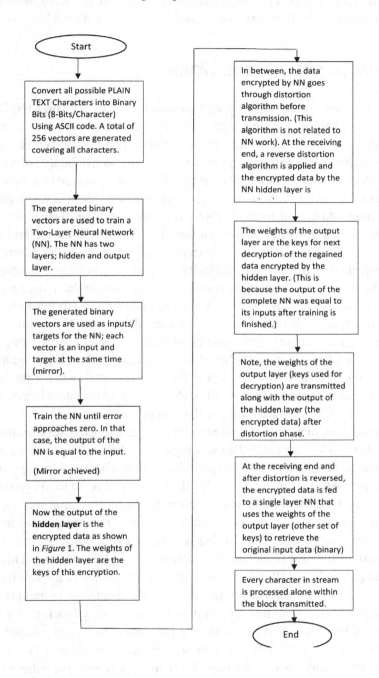

change as the key change. This extra confusion makes our proposed method much more challenging to the tools and techniques used by information hackers.

CONCLUSION AND FUTURE WORK

Although many researchers have strong believes that neural networks (NN) are not appropriate at all for encryptions and decryptions, in this work are showing the applicability of NN in efficient encryption/decryption processes. With appropriate selection of architecture and training parameters and with the availability of reasonable hardware, blocks of text or input data can be efficiently encrypted in a manner very competent to traditional methods. Our hybrid system is unique in a way it combines a computational AI-Based methods (NN) with another very illusive substitution method that uses a distortion algorithm based on table look up method with its own random number generator. This mixture of expertise raises the capabilities of encryption method and makes more difficult for any attempt to discover the encryption method. The strength of this method comes also from the fact that it uses embedded encryption accomplished by the NN. They keys themselves are not know by the system administrators or users. They are generated (through NN training+ RNG of the distortion algorithm), and transmitted with the data. The two stages work sequentially. They follows this path; NN (data encrypted by hidden layer)→ Distortion (substitution)→ Transmit a block, then at the receiving end; receive the block → Reverse Distortion (reverse substitution)→NN (decryption by output layer). The data goes back to its original binary form and then encoded according to the ASCII code table to the original plain text. The time used and the energy is very limited as we explained above. The encrypted data was regained %100 at the receiving end. All possible plain text characters are encrypted character by character during training of NN and during distortion phase. If any block of plain text is fed to the system, each character in the block will be handled separately and in the same way regardless of the word itself or the sentence constituted by the words. The system handles the input characters one by one. The training is done for every block of characters and then repeated for the next block for more security as explained above. This is very flexible and has no lag at all. While the sent block is handled at the receiving end, new training takes place at the sending end. The neural network is small (8 inputs) and has only two layers, no time-consuming training. Every block sent will have different set of keys (weights) sent with it. It was tested on core i5 computers with Matlab 19 and it was extremely fast with no bottlenecks or delays. The distortion layer obviously provides additional masking to the cipher text. We believe that this distortion is effective because it depends on variety of masking techniques such as the substitution, random effect insertion, and the random-based mutation. Encrypted data is not related or correlated with the input data in any sense.

Future work will focus on using faster and more efficient techniques for training the NN such as in (Zitar et al, 2004; Nuseirat et al, 2003; Zitar et al, 1995; Al-Tahrawi et al, 2008; Zitar et al, 2011; Zitar et al, 2001; Al-Fahed et al, 2001). Hybrid encryption or another stage of encryption could be added, more layers of NN to minimize any correlation between the plain text (inputs) and the encrypted data can be tested. We plan, however, to conduct thorough simulations to better evaluate the effectiveness of this layer. This is left for our future work.

REFERENCES

Al-Fahed Nuseirat, A. M., & Zitar, R. A. (2001). A neural network approach to _rm grip in the presence of small slips. *International Journal of Robotic Systems*, *18*(6), 305–315. doi:10.1002/rob.1025

Al-Muhammed, M. J., & Abuzitar, R. (2017). Dynamic Text Encryption. *International Journal of Security and its Applications, 11*(11), 13-30.

Al-Muhammed, M. J., & Abuzitar, R. (2017). K-Lookback Random-Based Text Encryption Technique. *Journal of King Saud University-Computer and Information Sciences*, *2019*(31), 92–104.

Al-Muhammed & Zitar. (2019). Mesh-Based Encryption Technique Augmented with Effective Masking and Distortion Operations. *Proceedings of the computing conference 2019*.

Al-Tahrawi, M. M., & Zitar, R. A. (2008). Polynomial networks versus other techniques in text categorization. *International Journal of Pattern Recognition and Artificial Intelligence*, *22*(2), 295–322. doi:10.1142/S0218001408006247

Anderson, R., Biham, E., & Knudsen, L. (2018). *Serpent: A Pro-posal for the Advanced Encryption Standard*. Retrieved from http://www.cl.cam.ac.uk/ rja14/ Papers/serpent.pdf

Biham, E., & Shamir, A. (1991). Differential Cryptanalysis of DES-like Cryptosystems. *Journal of Cryptology*, *4*(1), 3–72. doi:10.1007/BF00630563

Biham, E., & Shamir, A. (1993). *Differential Cryptanalysis of the Data Encryption Standard*. Springer-Verlag. doi:10.1007/978-1-4613-9314-6

Bogdanov, A., Mendel, F., Regazzoni, F., & Rijmen, V. (2014). ALE: AES-Based Lightweight Authenticated Encryption. In S. Moriai (Ed.), Lecture Notes in Computer Science: Vol. 8424. *Fast Software Encryption. FSE 2013.* Berlin: Springer.

Bogdanov, A., Mendel, F., Regazzoni, F., Rijmen, V., & Tischhauser, E. (2014). ALE: AES-Based Lightweight Authenticated Encryption. In S. Moriai (Ed.), *FSE 2013. LNCS* (Vol. 8424, pp. 447–466). Heidelberg, Germany: Springer.

Burwick, C., Coppersmith, D., D'Avignon, E., Gennaro, R., Halevi, S., Jutla, C., & Zunic, N. (1999). *The MARS Encryption Algorithm.* IBM.

Daemen, J., & Rijmen, V. (2002). *The Design of RIJNDAEL: AESThe Advanced Encryption Standard. Springer.* Berlin: German. doi:10.1007/978-3-662-04722-4

Isenburg, M., & Snoeyink, J. (2003). Binary Compression Rates for ASCII Formats. *Proceedings of Web3D Symposium'03*, 173-178. 10.1145/636593.636619

Knuden, L. R. (2015). Dynamic Encryption. *Journal of Cyber Security and Mobility*, *3*(4), 357–370. doi:10.13052/jcsm2245-1439.341

Komal, T., Ashutosh, R., Roshan, R., & Nalawade. S.M. (2015). Encryption and Decryption using Artificial Neural Network. *International Advanced Research Journal in Science, Engineering and Technology, 2*(4).

Mathur, N., & Bansode, R. (2016). AES Based Text Encryption using 12 Rounds with Dynamic Key Selection. *Procedia Computer Science*, *79*, 1036–1043. doi:10.1016/j. procs.2016.03.131

Matsui, M. (1994). Linear Cryptanalysis Method for DES Cipher. Lecture Notes in Computer Science, 765, 386-397. doi:10.1007/3-540-48285-7_33

Nie, T., & Zhang, T. (2009). A Study of DES and Blowsh Encryption Algorithm. *Proc. of IEEE Region 10th Conference.*

NIST Special Publication 800-67 Recommendation for the Triple Data Encryption Algorithm (TDEA) Block Cipher Revision 1. (2012). Gaithersburg, MD: NIST.

Nuseirat, A. F., & Zitar, R. A. (2003). Trajectory path planning using hybrid reinforcement and back propagation through time training. *International Journal of Cybernetics and Systems, 34*(8).

Patil, P., Narayankar, P., Narayan, D. G., & Meena, S. M. (2016). A Comprehensive Evaluation of Cryptographic Algorithms: DES, 3DES, AES, RSA and Blow sh. *Procedia Computer Science, 78*, 617–624. doi:10.1016/j.procs.2016.02.108

Rathee, N., Sachdeva, R., Dalel, V., & Jaie, Y. (2016, August). A Novel Approach for Cryptography Using Artificial Neural Networks. *International Journal of Innovative Research in Computer and Communication Engineering*, *4*, 4.

Rukhin, A., Soto, J., Nechvatal, J., Smid, M., Barker, E., Leigh, S., … Vo, S. (2001). *A Statistical Test Suite for Random and Pseudorandom Number Generators for Cryptographic Applications*. Academic Press.

Soto, J. (1999). *Randomness Testing of the Advanced Encryption Standard Candidate Algorithms*. NIST IR 6390.

Soto, J. J. (2018). *Randomness Testing of the AES Candidate Algorithms*. Retrieved from http://csrc.nist.gov/archive/aes/round1/r1-rand.pdf

Stallings, W. (2016). *Cryptography and Network Security: Principles and Practice* (7th ed.). Pearson.

Zitar. (2004). Optimum gripper using ant colony intelligence. *Industrial Robot Journal, 23*(1).

Zitar & Al-Jabali. (2005). Towards general neural network model for glucose/insulin in diabetics-II. *Informatica: An International Journal of Computing and Informatics, 29*.

Zitar, R. A., & Al-Fahed Nuseirat, A. M. (2001). A theoretical approach of an intelligent robot gripper to grasp polygon shaped object. *International Journal of Intelligent and Robotic Systems, 31*(4), 397–422. doi:10.1023/A:1012094400369

Zitar, R. A., & Hamdan, A. (2011). Spam detection using genetic based artificial immune system: A review and a model. *Artificial Intelligence Review*.

Zitar, R. A., & Hassoun, M. H. (1995). Neurocontrollers trained with rule extracted by a genetic assisted reinforcement learning system. *IEEE Transactions on Neural Networks, 6*(4), 859–879. doi:10.1109/72.392249 PMID:18263375

ENDNOTE

[1] Although we assume that each symbol is 8 bits, the substitution method is general is actually independent of the number of bits that represent a symbol.

APPENDIX

Table 5. Weights of the hidden layer-keys (example)

Neuron 1	Neuron 2	Neuron 3	Neuron 4	Neuron 5	Neuron 6	Neuron 7	Neuron 8
-0.001111	-0.010000	-0.001100	-0.010011	-0.010010	-0.001010	-10110.01001	0.001
-0.001100	-0.001110	-0.000100	-0.010001	10110.0100	-0.010000	0.010001	0.001101
-0.000111	-0.001100	10110.010010	-0.010010	-0.001010	-0.001111	0.001111	0.000111
-0.001110	-0.010010	-0.000111	-0.010011	-0.010000	-0.001011	0.001011	10110.011
-0.001100	-0.001110	-0.00111	-0.010100	-0.010010	10110.010100	0.001011	0.001001
0.100011	0.011000	0.010010	10001.110110	0.001111	-0.010011	0.001101	0.011101
-0.001111	10110.001110	-0.001010	-0.010010	-0.010011	-0.0011	0.001101	0.01
10110.010110	-0.010010	-0.000110	-0.010010	-0.010000	0.001101	0.01001	0.001101

Table 6. Weights of the output layer-keys (example)

Neuron 1	Neuron 2	Neuron 3	Neuron 4	Neuron 5	Neuron 6	Neuron 7	Neuron 8
0.00011	0.000111	0.000110	0.00011	0.000111	0.000111	0.00011	100.11011
0.00011	0.001000	0.000110	0.000101	0.00011	0.00011	100.11101	0.00011
0.001001	0.001001	101.000011	0.001001	0.001000	0.000111	0.001001	0.001001
0.000010	0.000111	0.000111	0.000001	0.000001	11.01111	0.0000011	0.000010
0.000111	101.00001	0.000111	0.000111	0.000111	0.000101	0.001000	0.001000
0.001000	0.001000	0.001000	0.001000	101.0001	0.000100	0.001000	0.001000
100.111000	0.000110	0.000101	0.000110	0.000111	0.000100	0.000111	0.000101
0.00011	0.000011	0.000011	100.100111	0.000111	0.000011	0.000100	0.000011

Table 7. Values of the bias in both layers-keys

B1	B2
-0.001	-1010.001111
-0.000111	-1010.01
-0.001001	-1010.010101
-0.000101	-1010.0101
-0.000111	-1010.010001
-0.001	-1001.0011
-0.000111	-1010.001011
-0.000111	-1010.01001

Chapter 3
Improving Spam Email Filtering Systems Using Data Mining Techniques

Wasan Shaker Awad
Ahlia University, Bahrain

Wafa M. Rafiq
Ahlia University, Bahrain

ABSTRACT

Email is the most popular choice of communication due to its low-cost and easy accessibility, which makes email spam a major issue. Emails can be incorrectly marked by a spam filter and legitimate emails can get lost in the spam folder or the spam emails can deluge the users' inboxes. Therefore, various methods based on statistics and machine learning have been developed to classify emails accurately. In this chapter, the existing spam filtering methods were studied comprehensively, and a spam email classifier based on the genetic algorithm was proposed. The proposed algorithm was successful in achieving high accuracy by reducing the rate of false positives, but at the same time, it also maintained an acceptable rate of false negatives. The proposed algorithm was tested on 2000 emails from the two popular spam datasets, Enron and LingSpam, and the accuracy was found to be nearly 90%. The results showed that the genetic algorithm is an effective method for spam classification and with further enhancements that will provide a more robust spam filter.

DOI: 10.4018/978-1-7998-2418-3.ch003

INTRODUCTION

E-mail is a means of communication which is widely used due to its global accessibility, low-cost and speed of information exchange. This makes it a popular choice of communication in both personal and professional aspects. Due to its popularity, spammers incline towards using email to send spam. Email spam has become one of the major problems of today's Internet, causing financial losses and data breaches to individual users as well as the organizations. Email spam is any unrequested email sent to a group of recipients. It can also include executable attachments/malware. Email spam is defined as any email that satisfies the following criteria (Rathi and Pareek, 2013):

1.   **Anonymity:** The sender's name and email address are unknown to the receiver.
2.   **Mass Mailing:** The sender sends the email to a large group of recipients.
3.   **Unsolicited:** The email is unrequested by the recipients.

Spam emails are a nuisance and adversely affect the productivity by consuming users' time to filter out the irrelevant emails, filling up the mailboxes, bury important emails, wasting the bandwidth etc. Moreover, according to the IBM Threat Intelligence Index 2017 (IBM, 2017), spam emails are one of the primary channels used by cybercriminals to spread malware. Users receive hundreds of spam emails every single day. These emails are sent from new email addresses with different content which makes it almost impossible to filter these spam emails using the traditional methods of blacklist and whitelist. A spam filter is one of the most important techniques to detect and prevent unwanted emails from getting into the users' inbox. It looks for certain criteria to judge the relevance of the email. The simplest version of a spam filter can be configured to identify certain groups of words occurring in the subject of the email and excluding them from the user's inbox. This is an overly simplistic and ineffective technique of spam filtration as the probabilities of false positives and false negatives are very high.

In 2004, Bill Gates famously said, "Two years from now, spam will be solved" and today 15 years later, spam is still a huge and ever-increasing problem. Therefore, it is clear that further research is required in order to study and improve spam filtering algorithms. This research is to study data mining techniques to solve the problem under study.

Over the years, email spam has become a significant problem faced by users on the Internet. These emails waste time, space and bandwidth. Spam emails are a threat to the privacy of the users. It has become an important security issue as it is also a means for propagating threats like viruses, worms, malware etc. According to recent statistics, 85% of the received emails are spams (CISCO, 2019). Despite all the research in the area of spam email filtering, on average the amount of email spam is increasing by 4% every month. Numerous methods have been developed to solve this problem, but spammers have found ways to evade the spam filters and get their emails into users' inboxes. To address this issue, this research will focus on increasing the accuracy of spam filters while reducing the number of false positives.

The following research questions have been formulated:

1.   What are the best possible techniques currently to filter spam emails and reduce false positives using data mining?
2.   How can the accuracy of the current data mining algorithms be improved for spam filtering?

Accordingly, the following are the chapter objectives:

1.   To analyze the effectiveness of current data mining techniques for spam filtering.
2.   To propose an algorithm for improving the accuracy of spam filters in order to reduce the rate of false positives.
3.   To validate the proposed algorithm using multiple email datasets.
4.   To compare the proposed algorithm with other similar existing techniques for spam filtering.

This research aims to benefit everyday users as well as future researchers in the field of spam filtering. By increasing the accuracy of the spam filters with the help of Genetic Algorithm, it can help improve the classification rate of emails, thus decreasing the high email traffic accounted to spam and also reducing the heavy load taken by mail servers. This study can also help future researchers in identifying the existing different classification techniques used for filtering spam emails by showing which algorithm is more efficient by comparing the results of the accuracy of the algorithm and the rate of false positives.

The scope of this research is limited to textual emails only. Emails that contain images, hyperlinks and attachments are out of scope. This research focuses on spam in the English language and any of the datasets used will be in English. This research concentrates on improving the accuracy of the spam filters to reduce the rate of false positives and not false negatives.

BACKGROUND AND LITERATURE REVIEW

Spam emails are divided into different categories based on their context. The various categories of email spam are (Kaspersky, 2019):

1. Health, medicine, and healthcare spam
2. Personal finance
3. Education and training
4. Adult content
5. Phishing
6. Lottery scam
7. Survey scam
8. Nigerian check scam

There are several methods used to identify spam emails. These methods can be divided into two main categories of spam filters: list-based and content-based filters. List-based filters classify emails as spam or ham by categorizing a user's email address as trusted or untrusted, and allowing or blocking the emails accordingly. The different types of list-based filters are (Hasib, Motwani & Saxena, 2012):

*   **Blacklist**

This method blocks emails from a predefined set of email addresses or IP addresses. As spammers persistently change their email and IP addresses, this method requires a lot of maintenance and cannot be used to block new spam emails immediately.

*   **Real-Time Blackhole List (RBL)**

This method is like a blacklist method mentioned above but requires less maintenance. These RBLs are provided by third parties who are responsible for keeping the list up to date. Since they are managed by a third-party provider, the chance of new spam emails getting blocked immediately increases but also the user has no control of what addresses are part of the blacklist.

*   **Whitelist**

It is the exact opposite of a blacklist. Rather than blocking emails from a predefined list of email addresses and IP addresses, it only allows emails from the predefined list. This is a very strict method and an email from a new sender will be blocked.

*   **Greylist**

This method rejects every incoming email from unknown senders and sends a delivery failure message to the originating server. If the originating server resends the email, this is considered ham and is allowed to go through because usually spammers only send out the batch of spam once and will not send it again if failed. This method is not very convenient and delays the delivery of emails.

Content-based filters classify emails as spam or ham by evaluating the words in every email. The different types of content-based filters are (Hasib, Motwani & Saxena, 2012)::

- **Word-Based Filters**

This method simply blocks any email that contains certain blacklisted words. This is a very basic method and results in a high number of false positives.

- **Rule-based/Heuristic Filters**

This method is similar to word-based filters but instead of blocking emails that contain the blacklisted word, it considers the multiple words in the email and assigns a score to each word. The total score of the email is calculated and if it is higher than a certain score then the email is classified as spam. This method is practical and effective and is the focus of this work.

- **Bayesian Filters**

This method uses statistics and probability to classify emails as spam or ham. The user must initially train the filter by marking every email as spam or ham. The filter learns from these emails and adds the words found in spam and ham emails to different lists. Each incoming email is compared to both the lists and then based on probability marked as spam or ham. Such filters become more effective the longer they are used but the drawback is that the user needs to train it manually before it can actually start working.

Since spammers use different email addresses and IP addresses to send out spam emails, content-based filters are better suited for spam filtering.

Data Mining

Data mining is described as the process of extracting useful information from raw data. It is the practice of analyzing large datasets using advanced algorithms which help to foresee future trends. It is a combination of database systems, statistics, machine learning (ML) and artificial intelligence (AI). Data mining is also known as "Knowledge Discovery in Data (KDD)" (Brownlee, 2019). ML models that run today's AI applications are dependent on data mining.

Spam filtering is a very popular application of data mining; hence it can be used to identify patterns and trends in spam emails. A spam filtering model based on data mining can be used to analyze the vast amounts of data and predict whether an email is spam or not based on its memory of learnt spam words from the dataset.

Data mining incorporates the use of algorithms to obtain the desired results. All the data mining algorithms analyze the given datasets and identify the model that is similar to the attributes of the data being analyzed. These algorithms are categorized on the basis of their suitability to a model of the data and preference. The models are of two types: descriptive or predictive (Agyapong, Hayfron-Acqua, & Asante, 2016).

Predictive data mining is a data mining model that is performed for the objective of analyzing the available data to foresee future trends. The four types of predictive models are mentioned below:

1. Classification is used to predict the class of an object based on its features. It is based on the analysis of a set of objects of known classes.
2. Regression is used to predict the numerical values of a variable based on the previously known values of correlated variables.
3. Time series analysis is used to analyze data at consistent intervals of time over a duration to predict meaningful statistics about the data.
4. Prediction is used to construct a model based on the available data to predict the possible values of data in the future.

Descriptive data mining is a data mining model that is done to discover data describing patterns and to come up with new, substantial information from the available data (Agyapong, Hayfron-Acqua, & Asante, 2016).The four types of descriptive models are mentioned below:

1. Clustering is used to find objects that are like one another and group them based on commonality.
2. Summarization is used to generalize a dataset to obtain aggregated information.
3. Association is used to identify the connection between objects.
4. Sequence Discovery is used to find rules by discovering patterns that describe strong sequential dependencies among different events.

Knowledge discovery in databases (KDD) is the process of discovering useful knowledge from a huge dataset. The steps of a KDD process described below (Han, Kamber & Pei, 2011):

Step 1: Understanding the application domain

The first step in the KDD process is to comprehend the needs of the end user to get a well-defined vision of what is expected and what the goal should be. This step to familiarize with the apt prior knowledge and helps define the process to reach the desired objectives.

Step 2: Data Selection

In this step, the relevant data is selected on which analysis will be performed to achieve the desired results. This is a critical step as the selection of wrong datasets can lead to irrelevant or inapplicable conclusions in the end.

Step 3: Data Preprocessing

During this step, the data is filtered and cleansed to improve and increase the reliability of the selected dataset. The dataset is usually cleansed of any kind of noise that may hinder the dataset. If the dataset at hand is inadequate, then it should be ensured that the algorithm is sufficient to account for the inadequate data and achieves the desired results.

Step 4: Data Transformation

In this step, useful features are extracted from the dataset to represent the data depending on the goal of the project. After feature extraction, the number of variables under consideration is reduced using transformation and reduction methods.

Step 5: Data Mining Technique Selection

In this step, a particular data mining technique is selected based on the expected goals of the project. Techniques among classification, clustering, regression, summarization etc. are chosen based on the expected output.

Step 6: Data Mining Algorithm Selection

In this step, the appropriate algorithm is chosen for the project. This selection of algorithm depends on the type of searching pattern and the desired result. The appropriate parameters for the algorithm are also selected during this step.

Step 7: Data Mining

During this step, the data mining algorithm is implemented and run multiple times by adjusting the parameters until the desired result is achieved.

Step 8: Pattern Evaluation

In this step, the mined data is evaluated to infer the results in regard to the defined goals defined at the beginning of the process. Patterns are identified from the mined data. There might be a need to remove redundant features if any. Once it is finalized, the newly discovered knowledge is documented.

Step 9: Knowledge Presentation

In the last step, the newly discovered knowledge is tested to check if it fulfils the end goal and is refined if needed. This knowledge is then applied and presented as desired.

Literature Review

Table 1 shows the existing research on spam filtering using not GA-based data mining methods whereas Table 2 shows the existing research in this field using evolutionary algorithms, especially the Genetic Algorithm (GA).

The research conducted in this field over the years has proposed a variety of different techniques for spam filtering, but email spam is still a prevalent issue. Although the existing spam detection methods have shown to be effective and reliable, spammers have found new ways to evade the spam filters. Some filtering methods require periodic maintenance. Other methods, which have solved for those weaknesses, are less effective at filtering spam from ham. The motivation for this work is to improve the existing methods in terms of accuracy. Furthermore, the aim is to propose a method that functions autonomously, without the need for frequent periodic updates.

Table 1. Non-evolutionary spam filtering methods

Reference	Algorithms	Results
Spam Behavior Recognition Based on Session Layer Data Mining (Zhang, Liu, Zhang, & Wang 2006).	• Behavior Classification • Bayesian Classification • Integration	**Items Behavior Classification:** Precision 98% Recall 53.27% **Bayesian Classification:** Precision 92.03% Recall 73.47% **Integration:** Precision 91.71% Recall 78.32% **Behavior Classification was better.**
Data Mining Techniques for Suspicious Email Detection: A Comparative Study (Balamurugan, Rajaram, Athiappan & Muthupandian, 2007)	• Decision tree (ID3 and J48) • Naïve Bayes • SVM • Neural Network	Accuracy: **Naives Bayes:** 76.9% **Neural Network:** 98.74% **SVM:** 89.9% **J48:** 96.04% **ID3:** 99.4% Simple ID3 classifier proved to be better.
Combination of Ant Colony Optimization and Bayesian Classification for Feature Selection in a Bioinformatics Dataset (Aghdam, 2009)	• Particle Swarm Optimization (PSO) • Ant Colony Algorithm (ACO)	Accuracy: **PSO:** 79% **ACO:** 85% ACO outperformed PSO by using less number of features and yielding higher accuracy.
Supervised Learning Approach for Spam Classification Analysis Using Data Mining Tools (Lakshmi & Radha, 2010)	• Naïve Bayes • MLP • LDA	Accuracy: **Naïve Bayes:** 90% **MLP:** 93% **LDA:** 92% MLP exhibited higher accuracy.

continues on following page

Table 1. Continued

Reference	Algorithms	Results
A Comparative Study of Classification Algorithms for Spam Email Data Analysis (Sharaff, Nagwani & Dhadse, 2016)	• ID3 • J48 • Simple CART • Alternating Decision Tree	Accuracy: **J48:** 92.76% **Simple CART:** 92.63% **ADTree:** 90.92% **ID3:** 89.11% J48 demonstrated the highest accuracy
Ant Colony Optimization and Data Mining (Michelakos, Mallios, Papageorgiou, & Vassilakopoulos, 2011)	• Ant Colony Algorithm (ACO)	Accuracy: 97%
Comparative Study on Email Spam Classifier Using Data Mining Techniques (Youn, & McLeod, 2007)	• C4.5 • ID3 • K-NN • Naïve Bayes • Rnd Tree • SVM	**Rnd Tree** achieved highest accuracy of 99%
An Enhanced ACO Algorithm to Select Features for Text Categorization and Its Parallelization (Janaki Meena, Chandran, Karthik, & Vijay Samuel, 2012)	• CHI • IG • ACO • Enhanced ACO • Enhanced ACO – LS	Accuracy: **CHI:** Precision: 83% Recall: 79.9% **IG:** Precision: 83% Recall: 79.9% **ACO:** Precision: 84.2% Recall: 80.5% **Enhanced ACO:** Precision: 85.15% Recall: 81.19% **Enhanced ACO – LS:** Precision: 86.35% Recall: 83%
Spam Mail Detection Through Data Mining – A Comparative Performance Analysis (Rathi, & Pareek, 2013)	• Naïve Bayes • Bayes Net • SVM • FT • J48 • Random Forest • Random Tree • Simple Cart	**Random Tree** had highest accuracy of 99.72%
Efficient Spam Classification by Appropriate Feature Selection (Ozarkar, & Patwardhan, 2013)	• Random Forest • Partial Decision Trees	Accuracy: **Random Forest:** 96% **PART:** 97%
Emails Classification by Data Mining Techniques (Naser, &Mohammed, 2014)	• Apriori algorithm	**Apriori** achieved 91% accuracy.
Comparison of Machine Learning Techniques in Spam E-Mail Classification (Jukic, Azemovic, Keco, & Kevric, 2015)	• Random Forest • C4.5 • Artificial Neural Network	**Random Forest** achieved 95.56% accuracy.
Developing A Spam Email Detector (Bayati, & Jabbar, 2015)	• Naïve Bayes	Accuracy: 100% Recall: 100% Precision: 100%
A Hybrid ACO Based Feature Selection Method for Email Spam Classification (Renuka, 2015)	• ACO-SVM Hybrid • SVM	Accuracy **ACO-SVM:** 81% **SVM:** 77%.

continues on following page

Table 1. Continued

Reference	Algorithms	Results
A Swarm Negative Selection Algorithm for Email Spam Detection (Idris, & Selamat, 2015)	• Negative Selection Algorithm (NSA) • Swarm NSA	**NSA:** 68.863% **Swarm NSA:** 82.69% Swarm NSA performs better than the standard NSA.
A Probabilistic Neural Network Based Classification of Spam Mails Using Particle Swarm Optimization Feature Selection (Kumar, & Arumugam, 2015)	• Neural Networks using Particle Swarm Optimization	Accuracy: 90% Precision: 93.23% Recall: 91.42%
Classifying Spam Emails Using Artificial Intelligent Techniques (Roy, & Viswanatham, 2016)	• Extreme Learning Machine (ELM) • Support Vector Machine (SVM)	Accuracy: **ELM:** 92.73% **SVM:** 92.17%
Application of Support Vector Machine Algorithm in E-Mail Spam Filtering (Bluszcz, etl. 2019)	• ZeroR • Naïve Bayes • Linear SVM	**Linear SVM** highest accuracy of 98.6%
Proposed Efficient Algorithm to Filter Spam Using Machine Learning Techniques (Aski, & Sourati, 2016)	• Multilayer Perceptron • J48 • Naïve Bayes	Accuracy: **Multilayer perceptron:** 99.3% **J48:** 96.6% **Naïve Bayes:** 98.6%
A Data Mining Approach on Various Classifiers in Email Spam Filtering (Balakumar, & Ganeshkumar, 2015)	• J48 • RndTree • BFTree • REPTree • LMT • Simple cart	**ReliefF filtering method:** Accuracy: **J48:** 97.17% **RndTree:** 99.93% **BFTree:** 96.82% **REPTree:** 94.65% **LMT:** 98.54% **Simple cart:** 96.30% **Chi-Square attribute method:** Accuracy: **J48:** 97.30% **RndTree:** 99.93% **BFTree:** 96.74% **REPTree:** 94.69% **LMT:** 98.54% **Simple cart:** 96.30% Both methods yield best results for the two classifiers **RndTree** and **LMT**.
Spam Mail Detection Using Classification (Parveen & Halse, 2016)	• Naïve Bayes • SVM • J48	Accuracy: **Naïve Bayes:** 76% **SVM:** 62% **J48:** 54%
Novel Email Spam Classification Using Integrated Particle Swarm Optimization and J48 (Kaur & Sharma, 2016)	• Integrated particle swarm optimization based J48 algorithm	Precision: 98.3% Recall: 98.3%
An Efficient Incremental Learning Mechanism for Tracking Concept Drift in Spam Filtering (Sheu, etl, 2017)	• Decision tree	Precision: 96% Recall: 99.5% F-measure: 97.7%
Analysis of Naïve Bayes Algorithm for Email Spam Filtering Across Multiple Datasets (Rusland, etl, 2017)	• Naïve Bayes on SpamData & SPAMBASE	**Accuracy:** Spam Data corpus: 82.88% SPAMBASE corpus: 72.57% **Precision:** Spam Data corpus: 74% SPAMBASE corpus: 76%

continues on following page

Table 1. Continued

Reference	Algorithms	Results
E-Mail Spam Detection and Classification Using SVM and Feature Extraction (Verma, 2017)	• SVM and feature extraction	Accuracy: 98%
Email Spam Detection: A Method of Metaclassifiers Stacking (Zhiwei, etl, 2017)	• SMO+J48 with SMO meta-classifier • J48+Naïve Bayes with J48 meta-classifier	**SMO+J48 with SMO meta-classifier:** Accuracy: 92.98% **J48+Naïve Bayes with J48 meta-classifier** Accuracy: 93.22%
An Anti-Spam System Using Naive Bayes Method and Feature Selection Methods (Esmaeili, etl, 2017)	• Bayesian Classifier • Principal Component Analysis (PCA)	Accuracy: **Bayesian Classifier:** 97.76% **PCA:** 92%
Spam Mail Detection through Data Mining Techniques (Shrivastava & Anju, 2017)	• Naive Bayes • Bayes Net • SVM • FT • J48 • Random • Forest • Random Tree • Simple Cart	Accuracy: **Naive Bayes:** 78.94% **Bayes Net:** 92.7% **SVM:** 86.54% **FT:** 95.54% **J48:** 95.65% **Random Forest:** 99.54% **Random Tree:** 99.72% **Simple Cart:** 93.94%
Overview of Content- Based Spam Filters Techniques and Similarity Hashing Algorithms (Devi, Supriya, & Alekya, 2017)	• Bayesian filter • Support Vector Machine • Neural Network • Artificial Immune system • K- nearest neighbor • Boosting	**Bayesian filter** outperformed all other with the highest accuracy of 99.7%
Performance of Machine Learning Techniques for Email Spam Filtering (Deepika, & Rani, 2017)	• Combining supervised Machine Learning with Support Vector Machines (SVM)	Accuracy: 98.46% Naive Bayes performs better than SVM with less data, but SVM shows better asymptotic performance as the amount of the training data increases.
A Comparison of Machine Learning Techniques: E-Mail Spam Filtering from Combined Swahili and English Email Messages (Omar, 2018)	• Naïve Bayes • Sequential Minimal Optimization (SMO) • K-Nearest Neighbour (k-NN)	**SMO** achieved highest accuracy of 97.51%
Hybrid Spam Detection Using Machine Learning (Jawale, etl. 2018)	• Naïve Bayes • SVM • Combined Naïve Bayes and SVM	Accuracy: **Naïve Bayes:** 95.78% **SVM:** 97.13% **Combined Naïve Bayes-SVM:** 97.57%s
Comparative Analysis of Classification Algorithms for Email Spam Detection (Muhammad, etl. 2018)	• Bayesian Logistic Regression • Hidden Naïve Bayes • Radial Basis Function (RBF) Network • Voted Perceptron • Lazy Bayesian Rule • Logit Boost • Rotation Forest • Nnge • Logistic Model Tree • REP Tree • Naïve Bayes • Multilayer Perceptron • Random Tree • J48	Rotation Forest classification algorithm performs relatively well in email classification with 94% accuracy.

continues on following page

Table 1. Continued

Reference	Algorithms	Results
A Comparative Study of Classification Algorithms on Spam Detection (Gayathri, 2018)	• Random forest • Logistic model • Decision tree • Naïve Bayes	Accuracy: **Random forest:** 97.27% **Logistic model:** 96.12% **SVM:** 96.27% **Decision tree:** 91.46% **Naïve Bayes:** 20.46%
Spam Classification by Using Association Rule Algorithm Based on Segmentation (Suhail, & Hashim, 2018)	• Term Frequency Inverse Term Frequency & Information Gain	Accuracy: 94%

Also, this proposed method must prove to be more effective and must yield promising results. The literature review conducted on the various spam filtering techniques showed that the GA is one of the scarcely used techniques to solve this problem although it has been used to solve various complex problems including certain types of classification problems. Hence based on this observation, the GA is chosen to find out its feasibility in filtering spam emails and to see if the accuracy can be improved using this method.

PROPOSED ALGORITHM

The goal of the data mining classification methodology is to design an effective model that can classify the most effective factors that require good input data (parameter), with suitable data mining model. The task of data mining in this research is to build models for the prediction of the class based on selected attributes. The research is based on three fundamentals which are the email dataset, data mining classification technique, and an implemented application, to classify and develop a model to identify spam and ham.

Two datasets: LingSpam (ACL Wiki, 2006) and Enron (Mark, & Perrault, 2005), were used in the proposed algorithm.

The entire corpus for this research contains 12,000 emails which were roughly divided into a training and testing set with a ratio of 80:20. The training set consists of a total of 10,000 spam emails. 9854 spam emails were randomly chosen from the Enron corpus and 146 spam emails were randomly chosen from the LingSpam corpus. The testing set consists of 2000 emails; 1000 ham and 1000 spam. 466 emails ham emails from the LingSpam corpus, 534 ham emails from the Enron corpus and 1000 spam emails from the Enron corpus were randomly chosen.

Table 2. Genetic algorithm based spam filtering methods

Title	Algorithms	Dataset	Results
An Anti-Spam System Using Artificial Neural Networks and Genetic Algorithms (Goweder, Rashed, Elbekaie, & Alhammi, 2008)	MLP as a classifier and GA as a training algorithm	• SpamAssassin • TREC 2005 • The Arabic Corpus	Accuracy: 94%
E-Mail Spam Filtering Using Adaptive Genetic Algorithm (Shrivastava, & Bindu, 2014)	GA	• SpamAssassin	Accuracy: 82%.
Spam Filtering by Using Genetic Based Feature Selection (kalaibar, & Razavi, 2014)	Bayesian and KNN using GA feature selection	• Spambase	Accuracy: **Bayesian:** 89.1% **K-NN:** 90%
Automatic E-Mails Classification Using Genetic Algorithm (Choudhary, & Dhaka, 2015)	GA	• SpamAssassin	Accuracy: 81%.
E-Mail Spam Filtering Using Genetic Algorithm: A Deeper Analysis (Chowdhary, & Dhaka, 2015)	GA	• SpamAssassin	Accuracy: 82%
A Score Point Based Email Spam Filtering Genetic Algorithm (Trivedi, & Singh, 2015)	GA	• SpamAssassin	Accuracy: 84%
Finding Template Mails from Spam Corpus Using Genetic Algorithm and K-Means Algorithm (Varghese, & Jacob, 2015)	GA and K-means	• Custom	**Accuracy before applying feature selection and learning algorithms:** 97.359% **Feature selection before genetic learning:** 89.899% **Feature selection and genetic learning:** 94.949% **Feature selection and K-Means:** 91%
Hybrid Email Spam Detection Method Using Negative Selection and Genetic Algorithms (Abdolahnezhad, & Banirostam, 2016)	Negative selection and GA	• Spambase	Accuracy: 91.90%
Providing an Improved Feature Extraction Method for Spam Detection Based on Genetic Algorithm in an Immune System (Razi, & Asghari, 2017)	GA and SVM	• SpamAssassin	Accuracy: 95%

Feature extraction is the first step to preprocess the dataset to represent it in standard format. The emails contain many features, most of which are noise or irrelevant and hamper the training process of the classifier. The common steps of the feature extraction process are:

1.   Tokenization
2.   Stop-words removal
3.   Noise removal
4.   Stemming

The datasets used were already in a preprocessed form and had already gone through the above-mentioned steps.

Feature selection is of paramount importance in data mining applications. It is a process where subsets from available features are extracted to apply an algorithm. It reduces the noise and irrelevant features and speeds up the training process of the algorithm. These selected features should contribute to the prediction/output of the classification algorithm. The feature selection method used is Term Frequency.

Term Frequency (TF) is a commonly used feature selection method in data mining. It exhibits the frequency of a term in a document. In the context of this research, terms correspond to words in an email. TF is used to measure the importance of a word in an email by counting its frequency. This is used to create the spam data dictionary with the most commonly occurring words in spam emails.

There are various techniques to classify spam emails such as header analysis, address list, keyword list, signature analysis, statistical content analysis but the most popular technique is classification using data mining. Thus, in this work, a method based on the GA has been proposed. The proposed method takes advantage of the evolution mechanism of GA which helps it to adaptively generate new variations of spam emails i.e. spam email prototypes to filter incoming emails automatically. Figure 1 shows the process of generating spam email prototypes from the spam corpus.

In this work, a spam filtering mechanism based on GA has been proposed. GA was chosen from all other algorithms due to its evolutionary traits. The evolution mechanism helps the system to generate newer varieties of spam email prototypes which inherit from the old emails. Due to the generation of spam email prototypes, this mechanism does not require a huge training set like other algorithms. the proposed algorithm is composed of two main processes. The first process is to extract keywords and construct the chromosomes which represent the emails and apply the genetic operators to generate spam email prototypes and the second process is to evaluate the prototypes and classify the incoming test emails.

The pseudocode for the proposed algorithm is below:

Procedure GENETIC ALGORITHM:

```
begin
    INITIALIZE population P using spam corpus;
    For each email i∈P, EVALUATE each email by the FITNESS
```

Figure 1. Generating spam email prototypes flowchart

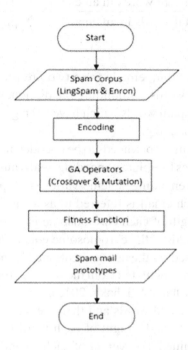

```
FUNCTION;
    repeat
        SELECT pairs of parents (i_a, i_b) ∈ P randomly;
        RECOMBINE pairs of parents using TWO-POINT CROSSOVER
operator with
        pre-specified probability, i_c=Crossover(i_a, i_b);
        MUTATE the resulting offspring i_c using RANDOM RESETTING
MUTATION operator
        with pre-specified probability, i_c=Mutate(i_c);
        EVALUATE offspring using the fitness function;
        COMPARE test emails with spam email prototypes and
CLASSIFY them;
    until TERMINATION-CONDITION is satisfied
end
```

$$\text{Weigt of word} = \frac{\text{Total spam words in an email}}{\text{Total words in an email}} \times \frac{\dfrac{\text{frequency of spam word}}{\text{Total words in dictionary}}}{\sum \text{probability of getting a word}} \tag{1}$$

In the proposed algorithm, emails from two pre-processed spam corpora have been used to extract keywords for building the dictionary. This dictionary consists of 453 commonly used spam words which have been grouped into seven categories based on their similar meaning.

To apply GA, the spam corpus needs to be encoded into chromosomes. There are various encoding schemes like binary encoding, real-value encoding, order encoding and tree encoding. The encoding scheme varies from problem to problem. In the proposed algorithm, each email is referred to as a chromosome and is encoded to a binary string. The length of each chromosome is 7 genes where 1 gene equal to 10 bits, so the entire length of the chromosome equals 70 bits. The chromosome is divided into 7 genes based on the above mentioned 7 categories of spam as shown in Figure 2. The genes are calculated from the words extracted from the spam corpus using Equation 1 (Chowdhary & Dhaka, 2015).

After finding the matched words and their frequencies from the email and the dictionary, the probability and weight of each word is calculated using Equation 1. Using the values obtained, the weight of each category is then calculated using Equation 2.

$$W_c = \frac{\sum W_{w_i}}{T_{sc}} \tag{2}$$

where i: Each word of category C and T_{sc}: Total words spam words matched in each category.

The weight of each category is then normalized to scale it in the range 0.000 - 1.000.

Figure 2. Pattern of spam email chromosome

C1	C2	C3	C4	C5	C6	C7
Weight of C1	Weight of C2	Weight of C3	Weight of C4	Weight of C5	Weight of C6	Weight of C7

In GA, the population can be initialized by either Random initialization or Heuristic initialization. In the proposed algorithm, Heuristic initialization method is used. This helps to give the GA a good starting point and speeds up the evolutionary process. The individuals of the initial population are the emails from the spam corpus.

After encoding the emails from the corpus and applying the genetic operators, the fitness value is calculated using the fitness function in Equation 3.

$$\sum_{i=1}^{i=n} \frac{F_w}{S_{WM}} \times W_i \tag{3}$$

where F_w: Frequency of spam word and S_{WM}: Total spam words in an email.

$$W_i = \sum_{m=1}^{m=7} \sum_{i=0}^{i=m} W_{w_i} / T_{SM} \tag{4}$$

where, W_{w_i} is calculated using Equation 1, and T_{SM} is the total number of spam emails.

Selection is the process of choosing which chromosomes will recombine to generate offspring. In the proposed algorithm, these chromosomes are chosen by roulette wheel selection. Roulette wheel selection is also known as "Selection of the fittest". In roulette wheel selection the fittest individuals have a greater chance of survival to be selected as compared to the weak ones. However, the weaker ones do have a chance of survival, but the probability of survival is less. The weaker solutions might be useful as they may have some stronger genes which are not present in the fitter ones and might prove useful in the successive generations.

The generated offspring is added in the next generation. All the chromosomes which are mated using crossover are also added in the new generation. Next generation also includes a portion of the highly fit chromosomes based on the fitness function ranking. The rest of the population is filled by randomly adding the chromosomes from the previous generation using tournament selection. As elitism prevents losing best found optimal solutions, it can swiftly increase GA performance.

Crossover is a technique in which the genetic material of two chromosomes is combined and at least one offspring is generated. The crossover operator used in this algorithm is the Two-point crossover. Crossover begins by randomly choosing a pair of parents from the mating pool using roulette wheel selection. Then, two crossover points are randomly generated, and each is multiplied with the total number of bits in the chromosome. The resultant crossover points namely crossover point1 and crossover point2 are then ensured to be different and also that the second value is greater than the first. The bits between crosspoint1 and crosspoint2 are swapped between the two chromosomes. This would result in the formation of 2 new chromosomes, offspring1 and offspring2. Now the fitness of parent 1 and parent 2 is compared and if the fitness of parent1 is greater than parent2 then offspring 1 is added to the next population otherwise offspring 2 is added to the next population.

Mutation is the process of applying a small random tweak to the chromosome to get a new chromosome. It is used to introduce and maintain diversity of the population. It is applied on a randomly chosen chromosome to a randomly chosen position which results in a new modified chromosome. This new chromosome replaces the old chromosome on which mutation was applied.

Random Resetting Mutation is used in this algorithm. In random resetting mutation, a random bit is selected, and its value is replaced with another random value from the given range. As binary bit encoding is used therefore the value of the replaced bit is either 0 or 1.

The termination condition determines when a GA will end. There can be one or termination condition for a GA. The termination condition for this algorithm is the reaching of a pre-specified number of generations.

The pseudocode for the classification of incoming emails is below:

Procedure CLASSIFICATION of each test email (i):

```
Begin
    CALCULATE the weight of words of each category;
    EVALUATE the test email (i) using spam email prototypes;
    IF Threshold ≥ x
        the test email (i) is considered as SPAM;
    ELSE
        the test email (i) is considered as HAM;
    Return SPAM or HAM;
End
```

The two weight of words are compared and matched, weight of words of testing email and weight of words of spam email prototypes. In this proposed algorithm, if the number of matches is greater or equal to a specific number x, then that spam email prototype will receive one spam score point. The score point of each individual of the population is calculated by using its fitness value, i.e. if the number of matched genes is greater than or equal to 4. The percentage of the population's score point is obtained by adding all the score points of the population and dividing it by population size. Test emails are classified by using the percentage of the population's score point. If this percentage value is greater than or equal to the threshold percentage, then the test email is classified as spam otherwise it is ham.

RESULTS

The performance of the proposed algorithm is evaluated based on the following criteria:

1. Accuracy
2. Precision
3. Recall

Accuracy is an important evaluator in spam filtering methods. It tells the correctly classified instances of ham or spam, but it cannot be used independently to measure the performance of a method as it does evaluate correctly when there is a severe imbalance in the number of true positives and true negatives. Due to this reason, other performance metrics: precision and recall are also used. Precision indicates the percentage of ham emails that were classified as spam and recall indicates the correct classification of actual spam emails.

$$Accuracy = \frac{TP + TN}{TP + TN + FP + FN} \tag{5}$$

$$Precision = \frac{TP}{TP + FP} \tag{6}$$

$$Recall = \frac{TP}{TP + FN} \tag{7}$$

The confusion matrix was used to assess the proposed algorithm. True positive (TP) indicates the accurate classification of a spam email and true negative (TN) indicates the accurate classification of a ham email. False positive (FP) indicates the wrong classification of a spam email and false negative (FN) indicates the wrong classification of a ham email.

The testing set contains 2000 emails; 1000 ham and 1000 spam. These emails are tested by changing the different parameters of the proposed algorithm while keeping the values of the genetic operators fixed. These values are:

1. Crossover probability = 35%
2. Mutation probability = 5%
3. Tournament size = 10
4. Number of generations = 15

The above mentioned parameters were tested with a range of different values and it was observed that their effect on the end result was negligible. Hence, after testing the values of these parameters were fixed. The following parameters of the proposed algorithm were tested with different values:

1. Population size
2. Number of matching genes
3. Threshold

Table 4 shows the results of the proposed algorithm. Since accuracy is one of the primary evaluation metrics in the case of spam filtering, it is observed that the proposed algorithm performs well in terms of accuracy when compared to the previous research which purely uses GA for classification mentioned in table 2.

Test Case 1

The values of two parameters; the number of matched genes and threshold were fixed while the population size varied during this test case as shown in table 5.

Table 5 shows that the accuracy and recall surged with the increase in population size. The precision is high initially and then continues to drop with the increase in population size and then finally when the population is significantly greater, the precision shoots up again.

Test Case 2

The values of two parameters; population size and threshold, were fixed while the number of matched genes was varied during this test case as shown in table 6.

Table 4. Results of the proposed algorithm

Total emails	TP	FN	TN	FP	Accuracy	Precision	Recall
2000 (1000 ham and 1000 spam)	882	118	906	94	89.4%	90.36%	88.2%

Table 5. Results of test case 1

No. of matched genes>= 4 and Threshold =50%							
Pop size	TP	FN	TN	FP	Accuracy (%)	Precision (%)	Recall (%)
500	101	899	989	11	54.5	90.17	10.1
1000	319	681	950	50	63.45	86.45	31.9
5000	779	221	840	160	80.95	82.96	77.9
10000	882	118	906	94	89.4	90.36	88.2

Table 6. Results of test case 2

Population size=1000 and Threshold =50%							
Genes	TP	FN	TN	FP	Accuracy (%)	Precision (%)	Recall (%)
2	999	1	236	764	61.75	56.66	99.9
3	997	3	430	570	71.35	63.62	99.7
4	882	118	906	94	89.4	90.36	88.2
5	17	983	1000	0	50.85	100	1.7

The results show that the accuracy is at its peak when the number of matched genes is greater than or equal to 4. The precision continues to increase with the increase in the number of matched genes, whereas the recall is at its peak when the number of matched genes is 2 and then plummets as the number of matched genes increases.

Test Case 3

The values of two parameters; population size and the number of matched genes were fixed while the score point threshold percentage was varied during this test case as shown in table 7.

The results show that the accuracy steadily rose as the score point threshold was increased and was at the highest point when the threshold is 50% and then showed a downward trend when the threshold is increased. The precision continues to rise with the increase in the threshold percentage and drops when threshold is at 60% and then rises again at threshold 70%. Whereas, the recall is at its peak when the threshold is 30% and then declines as the threshold percentage increases.

Table 7. Results of test case 3

Population size=1000 and genes matched >=4							
Threshold (%)	TP	FN	TN	FP	Accuracy (%)	Precision (%)	Recall (%)
30	979	21	677	323	82.8	75.19	97.9
40	951	49	734	266	84.25	78.14	95.1
50	882	118	906	94	89.4	90.36	88.2
60	691	309	881	119	78.6	85.31	69.1
70	345	655	970	30	65.75	92	34.5

Test Case 4

The proposed algorithm was tested with different values of crossover probability to observe its effect on the accuracy, precision and recall as shown in Table 8.

The results show that accuracy and precision drops drastically with the increase in the crossover probability. On the other hand, recall continues to rise with the increase in the crossover probability and at a certain point becomes stagnant. This shows that a lower crossover probability yields better results.

Test Case 5

The proposed algorithm was also tested with different values of mutation probability to observe its effect on the accuracy, precision and recall as shown in table 9.

The results show that a lower mutation probability yields better results in terms of accuracy, precision and recall. Although, the precision and recall increases with the increase in the mutation probability, those results are not feasible as the imbalance between false positives and false negatives is unacceptable.

Table 8. Results of test case 4

Population size=1000, Genes matched >=4 and Threshold=50%							
Crossover probability (%)	TP	FN	TN	FP	Accuracy (%)	Precision (%)	Recall (%)
25	870	130	900	100	89	89.6	87
35	882	118	906	94	89.4	90.36	88.2
45	981	19	658	342	81.95	74.15	98.1
60	986	14	648	352	81.7	73.7	98.6
75	977	23	652	348	81.45	73.73	98.7

Table 9. Results of test case 5

Population size=1000, Genes matched >=4 and Threshold=50%							
Mutation probability (%)	TP	FN	TN	FP	Accuracy (%)	Precision (%)	Recall (%)
4	959	41	772	228	86.55	80.79	95.9
5	882	118	906	94	89.4	90.36	88.2
7	6	994	1000	0	50.3	100	0.6
10	0	1000	1000	0	50	∞	∞
25	963	37	663	337	81.3	74.07	96.3

Test Case 6

The proposed algorithm was benchmarked with the same dataset, SpamAssassin, used in previous related works. The results are shown in table 10.

It can be seen that due to the lower number of emails and consequently less variety, the accuracy, precision and recall values are very low when compared with a larger dataset with a wider variety of emails.

Test Case 7

The proposed algorithm was also tested with different percentage of spam and ham emails in the dataset. The results are shown in table 11.

When 75% ham and 25% spam emails are used which is a more realistic approach, the proposed algorithm exhibits the highest accuracy of 95.3%. When 50% ham and 50% spam emails are used, the accuracy is nearly 90%. Lastly when 75% spam and 25% ham emails are used which is the least realistic approach, the proposed algorithm exhibits the lowest accuracy.

Table 10. Results of test case 6

Population size=1000, Genes matched >=4 and Threshold=50%							
Dataset	TP	FN	TN	FP	Accuracy (%)	Precision (%)	Recall (%)
SpamAssasin	270	62	54	454	38.57	36.94	81.1
Enron + LingSpam	882	118	906	94	89.4	90.36	88.2

Table 11. Results of test case 7

Population size=1000, Genes matched >=4 and Threshold=50%							
Spam:Ham (%)	TP	FN	TN	FP	Accuracy (%)	Precision (%)	Recall (%)
75:25	1302	198	302	198	80.2	86.8	86.8
50:50	882	118	906	94	89.4	90.36	88.2
25:75	440	60	1466	34	95.3	92.82	88

CONCLUSION

In this chapter, the goal was to implement a spam-filtering method that is more accurate than the current existing methods. In the first part of this chapter, all existing spam filtering methods in data mining were studied to understand their pros and cons. Based on the conducted literature review, a lot of the existing methods exhibit high accuracy, but each method has certain drawbacks. Some methods require frequent periodic updates while others are not practical or efficient. The objective of this chapter was to improve on some of the weaknesses and increase the accuracy. Based on the literature review, it was found that although evolutionary algorithms like the GA have a lot of scope in the field of classification, existing research on this algorithm is scarce. Hence GA was chosen as the classification method for this work as this algorithm has not been used to its full capacity in the field of email spam filtering and has the capability to meet the goals of this research.

A spam filtering method which uses GA as the classifier was proposed. The strengths of the proposed algorithm are:

1. It can classify newer variations of spam emails by creating spam email prototypes through the process of crossover and mutation.
2. It can classify unknown emails with a high degree of accuracy as the proposed algorithm was tested with randomly chosen emails from a different dataset than the training set.
3. The threshold value can be increased or decreased to the appropriate level of filtering that is needed.
4. It also provides the ability to customize the spam filter by manually choosing to not block certain categories of spam by excluding the category from the dictionary.
5. The new equation for calculation of weight of words and weight of categories is more efficient.

During the experiments, it was noted that the variation in values of the genetic operators has a very low impact on the results when the size of the corpus is sufficiently large whereas variations of the parameters of the proposed algorithm has a significant impact on the results regardless of the corpus size. It was also observed that there was a significant increase in the accuracy with a greater population size. The proposed algorithm was tested with 2000 emails from two different corpora: LingSpam and Enron and achieved an accuracy of nearly 90% which is better than the existing methods based on GA.

In the proposed algorithm, only the plain text of the email was taken into account and not the hyperlinks or attachments. This can be considered in the future research. The dataset was used 'as is' as preprocessed corpora were used, in the future the dataset can be better preprocessed to account for the new techniques spammers use like inserting spaces and special characters in between letters of a word. A broader dictionary with more categories can also be added. Only the two-point crossover and random resetting mutation operators were used so in the future the different variations of genetic operators can be used. Lastly, another enhancement in the future can be that words that only appear in spam emails receive a higher weightage than the words that can appear in both spam and ham emails.

REFERENCES

Abdolahnezhad, M., & Banirostam, T. (2016). Hybrid Email Spam Detection Method Using Negative Selection and Genetic Algorithms. *IJARCCE*, *5*(4), 1–5. doi:10.17148/IJARCCE.2016.5401

Abdulhamid, Shuaib, Osho, Ismaila, & Alhassan. (2018). Comparative Analysis of Classification Algorithms for Email Spam Detection. *International Journal of Computer Network and Information Security*, *10*(1), 60–67. doi:10.5815/ijcnis.2018.01.07

ACL Wiki. (2006). *Spam filtering datasets*. Available: https://aclweb.org/aclwiki/Spam_filtering_datasets

Aghdam, M. (2009). Combination of Ant Colony Optimization and Bayesian Classification for Feature Selection in a Bioinformatics Dataset. *Journal of Computer Science and Systems Biology*, *2*(3), 186–199. doi:10.4172/jcsb.1000031

Agyapong, K., Hayfron-Acqua, D., & Asante, D. (2016). An Overview of Data Mining Models (Descriptive and Predictive). *International Journal of Software & Hardware Research in Engineering*, *4*(5), 53–60.

Aski, A., & Sourati, N. (2016). Proposed efficient algorithm to filter spam using machine learning techniques, Pacific Science Review A. *Natural Science and Engineering*, *18*(2), 145–149.

Balakumar, C., & Ganeshkumar, D. (2015). A Data Mining Approach on Various Classifiers in Email Spam Filtering. *International Journal for Research in Applied Science and Engineering Technology*, *3*(1), 8–14.

Balamurugan, S., Rajaram, D., Athiappan, G., & Muthupandian, M. (2007). Data Mining Techniques for Suspicious Email Detection: A Comparative Study. *IADIS European Conference Data Ming 2007*, 213-217.

Bayati, M., & Jabbar, S. (2015). Developing a Spam Email Detector. *International Journal of Engineering and Innovative Technology*, *5*(2), 16–21.

Bluszcz, Fitisova, Hamann, & Trifonov. (2019). *Application of Support Vector Machine Algorithm in E-Mail Spam Filtering*. Academic Press.

Brownlee, J. (2019). *What is Data Mining and KDD*. Available: https://machinelearningmastery.com/what-is-data-mining-and-kdd/

Choudhary, M., & Dhaka, V. (2015). Automatic e-mails Classification Using genetic Algorithm. *International Journal of Computer Science and Information Technologies*, *6*(6), 5097–5103.

Chowdhary, M., & Dhaka, V. (2015). E-mail Spam Filtering Using Genetic Algorithm: A Deeper Analysis. *International Journal of Computer Science and Information Technologies*, *6*(3), 2272–2276.

CISCO. (2019). *Email and Spam Data || Cisco Talos Intelligence Group - Comprehensive Threat Intelligence*. Available: https://www.talosintelligence.com/reputation_center/email_rep

Deepika & Rani. (2017). Performance of Machine Learning Techniques for Email Spam Filtering. *International Journal of Recent Trends in Engineering & Research*, 245-248.

Devi, K., Supriya, N., & Alekya, P. (2017). Overview of Content- based spam filters Techniques and Similarity hashing Algorithms. *International Journal of Innovations & Advancement in Computer Science*, *6*(11), 265–271.

Esmaeili, M., Arjomandzadeh, A., Shams, R., & Zahedi, M. (2017). An Anti-Spam System using Naive Bayes Method and Feature Selection Methods. *International Journal of Computers and Applications*, *165*(4), 1–5. doi:10.5120/ijca2017913842

Gayathri, G. (2018). A Comparative Study of Classification Algorithms on Spam Detection. *International Journal for Research in Applied Science and Engineering Technology*, 6(4), 4791–4795. doi:10.22214/ijraset.2018.4785

Goweder, A. M., Rashed, T., Elbekaie, A., & Alhammi, H. A. (2008). An Anti-Spam System Using Artificial Neural Networks and Genetic Algorithms. *Proceedings of the 2008 International Arab Conference on Information Technology*.

Han, J., Kamber, M., & Pei, J. (2011). *Data mining*. Amsterdam: Elsevier/Morgan Kaufmann.

Hasib, S., Motwani, M., & Saxena, A. (2012). Anti-Spam Methodologies: A Comparative Study. *International Journal of Computer Science and Information Technologies*, 3(6), 5341–5345.

IBM. (2017). *IBM X-Force Threat Intelligence Index 2017*. Available: https://www-01.ibm.com/common/ssi/cgi-bin/ssialias?htmlfid=WGL03140USEN&

Idris, I., & Selamat, A. (2015). A Swarm Negative Selection Algorithm for Email Spam Detection. *Journal of Computer Engineering & Information Technology*, 4(1).

Janaki Meena, K., Chandran, K. R., Karthik, A., & Vijay Samuel, A. (2012). An enhanced ACO algorithm to select features for text categorization and its parallelization. *Expert Systems with Applications*, 39(5), 5861–5871. doi:10.1016/j.eswa.2011.11.081

Jawale, D., Mahajan, A., Shinkar, K., & Katdare, V. (2018). Hybrid spam detection using machine learning, International Journal of Advance Research. *Ideas and Innovations in Technology*, 4(2), 2828–2832.

Jukic, S., Azemovic, J., Keco, D., & Kevric, J. (2015). Comparison of Machine Learning Techniques in Spam E-Mail Classification. *Southeast Europe Journal of Soft Computing*, 4(1), 32–36. doi:10.21533cjournal.v4i1.88

Kalaibar, S., & Razavi, S. (2014). Spam filtering by using Genetic based Feature Selection. *International Journal of Computer Applications Technology and Research*, 3(12), 839–843. doi:10.7753/IJCATR0312.1018

Kaspersky. (2019). *Types of spam*. Available: https://encyclopedia.kaspersky.com/knowledge/types-of-spam/

Kaur, H., & Sharma, A. (2016). Novel Email Spam Classification using Integrated Particle Swarm Optimization and J48. *International Journal of Computers and Applications*, 149(7), 23–27. doi:10.5120/ijca2016911466

Kumar, S., & Arumugam, S. (2015). A Probabilistic Neural Network Based Classification of Spam Mails Using Particle Swarm Optimization Feature Selection. *Middle East Journal of Scientific Research*, *23*(5), 874–879.

Lakshmi, R., & Radha, N. (2010). Spam classification using supervised learning techniques. *Proceedings of the 1st Amrita ACM-W Celebration on Women in Computing in India - A2CWiC '10.* 10.1145/1858378.1858444

Mark, B., & Perrault, R. C. (2005). *Enron email dataset*. Retrieved from http://www-2.cs.cmu.edu/~enron/

Michelakos, I., Mallios, N., Papageorgiou, E., & Vassilakopoulos, M. (2011). Ant Colony Optimization and Data Mining. In N. Bessis & F. Xhafa (Eds.), *Next Generation Data Technologies for Collective Computational Intelligence. Studies in Computational Intelligence* (Vol. 352, pp. 31–60). Berlin: Springer.

Naser, M. A., & Mohammed, A. H. (2014). Emails classification by data mining techniques. *Journal of Babylon University*, *14*(2), 634–640.

Omar, R. (2018). *A Comparison of Machine Learning Techniques: E-Mail Spam Filtering From Combined Swahili and English Email Messages* (Thesis). Institut teknologi Sepuluh Nopember Surabaya.

Ozarkar, P., & Patwardhan, D. (2013). Efficient Spam Classification by Appropriate Feature Selection. *Global Journal of Computer Science and Technology Software & Data Engineering*, *13*(5), 49–57.

Parveen, P., & Halse, G. (2016). Spam Mail Detection using Classification. *International Journal of Advanced Research in Computer and Communication Engineering*, *5*(6), 347–349.

Rathi, M., & Pareek, V. (2013). Spam Mail Detection through Data Mining – A Comparative Performance Analysis. *International Journal of Modern Education and Computer Science*, *5*(12), 31–39. doi:10.5815/ijmecs.2013.12.05

Rathi, M., & Pareek, V. (2013). Spam Mail Detection through Data Mining – A Comparative Performance Analysis. *International Journal of Modern Education and Computer Science*, *5*(12), 31–39. doi:10.5815/ijmecs.2013.12.05

Razi, Z., & Asghari, S. (2017). Providing An Improved Feature Extraction Method For Spam Detection Based On Genetic Algorithm In An Immune System. *Journal of Knowledge-Based Engineering and Innovation*, *4*(8), 569–605.

Renuka, K. D. (2015). A Hybrid ACO Based Feature Selection Method for Email Spam Classification. *WSEAS Transactions on Computers*, *14*, 171–177.

Roy, S., & Viswanatham, V. (2016). Classifying Spam Emails Using Artificial Intelligent Techniques. *International Journal of Engineering Research in Africa*, 22, 152–161. doi:10.4028/www.scientific.net/JERA.22.152

Rusland, N., Wahid, N., Kasim, S., & Hafit, H. (2017). Analysis of Naïve Bayes Algorithm for Email Spam Filtering across Multiple Datasets. *IOP Conference Series. Materials Science and Engineering*, 226, 012091. doi:10.1088/1757-899X/226/1/012091

Sharaff, A., Nagwani, N., & Dhadse, A. (2016). *Comparative Study of Classification Algorithms for Spam Email Detection. In Emerging Research in Computing, Information, Communication and Applications* (pp. 237–244). New Delhi: Springer. doi:10.1007/978-81-322-2553-9_23

Sheu, J., Chu, K., Li, N., & Lee, C. (2017). An efficient incremental learning mechanism for tracking concept drift in spam filtering. *PLoS One*, 12(2), e0171518. doi:10.1371/journal.pone.0171518 PMID:28182691

Shrivastava, J., & Bindu, M. (2014). E-mail Spam Filtering Using Adaptive Genetic Algorithm. *International Journal of Intelligent Systems and Applications*, 6(2), 54–60. doi:10.5815/ijisa.2014.02.07

Shrivastava, S., & Anju, R. (2017). Spam mail detection through data mining techniques. *International Conference on Intelligent Communication and Computational Techniques*, 61-64.

Suhail Najam, S., & Hashim AL-Saedi, K. (2018). Spam classification by using association rule algorithm based on segmentation. *IACSIT International Journal of Engineering and Technology*, 7(4), 2760–2765. doi:10.14419/ijet.v7i4.18486

Trivedi, P., & Singh, S. (2015). A Score Point based Email Spam Filtering Genetic Algorithm, International Journal. *Computer Technology and Application*, 6(6), 955–960.

Varghese & Jacob. (2015). Finding Template Mails from Spam Corpus Using Genetic Algorithm and K-Means Algorithm. *International Journal of Computer Science and Information Technologies*, 6(4), 3548–3551.

Verma, T. (2017). E-Mail Spam Detection and Classification Using SVM and Feature Extraction, International Journal of Advance Research. *Ideas and Innovations in Technology*, 3(3), 1491–1495.

Youn, S., & McLeod, D. (2007). A Comparative Study for Email Classification. In K. Elleithy (Ed.), *Advances and Innovations in Systems, Computing Sciences and Software Engineering* (pp. 387–391). Dordrecht: Springer. doi:10.1007/978-1-4020-6264-3_67

Zhang, X., Liu, J., Zhang, Y., & Wang, C. (2006). Spam behavior recognition based on session layer data mining. *Proceedings of third international conference on fuzzy systems and knowledge discovery*, 1289-1298. 10.1007/11881599_160

Zhiwei, M., Singh, M., & Zaaba, Z. (2017). Email spam detection: A method of metaclassifiers stacking. *Proceedings of the 6th International Conference on Computing and Informatics*, 750-757.

Chapter 4
Odor Sensing Techniques:
A Biometric Person Authentication Approach

Yousif A. Albastaki
Ahlia University, Bahrain

ABSTRACT

With advances in technology and the never-ending goal of making life simpler for humans, it is obvious that odor sensing could lead to a better tomorrow. This chapter addressed the multiple cases in which odor sensing could be used and applied specially when identifying individuals. Various research has been carried out in this field using multiple other methods to assist create this field of studies. Most of research has been specifically focused on a single industry or field of application of odor sensing techniques. The work focused on and developed a system using artificial neural network with odor sensing techniques and laid the foundation for a general-purpose system that can be used for authentication and identification of individuals.

INTRODUCTION

The expression "biometrics" is originated from the Greek words "bio" which means "life" and "metrics" which means "to measure". The huge advancements in the field of computing processing enabled the emergence of automated biometric systems over the last few decades. A considerable number of these new mechanized approaches is developed by utilizing the ideas that were primarily imagined hundreds, even decades ago (Nancy, 2012).

DOI: 10.4018/978-1-7998-2418-3.ch004

Human face is one of the oldest and most fundamental characteristics utilized in identifying people. Since the start of the civilization, people have utilized appearances (faces) to distinguish known (familiar) and obscure (unfamiliar) individuals. This straightforward errand turned out to be progressively more testing as populaces expanded and as increasingly helpful techniques for movement brought numerous new people into-one little communities. The idea of human-to-human acknowledgment is likewise observed in social dominating biometrics, for example, voice and gait acknowledgment. People utilize these qualities, to some degree unwittingly, to perceive known people on an everyday premise.

Additional human special features have likewise been utilized since the commencement of human advancement as increasingly formal approaches to identify individuals. Stephen Mayhew in his article "biometrics update" (Stephen, 2019) highlights on the history and explorations of Biometrics methodologies and usage throughout the history of mankind. The following paragraphs spotlights on some different methods used throughout the history to identify individuals reported by Stephen Mayhew.

- Handprints surrounding pictures painted on walls of Chauvet cave believed to be at least 36,000 years old is discovered in France. It is reckoned that these handprints verified the signature of the prehistoric men who originated and painted these pictures.
- There are reports by explorers that fingerprints were utilized in Ancient Babylon to seal records or in marking authority papers as early as 500 B.C. The old Babylonians squeezed the tips of their fingertips into clay tablets to record business exchanges.
- It is reported by (Garfinkel, 2000) that the first coherent report of the use of a form of fingerprints as biometrics is utilized by the Chinese merchants to settle business transactions in the 14th century.
- Egyptian history reveals that the physical appearance of individual was used to identify and differentiate between confided traders of known notoriety and past effective exchanges, and those new to the market.
- With the fast development of urban areas because of the industrial revolution and increasingly profitable cultivating by the mid-1800, there was an officially perceived need to recognize individuals. Traders and authorities were looked with progressively bigger and increasingly portable populaces and could never again depend exclusively without anyone else encounters and local knowledge. Jeremy Bentham and other Utilitarian thinkers played a significant role in influencing the courts of this period began to codify concepts of justice that endure with us to this day. Most outstandingly, justice frameworks tried to treat first time guilty parties more indulgently and

recurrent wrongdoers even more brutally. Thus, a need for a formal approach that links the offenses along with measured identity traits of the offender is significantly identified. The earliest two methods used in this context was the Bertillon system of measuring different body dimensions, which initiated in France. These measurements were recorded on cards that could be sorted by height, arm length or any other parameters.

Currently, biometrics denoted a defining moment in the worldwide acknowledgment. It is widely used across industries, including mobile, businesses, airports, borders and healthcare and it is publically accepted. The most consumer awareness of biometrics technology is the incorporation of advanced biometric techniques into consumer devices. There are many applications for the use of Biometric Technology, but the most common ones are as follows: logical access control; physical access control; time and attendance; law enforcement; surveillance.

Customarily, authentication is achieved by utilizing an individual's belonging, something he has, or an individual's information, something he knows. For example, by possessing a house key, individuals are assumed to have authorization to enter the house, because he/she possesses the house key. The authentication device, in this case, is the house lock. Biometrics is been presented as the next huge thing in verification and authentication, supplanting or enhancing the idea of "things that you know" such as PINs and passwords. These traditional methods are the not the preferred approaches, if we aim to make individuals identification as transparent as possible. Biometrics technologies enables a substitution approach to authenticate individuals, using distinguishing physical characteristics of the human body, such as fingerprints, face recognitions, iris recognition or characteristics actions of individual such as written signature.

But despite lots of advances in the realm of biometric authentication, it's clear that there's still plenty of room for improvement. One of recent techniques used to identify individuals is through body odor or what is known as individual odor signature.

Scent, which alludes to odors or smells, can be used as a signature to recognize certain issues or sources of attention. These incorporate air contamination, environmental pollution, malady diagnostics, food classification, food spoilage detection and as a tool for crime investigations. Consequently, in the course of recent years there has been a developing interest, particularly in the territories of safeguard and national security, in the likelihood of utilizing human smell signatures as biometric identifiers. For many decades, dogs have been utilized by law requirement work force to recognize or track people by their smell signatures. The huge accomplishments of these exceedingly prepared animals give some confirmation of essential proof that people can relate to an unmistakable odor signature. Yet, there is no instrument that can substitute for the nose of an all-around prepared dog.

Odor composed of volatile organic compounds (VOCs) and it is well known that there are hundreds of VOCs in human odor (Sichu, 2009). If sufficiently nearby, the human olfactory system can smell out the human body odor with an affectability of 1 Parts-Per-Million (ppm) to sub Parts-Per-Billion (ppb) level (Pearce, 1997). Along these lines we utilize the affectability of a human olfactory system as a kind of perspective for human odor recognition in air matrices. It should be called attention to that this affectability level could be considered as a base prerequisite for human smell identification in air matrices. This is because, in many cases of human identification, it is still important to utilize the more delicate dog nose to smell out the odors. Li reported that it is believed that the limit of detection (LOD) of the dog nose in detecting VOCs in air matrices can be as low as Parts-Per- Trillion (ppt) levels (Sichu, 2009). Biological noses have both high affectability and specificity for smell out odors, and they are utilized as a model for Electronic Nose (Enose) design and advancement.

On the other hand, electronic noses are being created as frameworks for the automated recognition and characterization of smells, vapours and gasses. The two principle parts of an electronic nose are the odor detection framework and the computerized pattern recognition framework. The odor detection framework can be an array of several different sensing elements (e.g., chemical sensors), where each element measures a different property of the sensed odor, or it can be a single sensing device (e.g., spectrometer) that produces an array of measurements for each odor, or it can be a combination of both chemical sensors and a spectrometer. By showing a wide range of smells to the sensor array, a database of signatures is developed. This database of marked odor signatures is utilized to train the pattern recognition system. The objective of this preparation procedure is to arrange and configure the recognition system to deliver extraordinary mappings of every odor so that an automated distinguishing proof can be executed.

The aim of this chapter is to build on top of our research work in the field of odor sensing and electronic nose (Karlik & ALbastaki, 2005), (Albastaki, 2009), (Albastaki & Almutawa, 2013) and (Albastaki & Albalooshi 2018) to describe a framework for the detection of human odor signature using computerized artificial neural network system. This computerized system enormously builds the chances for utilizing human odor signature for personal authentication. Active researches in biometric person authentication emphasize the urgent demand for inexpensive, simple, and fast early qualitative authentication process. The chapter discusses the development of a computerized system using OMX-GR sensor to recognize human odor signature.

The remaining of the chapter is organized as follows: Related work of the field is discussed followed by a highlight on different types of existing biometric technologies used for authentication purposes. Finally, data collection and analysis will be described with the major findings of this research study.

RELATED WORK

Recent research reviled that the presence and variation of multiplicity of odor known as volatile organic compounds (VOC) in the surrounding of human body can be used as a mark for uniqueness of everyone known as human body odor signature. Therefore, to build a sold research foundation for measuring human body odor, the following paragraph will summarize the main findings in this field through reviewing the literature with a special attention given to detecting and sensing human body odor technologies and theories.

Rajan et al. in their article "Chemical Fingerprinting of Human Body Odor: An Overview of Previous Studies" (Rajan et al., 2014). They reviewed several theories touching the human body creation of scent and its characteristics. The article identified the primary human body scent to be responsible for individual identification through classifying human body odor into three different components and named them as primary odor, secondary odor and tertiary odor. The study focused and highlighted the past research that have been conducted to measure and anatomize the combination of VOCs existence in human body odor. Different methods of sampling are used in this study to collect human body odor by using a gauze pad continuing scent materials collected by direct contact with the human cuticle or evidence articles, using Scent Transfer Unit (STU), or by swiping the surface containing the scent with the gauze pad. Separation technology is utilized in this study to conduct the required analysis to extract scent compounds using the gas chromatography coupled with mass spectrometer. Alternative studies utilized the concept of electronic nose to collect human scents. Body odor and its use in forensic investigation are elaborated in this article by comparing the utilization of canine in identifying individuals and contrasting it with identifying individuals through their body productions of scents. Theories of Scent Productions are also investigated in this article. It identifies two theories for the production of scent: the Skin Raft Theory and Logical Source of human scent. The Skin Raft Theory by Syrotuck 1972 (Stockham, Slavin & Kift, 2004) demonstrates how the bacterial on the cuticle and the physical liquids shed by the Integumentary system participates in the uniqueness of the raft and as a result the scent produced. Whereas the second theory of scent production claims that the logical source of human scent might be one of the different secretions normal to the human cuticle (Tebrich, 1993). As a conclusion this article shows how different methods are used to establish the basis for utilizing human scents as the individualization biometrics. As a result, this study reviles that all the analytical studies indicate that human scent analysis is a viable method that can be used to identify human.

Bhattacharyya and his team (Bhattacharyya et al., 2009) in their article "Biometric Authentication: A Review", reviewed the biometric authentication techniques such as figure print, face recognitions and IRIS in general with a special focus on some future development in the field. This research article demonstrates how different biometrics characteristics of humans are utilized to identify individuals. The majority of information technology related systems needs a reliable personal features and recognition schemes to either assure or find out the identity of an individual seeking these systems services. The aim of such systems is to guarantee that only a lawful customer and not anyone else accesses the rendered services. Utilizing biometrics, the identity of an individual can be confirmed or established. In this technique, the position of biometrics in the present security sector was portrayed. This article also described different views on the usability of biometric authentication technologies, comparison of distinct methods and their benefits and disadvantages. This research work then illustrates the degree of security in different biometrics techniques adopted by the researchers. Different techniques are evaluated to show the degree of security when applying these types of biometrics authentications methods. Evaluation factors such as False Accept Rate (FAR) and False Match Rate (MAR), False Reject Rate (FRR) or False Non-Match Rate (FNMR), Relative Operating Characteristic (ROC) and Equal Error Rate (EER) are adopted in this research work. The article concludes that Biometric authentication is extremely reliable, as it is much more difficult to fake physical human features than security codes, passwords and hardware keys.

Zhanna (Zhanna, 2019) in his article "Biometric Person Authentication: Odor" a human identification issue is described through the authentication of the odor. This is the method of view that is still under growth. There are no commercial apps available yet on the market. While recognition of human odor is not yet accessible, nowadays odor recognition is commonly used. The author claims that technology needs become progressively advanced and less costly, biometric instruments are becoming more common as a type of identification. Vendors are already selling fingerprint recognition technology to producers of automated teller machines on computer keyboards or iris recognition. The article raises and important question: can we use the odor to recognize individuals? Medical researcher Lewis Thomas first suggested a connection in the mid-1970s between immunity and body smell. A collection of immune genes has already been related by scientists to a distinctive human body. As a result of previous research, the author claims that it is totally evident that distinct body odors are produced by individuals with distinct immune genes. Each person has a distinctive body odor that is about thirty distinct odorants in conjunction. Human body odor's primary aim is not only to identify these whole parts, but also to estimate their concentration.

(Inbavalli & Nandhini, 2014) in their article "Body Odor as a Biometric Authentication" argue that research on biometrics has noticeably increased. Biometric systems such as Fingerprint, retinal scan, face, voice, iris, signature and hand geometry are in use today, but they have several drawbacks. The authors claim that recent studies disclosed human odor's uniqueness. Compared to other biometric identifiers such as iris, fingerprints and face recognition, the body odor as a biometric identifier has the smallest error rate (15%) and this mainly because that human odor cannot be replicated. Body odor shows strong authentication over other biometric technologies that have lately emerged. This article is about developing a model scheme that authenticates individuals based on their body odor. In conclusion this article claims that odor detection for authentication in the biometric domain is a novel concept. This would lead in improved safety systems if implemented. The added benefit is that this strategy is contactless.

An interesting research paper in this field is presented by (Oyeleye et al., 2012) "An Exploratory Study of Odor Biometrics Modality for Human Recognition". They claim that the global security issues that are presently recurring and alarming have resulted to the growth and use of biometric methods for access control and human recognition. Although several biometrics for human recognition and access control usage have been suggested, investigated and assessed; it becomes apparent that each biometric has its strengths and constraints as each best fits a specific identification security application. There is no biometric modality, therefore, that is ideal for all applications. This opens a wide gap in introducing and applying newly emerging biometric methods for individual recognition and identification. Biometrics frequently applied or studied in security systems, however, include fingerprinting, face, iris, speech, signature, and hand geometry. The article argues that several newly emerging biometric modalities, including Gait, Vein, DNA, Body Odor, Ear Pattern, Keystroke and Lip, are less studied, understood, researched, promising to deliver better output, acceptability and circumvention. Finally, the article concludes that body odor, which considerably displays powerful safety potential over other newly emerging modalities, may prove very efficient for precise personal identification, little is known about its basic characteristics and human recognition suitability.

As a result of the above related work review, people with differing immunity genes produce different body odors. Odor detection for authentication in the biometric domain is a novel concept. This would lead in improved security systems if implemented.

EXISTING BIOMETRICS TECHNOLOGIES

Many biometric methods are now accessible; some of them are only at the research stage (e.g. the analysis of odors). However, a large amount of techniques is already mature and accessible commercially. Approximately ten distinct biometric technologies and methods are now a days accessible on the market. In this section we attempt to briefly describe the most common biometrics methods available nowadays.

Fingerprints Biometrics Technology: One of the oldest of all biometric methods is the identification of fingerprints. Figure 1 illustrates fingerprint biometrics process. This method maps the individual's fingerprint pattern and then compares the ridges, furrows, inside the template.

The fingerprint provided to the device is first searched in the database at the coarse stage and finer comparisons are then made to obtain the outcome. Since the last century, their use in law enforcement is well the earliest known and effectively let a fingerprint equal to crime association.

Figure 1. Fingerprint biometrics process

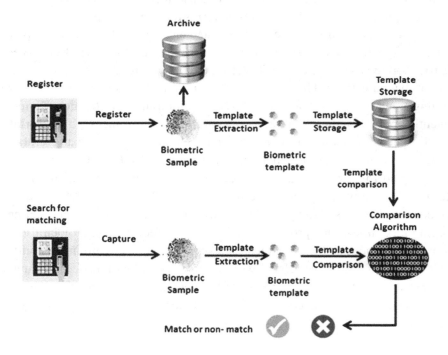

Iris Biometrics Technology: Each iris is a unique, complex pattern structure. This can be a mixture of features called corona, crypts, filaments, freckles, pits, furrows, striations, and ring. The iris is the colored tissue ring that surrounds the eye's pupil. Even twins have distinct patterns of iris, and the left and right iris of individuals is also distinct. Figure 2 illustrates iris biometrics process. Low intensity light source scans the iris and retina and compares the picture to the patterns stored in the database model. This is one of biometry's fastest technique.

Facial Recognition Biometrics Technology: The most natural means of biometric identification is facial recognition. The technique of separating one person from another is nearly every human being's capacity. The recognition of the face has never been regarded as a science until recently. It is possible to use any camera with adequate resolution to acquire the face picture. Usually the facial recognition systems use only the data on a gray scale. Colors are used only to assist locate the face in the picture. Facial scanning includes scanning the whole face and checking with the template of critical points and regions in the face. Figure 3 illustrates iris biometrics process.

Hand and Finger Geometry Biometrics Technology: Hand geometry biometrics technique is based on the reality that the hand of almost every individual is shaped differently and that after a certain age the shape of the hand of a person does not alter. This technique utilizes information such as length, shape, finger distance, general hand size as well as the comparative angle between the fingers. In conjunction with the Fingerprint scanning method, modern devices use this method. Different

Figure 2, Iris biometrics process

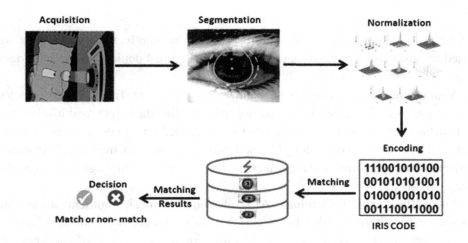

Figure 3. Facial recognition biometrics process

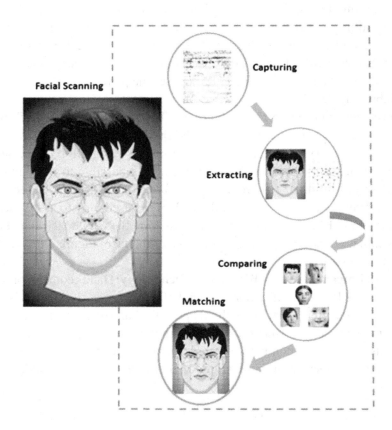

techniques are used for hand measurement. Most frequently, these techniques are based on either mechanical or optical principles. Figure 4 depicts a hand and finger geometry biometrics system.

Your whole hand provides unique identifiers beyond a mere finger. Hand geometry readers use a simple concept of measuring and recording the length, width, thickness and surface area of an individual's hand while guided on a plate, according to the National Science and Technology Council. Some scanners can measure the distance between the fingerprints and the knuckles, the curvature of the digits and even the shadow cast.

Voice Biometrics Technology: Also referred to as speaker authentication. The speaker verification principle is to evaluate the user's voice in order to store a voiceprint that is later used to identify or verify and individual. Verification of speakers and

Figure 4. Hand and finger geometric system

recognition of speech are two distinct tasks. The purpose of speech recognition is to find out what principle has been said while the speaker's objective is to verify who said that. Figure 5 illustrates the process of voice biometrics technology. This technique can confirm an individual based on speech patterns. Everything can be attributed to people by combining pitch, velocity and talking style. Users enroll by offering their credential template with a voiceprint. Speakers will utter an agreed sentence or word to obtain access, which may be prevalent to all people registered or a password particular to each individual.

Other Biometric Techniques: In the previous paragraphs we discussed the most popular biometrics techniques available and widely used in different applications. There are many less popular biometric techniques such as:

- Palm print
- Hand vein
- DNA
- Thermal imaging
- Ear shape
- Signature Verification
- Gait Identification
- Keystroke dynamics
- Fingernail bed

Figure 5. Voice biometric process

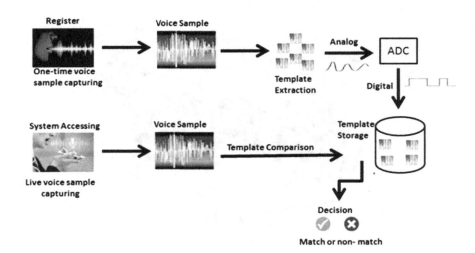

OBJECTIVES OF THE RESEARCH WORK

This research work tackles relatively a new and active research field for individual biometric authentication technique based on body odor. The biometrics of the body's odor is based on the reality that almost every human odor is distinctive. Sensors those can obtain the smell from non-intrusive areas of the body such as the underarm and back of the hand capture the smell. Every human odor consists of chemicals known as volatiles. The proposed system extracts them and transforms them into a template. Using body odor detectors raises the problem of privacy as the body odor carries a significant quantity of delicate private data.

This chapter aims on developing an Odor sensing system using OMX-GR odometer sensor as a hardware and Artificial Neural Network as software for general odor sensing system and applying it to identify individuals (Figure 6).

ARTIFICIAL INTELLIGENCE TECHNIQUES

Various Artificial Intelligence techniques have been developed and are used in different fields. For this research, we analyzed three most relevant techniques: Artificial Neural Networks (ANNs), Decision Trees and XGBoost (Natale et al., 2003) and Decision Trees and Random Forest.

Figure 6. Odor sensing system

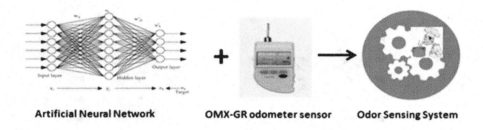

Artificial Neural Network   **OMX-GR odometer sensor**   **Odor Sensing System**

For this research, the algorithm we choose is Artificial Neural Networks over Decision Trees with XGBoost and Decision Trees with Random Forest. The reasons behind this are as follows. First, in terms of outputs, ANN is more flexible and can be used for single or multiple outputs. In addition, ANN provides the "Back propagation" feature, which requires minimal supervision and requires only input data to train itself, making it much easier to train for large amounts of data and more flexible for different types of applications, enabling the same network to be used in different fields. Lastly, with more training, the ' weights ' of an ANN's nodes are automatically adapted whenever trained to deliver more accurate outcomes, this characteristic can lead to our application being simplified so that less tech-savvy individuals can use it, thus improving its usefulness. The following paragraphs describe ANN briefly.

Artificial Neural Networks: ANN consists of nodes in various layers. As shown in Figure 7 the layers are input layer, intermediate hidden layer(s) and output layer. The links between nodes of adjacent layers has weights. The goal of training is to assign correct weights for these edges. These weights determine the output vector for a given input vector (Wilson & Baietto, 2009).

At the beginning, all edge weights are assigned randomly. The ANN is performed for each input in the training dataset. The obtained output is compared to the already known intended output, and if an error occurs, the error will be propagated back to the previous layer. The weights are adjusted by the error. This process is repeated until the error in the output is equal to or below a default limit.

A trained ANN is resulted once the algorithm is finished. The ANN is then at a functional stage to work with fresh inputs. This ANN can then be further trained by making the findings more precise by offering more input information.

Figure 7. Architecture of an artificial neural network

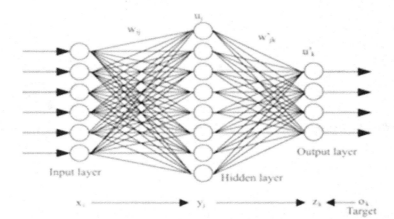

SCOPE OF THE WORK AND LIMITATIONS

As shown in Figure 8, the scope of this study is to produce a odor sensing scheme capable of distinguishing between individual sample odors using the hardware OMX-GR sensor and Artificial Neural Network (ANN)-based software. Hardware work and software execution details are outlined in this chapter's upcoming parts.

An OMX-GR smell sensor as shown in the figure 9 was used for odor sensing. It detects odors using two semiconductor gas sensors. Odor strength and classification (ID) calculated using an initial Shinyei technology technique is presented on the screen via its LCD display. There is no correlation between the OMX-GR value stated and the human sense of odor intensity value.

The ID is an integer with a range of 0 to 90 and an integer with a range of 0 to 999 is also the power or the strength of the odor. The response rate to various compounds and liquids is distinct as follows:

- Ethanol 100ppm in 20 seconds.
- Methyl Mercaptan 0.16ppm in 50 seconds.
- Xylene 46ppm in 50 seconds.

Using the custom-made application, an RS-232 cable was used to connect and read the strength and odor ID of the sensor.

Figure 8. The scope of the research

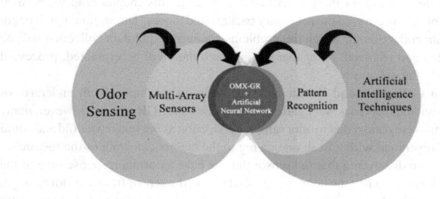

Figure 9. OMX-GR handheld odor meter

DATA COLLECTION, ANALYSIS AND RESULTS

Data collection and its analysis will be addressed in this chapter after we defined our problem and covered the necessary background theory. The argument will begin with data collection, in which the problems encountered in data collection will be examined and resolved. After that the gathered data will be evaluated, processed and lastly the outcomes.

Data Collection and Problems: Five body odor samples from underarm of two individuals' persons were gathered using the OMX-GR sensor. However, many problems were confronted in odor samples collection as the sensor was old and could not be substituted with a fresh one owing to the budget constrain of the research.

First, we discovered that the sensor did not have a normal response time to the body odors even when the odors were submitted to the sensor from a uniform range. This meant that the response time of odors could not be used as an input parameter for the neural network, which could have resulted in more precise outcomes. The response time of three odors is stated in the sensor handbook from which it can be concluded that the sensor initially had a normal response time. Nonetheless, as the sensor had grown old, its response time might have been impacted.

Next, when we attempted to read distinct odors in fast succession, the sensor gave entirely distinct measurements to the odor measurements earlier acquired. After research, we learned that distinct sensors have distinct retrieval times in relation to response time. Unlike reaction moment, however, the retrieval time was not stated in the handbook of the sensor. Therefore, to define the retrieval time, we began by enabling the sensor a retrieval time of 5 seconds and checking the readings consistency. The consistency of the readings did not improve, so we increased the recovery time further, this continued until we had increased the recovery time to 10 minutes and the consistency of the readings had not improved, as sometimes the sensor would not respond to an odor even after 10 minutes of recovery time. We therefore found that the sensor no longer had a normal reaction or retrieval time.

Then it also came to our understanding that environmental variables, i.e. temperature and humidity, influence sensor measurements. This has also been verified in numerous researches. To decrease the impact of environmental variables, tubes of variable dimensions were used to directly expose odors to the sensor and limit the impact of the environment on them.

Even after taking all the above measures to enhance the measurements, coherent measurements were not acquired. Therefore, the following technique of purification was used to achieve coherent measurements.

1.   Each body odor reading should be taken from a specific distance every time.
2.   The readings should be taken through the pipe chambers.

3. The sensor should be given a recovery time of at least 10 minutes after every reading.
4. A reading is considered acceptable only if the reading's ID has a range difference of 3 for 60 seconds and this reading is consistent with previous readings of the same substance.
5. Readings of two individual's underarm odors were taken, each for 60 seconds. Samples of the realigning are shown in figure 10. The acceptable readings are discussed and analyzed in the following section.

Data Analysis and Data Cleaning: In data analysis, the readings of the 5 body odors for two individuals will be analyzed. A total of 600 readings were taken for two volunteer's body odors (300 samples for each) over 5 sessions of 60 readings each. Each reading has an ID and strength. Figure 11 and 12 shows the density for IDs readings and strengths readings respectively.

Figure 11 shows the ID density values of the odor readings. The ID values of the first-person odor range between 63.5 and 66.5. Figure 12 shows the strength density values of the odor readings. The strength values of the first person's odor range between 135 and 165.

Figure 10. Samples of body odors

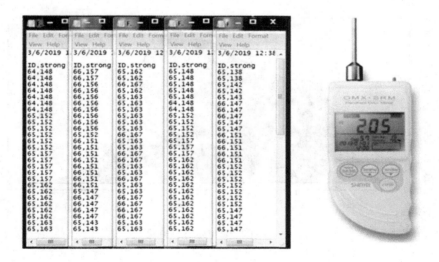

Figure 11. IDs density

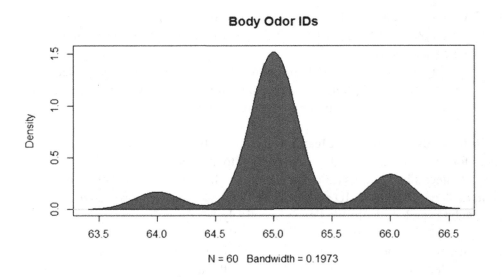

Figure 12. Strengths density

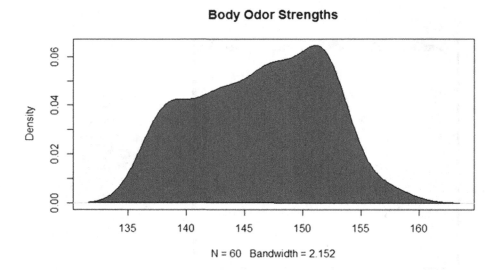

BASIC DESIGN AND ARCHITECTURE

The basic design and architecture are described in figure 13. The design basically collects individual body odors by a chemical sensor array and fed to the artificial neural network system for odor identification and classification. Consequently, the classification will be retrieved for authentication purposes.

DATA PROCESSING AND RESULTS

In order to process the information and to identify the odors using the neural network, the measurements were split into a proportion of 20, 70 and 30 for validation, training and testing according to the results of the Neural Networks Division. This implies that 20 percent of the complete readings (1500) were randomly chosen for validation set. Of the remaining 1200 readings, 70 percent were randomly chosen to train the network and the remaining 360 readings (30 percent) were used to test the qualified network.

Different architectures were used to train the neural network to assess which one would be the most suitable. Training was done until an error rate of 0.1000 was obtained. The details of trainings using different architectures are given in table 1, where the architecture of the neural network is represented as number of input layers: number of neurons in the hidden layer: number of neurons in the output layer.

After analyzing the results obtained in table 1 we can conclude that the best architecture for the information submitted to the neural network was 2:6:1. Training time reduced as the amount of neurons in the hidden layer increased until the amount

Figure 13. Basic design and architecture

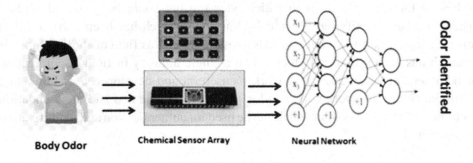

Body Odor   Chemical Sensor Array   Neural Network

Table 1. Training results of different architectures

Architecture	Training Time	Epochs Completed	Validation Rate
2:2:1	1h 14m 04s	3,740,445	0.03968
2:3:1	0h 03m 59s	178,999	0.03673
2:4:1	0h 02m 41s	68,0998	0.03809
2:5:1	0h 02m 02s	65,957	0.03098
2:6:1	0h 01m 41s	4,876	0.03752
2:7:1	0h 01m 59s	36,613	0.03801

of neurons in the hidden layer was 7. The number of epochs reduced as the number of neurons in the concealed layer increased. However, there was no important change in the validation rate, but the 2:6:1 architecture also obtained the highest validation rate. A simple 2:2:1 architecture was not suitable as there were overlapping data in both ID and Strength values, and therefore the neural network took a lot of time to train itself to attain a maximum error rate of 0.1000. It should be noted that, regardless of which architecture is chosen for training, if the required maximum error rate is achieved during training, the testing and querying accuracy of the neural network will not be significantly affected by the architecture of the network.

After training the network with the purified information, testing was conducted to evaluate the network's efficiency. The neural network properly categorized all 360 test samples, which meant that a 100 percent precision rate was achieved as shown in Figure 14 produced by the program.

CONCLUSION AND FINDINGS

With advances in technology and the never-ending goal of making life simpler for humans, it is obvious that odor sensing could lead to a better tomorrow. This chapter addressed the multiple cases in which odor sensing could be used and applied specially when identifying individuals. Various research has been carried out in this field using multiple other methods to assist create this field of studies. Most of research has been specifically focused on a single industry or field of application of odor sensing techniques. Our work focused on and developed a system using Artificial Neural Network with an odor sensing technique and laid the foundation for a general-purpose system which can be used for authentication and identification of individuals.

Figure 14.

Network Testing Performance Report

Network Details

Name:	BodyOdor
Type:	ActivationNetwork
Layout:	6-1
Function:	SigmoidFunction
Description:	

Network Schema

Inputs:	ID, Strength
Outputs:	Output

* Underlined fields indicates a categorical (non numeric) field

Training Details

Training Entries:	840
Validation Entries:	300
Training Deviation:	0.0999998878999852

Testing Summary

Testing Entries:		360
Testing Items:		360
Hits:	360	100.00%
Correct:	360	100.00%
Incorrect:	0	0.00%
Errors:	0	0.00%

The odor meter used in this research was an OMX-GR sensor which is mainly a semiconductor-based gas sensor. Artificial Neural Network was used as software, together with the smell sensor as hardware, which was built on top of the Sinapse framework and the framework itself was heavily modified to fit the research needs. Due to the sensor being old, and its other various limitations. Many methods had to be tried for data collection. Adjustments had to be made to the distance between the sample and the detector while gathering measurements, its retrieval times, and other internal variables to guarantee accurate measurements. The data was also cleaned and went through a purification process.

Data was collected and purified before it was fed to the ANN to train on and then the Artificial Neural Network was tested for accuracy. This method has been repeated for all the samples collected. Backpropagation algorithm was used to train and adjust weights to guarantee accurate outcomes.

Findings: The scheme established in this study could distinguish between different kinds of odors with a precision of between 93-100 percent. It indicates that Artificial Neural Networks can be used very effectively with smell sensors to detect multiple odors owing to the big quantity of information engaged in the nature of the issue and ANN's ability to learn and train further as more information is supplied, thereby improving its accuracy.

Limitations: There were numerous constraints affecting the study, primarily those linked to the smell sensor. The smell sensor used in this study is an OMX-GR sensor that was old. Because of this, the technique of information collection had to be adjusted to the restriction of the sensor. Some of these constraints linked to connectivity problems as the sensor's Serial Port utilizes legacy drivers that are uncommon to discover. Therefore, in order to make the sensor compatible, required drivers had to be implemented within the scheme. In addition, due to the absence of comprehensive sensor documentation, numerous experiments and tweaks had to be made to the information collection techniques to guarantee that the most precise information was obtained. Some of the information collection problems linked to the sensor's recovery and response time

Some constraints linked to software were also the restriction of the system used. This resulted to the development of numerous new features to make the system perform better and quicker and make it much easier to use.

Future Implementations: In the future, research could be performed to test the system with multiple other sensors that are contemporary and accurate to get measurements of more odors with more parameters, i.e. response time, to have a high precision with a greater number of odors. In addition, the capacity to develop a cloud-based data hub where different research could contribute with their information and samples to train the ANN could also lead to further innovations in the field of odor sensing. As far as sophisticated software is concerned, it can be improved by combining the ANN with a Genetic algorithm to avoid being stuck in local minima while training.

REFERENCES

Albastaki, Y. (2009). An Artificial Neural Networks-Based On-Line Monitoring Odor Sensing System. *Journal of Computational Science*, 878–882.

Albastaki, Y., & Albalooshi, F. (Eds.). (2018). *Electronic Noses and Technologies and Advances in Machine Olfaction*. IGI Global. doi:10.4018/978-1-5225-3862-2

Albastaki, Y., & Almutawa, K. (2013). *ANN Based Approach to Integrate Smell Sense in Multimedia Systems, Technology Diffusion and Adoption: Global Complexity, Global Innovation: Global Complexity, Global Innovation*. IGI Global.

Bhattacharyya, D., Ranjan, R., Alisherov, F. A., & Choi, M. (2009). Biometric Authentication: A Review. International Journal of u- and e- Service. *Science and Technology, 2*(3), 13–27.

Inbavalli, P., & Nandhini, G. (2014). Body Odor as a Biometric Authentication. *International Journal of Computer Science and Information Technologies, 5*(5), 6270–6274.

Karlik, B. & Albastaki, Y. (2005). Bad breath diagnosis system using OMX-GR sensor and Neural Network for telemedicine, Computer Medicine '2005, Scientific-practical Conference [eHealth]. *ElectronicHealthcare*, 23–25.

Nancy, Y. L. (2012). *Bio-Privacy: Privacy Regulations and Challenge of Biometrics*. Academic Press.

Natale, D. C., Macagnano, A., Martinelli, E., Paolesse, R., D'Arcangelo, G., Roscioni, C., & D'Amico, A. (2003). Lung cancer identification by the analysis of breath by means of an array of non-selective gas sensors. *Biosensors & Bioelectronics, 18*(10), 1209–1218. doi:10.1016/S0956-5663(03)00086-1 PMID:12835038

Oyeleye, C. A., Fagbola, T. M., Babatunde, R. S., & Adigun, A. A. (2012). An Exploratory Study of Odor Biometrics Modality For Human Recognition. *International Journal of Engineering Research & Technology, 1*(9).

Pearce, T. C. (1997). Computational parallels between the biological olfactory pathway and its analogue. The Electronic Nose ': Part II. Sensor-based machine olfaction. *Bio Systems, 41*(2), 69–90. doi:10.1016/S0303-2647(96)01660-7 PMID:9043677

Rajan, R., Fakhuruddin, N., Hassan, N., & Nasimul Islam, M. (2014). Chemical Fingerprinting of Human Body Odor: An Overview of Previous Studies. *Malaysian Journal of Forensic Sciences, 4*(1), 33–38.

Sichu, L. (2009). *Overview of Odor Detection Instrumentation and the Potential for Human Odor Detection in Air Matrices*. MITRE Nano systems Group, MITRE Innovation Program and U.S. Government Nano-enabled Technology Initiative, Project No. 07MSR216 and 15095320, Dept. E552.

Stephen, M. (2019). *Biometrics Updates*. Retrieved from https://www. biometricupdate.com

Stockham, R.A., Slavin, D.L., & Kift, W. (2004). Specialized Use of Human Scent in Criminal Investigations. *Forensic Sciences Communications*, 1-12.

Tebrich, S. (1993). *Human Scent and Its Detection*. Retrieved from: https:// www.cia.gov/library/center-forthe- study-of-intelligence/kentcsi/ vol5no2/html/ v05i2a04p_0001.htm

Wilson, A., & Baietto, M. (2009). Applications and Advances in Electronic-Nose technologies. *Sensors (Basel)*, *9*(7), 5099–5148. doi:10.339090705099 PMID:22346690

Zhanna, K. (2005). Biometric Person Authentication: Odor. *Techylib*. Retrieved from https://www.techylib.com/en/view/nauseatingcynical/biometric_person_ authentication_odor_2

Chapter 5
Agent–Based Intrusion Detection in Wireless Networks

Leila Mechtri
Badji Mokhtar University, Algeria

Fatiha Tolba Djemili
Badji Mokhtar University, Algeria

Salim Ghanemi
Badji Mokhtar University, Algeria

ABSTRACT

The need for effective, optimal, and adaptive intrusion detection systems that fit wireless networks' requirements caused agent-based intrusion detection systems to prevail though the complexity and challenges entailed by their deployment. This chapter presents the recent achievements in terms of the proposed frameworks, architectures, and implementations for the application of agent technology to intrusion detection in wireless networks. The chapter highlights their main features, strengths, and limitations. It also discusses the main issues that most existing works do not address like IDS security and proposes solutions to cope with some of the presented problems.

INTRODUCTION

Wireless networks are highly vulnerable to security threats and ensuring their security is a prime concern and an impeding issue that should be addressed. Since conventional security measures such as authentication and firewalls are not sufficient or non-applicable to these networks, plenty of other solutions are proposed in the

DOI: 10.4018/978-1-7998-2418-3.ch005

literature to solve their security issues. Example solutions are: prevention techniques (John and Samuel, 2015; Gharib, Moradlou, Doostari, & Movaghar, 2017; Gomathi, Parvathavarthini, & Saravanakumar, 2017), Secure routing (K. Sanzgiri et al., 2005; Hu, Johnson, & Perrig, 2003), and trust-based routing (Wang, Govindan, & Mohapatra, 2010; Sethuraman and Kannan, 2017; Saswati, Matangini, Samiran, & Pragma, 2018).

Most of the proposed solutions for attack prevention and to build secure routing protocols are attack-oriented. Such solutions can perform efficiently against some specific attacks but not if faced with insider attacks or unknown threats. In addition, the use of cryptography (mainly asymmetric cryptography) is resource consuming and secure routing protocols create extra overhead to achieve their goals. To cope with these problems intrusion detection systems (IDSs) are used as a second line of defence.

Wireless IDSs are, generally, classified into four main classes (architectures), namely, stand-alone IDSs (Cheng and Tseng, 2011), distributed and cooperative IDSs (Farhan, Dahalin, and Jusoh, 2010), hierarchical IDSs (Marchang and Datta, 2008), and agent-based IDSs. Contrary to stand-alone IDSs, where the detection process is performed on each node, and there is no cooperation or data exchange between the network nodes, distributed and cooperative IDSs suggest that every node in the network must participate cooperatively in intrusion detection and response. Hierarchical IDSs, on the other hand, are the most suitable for multi-layered networks where the network is divided into clusters. The main idea behind this architecture is that instead of performing host-based intrusion detection at each node, a cluster head is selected to collect security-related information from nodes in a cluster and to determine if an intrusion has occurred. The last architecture of IDSs, denoted agent-based IDS architecture, is based on the distribution of the intrusion detection tasks amongst a number of agents.

It is worth noting that contrary to former IDS architectures (stand-alone, distributed and cooperative, and hierarchical) which were excessively used for the development of wireless IDSs, the studies that approach agent-based IDSs were quite few in the early years of IDS deployment in wireless networks. This is mainly due to: (i) the additional complexity involved in developing agent-based IDSs especially as this technology is known for introducing new challenges with respect to security mainly when dealing with mobile agents and (ii) the lack of experience in formulating agent-based solutions to applications. However, as they, recently, proved several advantages, agents are gaining great attention especially for their suitability for the building of distributed applications. This is what encourages many researchers to explore more possibilities for the application of agents in the context of intrusion detection.

In this chapter, key notions related to the field of intrusion detection in wireless networks and a literature review highlighting the recent achievements in this field are presented. Key points in this review are static agent based IDSs, mobile agent based IDSs, and hybrid agent based IDSs.

The chapter is organized as follows: section 2 outlines the basic features of IDSs, software agents and agent-based technologies. Then, section 3 focuses on the recent advances in the field of agent-based intrusion detection in wireless networks (mainly mobile ad hoc networks (MANET) and wireless sensor networks (WSN)). Section 4 presents and discusses the drawn conclusions about agent deployment in intrusion detection. Finally, some concluding remarks are given in section 5.

BACKGROUND

This section introduces some concepts and terminology related to the field of agent-based intrusion detection.

Intrusion Detection

Intrusion detection is the process of monitoring and analysing events of computer systems or networks in order to uncover any set of actions that attempt to compromise the integrity, confidentiality or availability of a resource (Hung-Jen, Chun-Hung, Ying-Chih, & Kuang-Yuan, 2013).

There are two main intrusion detection methods, namely anomaly detection and misuse (or signature-based) detection. Anomaly detection (Garcia-Teodoro, Diaz-Verdejo, Maciá-Fernández, & Vázquez, 2009; Devi and Bhuvaneswaran, 2011) models normal behaviour i.e., it compares observed data to normal behaviour patterns, while misuse detection (Li et al., 2019) deals with attack behaviour i.e., it compares observed data to known attack patterns. A hybrid technique (Farhan, Zulkhairi, & Hatim, 2008; Nadeem and Howarth, 2014) that combines both anomaly and misuse detection can be considered as a third method of detection. Each of these methods has some advantages over the other one, but at the same time, they present some serious shortcomings. For instance, misuse detection is effective for accurately detecting known attacks but it generally fails to detect unforeseen attacks. Unfortunately, this inability to detect unknown attacks is deemed to generate a significant number of false negative alarms. Anomaly detection, on the other hand, allows the detection of new attacks since it focuses, during its analyses, on any deviation from the normal behaviour of the supervised system rather than being limited to the search of some specific attack scenarios. However, this might lead to the generation of a significant number of false positive alarms since it is often difficult to perfectly model the system's normal behaviour.

The source of data used by those methods can be either the host on which the intrusion detection system (IDS) is run or the network itself. Thus, we come to distinguish between two classes of IDSs which are Host-based IDSs (H-IDS) and Network-based IDSs (N-IDS).

The commonly used metrics for IDS evaluation are summarized in Table 1.

Where values of TP, TN, FP and FN are determined with respect to the relation between the predicted and actual classes of the audited profiles as illustrates table 2.

Software Agents

An agent (Breitman, Casanova, and Truszkowski, 2007) can be defined as a computer system that is able to execute autonomous actions in its environment, in a flexible

Table 1. IDS evaluation metrics

Metric	Formula	Description
Accuracy	$(TP + TN)/(TP + TN + FP + FN)$	The probability that the IDS can correctly predict normal profiles and attacks
Precision	$TP/(TP + FP)$	The proportion of predicted attack cases that are real attacks
Specificity	$TN/(TN + FP)$	The proportion of normal profiles that are successfully identified as normal profiles
Detection rate (Recall)	$TP/(TP + FN)$	The proportion of attacks that are successfully identified as attack cases
False positive alarm rate	$FP/(FP + TN)$	The proportion of learned normal profiles that are considered as attacks
False negative alarm rate	$FN/(FN + TP)$	The proportion of attacks that are not successfully detected

Table 2. IDS confusion matrix

		Predicted class	
		Normal profile	**Attack**
Actual class	Normal profile	True negative (TN)	False positive (FP)
	Attack	False negative (FN)	True positive (TP)

and intelligent manner, in order to achieve a predefined goal. Therefore, a multi-agent system is a system that consists of a collection of autonomous agents that can interact together to learn or to exchange experiences. Agent-based systems usually encompass three main types of agent architectures, namely: reactive, deliberative and the hybrid architecture where aspects of both reactive and deliberative agents are combined.

Reactive agents do not have representations of their own environment and act using a stimulus/response type of behaviour; they respond to the present state of the environment in which they are situated. They neither take history into account nor plan for the future. Reactive agents make decisions based on local information. Thus, they cannot take into consideration non-local information or predict the effect of their decisions on the global behaviour of the multi-agent system. Moreover, they lack adaptability as they cannot generate an appropriate plan if faced with a state that was not considered a priori. Despite these limitations, reactive agents still have the advantage of being speed which necessarily makes them desired in rapidly changing environments.

The key component of a deliberative agent is a central reasoning system that constitutes the intelligence of the agent. Thus, unlike reactive agents, deliberative agents maintain a model of the internal state and they are able of predicting the effects of their committed actions. More importantly, these agents are mainly characterized by their ability to generate plans that successfully lead to the achievement of their goals even in unforeseen situations. Unfortunately, a major problem with deliberative agents is that the sophisticated reasoning can slow them which may cause latency in the reaction time which is undesirable especially in case of real-time applications.

Regardless of their architecture, agents present several common features, among which we cite:

- **Autonomy:** Agents operate without the direct intervention of humans or others, and have some kind of control over their actions and internal state. In other words, it takes actions based on its built-in knowledge and its past experiences;
- **Social Ability:** Agents interact with other agents via some kind of agent-communication language;
- **Reactivity:** Agents perceive their environment and respond in a timely fashion to changes that occur in it;
- **Pro-Activeness:** Agents do not simply act in response to their environment, but they are able to exhibit goal-directed behaviour by taking initiative;
- **Negotiation:** The ability to conduct organized conversations to achieve a degree of cooperation with other agents;

- **Adaptation:** The ability to improve its performance over time when interacting with the environment in which it is embedded.

With these interesting features in mind, many researchers sought to investigate this technology in developing optimal, adaptive and comprehensive intrusion detection systems. Agents used for intrusion detection can be either static agents, used mainly for monitoring purposes and for local intrusion detection, or mobile agents best suited for distributed operations such as: gathering network-related information, broadcasting detection results and performing global responses while offering several advantages like: network load reduction, dynamic adaption, robustness and flexibility.

AGENT-BASED IDSs

Agent-based IDSs rely on the distribution of the intrusion detection tasks amongst a number of software agents. Recently, new paradigms for the deployment of agent-based IDSs were explored. The following subsections review some interesting works in this area highlighting their main features, strengths and limitations.

Static Agent Based IDSs

FORK (Ramachandran, Misra, & Obaidat, 2008) is a two-pronged strategy to an agent-based intrusion detection system for ad-hoc networks, in which only those nodes that are capable of participating in the intrusion detection process, in terms of their available resources and their reputation level are allowed to compete for and get the IDS agent tasks. The authors base the task allocation process on principles of auctioning. Whenever one or more nodes detect certain changes in the network, they initiate an auction process by submitting auction requests to the rest of the network nodes. The interested nodes submit their bids to the initiating node(s) that, then, choose them based on several metrics including a battery power metric. Finally, the chosen nodes perform the intrusion detection tasks using a variation of the Ant Colony Optimization (ACO) algorithm. For instance, each network node contains all the modules (lightweight agents) required to perform the anomaly detection tasks such as: host and network monitoring (data collection), the decision making given a set of audit data, and the activation of defensive actions if malicious behaviours have been detected.

Experiments show that the proposed detection algorithm is effective in terms of the accuracy of rules formed and the simplicity in their content. It was also shown that detection rates were improved compared to other IDSs. Nevertheless, node mobility, which highly affects the detection accuracy, was not considered in this evaluation. On the other hand, the distribution of detection tasks among a set of carefully selected nodes helps conserving local resources, mainly battery power. However, this IDS seems to be insecure as no suggestions about securing the mobile agents were given. Also, the cooperative nature of the proposed detection scheme offers the opportunity to malicious nodes to cause resource-consumption-like attacks by initiating fake detection tasks.

The biological immune system was a source of inspiration for several agent-based IDS designers, who tried to take benefit of the analogy that exists between the two fields to approach the distinguished ability of the biological immune system to distinguish self from non-self and to protect the human body from this latter.

An example of such IDS architecture is presented in (Byrski and Carvalho, 2008). Here, Byrsky and Carvalho designed an immunological intrusion detection system based on the agent concept for securing MANET. This IDS consists of a set of autonomous agents, denoted detectors, distributed among the different network nodes. Each detector implements an anomaly intrusion detection approach based on the negative selection algorithm and monitors the communication of its neighbouring nodes. For that, every node maintains both a set of self-patterns (characterizing normal behaviour) and a set of non-self-patterns (characterizing potential anomalous behaviour). Upon the observation of any kind of disturbance in the behaviour of a node, the concerned detectors communicate with neighbouring detectors in order to consult their observations. Then, a collective decision is undertaken based on the reliability weight of contributing detectors. This weight is applied by the super-detectors that represent the second level of detectors.

Although it seems simple and effective in detecting intrusions, this approach might have a negative effect on the nodes' performance mainly in networks with high mobility, where detectors and super-detectors have to regenerate neighbours' self-patterns and non-self-patterns as well as neighbouring detectors' reliability weights each time the network topology changes. So far, the approach ensures a high level of reliability because even if the detectors cannot maintain contact among themselves, they still may react to the behaviour they sense.

Some generic static agent-based IDSs that can be adopted for MANET were also proposed in the literature. For instance, Servin and Kudenko (2008) proposed a hierarchical architecture of distributed intrusion detection systems integrated by remote sensor agent diversity and reinforcement learning (RL) to detect and categorize DDoS Attacks.

This architecture is built from m cells with each cell composed of one central agent (RL-IDS) and n sensor agents. In RL, agents or programs sense their environment in discrete time steps and they map those inputs to local state information. Under this consideration, distributed sensor agents were configured so that to process the local state information and pass on short signals up a hierarchy of RL-IDS agents. That is, a sensor agent learns to interpret local state observations, and communicates them to a central agent higher up in the agent hierarchy. Central agents, in turn, learn to send signals up the hierarchy, based on the signals that they receive.

Then, via the signals from the lower-level RL-IDS agents, the agent on top of the hierarchy learns whether or not to trigger an intrusion alarm. If the signal is in accordance with the real state of the monitored network, all the agents receive a positive reward. If the action is inaccurate, all the agents receive a negative reward. Thus, after a certain number of iterations of the algorithm, every agent would know for each state the action that they need to execute to obtain positive rewards. Also, the Q-learning technique and a simple exploration/exploitation strategy are used to enable the agents to learn an accurate signal policy and to maximize the obtained reward over the time.

The proposed approach was evaluated in an abstract network domain with different architectures varying the number of agents, the number of states per sensor agent, the exploration/exploitation strategy, the distribution of attacks as input information, and the agent architecture.

Clearly, a clustered MANET would be a good ground for such IDS architecture with clusters mapping the cells, cluster-heads running RL-IDS agents, and cluster-member nodes running sensor agents.

Singh and Bedi (2016) proposed a new intelligent IDS that detects intrusions based on nodes' trust degrees. The detection task is divided into four main phases each handled by a software agent. A preliminary phase initiates for the detection by selecting the required features. In the second phase, the trust degree of a node is determined based on parameters like packet delivery ratio, node's behaviour and the residual energy. Extreme learning machine (ELM) is used in the third phase to classify nodes as either normal or malicious based on their trust degrees. The final phase consists of a response generation to the detected intrusions.

Jin et al. (2017) developed an agent-based IDS for a cluster-based WSN based on node's trust value. A multi-agent system is used in both the cluster heads and the ordinary sensor nodes to perform intrusion detection. Each sensor node uses its trust collection agent to collect trust-related features and relays this information to the corresponding cluster head using the communication agent. The communication agent on the cluster head receives trust information from its adjacent CHs and sensor nodes in its cluster and sends its own trust information to its adjacent CHs. It also uploads the collected data to the base station.

The cluster head is responsible for detecting malicious activities within its cluster. First, the cluster's trust calculation agent (activated by the cluster management agent) calculates the trust value of its adjacent CHs and nodes in its cluster based on the combination of the Beta distribution and a tolerance factor. Then, the cluster's intrusion judgment agent compares the obtained results to a predefined trust threshold.

If a node is deemed malicious, the intrusion response agent generates a response with respect to the judgment of the intrusion judgment agent. Example responses are: cutting off the node's communications, updating communication keys, and performing re-authentication. All agent interactions are coordinated by the cluster management agent.

As for the cluster heads, intrusion detection is implemented by the base station based on data received from adjacent cluster heads. If a cluster head is judged malicious, then the base station cuts off communications with it, recovers the sensor nodes that were judged malicious by the malicious cluster head, and broadcasts its identity to all of the other nodes. Experiments show that the proposed approach has a high detection rate and a low false positive rate for both single and simultaneous attacks.

Pires et al. (2017) proposed a decentralized framework for intrusion detection in WSNs based on intelligent agents. More specifically, a set of four agents is used, namely: Sniffer, Attack Detection, Action, and Console agent. Attack detection agent analyses network traffic captured by sniffer. If the captured traffic matches any of the predefined attack signatures, action agent will take the necessary measures to contain the threat. Finally, detection reports are sent to the console agent.

Mobile Agent Based IDSs

Mobile agents are special software agents that have the ability to roam through networks. Mobile agents offer several potential advantages over static agents when used to design MANET applications with respect to load reduction, dynamic and static adoption, and bandwidth conservation. In this overview, Roy and Chaki (2011) introduced a totally mobile agent based IDS to detect the blackhole attack in MANET. This IDS, referred to as MABHIDS, define two types of agents: a mobile agent and a specialized agent. First, the source node (willing to communicate with another node) generates a mobile agent and forwards it to the next hop node in the route to the intended destination. The mobile agent has to collect the raw data from the host machine then it computes the packet delivery ratio (R_i) for the ith host. The specialized agent then compares the R_i value with a threshold *ThR*, predefined by the source node, and gives responses to the source node accordingly.

Although this approach was proven to be efficient in detecting the blackhole attack, it still too limited and need to be extended so that to detect more attacks especially as the number of newly discovered attacks is always increasing. In addition, MABHIDS is based on merely mobile agents and their ability to roam in the network, but no security mechanism was integrated to protect them from attacks though they are well known for their security vulnerabilities.

Ping, Futai, Xinghao, and Jianhua (2007) also proposed an intrusion detection and response system for MANET based on mobile agents. It is composed of a monitor agent residing on every network node, a decision agent, and a collection of block agents. Each monitor agent collects information of its neighbour nodes' behaviour, filters it from unnecessary information, and sends this information after coding to the decision agent upon receiving a query message from this latter.

The decision agent, then, detects intrusions by analysing monitor agents' information. Due to resource constraints in MANET, decision agents are distributed over only some nodes. However network dynamics may cause a decision agent to move with its node thereby leaving the zone without any supervision. To tackle this problem, the authors suggested that if monitor agents in a zone have not received the query packet for a long period, a new node will be selected to run the decision agent.

If an intrusion is detected, the decision agent will produce block agents that will be sent to the neighbour nodes of the intruder to form the mobile firewall and isolate the intruder. To finish, a process of local repair will be executed to find new routes to replace all paths that include the intruder.

Though it succeeded in automating the response process, the proposed approach adopted no mechanism to prevent malicious or compromised nodes from initiating blackmail attacks through the generation of fake query messages.

Detection of unknown attacks together with the ability to detect attacks at different network layers is indispensable for a comprehensive IDS.

Realizing that, Devi and Bhuvaneswaran (2011) proposed an efficient cross layer anomaly-based intrusion detection architecture. This architecture implements a fixed width clustering algorithm for the training phase in order to build the normal profiles database. A data mining technique is then used by the intrusion detection module to distinguish attacks from normal profiles. This technique uses an association algorithm (Fast Apriori Algorithm) to extract necessary traffic features and to collect data streams from various network layers (physical, MAC, and network layers).

Data collection is usually followed by the local detection phase, in which the local detection module analyses the local data traces gathered by the collection module for evidence of anomalies. If any detection rule deviates beyond the anomaly threshold and if the local detection module has a high accuracy rate, it can independently determine that the network is under attack and thus, it initiates the alert management agent. However, if the support and confidence level is low or intrusion evidence is weak and inconclusive in the detecting node then it can make collaborative decision by gathering intelligence from its surrounding nodes via protected communication channel. The decision of the cooperative detection is based on the majority of the voting of the received reports indicating an intrusion or anomaly. Upon receiving alerts, the alert management agent collects them in the alert cache for t seconds. If there are more abnormal predictions than the normal predictions then it is regarded as abnormal and with adequate information an alarm is generated to inform that an intrusive activity is in the system.

Evaluation of the proposed approach revealed that it has some advantages. For instance, the way in which generated alerts are treated reduces both false positive and false negative alarms. Also, the use of the fixed width algorithm helps in detecting attacks at different layers while the fast apriori algorithm increased the speed of detecting them significantly. Nevertheless, this approach implies that the nodes should have considerable computational capabilities to run such algorithms. In addition, the authors considered that a protected channel is used as a means of communication between neighbouring nodes but no description of how to protect the channel was provided. Furthermore, the initialization of a cooperative detection depends on the level of intrusion evidence within the local detection module but there is no specification about when intrusion evidence is deemed weak or strong.

Hamerdheidari and Rafeh (2013) developed an effective agent based approach to detect sinkhole attacks in WSNs. The base station randomly chooses a number of nodes to send them the agent packets. After that, every node creates a neighbouring matrix containing an entry with the following information for every neighbour node: neighbour ID, Agentbit, and Validbit. Agentbit is set to true for every node hosting an agent packet. Agent nodes use mobile agents to determine whether other nodes are trusted or malicious. Agent nodes multicast trust packets to their respective trusted neighbours (which do not have agents) in order to inform them of the trusted and malicious nodes. If the energy level of an agent node is below a specified threshold, the mobile agent will move to a trusted neighbour.

Riecker et al. (2014) introduced a lightweight IDS for WSNs. This IDS uses a mobile agent to collect energy readings from sensor nodes. A linear regression model is applied to predict energy consumption and an alert is raised if unexpected changes in energy levels occur. The authors' main focus was on resource limitations. For instance, the mobile agent carries only energy-related data needed for the detection thereby, preserving the node's storage and keeping the communication overhead at a reasonable level. Unfortunately, this would limit the scope of detection to only attacks affecting energy consumption.

While some researchers use agents to build distributed agent-based IDSs, others (Li & Qian, 2010; Sen, 2010; Farhan, Zulkhairi, & Hatim, 2008; Pattanayak & Rath, 2014) prefer the use of agents to build hierarchical IDSs so that to get benefit of the specific characteristics offered by both architectures such as load balancing especially in networks where not all the nodes are capable of performing detection tasks.

In (Li & Qian, 2010) the authors proposed an agent-based intrusion detection model for MANET that forms a cluster head-centered backbone network by using a decision mode of joint detection used among cluster heads and vote by ballot in partial cluster heads. More specifically, the proposed model adopts a clustering algorithm for the building of nodes clusters, which form the platform for the agent-based intrusion detection. Intrusion detection agents are activated on elected cluster head nodes at the same time of cluster formation. These agents use a parameter based intrusion detection method that allows to detect any abnormal activities within a cluster and to generate local response in case of intrusion detection. In case of uncertainty, however, the cluster head node will trigger the joint detection among the cluster heads that will use a partial voting to determine malicious nodes. In case of an intrusion confirmed, a global network response in the form of blacklist broadcasting will be initiated. However, if the intruder is the cluster-head node itself, neighbouring cluster-head nodes, in addition to screening the intruder, will split and merge its cluster, or assign a new cluster-head using the adopted clustering algorithm.

According to its authors, the proposed model has advantages of short computing time, low consumption of both bandwidth and power and high detection rates. Nevertheless, mobility might present a serious problem to the proposed model. Actually, nodes mobility leads to cluster reformation which, by the way, implies the regeneration of detection agents thereby, resetting the detection process. This might result in: delaying the detection and response to intrusions, network overhead and nodes' resource consumption especially if a node is always chosen as a cluster head. Also, no mechanism for preventing a compromised node from being a cluster head was proposed.

In (Sen, 2010) the architecture of the proposed signature-based IDS is, however, organized as a dynamic hierarchy in which the intrusion data is acquired by network nodes and is incrementally aggregated, reduced in volume, and analysed as it flows upwards to the cluster-head.

It mainly consists of two broad modules: the Cluster-Head Module (CHM) running only on cluster-head nodes and the Cluster-Member Module (CMM) running on all the network nodes i.e., both cluster-heads and cluster-member nodes.

Every CMM maintains a database denoted intrusion interpreter base in which attacks' signatures and related thresholds are stored. It detects intrusions locally and may request the cluster-head node to initiate a cooperative intrusion detection and response action if additional information or a global response is required. In case of a cooperative intrusion detection, the cluster-head dispatches mobile agents to gather information from other members in the same cluster and other clusters, and then processes the gathered information to detect any intrusion in a global scale.

If an intrusion is detected by a CMM, it initiates a local response and, if need be, it communicates its response to its cluster head. This latter, via its CHM, logs the event and informs the nodes within its cluster and the adjacent cluster-heads (which in turn inform their cluster members) to isolate the offending node from the network.

Intrusion related message communication is handled by mobile agents. Cluster-heads can create, dispatch and process the results returned by the mobile agents. A database is maintained for the mobile agents that are created and dispatched. They are created only at the time of cooperative intrusion detection and are destroyed immediately after accomplishing the designated tasks successfully or if the associated timer expires.

Pattanayak and Rath (2014) proposed that a cluster head is to be elected, at the initiation of each application, based on a battery power metric. A dedicated mobile agent, consisting of a registration module (RM), a service agreement (SA), a detection module (DM) and a prevention module (PM), is incorporated in each cluster. During the initiation of a new application, all the nodes in the cluster need to register with the mobile agent and to accept a service agreement specific to the initiated application. The mobile agent, on its own, maintains a list of registered nodes in its registration module and uses the detection module to monitor each packet routed through the cluster head. If a mismatch occurs in source and destination addresses, the mobile agent will inform the cluster head to drop the packet and to block the respective node. If the mismatch occurs in the application ID or the packet length exceeds the threshold, then only the packet will be dropped by the cluster head.

This approach is time and resource consuming for all the packets are routed and monitored by the CH (mainly in case of several concurrent applications). Hence, a battery power metric is not sufficient to choose a reliable CH able of handling all the cluster communications in addition to performing intrusion detection tasks. Also, a node is not allowed to leave its cluster until the application is finished which is not the case of real world MANETs.

Another way of modelling the hierarchical agent-based IDS architecture was explored in (Farhan et al., 2008). Here, a zone-based framework is used to divide the whole ad hoc network into non overlapping zones. Nodes in a zone are either gateway nodes (inter-zone nodes), if a connection to a node in the neighbouring zone exists, or intra-zone nodes, otherwise.

In the proposed IDS framework, called MAZIDS, every intra-zone node runs a LIDS (Local Intrusion Detection System) locally to perform local data collection, anomaly detection and to initiate local response using mobile agents while gateway nodes will run GIDS (Gateway Intrusion Detection System).

GIDS are in charge of initiating global and zone intrusion detection and response. If a node detects an intrusion locally, it will initiate a local alarm, by sending an alarm message to the nearest GIDS, which in turn will trigger either cooperative agents or local and global response agents depending on the strength of evidence in the intrusion. Then, the GIDS, through its manager agent stores the alarm in the long term memory (LTM) if the intrusion is detected with strong evidence or in the short term memory (STM) in case of weak or inconclusive evidence, for future reference.

Not so far from clustered MANETs, the ad hoc network in (Mohamed & Abdullah, 2009) is divided into domains with each domain controlled by a master (server) node chosen based on relevant capabilities such as processing ability, battery power, and signal strength. In order not to exhaust the server's resources, a management method for dynamically changing the role of a domain node to act as a server is specified.

The proposed security approach defines four agents and is handled in two phases. First, the network domains pass with a recognition phase during which all of the four agents reside on the server side. This is a simulation of the maturation phase that takes place in thymus in the biological immune system. For instance, the monitor agent will learn to distinguish between the self (normal behaviour) and non-self patterns (anomalous behaviour) until it gets matured enough to detect intruders.

Following the recognition phase, the manager agent will release monitor and replicate agents in the domain and shifts to a listen state. While listening, the manager agent will act according to the notifications it receives from the monitor and replicate agents. Every monitor agent will supervise the packets passing through its node using a combination of both negative selection and danger theory. In case of suspicion, it will block the packets and will update the local database.

Recover agent is used in an attempt to add self-healing capability to the network. For instance, a restore point is periodically created for each node inside the domain and the healing process can be triggered automatically, using information reported by the monitoring agents, to correct nodes problems.

Krishnan (2015) put forward a distributed IDS for MANET. This IDS is based on a hierarchical architecture in which network monitoring agents are deployed not only on cluster heads but on some supportive nodes as well for a better coverage. Supportive nodes are selected by the cluster head depending on their residual energy. The number of these nodes depends on the size of the cluster. As for the system level, every node is equipped with a host monitoring agent to monitor local activities. Decision making agent uses simple associative rules to detect intrusive activities. A node that detects an intrusive activity dispatches an alert agent to notify the learning module. The learning module verifies the authenticity of the alert using the inference engine. If the attack is confirmed, it notifies other nodes and updates the attack database if necessary. Roaming agents' security is guaranteed using encryption.

Thamilarasu and Ma (2015) proposed an autonomous mobile agent based hierarchical IDS architecture to address security issues in wireless body area networks. In this architecture, a mobile agent manager dispatches sensor and cluster head agents on body sensor nodes and gateway nodes respectively. Body sensor nodes are capable of performing local detection using the attack features available within a clique, while gateway nodes and servers are capable of performing global attack detection. When a sensor agent migrates from one body sensor to another, it performs data analysis with local node data as well as collaborative sensor data carried with it. Upon detecting any anomalous behaviour, the sensor agent relays that information to its cluster head. The cluster head agent is used to perform intrusion detection on the wireless communication channel between sensors and cluster heads.

For that, it uses network traffic data, information retrieved from the sensor agents, as well as data obtained through migration between other cluster head nodes. In case of detected intrusions, the network is alerted by the report module agent. In this architecture, agent migration is organized and limited to cliques. Therefore, migration and data analysis time are reduced resulting in faster real-time response.

This architecture was extended by Odesile and Thamilarasu (2017) by another type of agents called Detective agents. These are deployed whenever the detection is suspicious but inconclusive. The sensor agent sends an intervention request to CH, which dispatches a special detective agent to further evaluate the situation. Also, Cluster head agents rely on the majority vote to determine whether to flag a CH as malicious or benign. This approach ensures the detection of compromised cluster heads and the prevention of a single point of failure within any cluster.

TraceGray (Taggu & Taggu, 2011) is an application layer scheme that uses mobile agents to detect grayholes in a DSR-based (Dynamic Source Routing) MANET. Actually, this IDS scheme invokes a mobile agent, which while migrating from its home context (the node on which the agent was created) towards the destination context, reports any grayhole it finds on its path. For that, the authors defined five states for an agent:

1. **Initial:** Refers to the agent's state at the time of its creation at its home context.
2. **1st hop:** The agent changes its state to the 1st hop state upon successful migration to the next hop node from the source node.
3. **2nd hop:** Reaching this state means that two hops from the home context have been successfully traversed and the mobile agent have to migrate backwards to its home context.
4. **Analysis:** The mobile agent reaches the analysis state upon successful return to the home context. If the second hop node is the destination context then this will imply that no grayholes were found. However, if the second hop node is not the destination context, then the mobile agent sets its new home context to the first hop node and restarts the whole traversal process by changing its state to the initial state. Whenever the return flow from second hop to the home context is not successful as indicated by timer expiry, a grayhole at the first hop node is announced.
5. **Dispose:** The mobile agent arrives at this state whenever ROUTE BROKEN condition occurs or timer expires

The deployment of such a solution is fairly easy and does not require any modification of the routing protocol but it is worth noting that it generates a considerable load and bandwidth consumption as well as a significant delay in attack reporting especially for the detection of grayholes over long paths. Moreover, the approach considers only one routing protocol (DSR), which makes it improper for other routing protocols like OLSR (Optimized Link State Routing) and AODV (Ad-hoc On-demand Distance Vector).

In (Hong-song, Zhenzhou, Mingzeng, Zhongchuan, & Ruixiang, 2007; Hong-Song, Jianyu, & Lee, 2008) two novel multi-agent-based dynamic lifetime intrusion detection and response schemes are proposed to protect AODV-based MANETs from blackhole and DoS attacks. In both schemes, agents are designed so as to dynamically adapt their creation, execution and expiration to the routing process status and are related to one RREQ–RREP stream. In (Hong-song et al., 2007) each agent is responsible for the monitoring of nodes within a three-hop zone. When the RREQ or RREP messages are out of this zone, a new agent is generated to execute the detection algorithm so as to avoid the delay in listening the routed packets. Once created, the current agent executes the intrusion detection algorithm based on the related link list and MAC-IP control table. In (Hong-song et al., 2008), however, only link list data is used by the IDS agent, implemented as a thread in network processor.

If the agent finds that the node itself has malicious behaviour, it can migrate to another high trustworthy node. Finally, if there is no RREQ–RREP stream in the network for some time, the related agent expires and the detection information is saved by the agent node for future detection.

While they efficiently improve trustworthiness, decrease computing complexity and save energy consumption, both approaches badly affect the network performance especially when many nodes initiate routing operations simultaneously. More specifically, the association of a new agent to every RREQ-RREP stream might overload the nodes (mainly those that are involved in many routes) with heavy extra processing loads entailed by the different detection agents.

Hybrid-Agent Based IDSs

While the previously discussed IDSs were comprised of collections of merely stationary or mobile agents, other works like (Bourkache, Mezghiche, & Tamine, 2011; Stafrace & Antonopoulos, 2010; Ye & Li, 2010; Chang & Shin 2010) were looking forward to enhancing the IDSs' fault tolerance and scalability through the combination of both stationary and mobile agents.

In (Bourkache et al., 2011), the authors proposed a new model for the building of a distributed and intelligent real-time intrusion detection system that fits MANET security requirements. The proposed IDS model is composed of multiple local IDS agents distributed among the different network nodes. Each LIDS is responsible for detecting intrusions locally using its three constituent agents, namely collector, the detection agent and the response agent. It implements a classification method as an anomaly detection engine in which classes of normal behaviour in the form of data vectors together with detection thresholds are built during the learning stage. In the test stage, however, the detection of local anomalies starts by collecting data using collector. Then, the detection agent builds a vector characterizing the audited activity to be compared with the centres of gravity of the various classes of normal behaviour using the Euclidean distance. To have a global vision of the network's security state and to defend against distributed attacks, collector agents were, further, designed so that to roam in the network to collect data from other network nodes. In this approach, no response mechanism was described though the use of a response agent.

Chang and Shin (2010) focused on the detection of intrusions at the application layer. Similarly to many other agent-based IDSs, they used a local IDS, consisting of a monitoring and detection agent, a response agent, and a communication agent to detect intrusions at every network node. Their main contribution is the use of mobile agents to augment each node's intrusion-detection capability. Specifically, they equipped the network with a mobile agent server capable of creating and dispatching three types of mobile agents: update, analysis, and verification agents.

If a local IDS fails to identify a suspicious behaviour, its response agent will request the mobile agent server to send analysis agents for further investigation. The analysis agent is capable of a more detailed analysis and diagnosis compared to the local IDS as it can launch multi-point network-based anomaly detection. Once the investigation completed, the analysis agent will report the results to the mobile agent server. Hence, if a new attack type is detected or the suspicious activity is judged as a change in the node's behaviour, an update agent will be created to update local IDSs' databases with the new attack signature or normal profile.

Further, the mobile agent server periodically checks the status of local IDSs using verification agents. If a vulnerability is detected, it will patch and install programs on the concerned mobile nodes via its update agents. Clearly, mobile agents can overcome network latency and reduce the network load related to intrusion detection. Also, this approach was a step forward in enhancing agent-based IDSs' fault tolerance, but it might lead to further problems. For instance, the mobile agent server might exhaust the node's resources (mainly processing and storage) in addition to being a single point of failure.

In (Ye & Li, 2010), a multi-agent system is again used to mimic the biological immune system in an attempt to secure a network after dividing it into independent logical zones.

The proposed security architecture defined two types of immune agents: detection agents uniformly distributed in the network and counterattack agents, residing on all the nodes.

Nodes, carrying out the detection agents, initiate zone creation by sending query messages to their one-hop neighbours. The other nodes will join the zone of the originator of the first query message they receive. A newly coming node sends a request message to its one-hop neighbours to join a detection zone. Detection agents that receive the request respond to it and the node will join the zone of the originator of the first response message it receives. If none of the neighbours is carrying a detection agent, the request message will be forwarded until it reaches a node with a detection agent. This latter copies itself and then moves to the new node.

Once the detection zones established, detection agents start data collection from the nodes within their zones and look for any matches with the records in their immune memories (misuse detection). If no matches are found, the agent will contrast the codes of the audited node's acts with protocols in its immune strategy library (anomaly detection).

If an intrusion is detected, the detection agent, through its communication module, will trigger dormant counterattack agents on the intruder's neighbour nodes to surround and isolate the intruder. Isolation is achieved through refraining from sending and receiving packets from the invader until it leaves the network or its power is exhausted.

This approach is simple but needs huge network resources for the management of detection zones (exponential to nodes' mobility).

A different artificial immune system (AIS) based IDS for MANET was proposed in (Kumar & Reddy, 2014). Here, each node was equipped with two agents: A mobile agent and a master agent. The mobile agent is in charge of gathering information related to bandwidth, packet delivery rate and delay from neighbouring nodes.

Collected information will be reported to the master agent residing on the mobile agent's home node that will use it to run the AIS to generate and /or update normal profiles patterns. Upon receiving new packets, a node calculates parameters like packet delivery rate and delay. If the calculated parameters match with the patterns generated by the master agent, then the connection is considered as valid. Otherwise, an alert is generated and carried by the communication agent to the source node. This latter halts the on-going transmission and resumes it after a stipulated period of time.

The detection approach is simple and the way normal patterns are generated ensures normal profiles patterns to be updated constantly. However, this way can be misleading, thereby causing the IDS to generate false alarms.

da Cunha Neto, Zair, Fernandes, and Froz (2013) presented a model of a wireless intrusion detection system (WIDS) aiming to expand Botnet detectors by using a set of agents that interact directly or indirectly to collect (through the monitoring agent) and analyse packets in wireless networks. The model, via the filtering agent, uses packet filtering through the WhiteList and BlackList, besides carrying the signature and anomaly analysis (via the signature analysis and anomaly analysis agents, respectively), to minimize the false positives.

If a security incident is detected, appropriate countermeasures are taken in accordance with the reaction database (notifying or blocking the signal from an intruder). In addition to the reaction database, a set of specialized databases (Collection Database, WhiteList Database, BlackList Database, Signature Database, and a Knowledge Database) is used for maintaining the persistent information from each agent.

Evaluation of the proposed approach revealed that WIDS can identify attacks with great efficiency and speed, due to the possibility of eliminating packages not needed to evaluation using the filter agent.

Another different way of approaching agent-based IDS solutions in ad-hoc networks is to visualize the network as an urban hostile zone, where the agents collaboratively follow specific tactics to police the zone. From this perspective, Stafrace and Antonopoulos (2010) presented the design of an agent framework modelled over a military command structure and an agent behavioural model, which employs adapted military tactics to police routes, and detect intruders in wireless ad-hoc networks.

The proposed detection solution works as follows: A Command Post (CP) is set up on Node *S* to control the route to Node *D*. The Command Post is a process that periodically orders a patrol mission along the route. A patrol mission consists of an Active Reconnaissance Phase and a Route Patrol Phase. The detection mission commences with the active reconnaissance process such that node *S* begins counting the outbound data packets for the destination node *D*. The duration of the reconnaissance activity is based on the data packet throughput and route stability. This phase results in a Reconnaissance Snapshot containing the number of outbound packets grouped by the next hop address. Each packet that was counted during this phase is also tagged with a Snapshot ID. In addition, an Intelligence (INTEL) process consisting of a similar reconnaissance function is performed on each intermediate node along the supervised route. The final result of the INTEL process is thereby a Reconnaissance Snapshot containing the respective packet counts for every intermediate node. On successful completion of phase one, the CP initiates the second phase whereby a Scout Patrol Squad is deployed to police the controlled route. The tactical mobile agent squad consists of three units, namely the Scout Leader (SL) and two scouts: Scout A (SA) and Scout B (SB). Both scouts perform a data collection-like function, which is basically querying the INTEL process on their host nodes for specific reconnaissance snapshots. Then, the leader of the squad will evaluate the observation provided by the scouts. Finally, it will perform a threat assessment based on the outcome of the evaluation and take the required actions accordingly.

Since tactical agents follow a risk-based approach which means that the frequency of patrols is directly proportional to the risk factor of the route (which is in turn a factor of the route throughput and frequency of use), resources were conserved without impacting the effectiveness of the IDS. Also, the proposed solution is independent of the routing protocol i.e., it is applicable to wireless ad-hoc networks regardless of the routing protocol. Nonetheless, the CP constitutes a single point of failure. In addition, the solution does not offer the possibility to detect unknown attacks.

Because traditional security-centric mechanisms consume a large amount of network resources and thereby degrading its performance, Wang et al. (2013) designed a network performance-centric anomaly detection scheme for resource constrained MANETs. This scheme employs a fully distributed multi-agent framework. More specifically, the system uses a platform of mobile agents to design the energy-aware and self-adaptive anomaly detection. In this concern, four kinds of agents, residing in every node, were defined, namely: the network tomography agent (NTA), the anomaly detection agent (ADA), the communication service agent (CSA), and the state detection agent (SDA).

The proposed anomaly detection system proceeds in two phases. The first phase aims at detecting link delay anomalies while the second phase tries to quickly detect and accurately localize malicious nodes on links. For instance, the detection is started by executing an energy-aware root election mechanism that selects the most cost-efficient node as the root that will sponsor system services. By the way, the NTA on that node will be considered as the root NTA that will be activated while other NTAs remain inactive to save resources. The root NTA performs the following functions: topology identification using a spatial time model, active probing, and inferring link delay distribution based on the Expectation Maximum method. Then, each ADA independently undertakes to set up the delay distribution profile of the link on which it is located. Once the profile of a link delay characteristics is obtained, it can be compared to the inferred delay of the link delivered by the NTA. If the inferred results go beyond a threshold value, the link is considered as an anomalous link and an alarm is raised. Since each ADA performs local detection using local audit data, the ADAs around an anomalous link can cooperate locally to confirm the maliciousness of a node. Furthermore, this cooperation should be done through secure channels. For that, CSA agents, used for communication services among the different nodes, were configured so that to communicate only intrusion detection related information. Again, for the sake of security, SDA agents are used to check the validity of CSAs and NTAs in the cooperative mobile nodes using encryption mechanisms.

Although this approach seems interesting and solves the problems related to mobile agents' security, raised by many other works, but it is too limited as it detects only link delay related attacks.

Chadli et al. (2016) presented a hierarchical agent-based IDS architecture for MANET. In this architecture, every node is equipped with a sensor agent (SA), an ontology agent (OA), agent actuator (ACA), and an agent Analyser (ANA). Cluster head nodes have, in addition to these four agents, a manager agent (MA). SA initiates the detection process by collecting data from the network. Collected data is filtered and analysed by ANA. If an intrusion is detected, OA is created to share the information with other nodes. If there is suspicion but the intrusion is not confirmed, ANA will ask MA to confirm the attack. In that latter case, MA communicates with other ANA agents and the result is communicated to the initiator of the query.

DISCUSSION

Table 3 summarizes the main features of existing agent-based IDSs, their main contributions, and the issues they do not address.

Figure 1 provides a statistical analysis of agent-based IDSs in the light of the studied IDS models.

Based on the studied works, the network seems to be the most popular source of data used in agent-based intrusion detection. This is due to the fact that network related data provide a more global vision of the network status and allows for the detection of distributed attacks. Also, most existing agent-based IDSs are based on computation-depended and artificial intelligence techniques (RL, rule based systems, and swarm intelligence), since they are best suited for deployment on agent basis. It is also worth noting that IDS designers have made a great effort in mapping biological concepts to intrusion detection. For instance, they established the immunological metaphor by mapping T-cells, B-cells, antibodies, antigens, lymphocytes, maturation in thymus, and the immune memory to detection agents, decision agents, response agents, intrusions, mobile agents, training phase, and the agent's local database. Most of these techniques are designed to perform anomaly detection, which better fits MANET and WSN requirements in terms of resource conservation and detection of unknown attacks.

Further, static agents are rarely adopted by these IDSs though the simplicity and low cost of their deployment. Contrary, mobile agents were extensively used to build agent-based IDSs, though they were deemed to introduce additional vulnerabilities to the network, for their capabilities of roaming and resource conservation. Nonetheless, there has been recently more tendency for the use of multiple agent types within the same IDS so that to have better overall control of the network. The study revealed also that while designing agent-based IDSs, the designers' main focus is to reduce energy consumption and the network load generated by the IDS, leaving crucial issues like node mobility and the IDSs' security problems open. Finally, evaluation of these IDSs shows that almost all of them do require neither high processing capabilities nor high memory storage.

Table 3. Comparison of agent-based IDSs

	Detection technique			Data source			Response		Advantages	Limitations
	Anomaly detection	Misuse detection	Specification based	Host	Neighbour-hood	Network	Passive	Active		
Ramachandran et al. (2008)	✓					✓		✓	- Accuracy and simplicity of rules - Improves detection rates - Energy conservation	- Mobility of nodes not addressed - IDS security issues not addressed
Byrski and Carvalho (2008)	✓				✓		✓		- Simple and reliable	- High computational cost under high mobility
Servin and Kudenko (2008)				✓		✓	✓		- Accuracy enhanced over time through learning	- High Communication overhead - Single point of failure
Singh and Bedi (2016)	✓					✓		✓	- Reduced training time - Adaptive response	- Normal behaviour changes not considered (False positive)
Jin et al. (2017)	✓				✓			✓	- Scalability - High detection accuracy - Reduces FPR	- IDS communication overhead
Pires et al. (2017)		✓				✓	✓		- Lightweight	- Security of the IDS agents not addressed
Roy and Chaki (2011)		✓			✓		✓		- Simple - lightweight	- Detects only blackhole attack - Security of mobile agents not addressed
Ping et al. (2007)	✓				✓			✓	- Automated response - Considers node mobility and resource limitations	- Vulnerable to blackmail attacks
Devi and Bhuvaneswaran (2011)	✓			✓				✓	- Detection of attacks at different layers - Reduces FPR and FNR - Fast detection	- High computational load
Hamedheidari and Rafeh (2013)					✓		✓		- Considers resource limitations - Secure IDS	- Detects only sinkhole attacks
Riecker et al. (2014)		✓				✓	✓		- Energy conservation - Low FPR - Considers resource limitations	- Inability to detect attacks that have no influence on energy consumption
Li and Qian (2010)		✓		✓				✓	- Reduced Energy and bandwidth consumption - Fast detection - FPR reduction	- High architecture maintenance cost under mobility - Single point of failure
Sen (2010)		✓		✓				✓	- Detection of distributed attacks	- High bandwidth consumption

continued on following page

Table 3. Continued

	Detection technique			Data source			Response		Advantages	Limitations
	Anomaly detection	Misuse detection	Specification based	Host	Neighbour-hood	Network	Passive	Active		
Pattanayak and Rath (2014)			✓		✓		✓		- High protection level	- Time and resource consuming - The method is not consistent due to unrealistic assumptions on nodes mobility
Farhan et al. (2008)	✓			✓			✓		- Dynamic adaption to environment changes - Scalable & robust	- Single point of failure (GIDS)
yasir and Azween (2009)	✓			✓				✓	- The self-healing capability	- Single point of failure (Master nodes)
Krishnan (2015)	✓	✓		✓		✓	✓		- Secure IDS	- High architecture maintenance cost under mobility
Thamilarasu and Ma (2015)	✓			✓		✓	✓		- Considers mobility and resource constraints - Fault Tolerance	- Redundancy
Taggu and Taggu (2011)		✓				✓	✓		- Simple and easy to deploy	- High resource and bandwidth consumption - Cause detection and response latency even when there is enough evidence locally - Routing protocol dependent
Hong-song et al.. (2008)		✓				✓		✓	- Considers security of IDS agent - Low computational complexity - Saves energy	- Routing protocol dependent - Overload nodes if the number of RREQ/RREP increases
Chang and Shin (2010)	✓	✓		✓			✓		- Enhances IDS fault-tolerance	- single point of failure (the mobile agent server)
Ye and Li (2010)	✓	✓			✓			✓	- The active response mechanism	- High architecture maintenance cost under mobility
Wang et al. (2013)	✓			✓				✓	- Considers security issues of mobile agents - Considers resource constraints	- Detects only link delay related attacks
Cunha Neto et al. (2013)	✓	✓				✓		✓	- Fast detection due to the possibility of eliminating packages not needed to evaluation using the filter agent	- Overload nodes
Chadli et al. (2016)		✓				✓		✓	- Scalability	- Single point of failure (CHs)

Figure 1. Statistical analysis of wireless agent-based IDSs

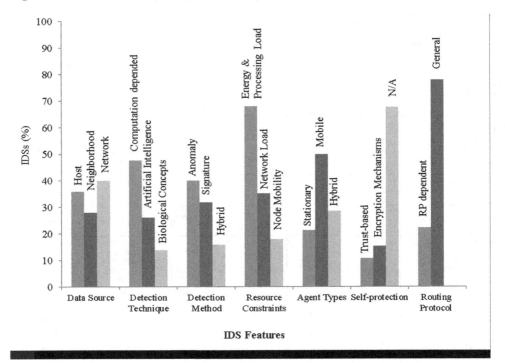

Building on the studied approaches and their analysis, it is clearly seen that wireless agent-based IDSs have some common features:

1. Distribution of the detection tasks on a group of collaborating agents distributed over the network;
2. Use of mobile agents for both communication (collaboration) and data collection on remote hosts;
3. Approaching real-time detection and response;
4. Besides, almost all these IDSs are lightweight, flexible and present an exceptional ease in maintenance (modifications and extensions can be made without halting the whole system).

Table 4 summarizes some of the several advantages obtained when using agent technology for the building of wireless IDSs in particular and MANET applications in general, with respect to MANET/WSN requirements.

Nevertheless, in addition to the complexity of their deployment, software agents might bring new vulnerabilities to the network such as:

Table 4. Advantages of using agents for wireless intrusion detection

Agent features	Wireless network shortcomings	Description
Scalability	Constrained processing and energy power	Agents reduce the computational load and consumed energy by dividing the (detection) tasks over different hosts.
Mobility	Limited bandwidth and storage capacity	Instead of transferring huge amounts of data (audited data), the processing unit (detection agent) is moved to data.
Portability	Heterogeneity of devices	Agents run on agent platforms, thereby guaranteeing independence from the platform of the host.
Autonomous execution	Dynamic topology	If the network is segmented or some agents cease to function (under the threat of an attack), the rest of the agents can still continue to function (guaranteeing a proportional level of security).
Fault tolerance	Vulnerability to attacks	An attacker can disable a small finite number of backups but not all of them (agent-based applications use redundancy to protect their components).

1. The security vulnerability introduced by mobile agents especially when they are operating in a hostile environment. In fact, in addition to their being vulnerable to security threats, they can be the source of new threats to the network. For instance, a compromised agent with some privileges (intrusion detection agents are usually given more privileges such as accessing to nodes' private information, accessing routing tables, and filtering routed packets) can cause serious damages without being suspected.

2. Code size may be too long (development of complex security solutions sometimes require large amounts of code), thereby causing latency in the processing time for static agents, slowing down the mobile agents in addition to network bandwidth high consumption.

3. Some of the proposed IDSs do not satisfy MANET/WSN requirements in terms of resource conservation and the dynamic topology change.

4. Some IDSs do not take into account mobility of the network. For instance, IDS architectures that are based on cluster-based approaches are costly to build and maintain in high mobility networks. The false positive rate may be greatly affected by the mobility level especially for anomaly-based IDSs.

5. Multi-agent systems are generally vulnerable to faults and system failures, thereby causing agent-based IDSs to be vulnerable and fault-prone.

6. Besides, some IDSs have critical points of failure (usually related to the cluster head).

Fortunately, security problems can be solved through the use of electronic signature, encryption and authorization methods. Also, trade-offs between security requirements and performance are often created so as to cope with performance related problems.

Overall, designing an IDS to protect networks like MANET and WSN (generally deployed in hostile and dynamic environments) entails the adoption of some basic concepts like autonomy, dynamism, collaboration, continuous operation, decentralization and rapidity. MASs present several interesting characteristics that can more or less satisfy these requirements such as portability, mobility, and autonomy. This makes the agent-based IDS architecture a good fit for wireless IDSs. However, it is sometimes necessary to borrow some features from other architectures to better fit wireless IDSs' requirements and more importantly to avoid the IDS from being an additional source of vulnerability to the protected system or network. For instance, features like task distribution and organization (hierarchical architecture) can help in optimizing resource consumption and in preventing the creation of unnecessary overhead. Thus, a merger between the agent-based architecture and other existing architectures can greatly help in obtaining an optimal security solution for wireless networks.

OPEN ISSUES, CHALLENGES, AND SCOPE FOR FUTURE WORK

The conducted study and analysis show the strong relevance to use agents in designing wireless intrusion detection tools. In fact, many of the features offered by agents show an exceptional match with MANET/WSN inherent characteristics (table 4) and agents are best suited for applications that are decentralized, changeable, ill-structured and complex like wireless intrusion detection.

However, other features like fault-tolerance and adaptability have not been fully exploited and there are still other issues that have not been fully addressed in that field. In fact, there are only few works that consider the effect of mobility on the intrusion detection process; therefore, it is an interesting topic for future research.

In addition, there are not much works that fully address the resource constraints issue. Network and node capabilities should be given an appropriate weight when designing MANET/WSN IDSs. For example, nodes should be assigned detection tasks based on their resources and communication between IDS agents should be adapted to the wireless links bandwidth. In other words, it should be minimized for low bandwidth links and optimized otherwise.

Also, the great majority of works done in the field does not consider security issues related to the IDS itself or are limited to making assumptions about them. The security of IDS agents, their communication, and IDS data should be considered by future works to fulfil the ideal wireless IDS requirements.

Similarly, IDS' fault-tolerance is almost absent in existing works. IDS' fault-tolerance is crucial for IDS and network survivability. It can be enhanced using, among others, techniques like replication of software agents, fault detection using heartbeat messages, and integrity checking for self-healing.

Besides, most existing IDSs can detect intrusions with high accuracy but fail to eliminate their source. The best they can do is to generate passive or proactive responses in terms of alarms or blacklist generation. Development of corrective responses seems more consistent and can help enhancing the network's survivability and healing ability.

Finally, most of the proposed IDSs have not been tested or evaluated. Hence, it is necessary to define evaluation criteria, datasets, and tools to guarantee the advancement of the field.

CONCLUSION

This chapter presented a survey and analysis of the work that has been recently done for the deployment of agent technology in the area of wireless intrusion detection.

This study revealed that the scalability, performance and fault tolerance can be improved through the use of agents to perform intrusion detection tasks. In addition, agents proved their utility in overcoming some MANET/WSN related problems such as the constrained resources and the heterogeneity of platforms.

Nevertheless, the study revealed, also, that the use of agents and mainly mobile agents might bring new vulnerabilities to the network. For instance, during its roaming, a mobile agent may be subjected to alteration or worse yet destruction by a malicious node. Also, complex security mechanisms sometimes necessitate large amounts of code which inevitably affects the desired fast roaming of mobile agents between the different network hosts.

Therefore, future research works on this appealing subject are to be carefully designed so that to take major profit of the offered agents' capabilities while controlling the potentially introduced vulnerabilities.

REFERENCES

Bourkache, G., Mezghiche, M., & Tamine, K. (2011). A Distributed Intrusion Detection Model Based on a Society of Intelligent Mobile Agents for Ad Hoc Network. In *Proceedings of the IEEE 2011 Sixth International Conference on Availability, Reliability and Security (ARES)* (pp. 569-572). Vienna: IEEE. 10.1109/ARES.2011.131

Breitman, K., Casanova, M. A., & Truszkowski, W. (2007). Software Agents. In *Semantic Web: Concepts, Technologies and Applications. NASA Monographs in Systems and Software Engineering* (pp. 219–228). London, UK: Springer.

Byrski, A., & Carvalho, M. (2008). Agent-Based Immunological Intrusion Detection System for Mobile Ad-Hoc Networks. In *Proceedings of the International Conference on Computational Science* (584-593). Kraków, Poland: LNCS. 10.1007/978-3-540-69389-5_66

Chadli, S., Saber, M., Emharraf, M., & Ziyyat, A. (2016). Implementation an Intelligent Architecture of Intrusion Detection System for MANETs. In *Proceedings of the Mediterranean Conference on Information & Communication Technologies. Lecture Notes in Electrical Engineering* (*vol. 381*, pp.479-487). Saidia, MA: Springer. 10.1007/978-3-319-30298-0_49

Chang, K., & Shin, K. G. (2010). Application-Layer Intrusion Detection in MANETs. In *Proceedings of the 43rd Hawaii International Conference on System Sciences* (1-10). Honolulu, HI: IEEE.

Cheng, B., & Tseng, R. (2011). A context adaptive intrusion detection system for MANET. *Computer Communications*, *34*(3), 310–318. doi:10.1016/j.comcom.2010.06.015

da Cunha Neto, R. P., Zair, A., Fernandes, V. P. M., & Froz, B. R. (2013). Intrusion Detection System for Botnet Attacks in Wireless Networks Using Hybrid Detection Method Based on DNS. In T. Sobh & K. Elleithy (Eds.), Emerging Trends in Computing, Informatics, Systems Sciences, and Engineering, Lecture Notes in Electrical Engineering 151 (pp. 689-702). Springer. doi:10.1007/978-1-4614-3558-7_59

Devi, V. A., & Bhuvaneswaran, R. S. (2011). Agent Based Cross Layer Intrusion Detection System for MANET. In *CNSA 2011, CCIS 196* (pp. 427–440). Springer Verlag-Berlin.

Farhan, A.F., & Dahalin, Z. M., & Jusoh, S. (2010). Distributed and cooperative hierarchical intrusion detection on MANETs. *International Journal of Computers and Applications*, *12*(1), 32–40.

Farhan, A. F., Zulkhairi, D., & Hatim, M. T. (2008). Mobile Agent Intrusion Detection System for Mobile Ad Hoc Networks: A Non-overlapping Zone Approach. In *Proceedings of the 4th IEEE/IFIP International Conference on Internet* (pp. 1-5). Tashkent: IEEE. 10.1109/CANET.2008.4655310

Garcia-Teodoro, P., Diaz-Verdejo, J., Maciá-Fernández, G., & Vázquez, E. (2009). Anomaly-based network intrusion detection: Techniques, systems and challenges. *Computers & Security*, *28*(1), 18–28. doi:10.1016/j.cose.2008.08.003

Gharib, M., Moradlou, Z., Doostari, M. A., & Movaghar, A. (2017). Fully distributed ECC-based key management for mobile ad hoc networks. *Computer Networks*, *113*(1), 269–283. doi:10.1016/j.comnet.2016.12.017

Gomathi, K., Parvathavarthini, B., & Saravanakumar, C. (2017). An Efficient Secure Group Communication in MANET Using Fuzzy Trust Based Clustering and Hierarchical Distributed Group Key Management. *Wireless Personal Communications*, *94*(4), 2149–2162. doi:10.100711277-016-3366-x

Hamerdheidari, S., & Rafeh, R. (2013). A Novel Agent-Based Approach to Detect Sinkhole Attacks in Wireless Sensor Networks. *Computers & Security*, *37*(1), 1–14. doi:10.1016/j.cose.2013.04.002

Hong-Song, C., Jianyu, Z., & Lee, H. W. J. (2008). A novel NP-based security scheme for AODV routing protocol. *Journal of Discrete Mathematical Sciences and Cryptography*, *11*(2), 131–145. doi:10.1080/09720529.2008.10698172

Hong-song, C., Zhenzhou, J., Mingzeng, H., Zhongchuan, F., & Ruixiang, J. (2007). Design and performance evaluation of a multi-agent-based dynamic lifetime security scheme for AODV routing protocol. *Elsevier Journal of Network and Computer Applications*, *30*(1), 145–166. doi:10.1016/j.jnca.2005.09.006

Hu, Y.-C., Johnson, D. B., & Perrig, A. (2003). SEAD: Secure efficient distance vector routing for mobile wireless ad hoc networks. *Ad Hoc Networks*, *1*(1), 175–192. doi:10.1016/S1570-8705(03)00019-2

Hung-Jen, L., Chun-Hung, R. L., Ying-Chih, L., & Kuang-Yuan, T. (2013). Intrusion detection system: A comprehensive review. *Elsevier Journal of Network and Computer Applications*, *36*(1), 16–24. doi:10.1016/j.jnca.2012.09.004

Jin, X., Liang, J., Tong, W., Lu, L., & Li, Z. (2017). Multi-agent trust-based intrusion detection scheme for wireless sensor networks. *Computers & Electrical Engineering, 59*(1), 262–273. doi:10.1016/j.compeleceng.2017.04.013

John, S. P., & Samuel, P. (2015). Self-organized key management with trusted certificate exchange in MANET. *Ain Shams Engineering Journal, 6*(1), 161–170. doi:10.1016/j.asej.2014.09.011

Krishnan, D. (2014). Article. In *Proceedings of International Conference on Information and Communication Technologies* (*vol. 46*, pp. 1203-1208). Elsevier.

Kumar, P., & Reddy, K. (2014). An Agent based Intrusion detection system for wireless network with Artificial Immune System (AIS) and Negative Clone Selection. In *Proceedings of the International Conference on Electronic Systems, Signal Processing and Computing Technologies* (pp. 429-433). IEEE. 10.1109/ICESC.2014.73

Li, W., Tug, S., Meng, W., & Wang, Y. (2019). Designing collaborative blockchained signature-based intrusion detection in IoT environments. *Future Generation Computer Systems, 96*(1), 481–489. doi:10.1016/j.future.2019.02.064

Li, Y., & Qian, Z. (2010). Mobile agents-based intrusion detection system for mobile ad hoc networks. In *Proceedings of the International Conference on Innovative Computing and Communication and 2010 Asia-Pacific Conference on Information Technology and Ocean Engineering* (pp. 145-148). Macao, China: IEEE. 10.1109/CICC-ITOE.2010.45

Marchang, N., & Datta, R. (2008). Collaborative techniques for intrusion detection in mobile ad-hoc networks. *Ad Hoc Networks, 6*(4), 508–523. doi:10.1016/j.adhoc.2007.04.003

Nadeem, A., & Howarth, M. P. (2014). An Intrusion Detection and Adaptive Response Mechanism for MANETs. *Ad Hoc Networks, 13*(1), 368–380. doi:10.1016/j.adhoc.2013.08.017

Odesile, A., & Thamilarasu, G. (2017). Distributed Intrusion Detection Using Mobile Agents in Wireless Body Area Networks. In *Proceedings of the International Conference on Emerging Security Technologies* (vol. 7, pp. 144-149). Canterbury, UK: IEEE. 10.1109/EST.2017.8090414

Pattanayak, B. K., & Rath, M. (2014). A Mobile Agent Based Intrusion Detection System Architecture for Mobile Ad Hoc Networks. *Journal of Computational Science, 10*(6), 970–975. doi:10.3844/jcssp.2014.970.975

Ping, Y., Futai, Z., Xinghao, J., & Jianhua, L. (2007). Multi-agent cooperative intrusion response in mobile adhoc networks. *Elsevier Journal of Systems Engineering and Electronics, 18*(4), 785–794. doi:10.1016/S1004-4132(08)60021-3

Pires, H., Abdelouahab, Z., Lopes, D., & Santos, M. (2017). A Framework for Agent-based Intrusion Detection in Wireless Sensor Networks. In *Proceedings of the Second International Conference on Internet of Things, Data and Cloud Computing* (vol. 2, pp. 1-7). Cambridge, UK: ACM. 10.1145/3018896.3056805

Ramachandran, C., Misra, S., & Obaidat, M. S. (2008). A novel two-pronged strategy for an agent-based intrusion detection scheme in ad-hoc networks. *Elsevier Comput. Commun, 31*(16), 3855–3869. doi:10.1016/j.comcom.2008.04.012

Riecker, M., Biedermann, S., El Bansarkhani, R., & Hollick, M. (2015). Lightweight energy consumption-based intrusion detection system for wireless sensor networks. *International Journal of Information Security, 14*(2), 155–167. doi:10.100710207-014-0241-1

Roy, D. B., & Chaki, R. (2011). MABHIDS: A New Mobile Agent Based Black Hole Intrusion Detection System. In N. Chaki & A. Cortesi (Eds.), *CISIM 2011, CCIS 245* (pp. 85–94). Springer Verlag-Berlin. doi:10.1007/978-3-642-27245-5_12

Sanzgiri, K., LaFlamme, D., Dahill, B., Levine, B. N., Shields, C., & Royer, E. (2005). Authenticated routing for ad hoc networks. *IEEE Journal on Selected Areas in Communications, 23*(3), 598–610. doi:10.1109/JSAC.2004.842547

Saswati, M., Matangini, C., Samiran, C., & Pragma, K. (2018). EAER-AODV: Enhanced Trust Model Based on Average Encounter Rate for Secure Routing in MANET. In C. Rituparna, C. Agostino, S. Khalid, & C. Nabendu (Eds.), *Advanced Computing and Systems for Security (6)* (pp. 135–151). Singapore: Springer.

Sen, J. (2010). An Intrusion Detection Architecture for Clustered Wireless Ad Hoc Networks. In *Proceedings of the Second International Conference on Computational Intelligence, Communication Systems and Networks* (pp. 202-207). Liverpool, UK: IEEE. 10.1109/CICSyN.2010.51

Servin, A., & Kudenko, D. (2008). Multi-agent Reinforcement Learning for Intrusion Detection. In *Adaptive Agents and Multi Agent Systems III: Adaptation and Multi Agent Learning* (pp. 211–223). Springer-Verlag Berlin Heidelberg. doi:10.1007/978-3-540-77949-0_15

Sethuraman, P., & Kannan, N. (2017). Refined Trust Energy-Ad hoc on Demand Distance Vector (ReTE-AODV) routing algorithm for secured routing in MANET. *Wireless Networks, 23*(7), 2227–2237. doi:10.100711276-016-1284-1

Singh, D., & Bedi, S. S. (2016). Multiclass ELM Based Smart Trustworthy IDS for MANETs. *Arabian Journal for Science and Engineering*, *41*(8), 3127–3137. doi:10.100713369-016-2112-8

Stafrace, S. K., & Antonopoulos, N. (2010). Military tactics in agent-based sinkhole attack detection for wireless ad hoc networks. *Elsevier Comput. Commun.*, *33*(5), 619–638. doi:10.1016/j.comcom.2009.11.006

Taggu, A., & Taggu, A. (2011). TraceGray: An Application-layer Scheme for Intrusion Detection in MANET using Mobile Agents. In *Proceedings of the IEEE 3rd International Conference on Communication Systems and Networks (COMSNETS)* (pp. 1-4). Bangalore: IEEE. 10.1109/COMSNETS.2011.5716475

Thamilarasu, G., & Ma, Z. (2015). Autonomous Mobile Agent based Intrusion Detection Framework in Wireless Body Area Networks. In *Proceedings of the IEEE 16th International Symposium on a World of Wireless, Mobile and Multimedia Networks* (vol. 16, pp. 1-3). Boston, MA: IEEE. 10.1109/WoWMoM.2015.7158178

Wang, W., Wang, H., Wang, B., Wang, Y., & Wang, J. (2013). Energy-aware and self-adaptive anomaly detection scheme based on network tomography in mobile ad hoc networks. *Elsevier Information Sciences*, *220*(20), 580–602. doi:10.1016/j.ins.2012.07.036

Wang, X., Govindan, K., & Mohapatra, P. (2010). Provenance-based information trustworthiness evaluation in multi-hop networks. In *Proceedings of 2010 IEEE Global Telecommunications Conference GLOBECOM* (pp. 1-5). 10.1109/GLOCOM.2010.5684158

Yasir, M. A., & Azween, B. A. (2009). Biologically Inspired Model for Securing Hybrid Mobile Ad hoc Networks. In *Proceedings of the International Symposium on High Capacity Optical Networks and Enabling Technologies* (187-191). Penang: IEEE.

Ye, X., & Li, J. (2010). A Security Architecture Based on Immune Agents for MANET. In *Proceedings of the International Conference on Wireless Communication and Sensor Computing* (pp. 1-5). Chennai: IEEE.

ADDITIONAL READING

Anderson, J. P. (1972). *Computer security technology planning study* (Vol. 2). doi:10.21236/AD0772806

Brenner, W., Zarnekow, R., & Wittig, H. (1998). *Intelligent Software Agents – Foundations and Applications*. Springer berlin Heidelberg.

Liu, G., Yan, Z., & Pedrycz, W. (2018). Data collection for attack detection and security measurement in Mobile Ad Hoc Networks: A survey. *Journal of Network and Computer Applications*, *105*(1), 105–122. doi:10.1016/j.jnca.2018.01.004

Potiron, K., Seghrouchni, A., & Taillibert, P. (2013). From Fault Classification to Fault Tolerance for Multi-Agent Systems. Springer berlin Heidelberg.

Pullum, L. (2001). *Software Fault Tolerance Techniques and Implementation*. Norwood, MA, USA: Artech House, Inc.

Ring, M., Wunderlich, S., Scheuring, D., Landes, D., & Hotho, A. (2019). A survey of network-based intrusion detection data sets. *Computers & Security*, *86*(1), 147–167. doi:10.1016/j.cose.2019.06.005

Wu, B., Chen, J., Wu, J., & Cardei, M. (2007). A survey of attacks and countermeasures in mobile ad hoc networks. In Y. Xiao, X. S. Shen, & D. Z. Du (Eds.), *Wireless Network Security, Signals and Communication Technology* (pp. 103–135). Springer. doi:10.1007/978-0-387-33112-6_5

Zhou, D., Yan, Z., Fu, Y., & Yao, Z. (2018). A survey on network data collection. *Journal of Network and Computer Applications*, *116*(1), 9–23. doi:10.1016/j.jnca.2018.05.004

KEY TERMS AND DEFINITIONS

AODV: The ad-hoc on-demand distance vector is a reactive routing protocol that enables multi-hop, self-starting and dynamic routing in MANET.

Blackhole: An active DoS (denial of service) attack in which a malicious node exploits the routing protocols such as AODV to advertise itself as having a valid and good path to the destination node with the goal of dropping the absorbed packets.

DSR: The dynamic source routing is similar to AODV but has the additional feature of source routing.

False Negatives: Cases where no alerts are raised when real intrusion attempts are present.

False Positives: IDS alerts that are raised on non-intrusive behaviours.

Grayhole: A variation of the blackhole attack in which the malicious node adopts a selective packet dropping.

Intrusion: Any set of actions that attempt to compromise the integrity, confidentiality, or the availability of a resource.

Intrusion Detection System: A software or hardware system that automate the process of monitoring the events occurring in a computer system or network, analysing them for signs of security problems. It can monitor and collect data from a target system (host or network), process and correlate the gathered information, and can initiate responses when evidence of an intrusion is detected.

MANET: A network consisting of a collection of mobile nodes that communicate with each other via wireless links without the help of any pre-existing infrastructure.

Security Threats: Are tools, techniques, or methods that can cause unwanted incidents, and potentially result in damaging the network.

True Negatives: Cases where no alerts are raised, and no intrusion attempts are present.

True Positives: IDS alerts that are raised for real intrusion attempts.

Chapter 6
Using an Artificial Neural Network to Improve Email Security

Mohamed Abdulhussain Ali Madan Maki
Ahlia University, Bahrain

Suresh Subramanian
ⓘ https://orcid.org/0000-0002-4055-8725
Ahlia University, Bahrain

ABSTRACT

Email is one of the most widely used features of internet, and it is the most convenient method of transferring messages electronically. However, email productivity has been decreased due to phishing attacks, spam emails, and viruses. Recently, filtering the email flow is a challenging task for researchers due to techniques that spammers used to avoid spam detection. This research proposes an email spam filtering system that filters the spam emails using artificial back propagation neural network (BPNN) technique. Enron1 dataset was used, and after the preprocessing, TF-IDF algorithm was used to extract features and convert them into frequency. To select best features, mutual information technique has been applied. Performance of classifiers were measured using BoW, n-gram, and chi-squared methods. BPNN model was compared with Naïve Bayes and support vector machine based on accuracy, precision, recall, and f1-score. The results show that the proposed email spam system achieved 98.6% accuracy with cross-validation.

DOI: 10.4018/978-1-7998-2418-3.ch006

INTRODUCTION

Electronic mail or known as e-mail it is a channel of electronically communicate with others by massages through the internet. Now a day's emails are not only used for communication but also for creating tasks and solving customer queries. Email is, simple, cheap, and fast type of communication, then it could be vulnerable to many threats (David, Lucia, and Bindura, 2013).

One of the most potential security threats in the emailing system is the "SPAM" where attackers are illegally disseminating malicious software's such us Malware's, Viruses', Trojan's and Internet worms (Ndumiyana, Magomelo and Sakala, 2013).

Spam means unwanted email or unsolicited commercial emails sent directly to a large number of addresses (Shama.N, 2017). The spam emails sent to the receivers without their permission. It is possible to send hundreds of emails to thousands of users around the world at no cost.

Spam scientifically different in content and can belong to the following categories: advertisement, money making, sexually explicit, business, scams. (Al-jarrah, Khater and Al-duwairi, 2012)

The spam has been increased in the last years and becomes a serious problem for communication. Mr. Vairagade, (2017) estimated that 48 billion out of the 80 billion emails are sent daily as spam also among 40,000 users are replying to spam emails. According to Symantec (2017), email spam rate decline in 2011 was 75%, in 2015 and 2016 dropped to 53% and the first quarter of 2017 the rate dropped to 54%. The high ratio of spams in recent years indicates that scammers are looking for fast revenue opportunity.

This research tried to improve the techniques of filtering the emails to prevent spam from spreading into customer's mailboxes. Also, we will preprocess the Enron spam dataset and extract the features required to feed NN text classifier. Accordingly this research improved the accuracy and performance of email spam filtering.

BACKGROUND

Theoretical Background

Machine learning is the development of algorithms that permit machines to learn. ML has been used in medical diagnosis, bioinformatics, Money fraud, stock market analysis, classifying DNS, speech recognition, computer games, and spam filtering (Bhuiyan *et al.*, 2018),(R Manikandan, 2018).

Neural Network (NN) is a beautiful biologically inspired programming paradigm, which enables a computer to learn from observational data. Currently, the NN algorithm used widely in many problems, such as text categorizations, image, and speech recognition.

However, extracting the emails and classify them needs knowledge of Natural Language Processing (NLP) to normalize the datasets, extract and select the features to feed the classifiers (Ndumiyana, Magomelo, and Sakala, 2013)(Jayanthi and Subhashini, 2016).

NN has more efficiency in detecting spam because its supervised learning method and also errors can be corrected NB, DT, SVM, KNN are also good classifiers (Sharma, 2014).

The study will use BPNN to improve accuracy and performance in detecting email spam.

Related Work

The tasks of managing a large volume of data are challenged because of the growing number of emails around the world. For example, detecting spam with many security roles may slow down system performance. Many studies include replies in the email, folder classification, automatic subject, contacts. Currently, email servers such as Google combined the email communication once the user replied (Alsmadi and Alhami, 2015).

The classification algorithm must not only classify the spam email accurately but also expected to classify emails as legitimate. The prediction metrics (True Positive, True Negative, False Positive, False Negative) are used to evaluate the quality of the email prediction (Alsmadi and Alhami, 2015).

Various approaches have been considered to compare the performance of many classification algorithms. Below are related work to the spam classification problems that include email spam problem.

NB is a probabilistic ML model used for classification problems. The core of the classifier depends on Bayes theorem which is discovered by British mathematician reverend Thomas Bayes in 1763. The demonstration of original Bayes Theorem as (Wei, 2018a):

$$p\left(A|B\right)=\frac{P\left(B|A\right)P\left(A\right)}{P\left(B\right)} \tag{1}$$

- P(A|B) is the posterior probability of class (target) given predictor (attribute).
- P(A) is the prior probability of class.
- P(B|A) is the likelihood, which is the probability of predictor given class.

- P(B) is the prior probability of predictor.

Rusland *et al.* (2017) used the NB algorithm for email spam filtering on two datasets (Spam Data & Spam base). The Spam data datasets have 9324 emails, and 500 attributes and Spam Based dataset has 4601 emails and 58 attributes.

SYSTEM DESIGN

The process that followed in our experiment has been developed based on supervised machine learning (ML) procedures by (Bassiouni, Ali and El-Dahshan, 2018). In our experiment, the dataset is divided into training and testing sets with a shuffle in each run. Cross-validation with Five folds to solve the overfitting problem.

- **Training Phase:** The training set has been pre-processed to eliminate noise, stop words, HTML tags, and numbers. Since we are implementing supervised ML, emails will be pre-classified with labels (Ham or Spam). Next, the features will be extracted, and the most ranked features will be selected using the filter method. These features will be used in the testing stage of the classifier model.
- **Testing Phase:** The testing set is also called "Unseen set" it will be pre-processed as we performed in training phase, features will be extracted and selected then these features will feed the classifier model to predict if the email is Ham or Spam. Next, the classifier will be evaluated by the performance evaluation methods.

Choosing Dataset

The Enron 1 dataset has 5172 emails, Hams 3672 and Spams 1500 (V. Metsis, 2006). Each folder identified as Ham or Spam. It is original dataset from Enron investigation but arranged by V.Metsis, I.Androutsopoulos, and G.Paliouras and collected by owners of the mailbox themselves. The dataset has baseline results for the classifiers with various conditions and sections (Sharma and Khurana, 2017). Figure (2) present a sample of ham email

The dataset has been selected to meet the proposed system requirements:

1. **The Dataset Must Contain the Header of the Email:** Al-jarrah, Khater, and Al-duwairi (2012) identified that header features could be used to identify the email spam. Therefore, using Header will increase the possibility of detecting spam. In our case, we will include "Subject" from the email.

Table 1. Summarization of the related work

Sr.	Author and year	Corpus Used	Tools used	Technique Used	Accuracy
1	(Rusland *et al.*, 2017)	Spam Based Spam Data	WEKA Tool	Naïve Bayes	Spam Data of 91.13% while Spam base get 82.54%
2	(Shahi and Yadav, 2014)	No corpus for Nepali, they have created their own.	Java Programming language -TF-IDF scheme to make feature vector	Naïve Bayes, Support Vector Machine (SVM)	Naïve Bayes classifier was 92.74% and for SVM classifier was 87.15%.
3	(G. Jain, Manisha, 2017a)	UCI SMS Spam Collection Twitter Text Data	Weighting scheme (TF-IDF)	Naïve Bayes SVM, ANN, KNN, RN	Naïve Bayes, SMS: %97.65 Twitter: %91.14 SVM, SMS: %97.45 Twitter: %93.14 ANN, SMS: %97.40 Twitter: %91.18 KNN, SMS: %90.40 Twitter: %91.96 RN, SMS: %97.77 Twitter: %93.04
4	(Gupta and Goyal, 2018)	Personnel Gmail dataset	-Python, -Keras to convert emails into a numeric matrix -Ripper to categorize the emails	Feed Forward Neural Network	One hidden layer was 33.33% 1500 hidden layers, where the accuracy result improved to 90% an increasing number of words to 12000 with 100 hidden layers increase the accuracy from 81.67% to 88.33%.
5	(Hota, Shrivas and Singhai, 2013)	UCI Spam Dataset		BPNN, Decision Tree, C5.0,	The best result achieved 91.96% when combining SVM & C5.0 (94.35%)
6	(Saad, 2018)	Reuters-21578	Singular Value Decomposition (SVD)	Back Propagation Neural Network	The average accuracy of the classification was %99.40
7	(Jameel, 2013)	Phishing Corpus (Monkey.org) And SpamAssassin		Feed Forward Neural Network	Accuracy Achieved 98.72%
8	(Awad and ELseuofi, 2011)	SpamAssassin Dataset	Frequent Words in spam email	NB, SVM, KNN, NN, AIS, RS	Naïve Bayes achieved the best accuracy result with 99.46%, Rough Sets achieved 97.42%, SVM achieved 96.90%, ANN achieved 96.83%.

135

Figure 1. Proposed email spam filtering system

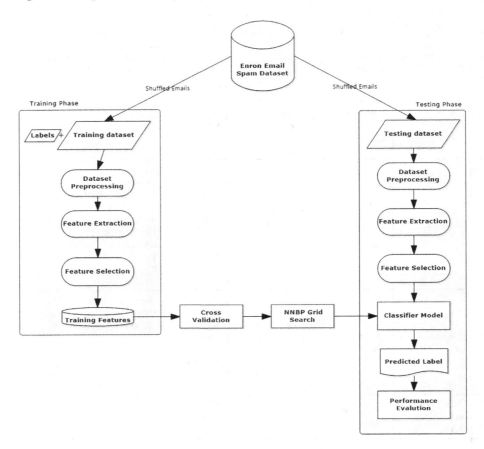

2.   **The Dataset Must Contain the Body of the Email:** To increase the accuracy prediction result the Iqbal *et al.* (2016) suggested to combine the body and the email header because header contains features that can be used in detecting spam.

3.   **The Dataset Must not be Encrypted:** Having the dataset in clear text will help in improving the pre-processing phase.

Train the Classifiers Algorithm

Based on the Mutual Information features selection algorithm, The BPNN, NB, SVM classifiers are trained by 70% of Enron1 dataset.

Figure 2. Sample of "Enron1" ham email

```
4402.2001-04-26.farmer.ham.txt - Notepad                                    —  □  ×
File  Edit  Format  View  Help
Subject: re : may wellhead " spot " purchases - request
vance ,
as we discussed yesterday , i will zero the confirmed column in pops for barrett and increase the same for seneca .
bob
from : vance l taylor / enron @ enronxgate on 04 / 26 / 2001 11 : 42 am
to : robert cotten / hou / ect @ ect
cc : george weissman / hou / ect @ ect , daren j farmer / hou / ect @ enron , melissa graves / enron @ enronxgate ,
susan smith / hou / ect @ enron
subject : re : may wellhead " spot " purchases - request
bob ,
i ' m still concern about april ' s nom ; if we don ' t take it to zero , than we could have the possibility of the
allocations group adding volumes to barrett ' s april deal . this would be incorrect .
vlt
- - - - - original message - - - - -
from : cotten , robert
sent : thursday , april 26 , 2001 9 : 27 am
to : taylor , vance l
cc : weissman , george ; daren j farmer / hou / ect @ enron ; graves , melissa ; susan smith / hou / ect @ enron
subject : re : may wellhead " spot " purchases - request
vance ,
based on the information below , nominations are being revised effective may 1 , 2001 :
counterparty meter # orig . nom rev . nom
barrett resources 0435 1 , 536 0
seneca resources 0435 3 , 073 4 , 609
total 4 , 609 4 , 609
bob
from : vance l taylor / enron @ enronxgate on 04 / 25 / 2001 08 : 42 am
to : robert cotten / hou / ect @ ect
cc : george weissman / hou / ect @ ect , susan smith / enron @ enronxgate , melissa graves / enron @ enronxgate
subject : re : may wellhead " spot " purchases - request
bob ,
hplc continues to purchase gas from both ocean and seneca on a term basis ; firm tickets were submitted for april
origination beginning with the month of april . as for as barrett , they are selling their gas under a joa with
```

By using Scikit-learn library in python called "fit_transform()," the classifier will learn the vocabulary and converts the training dataset into a document-term matrix (DTM).

- **Fit():** Learn the vocabulary of the training dataset.
- **Transform():** Converts the training data into document-term matrix. (DTM).

After creating the Training Document-Term Matrix (DTM), the DTM will be used to feed the BPNN classifier. The other classifiers (Naïve Bayes, SVM,) is selected to compare the results BPNN classifier.

The selected classifiers imported from Scikit-learning library in python. (scikit-learn developers, 2019b)

Grid Search

Grid-Search is used to find the optimal hyperparameters of a model which results in the most "Accurate" predictions (Joseph, 2018). We have implemented Grid-Search for BPNN.

We used one approach known as Grid Search algorithm with k-fold cross-validation. The hyperparameters can be given to a grid search to test the parameters with the classifier. Accordingly, the best parameters among them can be set as parameters to the NN classifier model. We created several tests for feature extraction algorithms, features selections with multiple numbers of features to test the parameters accordingly.

1. TF-IDF K features and BOW K features.
2. Unigram, Bigram, Trigram, and N-gram.
3. Chi-Squared best 4000, 8000,9000,1000,15000, 25000 features
4. Neural Network parameters
    a. Activation function: Identity, Tanh, Logistic, Relu
    b. Max_iter: 400, 300, 200
    c. Hidden_layer_Sizes: (10,80),(50,0),(80,0),(200,400)
    d. Learning_rate:
    e. Solver = ibfgs, sgd, Adam

The grid search implements "fit" and "score" method for each estimator used. The parameters of the estimator used to apply these methods are optimized by cross-validated grid-search over a parameter grid.(Sciket Learn developers, 2019)

The grid search algorithm has been implemented with sci-kit learn called "GridSearchCV()" (scikit-learn developers, 2019a).

Classifier Modeling

After tuning the parameters to get the best classifier performance, we need to save the trained models in a file and restore them in the production environment or compare the model with other models created to test the model on testing folds.

Saving of the classifier model called Serialization and restoring the data is called Deserialization (Python Software Foundation, 2019)

Creating a classifier model will allow us to predict the emails without executing training dataset every time, especially if the dataset is large.

We have used a package called "Pickle" it is python object serialization library (Python Software Foundation, 2019). Each training classifier model will be saved as "(Name of classifier.pki)".

Testing the Classifier

After creating and setting up the parameters of the classifier model, the model can be tested with production email data.

The remaining unseen 20% (One fold) will be given to the classifier model to get the actual testing result data to evaluate the classifier. The models generated results is called predicted results (Jayanthi and Subhashini, 2016)(Zavvar, Rezaei and Garavand, 2016)(Bassiouni, Ali and El-Dahshan, 2018).

Performance and Evaluation Parameters (Confusion Matrix):

In our experiment, the performance and the evaluation of the classifiers will be evaluated base on the Accuracy, Recall, Precision, and F-Measure. Below are more details:

To get the accuracy of the classification, this research used the confusion matrix provided by the scikit-learn library.

RESULTS AND DISCUSSION

Experiment 1: Chi2 feature selection algorithm with TF-IDF with compare to BOW

The experiment results will show the accuracy result of chi2 with feature extraction algorithms (TF-IDF) with the compare to (BOW) algorithm.

The results show that using Chi2 algorithm as features selection with TF-IDF will perform better than BOW algorithm as the accuracy result increased by (%0.1.417) for SVM, (0.5155) for BPNN and also increased by (%0.6) for BPNN with G.S and C.V but the performance decreased by (0.3866) for NB.

The difference between BPNN classifier and BPNN with cross-validation approach is due to cross-validation because it's split the dataset into five folds and then calculate the accuracy. Therefore, the accuracy of BPNN cross-validation is more accurate than BPNN.

The accuracy result shows that the BPNN algorithm performed better than SVM and NB in classifying the email using TF-IDF as feature extraction and Chi2 as feature selection.

Experiment 2: MI algorithm with TF-IDF with Compare to BO

The experiment results show the accuracy result of Mutual information according to the feature extraction algorithms (TF-IDF) with the compare to (BOW) algorithm.

Table 2. Confusion matrix

Test Outcome	Condition	
	Condition Positive	Condition Negative
Outcome Negative (Ham)	True Positive	False Positive
Outcome Negative (Spam)	False Negative	True Negative

Figure 3. Experiment 1: Chi2 algorithm with TF-IDF compared with BOW

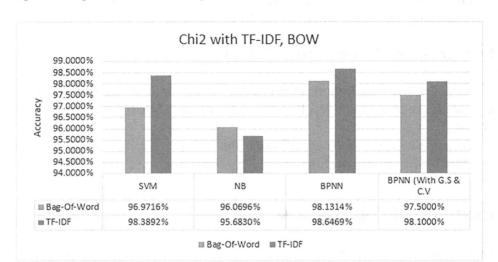

Figure 4. Experiment 2: MI algorithm with TF-IDF compare to BOW

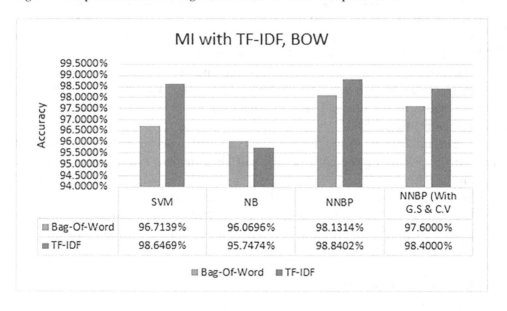

The results show that using Mutual information algorithm in feature selection with TF-IDF performed better than BOW. By using TF-IDF, the accuracy result increase for SVM by (%1.9330), BPNN (0.7088), BPNN with GS. & C.V (0.8000) and decreased by (%0.3222) for NB classifier.

The accuracy result shows the BPNN algorithm performed well in classifying the email using TF-IDF as feature extraction and Mutual Information as feature selection.

The accuracy result achieved by BPNN using Mutual information with TF-IDF achieved by better than Chi2 with TF-IDF.

The confusion evaluation report results for the experiment shows that BPNN Precision and f1-score achieved (%99.28), and it is the best among the classifiers but recall lower than SVM about (0.45).

The experiment shows that the BPNN algorithm is the best classifier for email spam due to the evaluation confusion report below:

The total number of Testing emails are 1552 emails. The number of correctly classified Ham emails (TP) are 1101 emails, and correctly classified spam emails (TN) are 433 emails. Therefore, the misclassified emails are 18 emails distributed among 8 Ham emails misclassified as Spam and 10 Spam emails misclassified as Ham.

Table 4 Confusion matrix for experiment 2

Table 5 Classification Report for experiment 2

With BPNN, the accuracy result achieved by Enron1 98.884%, BPNN with cross-validation 98.6%, SVM 98.6%, NB 95.7%.

Figure 5. Experiment 2: Classification report results

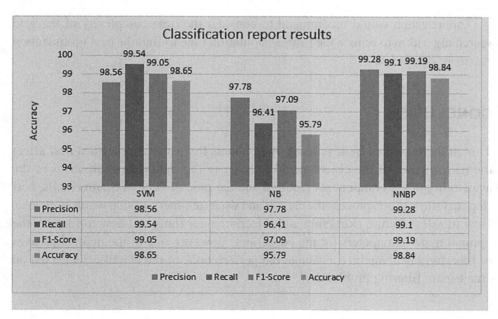

	SVM	NB	NNBP
■ Precision	98.56	97.78	99.28
■ Recall	99.54	96.41	99.1
■ F1-Score	99.05	97.09	99.19
■ Accuracy	98.65	95.79	98.84

Table 4. Shows the confusion matrix of experiment 2

Sr.	Classifier	TP	FP	FN	TN
1	SVM	1093	16	5	438
2	NB	1084	25	41	402
3	BPNN	1101	8	10	433

Table 5. Shows the classification report for experiment 2

Sr.	Classifier	Precision	Recall	F1-Score	Accuracy
1	SVM	98.56	99.54	99.05	98.65
2	NB	97.78	96.41	97.09	95.79
3	BPNN	99.28	99.1	99.19	98.84

FUTURE WORK

For future work, suggested to consider deep learning techniques which will help us in handling the feature representation and developing a learning model to generate feature representation. Since the spam is not limited to content, it has to be designed a system that supports image recognition, attachment malicious codes identification through learning model, support of other languages like Arabic, French, Chinese, Hindi.

This research would recommend to consider the time complexity of the grid search algorithm to reduce the time computation time to find the best optimization classifier parameter.

CONCLUSION

This study motivated by several research papers that various processes may affect the performance of the classifiers like choosing the right dataset in terms of the availability of the components required and the ratio of Ham or Spam emails, best steps to follow in pre-process the dataset and what stemmer and stop words to choose. How to select feature extraction and selection algorithms and how to identify the optimal hyper-parameters for the classifiers. However, one of the main objectives of this study is to analyze, evaluate the performance of the classifiers selected on email spam filtering problem.

Preprocessing of the dataset must be normalized well to support feature extraction and selection algorithms. The study observed that a good pre-processing could improve the performance of other classifiers.

The experiments prove that using TF-IDF with Mutual information algorithm can improve the accuracy results and by using the n-gram, the results are decreasing' due to dataset structure.

With BPNN, the accuracy result achieved by Enron1 98.884%, BPNN with cross-validation 98.6%, SVM 98.6%, NB 95.7%. With reference to the accuracy of Enron's datasets (1-6), BPNN classifier has achieved the best performance based on the obtained evaluation accuracy results.

REFERENCES

Al-jarrah, O., Khater, I., & Al-duwairi, B. (2012). Identifying potentially useful email header features for email spam filtering. *The Sixth International Conference on Digital Society*, 140–145.

Alsmadi, I., & Alhami, I. (2015). Clustering and classification of email contents. *Journal of King Saud University - Computer and Information Sciences, 27*(1), 46–57. doi:10.1016/j.jksuci.2014.03.014

Awad, W. A. (2011). Machine Learning Methods for Spam E-Mail Classification. *International Journal of Computer Science & Information Technology, 3*(1), 12. doi:10.5121/ijcsit.2011.3112

Bassiouni, M., Ali, M., & El-Dahshan, E. A. (2018). Ham and Spam E-Mails Classification Using Machine Learning Techniques. *Journal of Applied Security Research. Taylor & Francis, 13*(3), 315–331. doi:10.1080/19361610.2018.1463136

Bhuiyan, H. (2018). 'A Survey of Existing E-Mail Spam Filtering Methods Considering Machine Learning Techniques,' Global. *Journal of Computer Science and Technology, 18*(2), 21–29.

David, N., & Lucia, S. & Bindura. (2013). Hidden Markov Models And Artificial Neural Networks For Spam Detection. *International Journal of Engineering Research & Technology, 2*(2), 1–5. doi:10.1177/2393957514555052

Gupta, D. K., & Goyal, S. (2018). *Email Classification into Relevant Category Using Neural Networks*. Available at http://arxiv.org/abs/1802.03971

Hota, H. S., Shrivas, A. K., & Singhai, S. K. (2013). Artificial Neural Network, Decision Tree and Statistical Techniques Applied for Designing and Developing E-mail Classifier. *International Journal of Recent Technology and Engineering*, (16), 2277–3878.

Iqbal, M., Abid, M. M., Ahmad, M., & Khurshid, F. (2016). Study on the Effectiveness of Spam Detection Technologies. *International Journal of Information Technology and Computer Science*, 8(1), 11–21. doi:10.5815/ijitcs.2016.01.02

Jameel, N. G. M. (2013). Detection of Phishing Emails using Feed Forward Neural Network. *International Journal of Computers and Applications*, 77(7), 10–15. doi:10.5120/13405-1057

Jayanthi, S. K., & Subhashini, V. (2016). *Efficient Spam Detection using Single Hidden Layer Feed Forward Neural Network. International Research Journal of Engineering and Technology*, 690–696.

Joseph, R. (2018). *Grid Search for model tuning*. Available at: https://towardsdatascience.com/grid-search-for-model-tuning-3319b259367e

Manikandan, D. R. S. (2018). Machine Learning Algorithms for Classification. *International Journal of Academic Research and Development*, 384–389. doi:10.13140/RG.2.1.2044.4003

Metsis, V. I. A., & G. P. (2006). *Enron Dataset*. Available at: http://www2.aueb.gr/users/ion/data/enron-spam/

Ndumiyana, D., Magomelo, M., & Sakala, L. (2013). Spam Detection using a Neural Network Classifier. *Online Journal of Physical and Environmental Science Research*, 2(2), 28–37.

Python Software Foundation. (2019). *Pickle — Python object serialization*. Available at: https://docs.python.org/3/library/pickle.html

Rusland, N. F. (2017). Analysis of Naïve Bayes Algorithm for Email Spam Filtering across Multiple Datasets. *IOP Conference Series. Materials Science and Engineering*, 226(1). doi:10.1088/1757-899X/226/1/012091

Saad, Y. (2018). Dimension Reduction Techniques for Document Categorization with Back Propagation Neural Network. *Journal of Engineering and Applied Sciences (Asian Research Publishing Network)*, 1304–1309.

Sciket learns. (2019). *Mutual Information*. Available at: https://scikit-learn.org/stable/modules/generated/sklearn.feature_selection.mutual_info_classif.html

Scikit-learn developers. (2019a). *Grid Search*. Available at: https://scikit-learn.org/stable/modules/generated/sklearn.model_selection.GridSearchCV.html

Scikit-learn developers. (2019b). *Scikit learn Classifiers*. Available at: https://scikit-learn.org/stable/supervised_learning.html

Shahi, T. B., & Yadav, A. (2014). Mobile SMS Spam Filtering for Nepali Text Using Naïve Bayesian and Support Vector Machine. *International Journal of Intelligence Science*, *4*(01), 24–28. doi:10.4236/ijis.2014.41004

Shama, N. T. (2017). Neural Network Model for Email-Spam Detection. *International Journal of Multi-Disciplinary*, *2*(1), 1–4.

Sharma, A. A. (2014). SMS Spam Detection Using Neural Network Classifier. *International Journal of Advanced Research in Computer Science and Software Engineering, 4*(6), 2277–128. Available at: http://ijarcsse.com/Before_August_2017/docs/papers/Volume_4/6_June2014/V4I6-0151.pdf

Sharma, U., & Khurana, S. S. (2017, June). SHED: Spam Ham Email Dataset. *International Journal on Recent and Innovation Trends in Computing and Communication*, 1078–1082.

Symantec. (2017). Email Threats 2017 An ISTR Special Report Analyst: Ben Nahorney Internet Security Threat Report. *Symantec Security*. Available at: https://www.symantec.com/content/dam/symantec/docs/security-center/white-papers/istr-email-threats-2017-en.pdf

Vairagade, R. S. (2017). Survey Paper on User Defined Spam Boxes using Email Filtering. *International Journal of Computers and Applications*, *157*(6), 3.

Zavvar, M., Rezaei, M., & Garavand, S. (2016). Email Spam Detection Using Combination of Particle Swarm Optimization and Artificial Neural Network and Support Vector Machine. *International Journal of Modern Education and Computer Science*, *7*, 68–74. doi:10.5815/ijmecs.2016.07.08

Chapter 7
A Review of Machine Learning Techniques for Anomaly Detection in Static Graphs

Hesham M. Al-Ammal
University of Bahrain, Bahrain

ABSTRACT

Detection of anomalies in a given data set is a vital step in several applications in cybersecurity; including intrusion detection, fraud, and social network analysis. Many of these techniques detect anomalies by examining graph-based data. Analyzing graphs makes it possible to capture relationships, communities, as well as anomalies. The advantage of using graphs is that many real-life situations can be easily modeled by a graph that captures their structure and inter-dependencies. Although anomaly detection in graphs dates back to the 1990s, recent advances in research utilized machine learning methods for anomaly detection over graphs. This chapter will concentrate on static graphs (both labeled and unlabeled), and the chapter summarizes some of these recent studies in machine learning for anomaly detection in graphs. This includes methods such as support vector machines, neural networks, generative neural networks, and deep learning methods. The chapter will reflect the success and challenges of using these methods in the context of graph-based anomaly detection.

DOI: 10.4018/978-1-7998-2418-3.ch007

INTRODUCTION

In the past two decades, several researchers proposed graph algorithms that dealt with several types of graphs, including dynamic graphs, huge graph structures, and incomplete graphs. However, within the past 5 years, advances in machine learning made it possible to introduce new techniques for approaching this problem. This chapter aims at reviewing the latest techniques in machine learning for anomaly detection in static graphs, due to their prevalence in several real-life applications. Although dynamic graphs are also a good model for several situations, their case is out of the scope of this chapter.

Although several review papers were published previously, they tend to be outdated or do not cover machine learning and deep learning, both of which saw a huge number of activity and success in the past five years. The chapter will review recent machine learning algorithms for detecting anomalies in both labeled and unlabeled static graphs.

BACKGROUND

Graphs (also called networks in other sources) have been used extensively to model real-world situations in mathematics, operations research, and computer science. Their usefulness stems from the fact that they are generic representations that can be analyzed using an algorithm. Once this algorithm exists and is efficient, any graph that fits the requirements can be examined, leading to insights and pattern discovery. Famously, Euler laid out the ground work for graph theory when he studied in 1736 the so called Königsberg Bridges problem by formulating the layout as a graph which led to a solution (Bollobas 2012). More recently, advances in analyzing graph structures such as the World Wide Web lead to the success of Google after the PageRank algorithm was employed to strengthen information retrieval (Page et al. 1999). There are numerous other examples of the success (and limitations) of graph-based algorithms, to which the reader is referred to the book by Bollobas 2012 among many other sources.

When examining a massive data set, detecting an anomaly within the data is often more important than getting general facts about the data set (such as the mean or other general observations). Thus, *anomaly detection* techniques are used to detect or discover rare occurrences within a given data set. Consequently, several vital applications rely on anomaly detection including applications in cybersecurity, fraud detection, finance, health care and many others.

It should be noted that in the data mining field there is often some confusion between the terms "outlier detection" and "anomaly detection". However, an outlier is a term usually used for points within data placed in a multi-dimensional space independently. When dealing with data represented using a graph a more general term which better captures cases such as discrepancies as well as rare events is "anomaly".

Furthermore, although there are many outlier detection algorithms, not all data can be represented as points in multi-dimensional space. Several situations have inter-dependencies among the data that is better represented by a graph with links among the objects (Akoglu et al. 2015). In several situations, the richness provided by graph representation greatly enhances the data set and provides means of improving the algorithms or achieving a task. This is clearly evidenced by the case previously mentioned regarding Google search (Page et al. 1999).

In machine learning algorithms, statistical models are constructed from "training data" that enable a computer system to perform a task without being explicitly instructed on how the task is performed. This definition of "without being explicitly programmed" is attributed to Arthur Samuel and describes the core of the definition of machine learning (Torres 2016).

Machine learning is a branch of Artificial Intelligence (AI). As indicated by the timeline of discoveries within AI in Figure 1, machine learning techniques can belong to one of the main branches of AI, namely: (a) Symbolic AI, (b) Statistical AI, or (c) Hybrid AI techniques. It should be noted that machine learning spans the three branches and can utilize a statistical mode, neural network, or a hybrid model.

Recently, several major breakthroughs including deep learning and advanced hybrid techniques for anomaly detection were proposed by researchers. The current chapter aims at discussing some of these advances in machine learning algorithms

Figure 1. Brief overview timeline of artificial intelligence fields and techniques

for anomaly detection in graphs. To answer the important question: "why detect anomalies on graphs?", Akoglu et al. (2015) presents the following reasons which have been revised here:

1. **Inter-Dependent Nature of Data:** Not all data can be displayed in tables of independent records. Many practical situations such as: network traffic, social networks, disease infection, monetary transactions, etc. exhibit dependencies among the objects which are better represented by links within the nodes of a graph.
2. **Powerful Representation:** Several types of graph structures are available to represent relationships between objects including undirected, directed, and complex graphs.
3. **Relational Nature of Problem Domains:** Several anomalies carry the relational nature and are better described through relations. This is clearly evident in applications such as fraud detection, malware infection, etc.
4. **Robust Representation:** Graph structures are generic and thus an algorithm working on a graph tends to be universally useful for any other graph. This makes graph algorithms quite valuable and easily adaptable to different domains and applications.

However, there are several challenges with anomaly detection on graphs:

1. **Defining an Anomaly:** Akoglu et al. (2015) discusses the problem of the definition of "what is an anomaly?", as there have been several proposed definitions for the word "anomaly" in the literature. Furthermore, the graph-context has some extended definition of anomaly based on the relationships represented by the structure. For example, a node can be isolated, or hyperconnected, or far from the center; regardless of the properties or value of the node.
2. **Data Specific Challenges:** The three V's of big data (volume, velocity, and variety) all apply in this context. There are huge graphs such as the graph of the world-wide web, dynamic graphs that change continuously, as well as a variety of graph data which can be sparse, dense, or disconnected. Thus, scale and dynamics are important for graph data. Analyzing Facebook data or cell phone data with billions of constantly changing data carry many algorithmic challenges. Furthermore, complexity is a big issue as several graph algorithms are known to be NP-hard or NP-complete. The researcher or practitioner has to be aware of these challenges (Akoglu et al. 2015).
3. **Domain-Specific Challenges:** This includes lack of labels on the data, which would be a problem especially for supervised learning algorithms. Due to the

challenges in obtaining good labels, several researchers seek unsupervised learning solutions (Ott et al. 2011). Furthermore, as data science is very sensitive to knowledge of the domain, expert advice and supervision is essential when defining anomalous behavior. Although harder to implement, supervised learning is more effective in catching odd and non-conforming cases.

Graph and Algorithm Category

As the nature of the graph affects the algorithm and the problem type, we start by briefly describing the graph categories. In order to discuss current research trends a taxonomy for the various types of graphs and the methods used to study them must be adopted. The following taxonomy which is partly adopted from the field survey by Akoglu et al. 2015, divides graphs into two main categories:

1. **Static Graphs:** A static graph corresponds to a snapshot in time of the structure of the whole graph. The algorithm has complete knowledge of the structure of the whole graph and can utilize the data to locate anomalies.
2. Examples of static graphs include the road or street network, organizational structures, family trees, and basically any structure that does not evolve in real time.
3. **Dynamic Graphs:** A graph with a structure that varies with time and the algorithm attempts to detect anomalies among this change. This type of graph is usually more complex to analyze and many open problems exist within the dynamic graph category.
4. Examples of dynamic graphs are also more interesting, especially for anomaly detection. They include financial transactions, computer network activity, twitter comments, etc.

For these two types of graphs, the data can be labelled (also called attributed) or unattributed. *Labeled* graphs have information or attributes that are known in advance for each node or edge. On the other hand, *unlabeled* graph data has only the node and edge information without any labels, and the algorithm only examines the graph structure to detect anomalies. For the purposes of machine learning, this is a crucial piece of information that is needed to distinguish the approach used for the learning activity. The categories for the target graph are shown in Figure 2.

Furthermore, when categorizing the algorithm type we must consider two other important factors: the *processing mode* of the algorithm which can be (a) batch mode, or (b) stream mode; and the *type of learning* which is generally categorized as either (a) supervised learning, (b) semi-supervised learning, or (c) unsupervised learning.

Figure 2. Categorization of graph anomaly detection algorithms

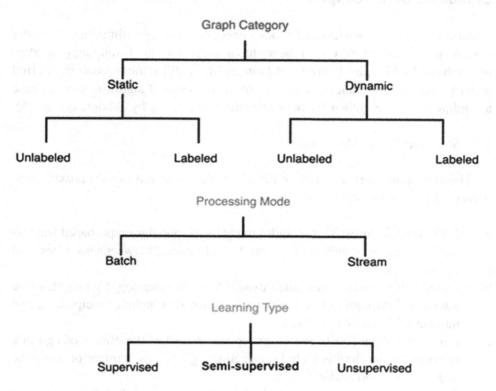

These factors are also shown in Figure 2 and this chapter will mainly concentrate on algorithms for anomaly detection in static graphs.

ANOMALY DETECTION IN STATIC GRAPHS

As discussed above, an algorithm examining a static graph is assumed to have knowledge of the whole graph which does not change. The aim of the algorithm is to examine this structure and detect patterns that will identify anomalies.

Given a static graph G = (V, E) where V is a set of n nodes of vertices, and E is a set of m pairs between the vertices, the aim of the algorithm is to find the vertices, edges, and/or subgraph that are different from the patterns observed in the rest of the graph. Note that the graph G is considered *static*, if the sets V and E do not change with time.

Unlabeled Static Graphs

In static graphs G without labelled nodes V or edges E, the algorithm can only access the structure of the graph. Graph theory has a long tradition of studying properties of graphs and subgraphs. Learning algorithms often utilize these properties to find patterns and spot anomalies. There are two main groups of algorithms in this case according to the comprehensive but somewhat dated survey by (Akoglu et a. 2015):

1.   Structure-Based Algorithms:

The algorithms in this section utilize either the (a) features or (b) proximity of parts of the graph to locate anomalies.

a.   Node-level features: This includes many of the popular graph-based features such as: degree, connectivity, centrality, closeness, betweenness, roles, and eigenvectors.
b.   Edge-level features: Also called dyadic features (sociology) which describe interaction through examining the edges; and this includes reciprocity, and number of common neighbors.
c.   Ego-centric features: In sociology, egonet describes the effects of ego in a relationship graph; this includes principle eigenvalues, number of triangles, and pairwise-correlation levels.
d.   Proximity-based features: PageRank (Brin & Page 1998) famously used recursive proximity-based features to assign "how important" is a node within the web-graph. These methods utilize random-walks to calculate probabilities of an anomaly within a node or an edge.

Most of the research within these features was not conducted with machine learning in mind. For example, Henderson et al. 2010 present several node-level features but often use direct analysis of these methods. The same graph features could be utilized during the feature selection phase of a machine learning approach such as Support Vector Machines (SVMs) or deep learning (Henderson et a. 2010). An interesting extension of these methods was the use of recursively obtained features (similar to what was captured by PageRank) to detect anomalies, but with no application of machine learning techniques (Henerson et al. 2011). The authors claim that their feature-based direct algorithms will scale very well with the graph size.

Other research which uses the same approach with no ML includes articles on social network analysis (Liben-Nowell and Kleinberg 2003), measures of ties in a social network (Gupte et al. 2012), among others. It should be noted that several researchers did utilize this work on identification of features within graphs within machine learning approaches (Dong et al. 2015, Huang et al. 2018, Abdelzaher et al. 2018), including an early use of supervised learning for graph anomaly detection by Dasgupta & Hsu 2008.

Proximity-based algorithms for anomaly detection include the work by Haveliwala (2003) and Chen & Giles (2013). Chowdhury et al. (2017) utilizes graph features to perform unsupervised learning SVMs to discover Botnets using graph-based feature clustering. Furthermore, Akula 2018 utilized self-organizing maps to cluster botnets in a graph, and Abou Daya's (2019) thesis also used supervised and unsupervised learning methods to detect Botnets. The algorithm outperforms flow-based methods and performs well in the online/dynamic graph setting.

2. Community-Building Algorithms:

The cluster or community-based techniques for anomaly detection in graphs detect abnormally dense subgraphs and the bridges that connect them. Finding such a bridge signals a connection to another community. Naturally, examining bipartite graphs and their properties was the starting point for this method (Sun et al. 2005). The study of bipartite graphs has many real-world applications in bibliometrics, financial transactions, and intrusion detection. Sun et al. 2005 examine the question of finding communities that a node belongs to, and quantifying the strength of this relationship. Several other researchers followed in this purely algorithmic method for finding communities, however, machine learning algorithms that utilize community-based metrics appear in Akoglu & Falotsus (2013), Galluccio et al. (2012), and Wang et al. (2008).

Recently, researchers started applying deep learning toward community building (Pandhre & Balasubramanian 2018). Other applications include ranking of anomalous nodes (Lamba, et al. 2017), Cybersecurity (Goodman 2015), peer-group based profiling (Turcotte et al. 2016) and outlier detection (Guo & Zhu 2017).

Labeled Static Graphs

In some situations, it might be possible to have a graph with extra information attached to its nodes or edges such as metadata or labels. For example, graphs obtained from social network applications, computer network traffic data, logistics data, etc. all have rich set of data attributes that can aid in finding anomalies. In this subsection we consider such graphs in the static setting (a snapshot of the network).

As might be expected the main difference with the previous case of unlabeled static graphs is that an algorithm is capable of exploiting these labels or attributes to improve the detection process, while previously only the structure mattered. Based on Akoglu et al. (2015), we will categorize the algorithms into structure-based, community-based, and relation-based.

1.   Structure-Based Algorithms:

Similar to unlabeled graphs above, structure-based algorithms attempt to find anomalies through patterns in the sub-structures of the graph. This includes examining rare events occurring due to specific graph attributes. One of the early attempts at this problem was by Noble and Cook (2003) who attempted to find the most frequent sub-structures and use Minimum Description Length (MDL) to detect substructures or subgraphs that are rare. This is achieved by formulating a measure that is inversely proportional to the MDL and using it to rank substructures. This measure can utilize the given graph attributes such as popularity of a node in social networks, or age of a packet in computer networks. Thus, these attributes contribute the numeric value to the formulated measure, which initially seems like a crude way of comparing substructures.

Later, Davis et al. (2011) suggested methods of transforming these labels into discrete values which lead to several algorithms based on clustering and probability density functions have been proposed Akoglu et al. (2015). On the other hand, Eberle & Holder (2007) use another approach by identifying very similar structures that differ in some attributes or metadata. This is again done through examining differences due to insertion, deletion, or modification.

One of the pioneer attempts to adopt machine learning in this context was the work by Liu et al. (2005) which employed features derived from the graph labels to train a model for identifying bugs in software programs. The researchers used positive and negative behavioral labels to train a model that would identify anomalous subgraphs. As usual, the challenge was in the feature selection and correct sampling of the training set. This clearly has to be done using domain experts and the algorithm belongs to the supervised learning category. Bachwani et al. (2012) and Cao et al. (2017) further utilize this technique for applications in recommender systems and fraud detection. Wei et al. (2019) build a data oriented system for detecting custom and covert intrusions in a network. Their algorithm uses PageRank and Support Vector Machines to build the machine learning models for detecting anomalies.

2.   Community-Based Algorithms:

The approach of these algorithms divides a graph into communities (via *clustering*) and then uses the labels or attributes to find nodes that deviate from their community. Again, both supervised and unsupervised learning is possible here.

Gao et al. (2017) performs unsupervised learning to detect local and global outliers. To perform the clustering, they utilize the work of Xu et al. (2007), and then the algorithms performs anomaly detection within the results of the clustering of the sub-communities.

On the other hand, several researchers followed an approach which starts with a *classification* phase, which is used to divide the graph into communities (similar to clustering) and then uses the labels or attributes to find nodes that deviate from their community. The difference here is that the classification is based on labelling of the anomalous and normal items using human experts, and thus this results in a supervised or semi-supervised learning algorithm.

This approach dates back to the work by Getoor et al. (2001) but has been studied extensively thereafter under the name relational learning Jensen et al. (2004). These methods can be classified into local and global methods. *Local algorithms* construct models at the local node level and use often "iterative inference" to collectively classify unlabeled objects. *Global algorithms* construct a global model of class attributes and use inference algorithms to obtain assignments that would maximize the joint probability distribution.

These so-called relational algorithms range in the inference engine used. Although optimal exact inference solution for Bayesian networks has been shown to be NP-hard by (Cooper 1990), several fast iterative approaches have been suggested for an approximation, including:

- Naïve Bayes: Neville & Jenson (2000), Chakrabarti (2007).
- Gibbs Sampling: Neville & Jenson (2003).
- Belief Propagation: Getoor et al. (2001), Kang et al. (2011).
- Markov Logic Networks: Richardson et al. (2006), Dong et al. (2019).
- Neural Networks: Vijayan et al. (2018).

CONCLUSION

This chapter presented a review of anomaly detection techniques for graph data with emphasis on recent machine learning approaches toward this problem. The emphasis was on static graph data, and as Table 1 summarizes, we can classify the proposed algorithms based on the given data set. Unlabeled graphs do not contain attributes for the graph data, and thus the algorithms must depend mainly on the graph structure. While in labeled/attributed graphs we can utilize the attributes to further analyze and detect anomalous behavior.

Table 1. Machine learning approaches toward anomaly detection in static graph structures

Category	Method	Supervised Learning	Unsupervised Learning
Static Unlabeled Graphs	*Structure Based Methods Community Based Methods*	• Dasgupta & Hsu (2008) • Dong et al. (2015) • Huang et al. (2018) • Abdelzaher et al. (2018) • Guo & Zhu (2017) • Yu et al. (2016)	• Chowdhury et al. (2017) • Akula (2018) • Abou Daya (2019) • Goodman (2015) • Turcotte et al. (2016)
Static Labeled Graphs	*Structure Based Methods Community Based Methods*	• Liu et al. (2005) • Bachwani et al. (2012) • Cao et al. (2017) • Getoor et al. (2001) • Neville & Jenson (2003) • Kang et al. (2011) • Müller et al. (2013) • Vijayan et al. (2018)	• Løken (2016) • Wei et al. (2019) • Richardson & Domingos (2006) • Xu et al. (2007) • Savage et al. (2014) • Gao et al. (2017) • Dong et al. (2019)

We have how machine learning techniques have been used in classification, clustering, and inference within anomaly detection in graphs. With the rise of social networks and network-based applications, this field of anomaly detection is becoming more and more important. Current methods have just been proposed with deep learning and more advance neural network algorithm for anomaly detection. This brief survey shows that there is huge potential for utilizing inference engines to solve the anomaly detection problem in both labelled and unlabeled graphs. The power of Convolutional Neural Networks and deep learning have just started to be employed within this context.

A recent survey of deep learning for anomaly detection was presented by Chalapathy and Chawla (2019), however, it is a general survey that does not concentrate on the graph context. Looking through the literature it is clear that deep learning methods are yet to be adopted to the case of graph structures, even though there are some recent attempts (Goyal et al. 2018, Yu et al. 2018, Li et al. 2019, Ding et al. 2019). Recently, most attention in the literature was given to representation learning, which can also be a promising area for anomaly detection on graphs and networks (Trivedi 2019, Pareja et al. 2019, Ding et al. 2019).

Furthermore, there has been a surge of recent activity in community-based anomaly detection in graphs. This section of the research area shows great promise for new results and better algorithms. Recent advances in high performance computing and big data have also not been fully utilized. This is mainly due to the nature of graphs which defy local and parallel analysis algorithms. This challenge can also provide an opportunity for further specialized parallel and distributed algorithms for anomaly detection.

REFERENCES

Abdelzaher, T., Han, J., Faloutsos, C., & Eliassi-Rad, T. (2018). *Robustness Analysis and Anomaly Detection of Interdependent Physical and Social Networks*. University of Illinois at Urbana Champaign Urbana United States.

Abou Daya, A. (2019). *BotChase: Graph-Based Bot Detection Using Machine Learning*. University of Waterloo.

Akoglu, L., & Faloutsos, C. (2013, February). Anomaly, event, and fraud detection in large network datasets. In *Proceedings of the sixth ACM international conference on Web search and data mining* (pp. 773-774). ACM. 10.1145/2433396.2433496

Akoglu, L., Tong, H., & Koutra, D. (2015). Graph based anomaly detection and description: A survey. *Data Mining and Knowledge Discovery*, *29*(3), 626–688. doi:10.100710618-014-0365-y

Akula, R. K. (2018). *Botnet Detection Using Graph Based Feature Clustering*. Mississippi State University.

Bachwani, R., Crameri, O., & Bianchini, R. (2012). *Mojave: A recommendation system for software upgrades*. Academic Press.

Bollobas, B. (2012). *Graph theory: an introductory course* (Vol. 63). Springer Science & Business Media.

Brin, S., & Page, L. (1998). The anatomy of a large-scale hypertextual web search engine. *Computer Networks and ISDN Systems, 30*(1-7), 107-117.

Cao, B., Mao, M., Viidu, S., & Philip, S. Y. (2017, November). HitFraud: A Broad Learning Approach for Collective Fraud Detection in Heterogeneous Information Networks. In *2017 IEEE International Conference on Data Mining (ICDM)* (pp. 769-774). IEEE. 10.1109/ICDM.2017.90

Chakrabarti, S. (2007, May). Dynamic personalized pagerank in entity-relation graphs. In *Proceedings of the 16th international conference on World Wide Web* (pp. 571-580). ACM. 10.1145/1242572.1242650

Chalapathy, R., & Chawla, S. (2019). *Deep learning for anomaly detection: A survey*. arXiv preprint arXiv:1901.03407

Chen, H. H., & Giles, C. L. (2013, August). ASCOS: an asymmetric network structure context similarity measure. In *2013 IEEE/ACM International Conference on Advances in Social Networks Analysis and Mining (ASONAM 2013)* (pp. 442-449). IEEE. 10.1145/2492517.2492539

Chowdhury, S., Khanzadeh, M., Akula, R., Zhang, F., Zhang, S., Medal, H., ... Bian, L. (2017). Botnet detection using graph-based feature clustering. *Journal of Big Data*, *4*(1), 14. doi:10.118640537-017-0074-7

Cooper, G. F. (1990). The computational complexity of probabilistic inference using Bayesian belief networks. *Artificial Intelligence*, *42*(2-3), 393–405. doi:10.1016/0004-3702(90)90060-D

Dasgupta, S., & Hsu, D. (2008, July). Hierarchical sampling for active learning. In *Proceedings of the 25th international conference on Machine learning* (pp. 208-215). ACM.

Davis, M., Liu, W., Miller, P., & Redpath, G. (2011, October). Detecting anomalies in graphs with numeric labels. In *Proceedings of the 20th ACM international conference on Information and knowledge management* (pp. 1197-1202). ACM. 10.1145/2063576.2063749

Ding, K., Li, J., Bhanushali, R., & Liu, H. (2019, May). Deep Anomaly Detection on Attributed Networks. In *Proceedings of the 2019 SIAM International Conference on Data Mining* (pp. 594-602). Society for Industrial and Applied Mathematics. 10.1137/1.9781611975673.67

Dong, S., Liu, D., Ouyang, R., Zhu, Y., Li, L., Li, T., & Liu, J. (2019). Second-Order Markov Assumption Based Bayes Classifier for Networked Data With Heterophily. *IEEE Access: Practical Innovations, Open Solutions*, *7*, 34153–34161. doi:10.1109/ACCESS.2019.2892757

Dong, Y., Zhang, J., Tang, J., Chawla, N. V., & Wang, B. (2015, August). Coupledlp: Link prediction in coupled networks. In *Proceedings of the 21th ACM SIGKDD International Conference on Knowledge Discovery and Data Mining* (pp. 199-208). ACM. 10.1145/2783258.2783329

Eberle, W., & Holder, L. (2007, October). Discovering structural anomalies in graph-based data. In *Seventh IEEE International Conference on Data Mining Workshops (ICDMW 2007)* (pp. 393-398). IEEE. 10.1109/ICDMW.2007.91

Galluccio, L., Michel, O., Comon, P., & Hero, A. O. III. (2012). Graph based k-means clustering. *Signal Processing*, *92*(9), 1970–1984. doi:10.1016/j.sigpro.2011.12.009

Gao, J., Liang, F., Fan, W., Wang, C., Sun, Y., & Han, J. (2010, July). On community outliers and their efficient detection in information networks. In *Proceedings of the 16th ACM SIGKDD international conference on Knowledge discovery and data mining* (pp. 813-822). ACM. 10.1145/1835804.1835907

Getoor, L., Friedman, N., Koller, D., & Pfeffer, A. (2001). Learning probabilistic relational models. In *Relational data mining* (pp. 307–335). Berlin: Springer. doi:10.1007/978-3-662-04599-2_13

Goodman, E., Ingram, J., Martin, S., & Grunwald, D. (2015, December). Using bipartite anomaly features for cyber security applications. In *2015 IEEE 14th International Conference on Machine Learning and Applications (ICMLA)* (pp. 301-306). IEEE. 10.1109/ICMLA.2015.69

Goyal, P., Kamra, N., He, X., & Liu, Y. (2018). *Dyngem: Deep embedding method for dynamic graphs.* arXiv preprint arXiv:1805.11273

Guo, J., & Zhu, W. (2018, April). Partial multi-view outlier detection based on collective learning. *Thirty-Second AAAI Conference on Artificial Intelligence.*

Gupte, M., & Eliassi-Rad, T. (2012, June). Measuring tie strength in implicit social networks. In *Proceedings of the 4th Annual ACM Web Science Conference* (pp. 109-118). ACM. 10.1145/2380718.2380734

Haveliwala, T. H. (2003). Topic-sensitive pagerank: A context-sensitive ranking algorithm for web search. *IEEE Transactions on Knowledge and Data Engineering, 15*(4), 784–796. doi:10.1109/TKDE.2003.1208999

Henderson, K., Eliassi-Rad, T., Faloutsos, C., Akoglu, L., Li, L., Maruhashi, K., & Tong, H. (2010, July). Metric forensics: a multi-level approach for mining volatile graphs. In *Proceedings of the 16th ACM SIGKDD international conference on Knowledge discovery and data mining* (pp. 163-172). ACM. 10.1145/1835804.1835828

Henderson, K., Gallagher, B., Li, L., Akoglu, L., Eliassi-Rad, T., Tong, H., & Faloutsos, C. (2011, August). It's who you know: graph mining using recursive structural features. In *Proceedings of the 17th ACM SIGKDD international conference on Knowledge discovery and data mining* (pp. 663-671). ACM. 10.1145/2020408.2020512

Huang, Q., Singh, V. K., & Atrey, P. K. (2018). On cyberbullying incidents and underlying online social relationships. *Journal of Computational Social Science, 1*(2), 241–260. doi:10.100742001-018-0026-9

Jensen, D., Neville, J., & Gallagher, B. (2004, August). Why collective inference improves relational classification. In *Proceedings of the tenth ACM SIGKDD international conference on Knowledge discovery and data mining* (pp. 593-598). ACM.

Kang, U., Chau, D. H., & Faloutsos, C. (2011, April). Mining large graphs: Algorithms, inference, and discoveries. In *2011 IEEE 27th International Conference on Data Engineering* (pp. 243-254). IEEE.

Lamba, H., Hooi, B., Shin, K., Faloutsos, C., & Pfeffer, J. (2017, September). zooRank: Ranking suspicious entities in time-evolving tensors. In *Joint European Conference on Machine Learning and Knowledge Discovery in Databases* (pp. 68-84). Springer. 10.1007/978-3-319-71249-9_5

Li, Y., Huang, X., Li, J., Du, M., & Zou, N. (2019). *SpecAE: Spectral AutoEncoder for Anomaly Detection in Attributed Networks.* arXiv preprint arXiv:1908.03849

Liben-Nowell, D., & Kleinberg, J. (2007). The link-prediction problem for social networks. *Journal of the American Society for Information Science and Technology, 58*(7), 1019–1031. doi:10.1002/asi.20591

Liu, C., Yan, X., Yu, H., Han, J., & Yu, P. S. (2005, April). Mining behavior graphs for "backtrace" of noncrashing bugs. In *Proceedings of the 2005 SIAM International Conference on Data Mining* (pp. 286-297). Society for Industrial and Applied Mathematics. 10.1137/1.9781611972757.26

Løken, E. (2016). *Graph Classification via Neural Networks* (Master's thesis).

Müller, E., Sánchez, P. I., Mülle, Y., & Böhm, K. (2013, April). Ranking outlier nodes in subspaces of attributed graphs. In *2013 IEEE 29th International Conference on Data Engineering Workshops (ICDEW)* (pp. 216-222). IEEE. 10.1109/ICDEW.2013.6547453

Neville, J., & Jensen, D. (2000, July). Iterative classification in relational data. In *Proc. AAAI-2000 Workshop on Learning Statistical Models from Relational Data* (pp. 13-20). Academic Press.

Neville, J., & Jensen, D. (2003). Collective classification with relational dependency networks. In *Workshop on Multi-Relational Data Mining (MRDM-2003)* (p. 77). Academic Press.

Noble, C. C., & Cook, D. J. (2003, August). Graph-based anomaly detection. In *Proceedings of the ninth ACM SIGKDD international conference on Knowledge discovery and data mining* (pp. 631-636). ACM. 10.1145/956750.956831

Ott, M., Choi, Y., Cardie, C., & Hancock, J. T. (2011). Finding deceptive opinion spam by any stretch of the imagination. *Proceedings of the 49th Annual Meeting of the Association for Computational Linguistics (ACL)*, 309–319.

Page, L., Brin, S., Motwani, R., & Winograd, T. (1999). *The PageRank citation ranking: Bringing order to the web*. Stanford InfoLab.

Pandhre, S., & Balasubramanian, V. N. (2018). *Understanding Graph Data Through Deep Learning Lens* (Doctoral dissertation). Indian Institute of Technology Hyderabad.

Pareja, A., Domeniconi, G., Chen, J., Ma, T., Suzumura, T., Kanezashi, H., . . . Leisersen, C. E. (2019). *Evolvegcn: Evolving graph convolutional networks for dynamic graphs*. arXiv preprint arXiv:1902.10191

Richardson, M., & Domingos, P. (2006). Markov logic networks. *Machine Learning*, *62*(1-2), 107–136. doi:10.100710994-006-5833-1

Savage, D., Zhang, X., Yu, X., Chou, P., & Wang, Q. (2014). Anomaly detection in online social networks. *Social Networks*, *39*, 62–70. doi:10.1016/j.socnet.2014.05.002

Sen, P., Namata, G., Bilgic, M., Getoor, L., Galligher, B., & Eliassi-Rad, T. (2008). Collective classification in network data. *AI Magazine*, *29*(3), 93–93. doi:10.1609/aimag.v29i3.2157

Sun, J., Qu, H., Chakrabarti, D., & Faloutsos, C. (2005, November). Neighborhood formation and anomaly detection in bipartite graphs. In *Fifth IEEE International Conference on Data Mining (ICDM'05)*. IEEE.

Torres, A., Torres, M. D., & de León, E. P. (2016, October). Automated analog synthesis with an estimation of the distribution algorithm. In *Mexican International Conference on Artificial Intelligence* (pp. 173-184). Springer.

Trivedi, R., Farajtabar, M., Biswal, P., & Zha, H. (2018). *Dyrep: Learning representations over dynamic graphs*. Academic Press.

Turcotte, M., Moore, J., Heard, N., & McPhall, A. (2016, September). Poisson factorization for peer-based anomaly detection. In *2016 IEEE Conference on Intelligence and Security Informatics (ISI)* (pp. 208-210). IEEE. 10.1109/ISI.2016.7745472

Vijayan, P., Chandak, Y., Khapra, M. M., Parthasarathy, S., & Ravindran, B. (2018). *Fusion graph convolutional networks*. arXiv preprint arXiv:1805.12528

Wang, B., Phillips, J. M., Schreiber, R., Wilkinson, D., Mishra, N., & Tarjan, R. (2008, April). Spatial scan statistics for graph clustering. In *Proceedings of the 2008 SIAM International Conference on Data Mining* (pp. 727-738). Society for Industrial and Applied Mathematics. 10.1137/1.9781611972788.66

Wei, T. E., Lee, H. M., Jeng, A. B., Lamba, H., & Faloutsos, C. (2019). WebHound: A data-driven intrusion detection from real-world web access logs. *Soft Computing*, 1–19.

Xu, X., Yuruk, N., Feng, Z., & Schweiger, T. A. (2007, August). Scan: a structural clustering algorithm for networks. In *Proceedings of the 13th ACM SIGKDD international conference on Knowledge discovery and data mining* (pp. 824-833). ACM. 10.1145/1281192.1281280

Yu, R., Qiu, H., Wen, Z., Lin, C., & Liu, Y. (2016). A survey on social media anomaly detection. *ACM SIGKDD Explorations Newsletter*, *18*(1), 1–14. doi:10.1145/2980765.2980767

Yu, W., Cheng, W., Aggarwal, C. C., Zhang, K., Chen, H., & Wang, W. (2018, July). Netwalk: A flexible deep embedding approach for anomaly detection in dynamic networks. In *Proceedings of the 24th ACM SIGKDD International Conference on Knowledge Discovery & Data Mining* (pp. 2672-2681). ACM. 10.1145/3219819.3220024

Chapter 8
Composite Discrete Logarithm Problem and a Reconstituted ElGamal Cryptosystem Based on the Problem:
New ElGamal Cryptosystems With Some Special Sequences and Composite ElGamal Cryptosystem

Çağla Özyılmaz
Ondokuz Mayıs University, Turkey

Ayşe Nallı
Karabuk University, Turkey

ABSTRACT

In this chapter, the authors have defined a new ElGamal cryptosystem by using the power Fibonacci sequence module m. Then they have defined a new sequence module m and the other ElGamal cryptosystem by using the new sequence. In addition, they have compared that the new ElGamal cryptosystems and ElGamal cryptosystem in terms of cryptography. Then the authors have defined the third ElGamal cryptosystem. They have, particularly, called the new system as composite ElGamal cryptosystem. The authors made an application of composite ElGamal cryptosystem. Finally, the authors have compared that composite ElGamal cryptosystem and ElGamal cryptosystem in terms of cryptography and they have obtained that composite ElGamal cryptosystem is more advantageous than ElGamal cryptosystem.

DOI: 10.4018/978-1-7998-2418-3.ch008

INTRODUCTION

The fundamental objective of cryptography is to enable two people, which are usually referred to as Alice and Bob, to communicate over an insecure channel in such a way that an opponent, Oscar, can't understand what is being said. The information that Alice wants to send to Bob, which is called 'plaintext', can be English text, numerical data, or anything else, that is, its structure is selected arbitrarily. Alice encrypts the plaintext, using a predetermined key, and sends ciphertext over the insecure channel. Oscar, by seeing the ciphertext in the channel, can't determine what the the message was; but Bob who knows the encryption key, can decrypt the ciphertext and revive the plaintext or the message. These situations are identified by using the following mathematical notation.

Definition 1. A cryptosystem is a five–tuple (P, C, K, E, D) where the following conditions are satisfied:

1. 1. P is a finite set of possible plaintexts (or the messages);
2. 2. C is a finite set of possible ciphertexts (or encrypted messages);
3. 3. K is a finite set of possible keys;
4. For each $K \in K$, there is an encryption function $e_K : P \to C$ ($e_K \in E$) and a decryption function $d_K : C \to P$ ($d_K \in D$) such that $d_K(e_K(x)) = x$ for every plaintext element $x \in P$ (Stinson, 2002).

In practice, there are two types of cryptosystems.

1. Symmetric Cryptography (Secret key cryptosystems)
2. Asymmetric Cryptography (Public key cryptosystems)

Normally, in any cryptosystem, the encryption and the decryption key are closely related. It is practically impossible to decrypt the ciphertext with the key that is unrelated to the encryption key. In symmetric cryptography is used a single key for both encryption and decryption and in asymmetric cryptography, such as the RSA (Rivest et al., 1978) and ElGamal cryptosystem (ElGamal, 1985), is used different keys for encryption and decryption (Hwang et al., 2002).

In this chapter, the authors have focused on asymmetric cryptography and they, especially, have cited that discrete logarithm problem which is one of the mathematical difficult problems that are used in asymmetric cryptography and ElGamal cryptosystem based on the discrete logarithm problem. They have defined new discrete logarithm problems and new ElGamal cryptosystem and they have made new applications.

BACKGROUND

At the very heart of cryptography is the notion of one way function, which was shown to be necessary and sufficient for many cryptographic primitives.

Definition 2. A one-way function(OWF) is a function f such that for each x in the domain of f, it is easy to compute $f(x)$; but for essentially all y in the range of f, it is computationally

infeasible to find any x such that $y = f(x)$.

The following are two examples of candidate one-way functions.

1. *OWF multiplication of large primes*: For primes p and q, $f(p,q) = pq$ is a one-way function: given p and q, computing $n = pq$ is easy; but given n, finding p and q is difficult. The difficult direction is known as the integer factorization problem, RSA and many other cryptographic systems rely on this example.

2. *OWF exponentiation in prime fields*: Given a generator α of $\mathbb{Z}_p^*$ for most appropriately large prime p, $f(a) = \alpha^a \pmod{p}$ is a one-way function. $f(a)$ is easily computed given α, a, and p; but for most choices p it is difficult, given (y; p; α), to find an a in the range $1 \le a \le p-1$ such that $\alpha^a \pmod{p} = y$. The difficult direction is known as the discrete logarithm problem.

However, a one-way function is not sufficient for public-key cryptography if it is equally hard for the legitimate receiver and the adversary to invert. So rather, it is needed a trapdoor one-way function. A trapdoor one-way function is a one-way function where the inverse direction is easy, given a certain piece of information (the trapdoor), but difficult otherwise. Public-key cryptosystems are based on trapdoor one-way functions. The public key gives information about the particular instance of the function; the private key gives information about the trapdoor (Zhu, 2001).

Now, the authors cite public-key cryptosystems based on the discrete logarithm problem. The first and best-known of these is the ElGamal cryptosystem. ElGamal proposed a public-key cryptosystem which is based on the discrete logarithm problem in ($\mathbb{Z}_p^*$, .). The encryption operation in the ElGamal cryptosystem is randomized, since ciphertext depends on both the plaintext x and on the random value k chosen by Alice. Hence, there will be many ciphertexts that are encryptions of the same plaintext.

ElGamal cryptosystem is presented below:

Definition 3. Let p be a prime number such that the discrete logarithm problem in $(\mathbb{Z}_p^*, .)$ is infeasible, and let $\alpha \in \mathbb{Z}_p^*$ be a primitive element. Let $P = \mathbb{Z}_p^*$, $C = \mathbb{Z}_p^* \times \mathbb{Z}_p^*$ and define $K = \{(p, \alpha, a, \beta): \beta \equiv \alpha^a \pmod{p}\}$. The values p, α, β are the public key, and a is the private key. For $K = (p, \alpha, a, \beta)$, and for a (secret) random number $k \in \mathbb{Z}_{p-1}$, define $e_K(x, k) = (y_1, y_2)$, where $\begin{aligned} y_1 &= \alpha^k \pmod{p} \\ y_2 &= x\beta^k \pmod{p} \end{aligned}$.

For $y_1, y_2 \in \mathbb{Z}_p^*$, define $d_K(y_1, y_2) = y_2(y_1^a)^{-1} \bmod p$ (Stinson, 2002).

Definition 4. Let G be a bi-infinite integer sequence satisfying the recurrence relation $G_n = G_{n-1} + G_{n-2}$. If $G \equiv 1, \alpha, \alpha^2, \alpha^3, ... \pmod{m}$ for some modulus m, then G is called a power Fibonacci sequence modulus m (Ide and Renault, 2012).

Example 1. Modulo $m = 19$, there are two power Fibonacci sequences: 1, 15, 16, 12, 9, 2, 11, 13, 5, 18, 4, 3, 7, 10, 17, 8, 6, 14, 1, 15. . . and 1, 5, 6, 11, 17, 9, 7, 16, 4, 1, 5, . . .

Curiously, the second is a subsequence of the first.

Ide and Renault, in their paper, obtained for modulo 5 there is only one such sequence (1, 3, 4, 2, 1, 3, ...), for modulo 10 there are no such sequences, and for modulo 209 there are four of these sequences. Thus, they obtained the following theorem.

Theorem 1. There is exactly one power Fibonacci sequence modulo 5. For $m \neq 5$, there exist power Fibonacci sequences modulo m precisely when m has prime factorization $m = p_1^{e_1} p_2^{e_2} ... p_k^{e_k}$ or $m = 5p_1^{e_1} p_2^{e_2} ... p_k^{e_k}$, where each $p_i \equiv \pm 1 \pmod{10}$; in either case there are exactly 2^k power Fibonacci sequences modulo m (Ide and Renault, 2012).

In this section, the authors have examined power Fibonaci sequences modulo m and they have obtained that a power Fibonaci sequence modulo m constitutes a cyclic and multiplicative group whose order is a divisor of $\varphi(m)$ at the same time. That is, If $G \equiv 1, \alpha, \alpha^2, \alpha^3, ... \pmod{m}$ is a power Fibonacci sequence module m, the power Fibonacci sequence constitutes a cyclic and multiplicative group whose generator is α. This sequence is a subgroup of $\mathbb{Z}_m^*$ ($\mathbb{Z}_m^* = \{x \in \mathbb{Z}_m : (x, m) = 1\}$).

In addition when the authors examine to mathematical difficult problems which are used asymmetric cryptography, they get a generator is necessary for the discrete logarithm problem. When the authors have thought all these things together, they have obtained that they can rearrenge discrete logarithm problem by using the power Fibonacci sequence module m and so they can rearrenge ElGamal cryptosystem based on the discrete logarithm problem. Thus, they have made a custom application of discrete logarithm problem and ElGamal cryptosystem which is used only in prime modulus is also usable for composite modulus.

Moreover, there are two limits in the ElGamal cryptosystem. One is that the plaintext must be less than $p-1$ (Hwang et al., 2002). So then if m is chosen a composite number by using the power Fibonacci sequence module m, how does this limit in the ElGamal cryptosystem change? To obtain the answer of this question, firstly the authors define new discrete logarithm problem by using the power Fibonacci sequence module m and then they constitute a new ElGamal cryptosystem based on the new problem.

MAIN FOCUS OF THE CHAPTER[1]

ElGamal Cryptosystem with Power Fibonacci Sequence

Definition 5. Given a generator α of a chosen subgroup of $\mathbb{Z}_m^*$ for most appropriately large m, $f(\lambda)=\alpha^\lambda \pmod{m}$ is a one-way function. $f(\lambda)$ is easily computed given λ, α, and m; but for most choices m it is difficult, given (y ; m ; α), to find an λ such that $\alpha^\lambda \pmod{m}=y$. The authors have, particularly, called difficult direction as the discrete logarithm problem with power Fibonacci sequence module m.

Now, the authors will obtain public-key cryptosystem based on the discrete logarithm problem with power Fibonacci sequence module m. They have, particularly, called the cryptosystem as the ElGamal cryptosystem with power Fibonacci sequence module m.

Definition 6. Let m be a positive integer such that the discrete logarithm problem with power Fibonacci sequence module m in a chosen subgroup of ($\mathbb{Z}_m^*$,.) is infeasible, and let $\alpha \in$ (*the chosen subgroup of* $\mathbb{Z}_m^*$) be a primitive element (generator). Let $P=\mathbb{Z}_m \setminus \{0\}$, $C=$ (*the chosen subgroup of* $\mathbb{Z}_m^*$) $\times (\mathbb{Z}_m \setminus \{0\})$ and define $K=\{(m,\alpha,\lambda,\beta): \beta \equiv \alpha^\lambda \pmod{m}\}$. The values m,α,β are the public key, and λ is the private key. For $K=(m,\alpha,\lambda,\beta)$, and for a (secret) random number $k \in \mathbb{Z}_{the\ order\ of\ the\ chosen\ subgroup}$, define $e_K(x,k)=(y_1,y_2)$, where $\begin{aligned} y_1 &= \alpha^k \pmod{m} \\ y_2 &= x\beta^k \pmod{m} \end{aligned}$ .For $(y_1,y_2) \in C$, define $d_K(y_1,y_2)=y_2(y_1^\lambda)^{-1} \bmod m$.

Thus, if it is closely examined, while $\alpha \in \mathbb{Z}_p^*$, the plaintext must be less than $p-1$ in the ElGamal cryptosystem, $\alpha \in$ (*the chosen subgroup of* $\mathbb{Z}_m^*$), the plaintext must be less than $m-1$ in ElGamal cryptosystem with power Fibonacci sequence module m. In addition, it is known that if in ElGamal cryptosystem p is a large prime number, in ElGamal cryptosystem with power Fibonacci sequence module m, m is more large number($m = p_1^{e_1} p_2^{e_2} ... p_k^{e_k}$ or $m = 5 p_1^{e_1} p_2^{e_2} ... p_k^{e_k}$, for each $p_i \equiv \pm 1 \, (\mathrm{mod} \, 10)$ is large prime number). That is, if m is selected a composite number by using the power Fibonacci sequence, the authors obtained that for the answer of the question of how this limit in the ElGamal cryptosystem change in new cryptosystem which the authors constitute this limit decrease as m increases. So, ElGamal cryptosystem with power Fibonacci sequence module m is more advantageous than ElGamal cryptosystem in terms of cryptography (Ozyilmaz and Nalli, 2019).

An Application of ElGamal Cryptosystem with The Power Fibonacci Sequence Modulo m

In this section, the authors illustrate an encryption example for an application of ElGamal cryptosystem which they constructed by using The power Fibonacci sequence module m.

Example 1. Suppose $m = 1045$ which provides theorem 1 and so $\mathbb{Z}_{1045}^* = \{ x \in \mathbb{Z}_{1045} : (x, 1045) = 1 \}$, Module $m = 1045$, there are four power Fibonacci sequences:

- 1, 338, 339, 677, 1016, 648, 619, 222, 841, 18, 859, 877, 691, 523, 169, 692, 861, 508, 324, 832, 111, 943, 9, 952, 961, 868, 784, 607, 346, 953, 254, 162, 416, 578, 994, 527, 476, 1003, 434, 392, 826, 173, 999, 127, 81, 208, 289, 497, 786, 238, 1024, 217, 196, 413, 609, 1022, 586, 563, 104, 667, 771, 393, 119, 512, 631, 98, 729, 827, 511, 293, 804, 52, 856, 908, 719, 582, 256, 838, 49, 887, 936, 778, 669, 402, 26, 428, 454, 882, 291, 128, 419, 547, 966, 468, 389, 857, 201, 13, 214, 227, 441, 668, 64, 732, 796, 483, 234, 717, 951, 623, 529, 107, 636, 743, 334, 32, 366, 398, 764, 117, 881, 998, 834, 787, 576, 318, 894, 167, 16, 183, 199, 382, 581, 963, 499, 417, 916, 288, 159, 447, 606, 8, 614, 622, 191, 813, 1004, 772, 731, 458, 144, 602, 746, 303, 4, 307, 311, 618, 929, 502, 386, 888, 229, 72, 301, 373, 674, 2, 676, 678, 309, 987, 251, 193, 444, 637, 36, 673, 709, 337, 1, 338, ...
- 1, 433, 434, 867, 256, 78, 334, 412, 746, 113, 859, 972, 786, 713, 454, 122, 576, 698, 229, 927, 111, 1038, 104, 97, 201, 298, 499, 797, 251, 3, 254, 257, 511, 768, 234, 1002, 191, 148, 339, 487, 826, 268, 49, 317, 366, 683, 4, 687, 691, 333, 1024, 312, 291, 603, 894, 452, 301, 753, 9, 762, 771, 488, 214, 702, 916, 573, 444, 1017, 416, 388, 804, 147, 951, 53, 1004, 12, 1016, 1028, 999, 982, 936, 873, 764, 592, 311, 903, 169, 27, 196, 223, 419, 642, 16, 658, 674,

287, 961, 203, 119, 322, 441, 763, 159, 922, 36, 958, 994, 907, 856, 718, 529, 202, 731, 933, 619, 507, 81, 588, 669, 212, 881, 48, 929, 977, 861, 793, 609, 357, 966, 278, 199, 477, 676, 108, 784, 892, 631, 478, 64, 542, 606, 103, 709, 812, 476, 243, 719, 962, 636, 553, 144, 697, 841, 493, 289, 782, 26, 808, 834, 597, 386, 983, 324, 262, 586, 848, 389, 192, 581, 773, 309, 37, 346, 383, 729, 67, 796, 863, 614, 432, 1, 433, …

- 1, 613, 614, 182, 796, 978, 729, 662, 346, 1008, 309, 272, 581, 853, 389, 197, 586, 783, 324, 62, 386, 448, 834, 237, 26, 263, 289, 552, 841, 348, 144, 492, 636, 83, 719, 802, 476, 233, 709, 942, 606, 503, 64, 567, 631, 153, 784, 937, 676, 568, 199, 767, 966, 688, 609, 252, 861, 68, 929, 997, 881, 833, 669, 457, 81, 538, 619, 112, 731, 843, 529, 327, 856, 138, 994, 87, 36, 123, 159, 282, 441, 723, 119, 842, 961, 758, 674, 387, 16, 403, 419, 822, 196, 1018, 169, 142, 311, 453, 764, 172, 936, 63, 999, 17, 1016, 1033, 1004, 992, 951, 898, 804, 657, 416, 28, 444, 472, 916, 343, 214, 557, 771, 283, 9, 292, 301, 593, 894, 442, 291, 733, 1024, 712, 691, 358, 4, 362, 366, 728, 49, 777, 826, 558, 339, 897, 191, 43, 234, 277, 511, 788, 254, 1042, 251, 248, 499, 747, 201, 948, 104, 7, 111, 118, 229, 347, 576, 923, 454, 332, 786, 73, 859, 932, 746, 633, 334, 967, 256, 178, 434, 612, 1, 613, … and

- 1, 708, 709, 372, 36, 408, 444, 852, 251, 58, 309, 367, 676, 1043, 674, 672, 301, 973, 229, 157, 386, 543, 929, 427, 311, 738, 4, 742, 746, 443, 144, 587, 731, 273, 1004, 232, 191, 423, 614, 1037, 606, 598, 159, 757, 916, 628, 499, 82, 581, 663, 199, 862, 16, 878, 894, 727, 576, 258, 834, 47, 881, 928, 764, 647, 366, 1013, 334, 302, 636, 938, 529, 422, 951, 328, 234, 562, 796, 313, 64, 377, 441, 818, 214, 1032, 201, 188, 389, 577, 966, 498, 419, 917, 291, 163, 454, 617, 26, 643, 669, 267, 936, 158, 49, 207, 256, 463, 719, 137, 856, 993, 804, 752, 511, 218, 729, 947, 631, 533, 119, 652, 771, 378, 104, 482, 586, 23, 609, 632, 196, 828, 1024, 807, 786, 548, 289, 837, 81, 918, 999, 872, 826, 653, 434, 42, 476, 518, 994, 467, 416, 883, 254, 92, 346, 438, 784, 177, 961, 93, 9, 102, 111, 213, 324, 537, 861, 353, 169, 522, 691, 168, 859, 1027, 841, 823, 619, 397, 1016, 368, 339, 707, 1, 708, …

The authors have choosed one of these power Fibonacci sequences. Curiously, {1, 338, 339, 677, 1016, 648, 619, 222, 841, 18, 859, 877, 691, 523, 169, 692, 861, 508, 324, 832, 111, 943, 9, 952, 961, 868, 784, 607, 346, 953, 254, 162, 416, 578, 994, 527, 476, 1003, 434, 392, 826, 173, 999, 127, 81, 208, 289, 497, 786, 238, 1024, 217, 196, 413, 609, 1022, 586, 563, 104, 667, 771, 393, 119, 512, 631, 98, 729, 827, 511, 293, 804, 52, 856, 908, 719, 582, 256, 838, 49, 887, 936, 778, 669, 402, 26, 428, 454, 882, 291, 128, 419, 547, 966, 468, 389, 857, 201, 13, 214, 227, 441, 668, 64, 732, 796, 483, 234, 717, 951, 623, 529, 107, 636, 743, 334, 32, 366, 398, 764, 117, 881, 998, 834, 787, 576, 318, 894, 167, 16, 183, 199, 382, 581, 963,

499, 417, 916, 288, 159, 447, 606, 8, 614, 622, 191, 813, 1004, 772, 731, 458, 144, 602, 746, 303, 4, 307, 311, 618, 929, 502, 386, 888, 229, 72, 301, 373, 674, 2, 676, 678, 309, 987, 251, 193, 444, 637, 36, 673, 709, 337} is both a subgroup of $\mathbb{Z}^*_{1045}$ and a power Fibonacci sequence for module 1045. α is a primitive element of the chosen subgroup of $\mathbb{Z}^*_m$. So, the primitive element $\alpha = 338$. Let $\lambda = 547$, so

$$\beta = 338^{547} \,(\mathrm{mod}\,1045) = 222.$$

Now, suppose that Alice wishes to send the message $x = 1001$ to Bob. Say $k = 162$ is the random integer she chooses. Then she computes

$$y_1 = \alpha^k (\mathrm{mod}\,m) = 338^{162} \,(\mathrm{mod}\,1045) = 229,$$

$$y_2 = x\beta^k (\mathrm{mod}\,m) = 1001.222^{162} (\mathrm{mod}\,1045) = 1001.609 \,(\mathrm{mod}\,1045) = 374$$

Alice sends $y = (y_1, y_2) = (229, 374)$ to Bob. When Bob receives the ciphertext $y = (229, 374)$, he computes

$$x = y_2 (y_1^{\lambda})^{-1} \bmod m = 374.(229^{547})^{-1} \bmod 1045$$

$$= 374.\,(609)^{-1} \qquad \bmod 1045$$

$$= 374.894 \qquad \bmod 1045$$

$$= 1001$$

which was the plaintext that Alice encrypted (Ozyilmaz and Nalli, 2019).

Power Jacobsthal Sequence and ElGamal Cryptosystem with Power Jacobsthal Sequence

In this section, the authors examined The Jacobsthal sequence and then they defined a new sequence.

Definition 7. The Jacobsthal sequence (J_n) is defined recursively by the equation $J_n = J_{n-1} + 2J_{n-2}$ for $n \geq 2$, where $J_0 = 0$ and $J_1 = 1$ (Deveci et al., 2016).

Definition 8. Let J^* be a bi-infinite integer sequence satisfying the recurrence relation $J^*_n = J^*_{n-1} + 2J^*_{n-2}$. If $J^* \equiv 1, \alpha, \alpha^2, \alpha^3, \ldots (\mathrm{mod}\,m)$ for some modulus m, then J^* is called a power Jacobsthal sequence modulo m.

In addition, when the authors examined power Jacobsthal sequence modulo m, they obtained that for modulo 3 there is only one such sequence $(1, 2, 1, 2, \ldots)$, for modulo 6 there are two of these sequences, for modulo 27 there are six of these sequences and also there exist power Jacobsthal sequences for an any modulo m, ($m \geq 3$). Thus, they, specially, obtained the following theorem.

Theorem 2. For $m \geq 3$, there precisely exist power Jacobsthal sequences modulo m. In addition, for the number of the power Jacobsthal sequences modulo m, there is exactly one power Jacobsthal sequence modulo 3 and for $m \neq 3$, when m has prime factorization $m = 3^e p_1^{e_1} p_2^{e_2} ... p_k^{e_k}$, there are exactly 2^k power Jacobsthal sequences for $e = 0, 1$, 3.2^k power Jacobsthal sequences for $e = 2$, 6.2^k power Jacobsthal sequences modulo m for $e > 2$.

Proof. 1, α, α^2, α^3, ... is a power Jacobsthal sequence modulo m if and only if α is a root of $f(x) = x^2 - x - 2 \pmod{m}$. The roots of $f(x)$ are those residues of the form $2^{-1}(1 + r)$ where $r^2 \equiv 9 \pmod{m}$.

Let $j^*(x) = x^2 - 9$. Counting the number of solutions to $j^*(x) \equiv 0 \pmod{m}$ thus determines the number of power Jacobsthal sequence modulo m.

By inspection, the only solution to $x^2 \equiv 9 \pmod{3}$ is 0, there are three solutions to $x^2 \equiv 9 \pmod{9}$ are $0, 3, 6$; there are six solutions to $x^2 \equiv 9 \pmod{27}$ are $3, 6, 12, 15, 21, 24$ and there are also six solutions to $x^2 \equiv 9 \pmod{81}$ are $3, 24, 30, 51, 57, 78$.

Consequently we have obtained that $x^2 \equiv 9 \pmod{3^e}$ has a solution when $e = 1$, has three solutions $e = 2$ and has six solutions $e > 2$ with induction.

Consider now the roots of $j^*(x) \pmod{p}$ for an odd prime $p \neq 3$. By use of the law of quadratic reciprocity and Legendre symbol (Asar and Arıkan, 2012), one finds that 9 is a quadratic residue module all primes p ($p \neq 3$). Thus, if p is a odd prime number $j^*(x) \pmod{p}$ has two distinct roots.

Now that we know existance and number of roots of $j^*(x) \pmod{p}$, we address the existance and number of roots of $j^*(x) \pmod{p^e}$ for positive integers e. According to Hensel 's lemma (Niven et al., 1991) if $h(x)$ is an integer polynomial with root $\alpha \pmod{p^i}$ and if $h'(a) \not\equiv 0 \pmod{p}$ then $h(x)$ has a root $\bar{a} \pmod{p^{i+1}}$ with the property that $\bar{a} \equiv a \pmod{p^i}$, in esence, distinct roots of $h(x) \pmod{p^i}$ ' lift' to distinct roots of $h(x) \pmod{p^{i+1}}$. with $j^*(x) = x^2 - 9$, p is a prime number, we find that if x_0 is a root of $j^*(x) \pmod{p}$, then $j^{*'}(x_0) = 2x_0 \not\equiv 0 \pmod{p}$.

By Hensel's Lemma it follows that $j^*(x) \pmod{p^e}$ has two distinct roots for every positive integer e.

Lastly, we turn to composite modulo and make use of the Chinese Remainder theorem from elementary number theory (Jones and Jones, 1998). If u and v are relatively prime, if $j^*(x) \equiv 0 \pmod{u}$ has s solutions, and if $j^*(x) \equiv 0 \pmod{v}$ has t solutions, then $j^*(x) \equiv 0 \pmod{uv}$ has st solutions $\square$.

Whereas all power Fibonacci sequences (Ide and Renault, 2012) is periodic for those module m for which power Fibonacci sequences exist, power Jacobsthal sequences is not periodic for those module m which is even for which power Jacobsthal sequences exist.

In this chapter, the authors have obtained that power Jacobsthal sequence module m constitutes a cyclic and multiplicative group whose order is a divisor of $\varphi(m)$ and whose generator is α, as power Fibonacci sequence module m is. So, they have reconstructed definitions similar to discrete logarithm problem with Power Fibonacci sequence and ElGamal cryptosystem with Power Fibonacci sequence as follows:

Definition 9. Given a generator α of a chosen subgroup of $\mathbb{Z}_m^*$ for most appropriately large m, $f(\omega) = \alpha^\omega \pmod{m}$ is a one-way function. $f(\omega)$ is easily computed given ω, α, and m; but for most choices m it is difficult, given (y; m; α), to find an ω such that $\alpha^\omega \pmod{m} = y$. The authors have, particularly, called difficult direction as the discrete logarithm problem with power Jacobsthal sequence module m.

Now, the authors will obtain public-key cryptosystem based on the discrete logarithm problem with power Jacobsthal sequence module m. They have, particularly, called the cryptosystem as the ElGamal cryptosystem with power Jacobsthal sequence module m.

Definition 10. Let m be a positive integer such that it provides theorem 2 in a chosen subgroup of $(\mathbb{Z}_m^*, .)$ is infeasible $\mathbb{Z}_m^* = \{x \in \mathbb{Z}_m : (x,m) = 1\}$, and let $\alpha \in$ (*the chosen subgroup of* $\mathbb{Z}_m^*$) be a primitive element. Let $P = \mathbb{Z}_m \backslash \{0\}$, $C = $ (*the chosen subgroup of* $\mathbb{Z}_m^*$) $\times (\mathbb{Z}_m \backslash \{0\})$ and define $K = \{(m, \alpha, \omega, \beta) : \beta \equiv \alpha^\omega \pmod{m}\}$. The values m, α, β are the public key, and ω is the private key. For $K = (m, \alpha, \omega, \beta)$, and for a (secret) random number $k \in \mathbb{Z}_{the\ order\ of\ the\ chosen\ subgroup}$, define $e_K(x,k) = (y_1, y_2)$, where $y_1 = \alpha^k \pmod{m}$ $y_2 = x\beta^k \pmod{m}$. For $(y_1, y_2) \in C$, define $d_K(y_1, y_2) = y_2(y_1^\omega)^{-1} \bmod m$.

Thus, if it is closely examined, when the authors made an application of ElGamal cryptosystem by using power Jacobsthal sequence, $\mathbb{Z}_m^*$ (m is composite number) is not always cyclic and multiplicative group and so they have used a cyclic and multiplicative subgroup of $\mathbb{Z}_m^*$ they have choosed whose order is a divisor of $\varphi(m)$.

An Application of ElGamal Cryptosystem with The Power Jacobsthal Sequence Modulo m

In this section, the authors illustrate an encryption example for an application of ElGamal cryptosystem which they constructed by using The power Jacobsthal sequence module m.

Example 2. Assume that m be 1215, there are twelve power Jacobsthal sequences:

- 1, 2, 4, 8, 16, 32, 64, 128, 256, 1024, 833, 451, 902, 589, 1178, 1141, 1067, 919, 623, 31, 62, 124, 248, 496, 992, 769, 323, 646, 77, 154, 308, 616, 17, 34, 68, 136, 272, 544, 1088, 961, 707, 199, 398, 796, 377, 754, 293, 586, 1172, 1129, 1043, 871, 527, 1054, 893, 571, 1142, 1069, 923, 631, 47, 94, 188, 376, 752, 289, 578, 1156, 1097, 979, 743, 271, 542, 1084, 953, 691, 167, 334, 668, 121, 242, 484, 968, 721, 227, 454, 908, 601, 1202, 1189, 1163, 1111, 1007, 799, 383, 766, 317, 634, 53, 106, 212, 424, 848, 481, 962, 709, 203, 406, 812, 409, 818, 421, 842, 469, 938, 661, 107, 214, 428, 856, 497, 994, 773, 331, 662, 109, 218, 436, 872, 529, 1058, 901, 587, 1174, 1133, 1051, 887, 559, 1118, 1021, 827, 439, 878, 541, 1082, 949, 683, 151, 302, 604, 1208, 1201, 1187, 1159, 1103, 991, 767, 319, 638, 61, 122, 244, 488, 976, 737, 259, 518, 1036, 857, 499, 998, 781, 347, 694, 173, 346, 692, 169, 338, 676, 137, 274, 548, 1096, 977, 739, 263, 526, 1052, 889, 563, 1126, 1037, 859, 503, 1006, 797, 379, 758, 301, 602, 1204, 1193, 1171, 1127, 1039, 863, 511, 1022, 829, 443, 886, 557, 1114, 1013, 811, 407, 814, 413, 826, 437, 874, 533, 1066, 917, 619, 23, 46, 92, 184, 368, 736, 257, 514, 1028, 841, 467, 934, 653, 91, 182, 364, 728, 241, 482, 964, 713, 211, 422, 844, 473, 946, 677, 139, 278, 556, 1112, 1009, 803, 391, 782, 349, 698, 181, 362, 724, 233, 466, 932, 649, 83, 166, 332, 664, 113, 226, 452, 904, 593, 1186, 1157, 1099, 983, 751, 287, 574, 1148, 1081, 947, 679, 143, 286, 572, 1144, 1073, 931, 647, 79, 158, 316, 632, 49, 98, 196, 392, 784, 353, 706, 197, 394, 788, 361, 722, 229, 458, 916, 617, 19, 38, 76, 152, 304, 608, 1, 2, 4, ...

- 1, 164, 166, 494, 826, 599, 1036, 1019, 661, 269, 376, 914, 451, 1064, 751, 449, 736, 419, 676, 299, 436, 1034, 691, 329, 496, 1154, 931, 809, 241, 644, 1126, 1199, 1021, 989, 601, 149, 136, 434, 706, 359, 556, 59, 1171, 74, 1201, 134, 106, 374, 586, 119, 76, 314, 466, 1094, 811, 569, 976, 899, 421, 1004, 631, 209, 256, 674, 1186, 104, 46, 254, 346, 854, 331, 824, 271, 704, 31, 224, 286, 734, 91, 344, 526, 1214, 1051, 1049, 721, 389, 616, 179, 196, 554, 946, 839, 301, 764, 151, 464, 766, 479, 796, 539, 916, 779, 181, 524, 886, 719, 61, 284, 406, 974, 571, 89, 16, 194, 226, 614, 1066, 1079, 781, 509, 856, 659, 1156, 44, 1141, 14, 1081, 1109, 841, 629, 1096, 1139, 901, 749, 121,

404, 646, 239, 316, 794, 211, 584, 1006, 959, 541, 29, 1111, 1169, 961, 869, 361, 884, 391, 944, 511, 1184, 991, 929, 481, 1124, 871, 689, 1, 164, 166, …

- 1, 242, 244, 728, 1, 242, 244, …
- 1, 404, 406, 1214, 811, 809, 1, 404, 406, …
- 1, 407, 409, 8, 826, 842, 64, 533, 661, 512, 619, 428, 451, 92, 994, 1178, 736, 662, 919, 1028, 436, 62, 934, 1058, 496, 182, 1174, 323, 241, 887, 154, 713, 1021, 17, 844, 878, 136, 677, 949, 1088, 556, 302, 199, 803, 1201, 377, 349, 1103, 586, 362, 319, 1043, 466, 122, 1054, 83, 976, 1142, 664, 518, 631, 452, 499, 188, 1186, 347, 289, 983, 346, 1097, 574, 338, 271, 947, 274, 953, 286, 977, 334, 1073, 526, 242, 79, 563, 721, 632, 859, 908, 196, 797, 1189, 353, 301, 1007, 394, 1193, 766, 722, 1039, 53, 916, 1022, 424, 38, 886, 962, 304, 1013, 406, 2, 814, 818, 16, 437, 469, 128, 1066, 107, 1024, 23, 856, 902, 184, 773, 1141, 257, 109, 623, 841, 872, 124, 653, 901, 992, 364, 1133, 646, 482, 559, 308, 211, 827, 34, 473, 541, 272, 139, 683, 961, 1112, 604, 398, 391, 1187, 754, 698, 991, 1172, 724, 638, 871, 932, 244, 893, 166, 737, 1069, 113, 1036, 47, 904, 998, 376, 1157, 694, 578, 751, 692, 979, 1148, 676, 542, 679, 548, 691, 572, 739, 668, 931, 1052, 484, 158, 1126, 227, 49, 503, 601, 392, 379, 1163, 706, 602, 799, 788, 1171, 317, 229, 863, 106, 617, 829, 848, 76, 557, 709, 608, 811, 812, 4, 413, 421, 32, 874, 938, 256, 917, 214, 833, 46, 497, 589, 368, 331, 1067, 514, 218, 31, 467, 529, 248, 91, 587, 769, 728, 1051, 77, 964, 1118, 616, 422, 439, 68, 946, 1082, 544, 278, 151, 707, 1009, 1208, 796, 782, 1159, 293, 181, 767, 1129, 233, 61, 527, 649, 488, 571, 332, 259, 923, 226, 857, 94, 593, 781, 752, 1099, 173, 1156, 287, 169, 743, 1081, 137, 1084, 143, 1096, 167, 1144, 263, 121, 647, 889, 968, 316, 1037, 454, 98, 1006, 1202, 784, 758, 1111, 197, 1204, 383, 361, 1127, 634, 458, 511, 212, 19, 443, 481, 152, 1114, 203, 1, 407, 409, …
- 1, 569, 571, 494, 421, 194, 1036, 209, 1066, 269, 1186, 509, 451, 254, 1156, 449, 331, 14, 676, 704, 841, 1034, 286, 1139, 496, 344, 121, 809, 1051, 239, 1126, 389, 211, 989, 196, 959, 136, 839, 1111, 359, 151, 869, 1171, 479, 391, 134, 916, 1184, 586, 524, 481, 314, 61, 689, 811, 974, 166, 899, 16, 599, 631, 614, 661, 674, 781, 914, 46, 659, 751, 854, 1141, 419, 271, 1109, 436, 224, 1096, 329, 91, 749, 931, 1214, 646, 644, 721, 794, 1021, 179, 1006, 149, 946, 29, 706, 764, 961, 59, 766, 884, 1201, 539, 511, 374, 181, 929, 76, 719, 871, 1094, 406, 164, 976, 89, 826, 1004, 226, 1019, 256, 1079, 376, 104, 856, 1064, 346, 44, 736, 824, 1081, 299, 31, 629, 691, 734, 901, 1154, 526, 404, 241, 1049, 316, 1199, 616, 584, 601, 554, 541, 434, 301, 1169, 556, 464, 361, 74, 796, 944, 106, 779, 991, 119, 886, 1124, 466, 284, 1, 569, 571, …
- 1, 647, 649, 728, 811, 1052, 244, 1133, 406, 242, 1054, 323, 1, 647, 649, …
- 1, 809, 811, 1214, 406, 404, 1, 809, 811, …

- 1, 812, 814, 8, 421, 437, 64, 938, 1066, 512, 214, 23, 451, 497, 184, 1178, 331, 257, 919, 218, 841, 62, 529, 653, 496, 587, 364, 323, 1051, 482, 154, 1118, 211, 17, 439, 473, 136, 1082, 139, 1088, 151, 1112, 199, 1208, 391, 377, 1159, 698, 586, 767, 724, 1043, 61, 932, 1054, 488, 166, 1142, 259, 113, 631, 857, 904, 188, 781, 1157, 289, 173, 751, 1097, 169, 1148, 271, 137, 679, 953, 1096, 572, 334, 263, 931, 242, 889, 158, 721, 1037, 49, 908, 1006, 392, 1189, 758, 706, 1007, 1204, 788, 766, 1127, 229, 53, 511, 617, 424, 443, 76, 962, 1114, 608, 406, 407, 4, 818, 826, 32, 469, 533, 256, 107, 619, 833, 856, 92, 589, 773, 736, 1067, 109, 1028, 31, 872, 934, 248, 901, 182, 769, 1133, 241, 77, 559, 713, 616, 827, 844, 68, 541, 677, 544, 683, 556, 707, 604, 803, 796, 1187, 349, 293, 991, 362, 1129, 638, 466, 527, 244, 83, 571, 737, 664, 923, 1036, 452, 94, 998, 1186, 752, 694, 983, 1156, 692, 574, 743, 676, 947, 1084, 548, 286, 167, 739, 1073, 121, 1052, 79, 968, 1126, 632, 454, 503, 196, 1202, 379, 353, 1111, 602, 394, 383, 1171, 722, 634, 863, 916, 212, 829, 38, 481, 557, 304, 203, 811, 2, 409, 413, 16, 842, 874, 128, 661, 917, 1024, 428, 46, 902, 994, 368, 1141, 662, 514, 623, 436, 467, 124, 1058, 91, 992, 1174, 728, 646, 887, 964, 308, 1021, 422, 34, 878, 946, 272, 949, 278, 961, 302, 1009, 398, 1201, 782, 754, 1103, 181, 1172, 319, 233, 871, 122, 649, 893, 976, 332, 1069, 518, 226, 47, 499, 593, 376, 347, 1099, 578, 346, 287, 979, 338, 1081, 542, 274, 143, 691, 977, 1144, 668, 526, 647, 484, 563, 316, 227, 859, 98, 601, 797, 784, 1163, 301, 197, 799, 1193, 361, 317, 1039, 458, 106, 1022, 19, 848, 886, 152, 709, 1013, 1, 812, 814, ...

- 1, 974, 976, 494, 16, 1004, 1036, 614, 256, 269, 781, 104, 451, 659, 346, 449, 1141, 824, 676, 1109, 31, 1034, 1096, 734, 496, 749, 526, 809, 646, 1049, 1126, 794, 616, 989, 1006, 554, 136, 29, 301, 359, 961, 464, 1171, 884, 796, 134, 511, 779, 586, 929, 886, 314, 871, 284, 811, 164, 571, 899, 826, 194, 631, 1019, 1066, 674, 376, 509, 46, 1064, 1156, 854, 736, 14, 271, 299, 841, 224, 691, 1139, 91, 1154, 121, 1214, 241, 239, 721, 1199, 211, 179, 601, 959, 946, 434, 1111, 764, 556, 869, 766, 74, 391, 539, 106, 1184, 181, 119, 481, 719, 466, 689, 406, 569, 166, 89, 421, 599, 226, 209, 661, 1079, 1186, 914, 856, 254, 751, 44, 331, 419, 1081, 704, 436, 629, 286, 329, 901, 344, 931, 404, 1051, 644, 316, 389, 1021, 584, 196, 149, 541, 839, 706, 1169, 151, 59, 361, 479, 1201, 944, 916, 374, 991, 524, 76, 1124, 61, 1094, 1, 974, 976, ...

- 1, 1052, 1054, 728, 406, 647, 244, 323, 811, 242, 649, 1133, 1, 1052, 1054, ...

- 1, 1214, 1, 1214, 1, ...

The authors have choosed one of these power Jacobsthal sequences. Curiously, {1, 407, 409, 8, 826, 842, 64, 533, 661, 512, 619, 428, 451, 92, 994, 1178, 736, 662, 919, 1028, 436, 62, 934, 1058, 496, 182, 1174, 323, 241, 887, 154, 713, 1021,

17, 844, 878, 136, 677, 949, 1088, 556, 302, 199, 803, 1201, 377, 349, 1103, 586, 362, 319, 1043, 466, 122, 1054, 83, 976, 1142, 664, 518, 631, 452, 499, 188, 1186, 347, 289, 983, 346, 1097, 574, 338, 271, 947, 274, 953, 286, 977, 334, 1073, 526, 242, 79, 563, 721, 632, 859, 908, 196, 797, 1189, 353, 301, 1007, 394, 1193, 766, 722, 1039, 53, 916, 1022, 424, 38, 886, 962, 304, 1013, 406, 2, 814, 818, 16, 437, 469, 128, 1066, 107, 1024, 23, 856, 902, 184, 773, 1141, 257, 109, 623, 841, 872, 124, 653, 901, 992, 364, 1133, 646, 482, 559, 308, 211, 827, 34, 473, 541, 272, 139, 683, 961, 1112, 604, 398, 391, 1187, 754, 698, 991, 1172, 724, 638, 871, 932, 244, 893, 166, 737, 1069, 113, 1036, 47, 904, 998, 376, 1157, 694, 578, 751, 692, 979, 1148, 676, 542, 679, 548, 691, 572, 739, 668, 931, 1052, 484, 158, 1126, 227, 49, 503, 601, 392, 379, 1163, 706, 602, 799, 788, 1171, 317, 229, 863, 106, 617, 829, 848, 76, 557, 709, 608, 811, 812, 4, 413, 421, 32, 874, 938, 256, 917, 214, 833, 46, 497, 589, 368, 331, 1067, 514, 218, 31, 467, 529, 248, 91, 587, 769, 728, 1051, 77, 964, 1118, 616, 422, 439, 68, 946, 1082, 544, 278, 151, 707, 1009, 1208, 796, 782, 1159, 293, 181, 767, 1129, 233, 61, 527, 649, 488, 571, 332, 259, 923, 226, 857, 94, 593, 781, 752, 1099, 173, 1156, 287, 169, 743, 1081, 137, 1084, 143, 1096, 167, 1144, 263, 121, 647, 889, 968, 316, 1037, 454, 98, 1006, 1202, 784, 758, 1111, 197, 1204, 383, 361, 1127, 634, 458, 511, 212, 19, 443, 481, 152, 1114, 203} is both a subgroup of $\mathbb{Z}^*_{1215}$ and a power Jacobsthal sequence modulo 1215 . α is a primitive element of the chosen subgroup of $\mathbb{Z}^*_m$. So, the primitive element $\alpha = 407$. Let $\omega = 264$, so $\beta = 407^{264} \, (\mathrm{mod}\, 1215) = 181$.

Now, suppose that Alice wishes to send the message $x = 898$ to Bob. Say $k = 125$ is the random integer she chooses. Then she computes

$$y_1 = \alpha^k \,(\mathrm{mod}\, m) = 407^{125} \,(\mathrm{mod}\, 1215) = 257,$$

$$y_2 = x\beta^k \,(\mathrm{mod}\, m) = 898.181^{125} \,(\mathrm{mod}\, 1215) = 898.226 = 43$$

Alice sends $y = (y_1, y_2) = (257, 43)$ to Bob.

When Bob receives the ciphertext $y = (257, 43)$, he computes

$$x = y_2(y_1^\omega)^{-1} \,\mathrm{mod}\, m = 43.(257^{264})^{-1} \,\mathrm{mod}\, 1215$$
$$= 43.\,(226)^{-1} \quad \mathrm{mod}\, 1215$$
$$= 43.586 \quad\quad\ \mathrm{mod}\, 1215$$
$$= 898$$

which was the plaintext that Alice sent.

Composite Discrete Logarithm Problem and Composite ElGamal Cryptosystem

Theorem 3. $\mathbb{Z}_m^*$ is cyclic and multiplicative group if and only if $m = 2$, $m = 4$ or $m = p^k$ or $m = 2p^k$ such that $p \neq 2$ prime number (Yeşilot and Özavşar, 2013).

Definition 11. Let α be a primitive eleman of $\mathbb{Z}_m^*$ for huge large number m. Given μ, α, and m, $f(\mu)$ is easily computed; but for most choices m, given (y ; m ; α) it is difficult to find an μ such that $\alpha^\mu (\mathrm{mod}\, m) = y$. The authors have, especially, called difficult direction as the composite discrete logarithm problem.

Now, the authors will obtain public-key cryptosystem based on composite discrete logarithm problem. They have, especially, called the new cryptosystem as the composite ElGamal cryptosystem.

Definition 12. Let m be a positive integer such that the composite discrete logarithm problem in ($\mathbb{Z}_m^*$, .) is infeasible, and let $\alpha \in \mathbb{Z}_m^*$ be a primitive element (generator). Let $P = \mathbb{Z}_m \setminus \{0\}$, $C = \mathbb{Z}_m^* \times (\mathbb{Z}_m \setminus \{0\})$

and define $K = \left\{ (m, \alpha, \mu, \beta) : \beta \equiv \alpha^\mu (\mathrm{mod}\, m) \right\}$. The values m, α, β are the public key, and μ is the private key. For $K = (m, \alpha, \mu, \beta)$, and for a (secret) random

number $k \in \mathbb{Z}_{\varphi(m)}$, define $e_K(x, k) = (y_1, y_2)$, where $\begin{aligned} y_1 &= \alpha^k (\mathrm{mod}\, m) \\ y_2 &= x\beta^k (\mathrm{mod}\, m) \end{aligned}$. For

$(y_1, y_2) \in C$, define $d_K(y_1, y_2) = y_2 (y_1^\mu)^{-1} \mathrm{mod}\, m$.

Now, the authors illustrate an example composite ElGamal cryptosystem.

Example 3. Let m be 625 according to theorem 3. $\mathbb{Z}_{625}^* = \left\{ x \in \mathbb{Z}_{625} : (x, 625) = 1 \right\}$.

So, the primitive element $\alpha = 2$. Let $\mu = 90$, so $\beta = 2^{90} (\mathrm{mod}\, 625) = 474$.

Let assume that $x = 598$ be the message which is sent and $k = 245$ be the random integer sender chooses. Then the sender computes

$$y_1 = \alpha^k (\mathrm{mod}\, m) = 2^{245} (\mathrm{mod}\, 625) = 332,$$

$$y_2 = x\beta^k (\mathrm{mod}\, m) = 598.474^{245} (\mathrm{mod}\, 625) = 598.124 = 402$$

The sender sends $y = (y_1, y_1) = (332, 402)$ to the receiver. When the receiver obtains the ciphertext $y = (332, 402)$, s/he computes

$$x = y_2 (y_1{}^{\mu})^{-1} \bmod m = 402.(332^{90})^{-1} \bmod 625$$
$$= 402.\,(124)^{-1} \quad \bmod 625$$
$$= 402.499 \qquad \bmod 625$$
$$= 598$$

which was the mesage that the sender sent.

SOLUTIONS AND RECOMMENDATIONS

In this chapter, the authors have compared that composite ElGamal cryptosystem and ElGamal cryptosystem in terms of cryptography. It is known that one of two limits in the ElGamal cryptosystem is that the message must be less than $p-1$ (Hwang et al, 2002). When the authors have compared that ElGamal cryptosystem and composite ElGamal cryptosystem in terms of this limit, they have obtained that while $\alpha \in \mathbb{Z}_p^*$, the plaintext must be less than $p-1$ in the ElGamal cryptosystem, $\alpha \in \mathbb{Z}_m^*$, the plaintext must be less than $m-1$ in composite ElGamal cryptosystem. Moreover, it is known that if in ElGamal Cryptosystem p is a large prime number, in composite ElGamal cryptosystem, m is more large number ($m = p^k$ or $m = 2p^k$, for p is large prime number). That is, if m is chosen a composite number by using the theorem 3, the authors obtained that this limit decrease as m increases. So, thanks to the new cryptosystem, the cryptosystem which is used only in prime modulus is also usable for composite modulus.

In addition, composite ElGamal cryptosystem is more advantages than ElGamal cryptosystem in terms of cryptography. Because, while number of data which must try to understand the message for one who doesn't know the private key is $\varphi(m) = p^k - p^{k-1}$ (for p is large prime number) in composite ElGamal cryptosystem, $\varphi(p) = p-1$ in ElGamal cryptosystem. That is, in comparison with ElGamal cryptosystem, for one who doesn't know the private key the number of data which must try to understand the message increase in composite ElGamal cryptosystem.

FUTURE RESEARCH DIRECTIONS

New cryptographic applications can be made by using the different sequences. Then these cryptographic applications are comparable with each other.

CONCLUSION

In this chapter, firstly, the authors examined power Fibonacci sequence module m and they have defined a new discrete logarithm problem and a new cryptographic system by using the power Fibonacci sequence module m. Then the authors have defined a new sequence module m and they have called the sequence as power Jacobsthal sequence module m and they have defined other discrete logarithm problem and other cryptographic system by using the power Jacobsthal sequence module m. In addition, they have compared that the new cryptographic systems and ElGamal cryptosystem in terms of cryptography. They obtained that the new ElGamal cryptosystems are more advantegous than ElGamal cryptosystem. In both ElGamal cryptosystem with power Fibonacci sequence and ElGamal cryptosystem with power Jacobsthal sequence is used a cyclic and multiplicative group whose order is a divisor of $\varphi(m)$. So, then the authors have defined third discrete logarithm problem and the third ElGamal cryptosystem such that the order of the sequence which is used in the cryptosystem is $\varphi(m)$ and the authors have, especially, called the third problem and the third system as composite discrete logarithm problem and composite ElGamal cryptosystem, respectively.

Finally, they have compared that ElGamal cryptosystem and composite ElGamal cryptosystem in terms of cryptography and they obtained that while $\alpha \in \mathbb{Z}_p^*$, the plaintext must be less than $p-1$ (p is a large prime number) in the ElGamal cryptosystem, $\alpha \in \mathbb{Z}_m^*$, the plaintext must be less than $m-1$ ($m = p^k$ or $m = 2p^k$, for p is large prime number) in composite ElGamal cryptosystem and they also obtained while number of data which must try to understand the message for one who doesn't know the private key is $\varphi(m) = p^k - p^{k-1}$ (for p is large prime number) in composite ElGamal cryptosystem, $\varphi(p) = p - 1$ in ElGamal cryptosystem. Consequently, when all these things have been thought together, they have obtained that, composite ElGamal cryptosystem is more advantageous than ElGamal cryptosystem in terms of cryptography. In addition, all of the new cryptographic systems which is defined in here are usable for composite modulus.

ACKNOWLEDGMENT

This research received no specific grant from any funding agency in the public, commercial, or not-for-profit sectors.

REFERENCES

Asar, A. O., & Arıkan, A. (2012). *Sayılar Teorisi*. Ankara: Gazi Kitabevi.

Deveci, Ö., Karaduman, E., & Sağlam, G. (2016). The Jacobsthal sequences in finite groups. *Bulletin of the Iranian Mathematical Society*, *42*(1), 79–89.

ElGamal, T. (1985). A public key cryptosystem and a signature scheme based on discrete logarithms. *IEEE Transactions on Information Theory*, *31*(4), 469–472. doi:10.1109/TIT.1985.1057074

Hwang, M. S., Chang, C. C., & Hwang, K. F. (2002). An ElGamal-like cryptosystem for enciphering large messages. *IEEE Transactions on Knowledge and Data Engineering*, *14*(2), 445–446. doi:10.1109/69.991728

Ide, J., & Renault, M. S. (2012). Power Fibonacci Sequences. *The Fibonacci Quarterly*, *50*(2), 175–180.

Jones, G. A., & Jones, J. M. (1998). *Elementary number theory*. Springer Science & Business Media. doi:10.1007/978-1-4471-0613-5

Niven, I., Zuckerman, H. S., & Montgomery, H. L. (1991). *An introduction to the theory of numbers*. John Wiley & Sons.

Ozyilmaz, C. & Nalli, A. (2019). Restructuring Of Discrete Logarithm Problem And Elgamal Cryptosystem By Using The Power Fibonacci Sequence Module M. *Journal of Science and Arts Quarterly*, (1), 61-70.

Rivest, R. L., Shamir, A., & Adleman, L. (1978). A method for obtaining digital signatures and public-key cryptosystems. *Communications of the ACM*, *21*(2), 120–126. doi:10.1145/359340.359342

Stinson, D. R. (2002). *Cryptography Theory and Practice*. New York: Chapman & Hall / CRC.

Yeşilot, G., & Özavşar, M. (2013). *Soyut Cebir Çözümlü Problemleri*. Ankara: Nobel Akademi.

Zhu, H. (2001). *Survey of Computational Assumptions Used in Cryptography Broken or Not by Shor's Algoritm* (Master Thesis). McGill University School of Computer Science, Montreal, Canada.

ADDITIONAL READING

Abdouli, A. S., Baek, J., & Yeun, C. Y. (2011, December). *In 2011 International Conference for Internet Technology and Secured Transactions*. Survey on computationally hard problems and their applications to cryptography, Abu Dhabi, United Arab Emirites.

Çimen, C., Akleylek, S., & Akyıldız, E. (2007). *Şifrelerin Matematiği Kriptografi*. Ankara: ODTÜ Yayıncılık.

Hoffstein, J., Pipher, J., Silverman, J. H., & Silverman, J. H. (2008). *An introduction to mathematical cryptography* (Vol. 1). New York: springer.

Hungerfold, T. W. (1987). *Algebra*. New York: Springer-Verlag.

Katz, J., Menezes, A. J., Van Oorschot, P. C., & Vanstone, S. A. (1996). *Handbook of applied cryptography*. CRC press.

Klein, S. T., & Ben-Nissan, M. K. (2009). On the usefulness of Fibonacci compression codes. *The Computer Journal*, *53*(6), 701–716. doi:10.1093/comjnl/bxp046

Teske, E. (2001). Square-root algorithms for the Discrete Logarithm Problem(A Survey*), In Public Key Cryptography and Computational Number Theory*, 29, 283-301.

Yilmaz, F., & Bozkurt, D. (2009). The generalized order-k Jacobsthal numbers. *Int. J. Contemp. Math. Sciences*, *4*(34), 1685–1694.

KEY TERMS AND DEFINITIONS

Composite Number: It is a positive integer that has at least one divisor other than 1 and itself.

Cryptography: It is a process of protecting information and communications such that the only one for whom the information is intended can understand.

Fibonacci Sequence: It is one of the most famous formulas such that every number in the sequence is the sum of the two consecutive numbers.

One Way Function: It is a function that is easy to compute on every input, but it is hard to invert given the image of a random input.

Public Key Cryptosystem: It is an encryption system that uses two keys such that one of them is public key and the other is private key and it is computationally infeasible compute the private key.

Trapdoor: It is a special information which is used to find inverse.

Chapter 9
Characteristic Analysis of Side Channel Attacks and Various Power Analysis Attack Techniques

Shaminder Kaur
Chitkara University, Punjab, India

Balwinder Singh
C-DAC Mohali, India

Harsimran Jit Kaur
Institute of Engineering and Technology, Chitkara University, Punjab, India

ABSTRACT

Embedded systems have a plethora of security solutions and encryption protocols that can protect them against a multitude of attacks. Hardware engineers infuse lot of time and effort in implementing cryptographic algorithms, keeping the analysis of design constraints into rumination. When it comes to designs in potential hostile environment, engineers face a challenge for building resistance-free embedded systems against attacks called side channel attacks. Therefore, there is a strong need to address issues related to side channel attacks. This chapter will provide an insight into the field of hardware security, and will provide a deep investigation of various types of side channel attacks and better understanding of various power analysis tools, which will further give researchers a vision to build efficient and secure systems in order to thwart attacks. This chapter mainly focuses on passive attacks as compared to active attacks since passive attacks are easy to perform and lot of research is going on these attacks.

DOI: 10.4018/978-1-7998-2418-3.ch009

INTRODUCTION

The era of IOT and cloud computing has given advent to the field of hardware security. Hardware security deals with designing resistant free IC i.e. to secure hardware against side channel attacks. In today's world, numerous systems rely no more on traditional PC but they are connected to embedded system such as FPGA, ASIC, SOC etc (Barenghi et al, 2012). Embedded devices are widespread in every aspect of life. There are manifolds such as smart cars, smart locks, smart cards, industrial machines etc. In case of smart cars if the antagonist is able to malfunction the operation or somehow able to get the unintended data, then it may lead to some erroneous output or in worst case endanger the human lives. In this electronic world if adversary is able to get the secret information, it may hamper the security, which can further lead to serious ramifications (Cilio et al, 2013).

In this era of embedded systems, there is a need to dig into the security related issues and examine security related mechanism thoroughly. Hardware security is a young field, which received relatively little attention in scientific community. Physical attacks pose a serious threat to embedded devices and there is a strong need to address security related challenges. We need to build secured hardware in order to have effective communication (Lumbiarrs, 2016).

Figure 1 shows the layered approach of hardware security. As shown in the figure a device consists of hardware, software and firmware. The device secured at only software part is not considered as secured one. Hardware part is equally important and needs protection against various kinds of physical attacks, only then we can build a secure device/circuit. Hardware security is a field which deals with securing a device at hardware level (circuit level, system level etc).

Brief History of Hardware Attacks: It was in the late 90's when kocher et al (1998) proposed Side Channel Attacks (Biham et al, 1997). In 1996 kocher introduced the first passive attack based on the execution's timing measurements. It showed a new method to extract secret data from smart card while processing. Boneh, DeMillo and Lipton then published the first active attack know as bellcore attack. Both the attacks types are opposite in nature. Active attacks tamper the parameters of IC such as variation in clock, power supply etc that leads to erroneous behavior of device, where as passive attacks are based on observation of information leaked during normal operation of device such as power consumption, EM waves, temperature, computation time of different instructions, observing the sound of fan used in microprocessor etc while the cryptographic operation is still taking place.

Classification of Side Channel Attacks: Side channel attacks are called as side channel because they do not involve actively but take part passively without tampering the device. The person will not even know about the attack. Figure 2 shows the categorization of side channel attacks.

Figure 1. Layered approach of hardware security

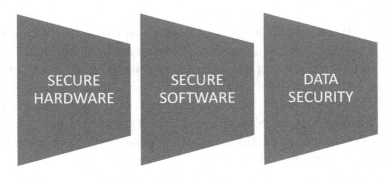

The literature categorizes attacks as invasive vs non- invasive, active vs passive attacks.

Invasive Vs Non-Invasive: Invasive attacks are the ones, which require direct access to the chip. They are penetrative attacks, which leave tamper evidence of attack or even destroy the device. They may harm the chip physically leaving the device damaged permanently. Non-invasive attacks are less destructive as compared to invasive attacks and they do not harm the chip physically. They non-penetrative attacks. In this attacker interacts with device via its interface (voltage, current, I/O etc). They just observe and manipulate device without physical harm to it. These types of attacks leave no evidence of attack. Device remains undamaged. Skorobogatov and Anderson add a new distinction with what they call *semi-invasive attacks*. It's a kind of attack which is less destructive than invasive one. In this, it requires depackaging of chip but they do not tamper with passivation layer- they do not require electrical contact to metal surface.

Between invasive and non-invasive, non-invasive attacks are interesting because equipment and hardware specific knowledge necessary to perform them is minimal. Strong expertise is not required to perform such types of attacks. This is why these types of attacks are gaining lot of attention in scientific community.

Active vs Passive Attacks: They aim at inducing faults in a circuit to get slightly different or erroneous behavior. There are several means to inject faults into a circuit, either by modifying chip's parameters or by modifying its external environment: variation in clock frequency, under powering, over powering, glitches, laser shots etc. Passive attacks are based on observation of information leaked during normal operation of device such as power consumption, EM waves, temperature, sound etc. These attacks can retrieve secret data using statistical analysis, which are discussed latter.

Figure 2. Classification of side channel attacks

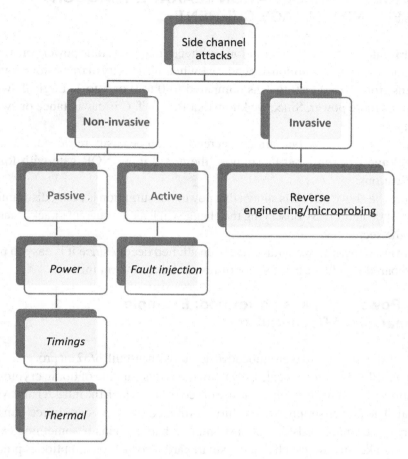

Power attacks: As shown in the figure below attacker tries to capture the information from the target device. Resistor is connected across the target device. Since

V=IR

P=VI

$P_{load} \alpha V_{series}$

From the above equation, we can easily find out power traces and can find out the secret key. Attacker doesn't need to the exact power consumption, but he just needs to determine that when target is consuming more power and when less.

SOURCES OF INFORMATION LEAKAGE THROUGH POWER AND LEAKAGE CURRENT

Power Leakage: Power consumption is either dynamic or static power consumption. Dynamic power consumption depends on switching activity of transistors. Switching happens from 1 to 0 or 0 to 1 as compared to 0 to 0 or 1 to 1. Logical switching consumes more power. Since we know that $P\alpha\ CV^2f$, C is capacitance or switching activity.

By observing power variations, secret data can be easily retrieved.

Leakage Current: Let us suppose there is 2 input NOR gate with following specifications:

From the above table it is shown that power consumption is easily distinguishable in case of 00 and 11. By observing the changes in leakage current attacker can easily guess the secret key.

Power Attack: Power attack has been studied deeply since it is easy to perform as compared to other attacks so lot of research is going on this.

How Power Attack is performed: Example of Smart Card Recapitulation

We know that smart card is an embedded device with in-built 8/32 bit processor, tighter with RAM/ROM (Biham et al, 1997). Smart card is capable of doing cryptographic operations. This device involves the use of secret key, which the intruder always wants to steal. The power supply to this chip is provided from outside source (smart card reader) since smart cards do not have internal battery. This is something exploited by the attacker in a way such that the smart card's power consumption is pretty easy to measure for the attacker as shown in the figure below.

The Model: To measure power consumption resistor is connected in series with power or ground input. Voltage across resistor is measured. Well-equipped equipments can digitally sample voltage with high accuracy and data is sent to computer. Further

Table 1. Leakage current Vs input data

Input	Leakage current
00	35.8
01	100
10	95
11	454

Figure 3. Power attack using smart card

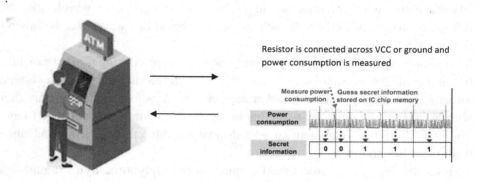

through DSO (digital signal oscilloscope), waveforms are observed. Various analysis techniques are used such as SPA, DPA etc, during cryptographic operations.

Power Analysis Techniques: There are various power analysis techniques as discussed below:

1. SPA (Simple Power Analysis)
2. DPA (Differential Power Analysis)
3. CPA (Correlation Power Analysis)
4. MIA (Mutual Information Analysis)
5. Horizontal & Vertical power analysis
6. CIA (Combined Implementation Attacks)

Figure 4. The power attack principle

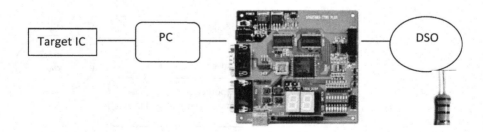

Simple Power Analysis and Differential Power Analysis: These Techniques were proposed in 1999 (Courrège et al, 2010). Simple power analysis is done by adversary to reveal secret information just by observing the power waveforms. Data is leaked through side channels such as timing, power, EM waves etc. as shown in the figure 5.

It simply involves interpreting power traces or graphs during normal execution (Giraud et al, 2006). Small set of power traces with relevant information obtained directly from trace patterns. Attacker captures the waveforms and compare them with leaked information. By using hamming weight distance model secret key is revealed. This is basic techniques used to do analysis. After this much more advanced techniques has arrived.

From the above figure 6 the traces for square and multiply are easily distinguishable. As observed multiplication traces consumed more power as compared to square traces. So the adversaries can extract the secret key just by observing the waveforms (Schmidt et al, 2008).

Advantage: Small traces are required

Disadvantage: Lot of manual effort is required along with detailed supervision.

Differential Power Analysis: It was introduced by Paul Kocher (1998). This is an advanced method as compared to SPA in which attacker uses statistical properties of traces in order to recover secret data. It is based on the evaluation of many traces with varying input data for the targeted algorithm. Then brute force attack with

Figure 5. Side channel analysis DPA ATTACK

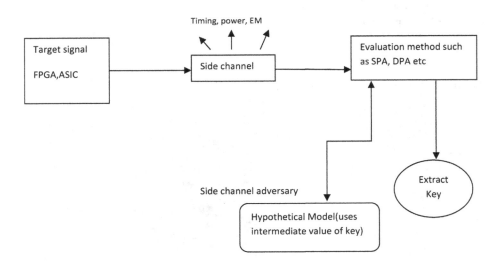

Figure 6. Example of SPA

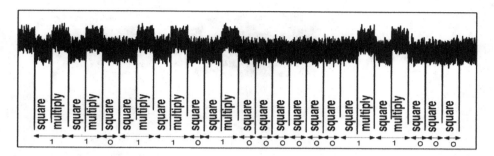

additional information is performed on a part of algorithm. Hence, it is also called as divide and conquer strategy.

Basic Approach of DPA: Approach being that the attacker selects small portion of key, makes hypothesis of its value and then compare hypothesis against measured power traces. By repeating this process (brute force analysis) for all sub keys, each sub key can be determined and thus full key is recovered. This is where this method varies with other methods. DPA is based on computing the difference between two trace sets, while CPA uses the correlation coefficient to perform this test for dependency.

Steps to perform DPA

It can be divided into two steps:

1. Measurement phase
2. Evaluation phase

In measurement phase the adversary has physical access to the Device and it records the information through side channel such as power, timings, EM waves etc. These side channel information's collected are related to the processed data. This step is repeated N times with varying input data M_I yielding N time discrete waveforms.

In evaluation phase the key is recovered by fixing subset and considering all the key candidates. Hypothesis on value of some intermediate is computed and key is extracted after several rounds.

Advantage: 1) Limited reverse engineering is required as compared to SPA. 2) Harder to confuse

Disadvantage: Large amount of traces are required to analyze the data deeply.

Figure 7. Steps to perform DPA attack

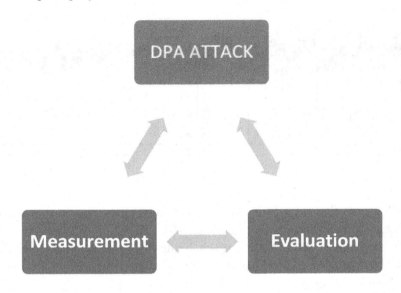

Correlation Power Analysis: It is subclass of Differential power analysis. It is type of DPA attack which uses correlation factor/coefficient between power samples and hamming weight of handled data (Brier et al, 2004).. In CPA several bits can be taken into account to better model the physical process behind the leakage and thus to reduce the number of required traces compared to DPA. Power models generally used are hamming weight (HW)or hamming distance(HD) models.

For linear power model, Pearson's correlation coefficient is a good choice 2. Other models: difference of means, mutual information.

Steps to Perform CPA Attack

1. The intermediate value is chosen.
2. Based on chosen values power traces are measured
3. Choose a power model
4. Calculate the hypothetical intermediate value and corresponding hypothetical power consumption
5. Apply the statistic analysis between measured power consumption and hypothetical power consumption. The value having highest correlation will be considered as secret key.

Figure 8.

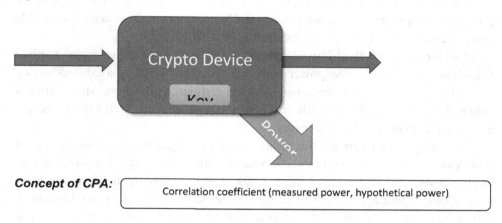

Concept of CPA:

Correlation coefficient (measured power, hypothetical power)

Disadvantage: The main drawback of CPA regards the characterization of the leakage model parameters. As it is more demanding than DPA, the method may seem more difficult to implement.

A statistical power analysis of any kind is never conducted blindly without any preliminary reverse engineering (process identification, bit tracing): this is the opportunity to quantify the leakage rate by CPA on known data. – DPA requires more sample curves anyway since all the unpredicted data bits penalize the signal to noise ratio. If DPA fails by lack of implementation knowledge (increasing the number of curves does not necessarily help), we have shown how to infer a part of this information without excessive efforts: for instance the reference state is to be found by exhaustive search only once in general. – There exists many situations where the implementation variants (like SBox implementation in DES) are not so numerous because of operational constraints. – If part of the model cannot be inferred (SBox implementation in DES, hardware co-processor), partial correlation with the remainder may still provide exploitable indications. Eventually DPA remains relevant in case of very special architectures for which the model may be completely out of reach, like in certain hard wired co-processors.

Mutual Information Analysis: It is one of the most established technique. Techniques discussed before are quite complicated and they need to consider many factors while doing power analysis such as (Gierlichs et al, 2008).

- Device power consumption characteristics
- Attackers power model
- the distinguisher by which measurements and model predictions are compared
- the quality of the estimations

In contrast to CPA, MIA can capture non-linear dependencies between predicted power consumption and measured values and hence improve the success rate of side channel attacks in certain situations (Batina et al, 2011).

Horizontal & Vertical Power Attack: A different kind of evaluation method called *horizontal* and *vertical* power analysis is also there which is based on detecting and utilizing correlations within a single trace e.g to identify the processing of similar values in a cryptographic algorithm. These methods apply to both symmetric and asymmetric cryptographic primitives.

According to literature review, all kind of countermeasures become ineffective if attacks are performed with modus operandi called *Horizontal*. Classical attacks require several traces, however these kinds of attacks require single observation trace. Colin Walter at CHES 2001 originally introduced these attacks (Bauer et al, 2013). Vertical attack differs from horizontal attack in a way that information is obtained from different algorithm executions.

Combined Implementation Attack: Different kind of attacks such as side channel attacks and fault injection attacks are considered as separate attacks (Amiel eta l, 2007). Adversary may successfully combine them to overcome countermeasures against them. This category is known as combined implementation attack (Kulikowski et al, 2006).

Basic Principle of Combining Active and Passive Attacks

By injecting a fault, computation of device gets disturbed further it becomes possible to realize a passive attack on the perturbed execution. The fault is detected at the end of the command. The secret value has already been recovered using classical power analysis. Fault countermeasures are only active after the end of the computation.

Countermeasure for Power Attacks

1. **Hiding:** Break the link between the power and the processed value.
2. **Masking:** Generate random numbers to hide data.
3. Using D^3L (dual spacer dual rail delay insensitive logic) logic to mitigate both power and timing attacks. In a D^3L circuit, power consumption is decoupled from data pattern by using a dual-spacer-protocol which guarantees balanced switching activities between the two rails of each signal, while timing-data correlation is broken by inserting random delays (Cilio et al, 2013).
4. Use of DITL (Delay-Insensitive Ternary Logic) DITL uses a single wire per bit, three-voltage scheme to represent the three states needed for delay-insensitive signaling, *i.e.*, DATA0,DATA1, and NULL (Ravi et al, 2015).

Table 2. Simple side channel attacks

1. Simple SCA (Side channel analysis) extract the secret data by just observing the power traces. 2. Power consumption depends on intermediate data. 1 -- 0 or 0 -- 1 transition will consume more power as compared to switching between 1 -- 1 and 0 – 0. 3. Lot of power traces are chosen and information is deduced from them 4.These attacks require less expertise and less knowledge of device and reverse engineering. 5. Techniques like SPA are used .

Table 3. Advanced side channel attacks

1. Advanced Attacks involve more of statistical analysis and evaluation. 2. Lot of power traces are choosen and a hypothetical model is build. Based on it assumptions of secret key are made and data is compared using advanced methods such as DPA, CPA etc. 3.These attacks require more expertise and some knowledge of reverse engineering. 4. These analysis are time consuming but are more successful.

Conclusion and Future challenges: Despite of various mathematical models and various encryption algorithms, countless embedded devices are becoming victim to side channel attacks every day and malicious attackers have become smart enough to impose threats on them. In order to build an attack resistant free embedded device, a hardware engineer has to understand their threats. In this chapter we tried to share and analyze the properties of side channel attacks viz power attacks in detail that aim to break the security of embedded systems. Various types of power analysis techniques are also discussed in detail. Some countermeasures to power attack are briefly discussed. In era of IOT and embedded systems, we believe that hardware and software developers both needs to join hands and put additional efforts in tranquillizing the effects of attacks on embedded devices

FUTURE CHALLENGES

1. Literature reveals that due to voltage glitches different sub circuits might be powered at different voltages, hence enabling fault injections. No evidence of this phenomenon is provided.
2. Assignment of criterion of flip flop sensitivity for faults injection simulation at logical level.

1. Counter measures: definition of design rules to avoid vulnerable combinational logic structures.
2. To demonstrate attacks into practice with low cost tools/low financial efforts, since commercial solutions for conducting implementation attacks

are usually expensive, so that next generation products can find appropriate countermeasures.

3. To propose digital and analog pre-processing techniques to increase the quality of Side Channel Attacks.

4. To study & analyze the effects of DSP operations such as filtering on Side Channel Attacks.

5. Lot of research is going on at circuit level, very few research is done at system level. To develop countermeasures against Side Channel Attacks at system level.

6. To study spatial effect associated with power glitches.

REFERENCES

Amiel, F. (2007). *Passive and active combined attacks: Combining fault attacks and side channel analysis. In FDTC* (pp. 92–102). IEEE.

Barenghi. (2012). Fault injection attacks on cryptographic devices:theory, practice and countermeasures. *Proceedings of IEEE, 100*(11).

Batina, L., Gierlichs, B., Prouff, E., Rivain, M., Standaert, F.-X., & Veyrat-Charvillon, N. (2011). VeyratCharvillon, N.: Mutual Information Analysis: a Comprehensive Study. *Journal of Cryptology, 24*(2), 269–291. doi:10.100700145-010-9084-8

Bauer, A. (2013). *Horizontal and Vertical Side-Channel Attacks Against Secure RSA Implementations – Extended Version.* Cryptology ePrint Archive.

Biham, E. (1997). Differential Fault analysis of secret key cryptosystems. *Proceedings CRYPTO, 1294*, 513-525. 10.1007/BFb0052259

Brier, E., Clavier, C., & Olivier, F. (2004). Correlation Power Analysis with a Leakage Model. In M. Joye & J. J. Quisquater (Eds.), Lecture Notes in Computer Science: Vol. 3156. *Cryptographic Hardware and Embedded Systems - CHES 2004. CHES 2004.* Berlin: Springer. doi:10.1007/978-3-540-28632-5_2

Cilio, W. (2013). *Mitigating power and timing based side channel attacks using dual spacer dual rail delay insensitive asynchronous logic," in journal of microelectronics.* Elsevier. doi:10.1016/j.mejo.2012.12.001

Cilio, W., Linder, M., Porter, C., Di, J., Thompson, D. R., & Smith, S. C. (2013). Mitigating power- and timing-based side-channel attacks using dual-spacer dual-rail delay-insensitive asynchronous logic. *Microelectronics Journal, 44*(3), 258–269. doi:10.1016/j.mejo.2012.12.001

Courrège, J.-C., Feix, B., & Roussellet, M. (2010). Simple Power Analysis on Exponentiation Revisited. *9th IFIP WG 8.8/11.2 International Conference on Smart Card Research and Advanced Applications (CARDIS)*, 65-79. .ffhal01056099f10.1007/978-3-642-12510-2_6ff

Gierlichs, B. (2008). *Mutual Information Analysis. In Lecture notes CHES* (Vol. 5154, pp. 426–442). Springer.

Giraud, C. (2006, September). An RSA Implementation Resistant to Fault Attacks and to Simple Power Analysis. *IEEE Transactions on Computers*, *55*(9), 1116–1120. doi:10.1109/TC.2006.135

Karaklajic. (2013). Hardware designers guide to fault attacks. *IEEE Transactions on Very Large Scale Integration (VLSI) Systems*, *21*(12).

Kocher, P.C. (1998). Introduction to Differential Power Analysis. *Journal of Cryptographic Engineering, 1*(1), 5–27.

Kulikowski, K.J. (2006). DPA on faulty cryptographic hardware and countermeasures. FDTC, 211–222.

Lumbiarres, R. (2016). *A new countermeasure against side channel attacks based on hardware software co-design," in journal of microelectronics*. Elsevier.

Rankl, W., & Effing, W. (1997). *Smart card handbook*. John Wiley & Sons.

Ravi, S. P. (2015). Delay Insensitive Ternary CMOS Logic for Secure Hardware. *Journal of Low Power Electron. Appl.*, *5*(3), 183–215. doi:10.3390/jlpea5030183

Schmidt. (2008). A Practical Fault Attack on Square and Multiply. *5th Workshop on Fault Diagnosis and Tolerance in Cryptography*, 53-58.

Chapter 10
Bahrain Government Information Security Framework:
CyberTrust Program

Yusuf Mohammed Mothanna
Information and eGovernment Authority, Bahrain

Yousif Abdullatif Albastaki
iD https://orcid.org/0000-0002-6866-2268
Ahlia University, Bahrain

Talal Mohamed Delaim
iD https://orcid.org/0000-0002-6866-1791
Information and eGovernment Authority, Bahrain

ABSTRACT

Information technology is perceived as an important enabler for government entities to accomplish their goals. The proliferation of electronic government services that can provide value for citizens and residents have pushed governments all over the world to adopt and deploy these services. However, governments have realized that it is critical to build proper defense to protect the information. Implementing information security by using international or national information security frameworks helps organizations to ensure the safeguard of information assets. This chapter reviews useful information security frameworks. Also, this chapter provides a proposed information security framework implemented in the Government of Bahrain, which is called CyberTrust Program. This framework was developed based on best practices and local resources and culture.

DOI: 10.4018/978-1-7998-2418-3.ch010

INTRODUCTION

Information is an important asset for all organizations to achieve their goals as well Information technology has become a major driving force in many organizations in order to make the functions running smoothly and faster. Consequently, protecting information is perceived as a critical function that needs to be successfully accomplished and needs devotion from the entire organization's members.

Information security is vital to all organizations that are using Information technology to protect their information and conduct their business. Whitman and Mattord define information security as "the protection of information and its critical elements, including the systems and hardware that use, store, and transmit that information" (Whitman and Mattord, 20017). Additionally, Merkow and Breithaupt define information security as "the process of protecting the confidentiality, integrity, and availability (CIA) of data from accidental or intentional misuse" (Merkow and Breithaupt, 2014).

When implementing information security, organizations and enterprises have an opportunity to follow proven standards or frameworks, that include guidelines and best practices to be followed in order to successfully achieve information security. Two examples of these standards/frameworks are United States National Institute of Standards and Technology (NIST)'s Special Publication 800-53r5 and International Standard Organization (ISO) 27001:2013 Standard.

These standards define certain information security controls to be implemented in multiple areas within the organization in order to protect information assets. These controls fall into three categories: preventive, detective, and responsive. Preventive controls will work to prevent the occurrence of any threat from the beginning, but if unluckily a threat occurred, it is the responsibility of detective controls to detect and identify the threat. Finally, a response to the threat will be the duty of responsive controls.

The controls will affect three areas within the organization: people, technology and process. Human resources within the organization should get enough knowledge regarding correct interaction with technology. This will minimize threats caused by human errors and mistakes. Technology itself should be designed with certain controls to participate in protecting information. Finally, process or procedures should be followed by each person in the organization. Procedures, when written clearly and followed by everybody, will further help in avoiding human errors.

The Kingdom of Bahrain has recognized the importance of information technology in its endeavor to achieve a better life for all citizens and residents in the Kingdom of Bahrain, within the principles of vision 2030, based on sustainability, competitiveness, and fairness. The Kingdom of Bahrain has witnessed substantial progress in the information technology sector to the extent that the provision of services and exchanging, storing, and using information electronically has become a fundamental means of work at all government entities. Therefore, it is imperative to uphold the confidentiality, integrity, and availability of government information for gaining the confidence of its constituents.

Therefore, it is necessitated to develop a framework aimed at assuring that information security in all government entities is conducted in a uniform manner yet appreciates the differences in environments. As such, the Information Government Authority (IGA) has designed a new framework titled 'Cyber Trust Programme' (CTP), which defines a framework to enable government entities within the kingdom to improve information security assurance, to have a unified, methodical, approach to information security, and to be able to determine information security maturity within the respective entities.

CTP designed to provide an information security framework of in competitive nature, which endeavours to raise the level of information security through governance and the support of human and technology elements, which results in a continuously trusted electronic environment for the government.

The research questions directing the Chapter are:

1.   What are the information security framework and the CyberTrust Program?
2.   How the CyberTrust program enhances information security in Bahrain government entities?

The Chapter aims at realizing the following objectives:

1.   Increasing knowledge in the information security frameworks
2.   Investigating the Bahrain government experience in Information security framework measures that institutions could use to improve the information security level in organizations.

The Chapter will be a source of insight for information security researchers and officers in higher learning institutions and organizations. Its findings will help increase the implementation of security controls and measures how the security controls are implemented in government organizations.

RELATED WORK

Nowadays, there is several different types of information security frameworks, some of them issued by national and international organizations and others issued by professional organizations. This section reviews literature conducted previously in information security frameworks. In addition, this review focuses on some well-known frameworks used to implement information security within organizations which are International Organization for Standardization (ISO) 27001:2013, National Institute of Standards and Technology (NIST), COBIT, Critical Security Controls (CSC).

ISO 27001- 2013: International Organization for Standardization (ISO) developed and published ISO 27001 (formally known as ISO/IEC 27001:2013) which provides a checklist of controls for an information security management system (ISMS). An ISMS is a structure of policies and procedures that handles information security risks which can be customized to the organization's needs.

An organization that achieved ISO 27001, indicates that the organization have defined the risks, evaluated the consequences and set the control to minimize any breaches, guaranteed that information is precise and only be modified by authorized users, and protected their information from getting into unauthorized hands.

As well as, increasing credibility and security of systems and information, improving business resilience and management process.

The National Institute of Standards and Technology (NIST): The National Institute of Standards and Technology (NIST) was founded in 1901. Currently, NIST is part of the United States Department of Commerce. There are six research laboratories within NIST and one of them is Information Technology Laboratory (ITL). ITL publishes valuable reports and guidelines. among these reports are NIST Special Publication (SP) 800-series and 1800-series.

SP 800 series contains the output of ITL research as guidelines in the information security field to be applied in various organizations. On the other hand, SP 1800 series focuses on information security practices and guidelines (Santos,2019). Of Special interest comes NIST SP 800-53 which is a large set of information security controls. The controls span 17 areas within the information security field (Calder, 2018).

COBIT: COBIT stands for Control Objectives for Information and related Technology. COBIT was first released in 1996. Erik Guldentops is recognized as the 'grandfather of COBIT', while Gary Hardy is recognized as the 'father of COBIT' (CSC, 2019). The first release of COBIT was intended to be used by IT auditors. With the release of COBIT 3 in 2000, the focus has evolved from IT audit into IT governance. The current version of COBIT is COBIT 5 which was released in 2012 .

COBIT is released by both ITGI (IT Governance Institute) and ISACA (Information Systems Audit and Control Association). IASCA claims that COBIT 5 is "based on more than 80 frameworks and standards" (Harmer, 2014). ISACA uses the term Governance of Enterprise IT (GEIT) to describe the focus of COBIT 5 stating that it is "the only business framework for the governance and management of enterprise IT" (COBIT, 2019).

COBIT 5 is designed to achieve five principles: 1) Meeting stakeholders needs, 2) Covering the enterprise end-to-end, 3) Applying a single integrated framework, 4) Enabling a holistic approach, and 5) Separating governance from management. Also, COBIT 5 declares the need for seven categories of enablers: 1) Principles, policies and frameworks, 2) Processes, 3) Organizational structures, 4) Culture, ethics, and behavior, 5) Information, 6) Services, infrastructure, and applications, and 7) People, skill, and competencies (Harmer, 2014).

Critical Security Controls (CSC): Center for Internet Security (CIS) is non-profit organization that work together with a global IT community to protect organizations against cyber threats (9). The CIS is selected most critical controls that help organizations to effectively defend their systems and networks in a prioritized manner by providing list of 20 controls fundamental security controls that improve cyber security of the organizations with the fewest number of control implementation (Virtue & Rainey, 2015). The CSC is a framework that provides safeguards for IT security based on two main factors which are actual attacks and effective defense to protect (Jasper, 2017).

BEFORE IMPLEMENTING CYBER TRUST PROGRAM

The Information and eGovernment Authority (IGA) in Bahrain encountered several challenges in the implementation of policies, procedures and technical controls related to information security across government entities. Most of the government entities were primarily dedicated to the development of Information systems and the tasks, services and the availability related to those systems. Without taking into consideration the implementation of Information security controls, as it was considered that these controls were unaffordable and will cause a delay in the delivery of services. Therefore, led to a lack of cooperation in a significant number of government entities. The IGA encountered difficulties to reach the required level of security that need to be achieved.

Consequently, a huge number of government systems were exposed to vulnerabilities and risks that led to the disruption of electronic services during that period. as it was noticed that:

- Government entities connected to the government network, had different levels of security implemented.
- Government entities did not comply with the policies and regulatory procedures related to information security issued by the Information Authority and e-Government

- A unified national framework to improve the level of information security in government entities was unavailable.
- A security Awareness Campaign for officials and employees throughout government entities was unavailable.
- The development of electronic services was prioritized rather than prioritizing the security requirements in order to secure such services.
- A method to measure and audit the levels of information security across government entities was unavailable.

The CyberTrust Program provided as a government framework that will solve the challenges mentioned earlier and raises the level of information security through governance by the application of security controls (policies, systems, and awareness of government employees to information security risks). The program is mandatory for all government entities as it helps to assist them in developing Information security within a scalable mechanism and clear standards.

PROPOSED SOLUTION

The CTP supports the process of designing and providing government services in a secure manner, in addition to educating users and training cadres through establishing three graduate levels of effective standards, based on which government entities are classified according to the achievement and implementation of the standards for each level. The CTP gradually raises the level and maturity of information security at government entities through carefully planned stages, which directly serves IGA's national strategic goals in managing information security within the Government of Bahrain. In addition, the government entities have previously carried out various initiatives to improve information security. These include the implementation of international standards and/or implementing various controls to safeguard the information and wider IT infrastructure. The CTP appreciates these initiatives by incorporating the activities within the maturity framework. Various other actions have also been incorporated into the framework to enable wider coverage of the activities to safeguard the government entities. The figure below demonstrates the three levels of maturity within the CyberTrust Programme.

At the heart of the CTP is the concept of continuous improvement. This is essential for any organization to meet the challenges of changing threats. The CTP was based partly on these references and the experience of IGA in working with the government entities within the Government of Bahrain. The CTP, as is the case with any novel concept or new idea, will be closely monitored and continuously improved.

Figure 1. Programme maturity level

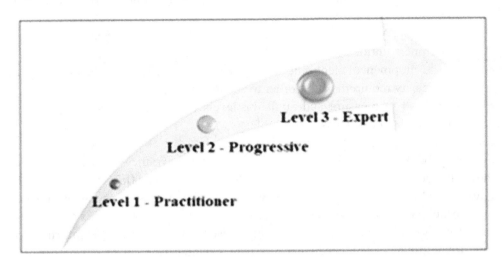

In the past, IGA launched several initiatives to support the government entities in various endeavours over the years. The government entities benefited from these initiatives such as acquiring IT infrastructure, standardization, knowledge sharing, facilitating statistical information databases, and many others.

The CTP is an such initiative aimed at improving the maturity of government entities associated with information security. The Programme encourages government entities to enhance information security in a competitive way and in such a manner that builds a framework consisting of the following:

- **Determination of Confidence Levels**: Assess information security maturity at government entities based on established standards.
- **Establishment of Standards**: Defines a roadmap of requirements for each maturity level that is verifiable and enable government entities to evaluate and progress towards an acceptable state in information security.
- **Issuance of Guidelines:** Guidelines will be issued that prescribe the requirements for each maturity level. Guidelines include administrative advice specific to how to manage and govern information security, as well as technical guidelines specific to related technologies.
- **Auditing and Evaluation:** Establish a mechanism for auditing government entities on the compliance with the requirements at each maturity level of the Program. Government entities will be placed at a maturity level based on initial capability assessment and advised on the roadmap to reach the highest level.

- **Recognition**: Government entities enrolled within the Program will be recognized and honored based on transparent, verifiable, criteria. The Program encourages government entities to innovate and perform proactive action to excel in information security and related disciplines.

PROGRAM MISSION AND GOALS

The Mission of the program is to provide an information security framework of in competitive nature, which endeavours to raise the level of information security through governance and the support of human and technology elements, which results in a continuously trusted electronic environment for the government and leads to regional and global leadership.

The goals of the Cyber Trust Programme are described below:

1. Enhancing the Protection of Information and Communication Technology From Risks

Encourage government entities to implement initiatives and projects that aim at protecting the IT infrastructure, information, and assets, to implement security policies and procedures, and to benefit from information security services and operations.

2. Supporting the Process Of Building and Continuously Developing National Cadres and Expertise in Information Security

Encourage nationals in the government entities to enhance and enrich their capabilities in information security, and on emerging threats and challenges by exposing them to innovative technologies, new developments, providing training, and creating a platform conducive for learning and growth in gearing them to meet the challenges of the future.

3. Enhancing Government User Awareness of Information Security

Educate the government users in the fundamentals of information security, related threats, and the safeguards to proactively protect users from security incidents and raise overall security readiness.

4. Enhancing Information Security Knowledge Management

Support the process of development, acquisition, and dissemination of knowledge in the field of information security through encouraging developmental practices and applications, research, studies and analysis, and through working on providing and disseminating a knowledge base.

5.   Enhancing the Regional and International Position of the Kingdom of Bahrain in the Field of Information Security

Enhancing the Kingdom of Bahrain's position locally, regionally, and internationally in the field of information security, through:

*   Enhancing competitiveness among government entities and between government and non-government entities in the Kingdom of Bahrain in information security governance.-
*   Learning and benefiting from lessons of other countries and ensuring that well-defined frameworks are used in the governance of information security, and continuously sharing information and experiences with other nations.
*   Organizing and hosting Programs and conferences locally and internationally, and effectively participating in relevant international events and championing information security issues.
*   Facilitating agreements, accords, and treaties, and participating with local, regional and international organizations in the field of information security governance to extend the benefits to the rest of the Government and contribute to greater maturity.

    6.   Evaluate Information Security Levels at Government Entities

Evaluating information security practices at government entities based on well-defined and clear standards, conditions, and best practices, leading to the achievement of desired goals of information technology.

MATURITY MODEL LEVELS

A maturity level is a well-characterized transformative level that builds up a degree of limit with regards to improving workforce capacity; every maturity level indicates certain qualities for procedures, with higher development levels having further developed attributes and is a stage towards accomplishing a develop procedure, giving a lot of objectives which, when fulfilled, places an association at the following degree of development. It additionally determines the way that a procedure follows in moving from juvenile and impromptu procedure to profoundly develop process. In this project we define three maturity levels as follows:

Maturity level 1- Practitioner: This level indicates that a government entity has achieved 'Practitioner' level, implementing the basic requirements of the Cyber Trust Programme. The entity has achieved initial maturity with respect to process, technology, and people requirements associated with information security and are progressing towards achieving 'Progressive' maturity level. Most importantly, this level reflects active efforts by the entity to prevent the overall security situation from deteriorating and is well on its way towards building an information security culture on an organizational level.

Maturity level 2 – Progressive: The 'Progressive' level indicates government entities have achieved all requirements of the 'Practitioner' level and the 'Progressive' level and are progressing towards the 'Expert' level. Such entities have implemented an extended set of information security practices leading to an increased confidence level. The entity has reached a high level of maturity of experience, practices, and awareness of information security, and their ability to respond to information security threats and incidents is greatly improved.

Maturity level 3- Expert: The 'Expert' level is the highest level of the Cyber Trust Programme, with entities adhering to a wider range of information security requirements, in addition to the requirements of all previous levels.

Such entities have implemented a comprehensive set of information security practices leading to an increased confidence level.

At 'Expert' maturity the organization has reached the highest level of confidence, focused on confidentiality, integrity, and availability of information and systems. The organization takes a leading role in promoting and sharing good information security practices with other government entities and can assist IGA in conducting audits of lower-maturity organizations.

PROGRAM ORGANIZATION

The Programme certifies government entities into maturity levels in accordance with their achievement in information security as per Programme requirements. IGA determines the starting maturity level at the time of enrolment pursuant to an organization's self-assessment and IGA's verification. Thereafter, subsequent maturity levels are determined based on audits.

Requirements for each level are grouped into three logical groupings as 'People', 'Technology' and 'Process'. The requirements for each maturity level are structured and described in the following figure.

PARTICIPATION IN THE PROGRAM

Participation in the CTP is obligatory for all government and semi-government entities. A resolution of the Supreme Committee of ICT obliged all such organizations to participate and achieve the lowest level within a set period of time. Private organizations are at liberty to enrol in the Programme at their discretion.

The Programme will extend a wealth of benefits to participating government entities, including:

- Raising the level of information security on an organizational scale
- Continuous training, education, and awareness for all employees
- The right to use the corresponding CTP logo in all communications and marketing collateral

Figure 2. Programme organization

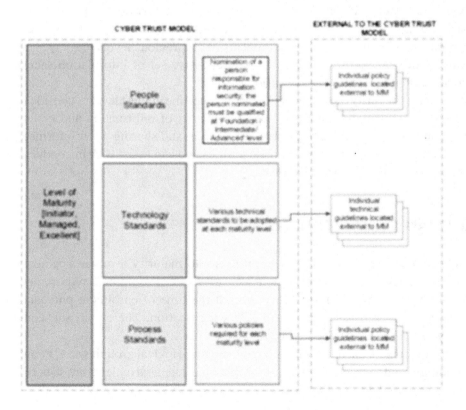

- Recognition for the Organization's commitment and progress in information security
- Building public confidence in the protection of information
- International recognition
- Confidence within the government for internal transactions

PROGRAM DETAILS

This section provides a brief overview of the CTP model, presenting a holistic view of the Program lifecycle. Key requirements in the Program are explained in brief. The following figure depicts the overall lifecycle of the Program.

Enrolment: A Government entity enrols to the CTP by completing the 'Cyber Trust Programme Application Form', which is available at **cybersecurity.iga.gov. bh** after signing the agreement.

The Programme is open for any government entity irrespective of its current information security maturity level. Once the application is received, the IGA will assess it and determine the most suitable target maturity level, statement of applicability, and boundary covered within the current scope. The IGA, in collaboration with the applicant, then determines the "Maturity roadmap" for the government entity to reach the highest maturity level from current standing.

The government entity together with the IGA then agrees on the "Implementation Plan" for the scope specified during the enrolment; the performance of the entity shall be measured based on the aforementioned "Implementation Plan".

The enrolled government entity is allowed one year to achieve the "Practitioner" level at a minimum.

Implementation and Self-Assessment: Government entities enrolled with the CTP must start the implementation based on the agreed implementation plan between the government entity and IGA.

Furthermore, government entities must perform a quarterly Programme self-assessment. The assessment includes all mandatory requirements of lower levels and requirements of the current maturity level of the entity (i.e. an entity in "Progressive" level should assess the requirements for both "Practitioner" level and "Progressive" level).

Objectives of the self-assessment are to:

- Ensure action has been taken on minor and major non-conformities reported from previous self-assessments or audits
- Monitor progress against the agreed plan
- Ensure compliance to achieve maturity requirements

External Audit: Government entities are required to conduct an annual external audit. The external audit may be carried out directly by the IGA, or by any suitably qualified and pre-approved third-party auditing firms or a governmental audit team from various government entities. The purpose of the annual audit is to:

- Validate the self-assessment report
- Compare progress with the plan
- Validate conformance to the achieved maturity level
- Identify any minor or major non-conformities
- Ensure actions were taken on previously identified minor and major non-conformities identified during self-assessment or external audits
- Recommend or suspend maturity level based on audit finding

Certification and Recognition: IGA awards the certification after the 'External audit' process if the entity conforms to the criteria required by the maturity level by substantially attaining its requirements. Certified government entities are granted the right to use branding material of the achieved maturity level.

Certification will remain valid if the entity conforms to the criteria of the Programme requirements pertaining to the respective maturity level. Certification may be suspended, downgraded, or revoked based on audit findings and the actions (or lack thereof) taken by the government entity.

Furthermore, at this part of the Programme Lifecycle, there is an annual recognition of those entities who perform exceptionally well during the period of focus. Entities are ranked within different groups based on maturity, complexity, the scope of Information security, etc. The process of recognition and granting honors and awards is governed by terms to be developed by a dedicated evaluation committee.

CONCLUSION

As the usage of the electronic services in Bahrain government increases, the potential of cyber-attacks also rises. Therefore, it is significant to raise the level of the information security for the government entities by using an information security framework. This study focuses on and describes one of the Bahrain government initiatives which is CyberTrust Program that helps to enhance the level of information security in government entities. The CTP was developed with considering best practices and local resources, cultures and qualifications as well it was implemented in several government entities. this study makes the following recommendations:

1. Study and evaluate the Effectiveness of Cyber Trust Program on Information Security at government entities in Bahrain.
2. Improve and enhance the CTP with the involvement and participation of academic sector.
3. Increase the implementation of Cyber Trust Program to be national wide.

REFERENCES

Calder, A. (2018). *NIST Cybersecurity Framework – A pocket guide.* IT Governance Publishing. doi:10.2307/j.ctv4cbhfx

COBIT. (2019). *COBIT's.* Retrieved from http://www.cobitonline.isaca.org

CSC. (2019). *Critical Security Controls.* Retrieved from https://www.cisecurity.org/about-us/

Harmer, G. (2014). *Governance of Enterprise IT based on COBIT®5: A Management Guide.* IT Governance Publishing.

ISO/IEC 27001:2013. (2019, June 3). Retrieved from https://www.iso.org/standard/54534.html

Jasper, S. (2017). *Strategic Cyber Deterrence: The Active Cyber Defense Option.* Rowman & Lttlefield.

Merkow, M. S., & Breithaupt, J. (2014). *Information Security: Principles and Practices.* Pearson.

National Institute of Standards and Technology (NIST). (n.d.). Retrieved from https://www. nist.gov

Santos, O. (2019). *Developing Cybersecurity Programs and Policies.* Pearson Education.

Virtue, T., & Rainey, I. (2015). *HCISPP Study Guide. Syngress.* Elsevier.

Whitman, M., & Mattord, J. H. (2017). Principles of Information Security. Cengage Learning.

Chapter 11
Critical Cybersecurity Threats:
Frontline Issues Faced by Bahraini Organizations

Adel Ismail Al-Alawi
https://orcid.org/0000-0003-0775-4406
University of Bahrain, Bahrain

Sara Abdulrahman Al-Bassam
https://orcid.org/0000-0003-0094-6149
The Social Development Office of His Highness the Prime Minister's Diwan, Kuwait

Arpita A. Mehrotra
Royal University for Women, Bahrain

ABSTRACT

One common reason for cybercrime is the goal of damaging a business by hacking or destroying important information. Another such reason is the criminal's goal of gaining financially from the hack. This chapter analyzes Bahraini organizations' vulnerability to digital security threats. It has used qualitative research to analyze industry performance. Moreover, with the support of secondary research, it has also explored cybersecurity threats faced by such organizations. The discussion based on secondary data analysis has explored two major aspects of Bahraini organizations and the cybersecurity threats they face. Firstly, the data and finances of both sectors are at huge risk in Bahraini organizations. Secondly, one important aspect of exploration has been to identify the most frequently encountered forms of cybercrime. Its analysis reveals that the kind of cybersecurity threat that a business is most likely to face is cyberwarfare. This may affect two rival businesses while they are competing with each other. Competitors' data may be destroyed or hacked—leading to long-term losses.

DOI: 10.4018/978-1-7998-2418-3.ch011

INTRODUCTION

Continuous improvement in organizational processes adheres to the principle of technological development. Constant progress usually involves technological development. Reasons include customizing work-related processes, optimizing workflow efficiency to improve turnaround time, and improving performance (Elmaghraby & Losavio, 2014). However, an increase in technological development may result in business data being stored in the cloud or on at-risk devices—making such data vulnerable to emergent threats (Abawajy, 2014).

Hence, cybersecurity issues have emerged in response to technological advancement. This chapter report intends to analyze present-day cybersecurity issues in industries and their impact on organizations. Information technology has become inseparable from all daily activities and is in the process of becoming a civilizational-structuring factor. However, vulnerabilities in digital infrastructure hardware and services, as well as the characteristics of the Internet itself, favor the expression of crime and of expanded opportunities for criminal malfeasance. The present day has witnessed the rise of cybercrime incidents affecting everyone (to varying degrees). Al-Alawi and Abdelgadir (2006) stated: "Computer crime has emerged as one of the major forms of sabotage[—]causing millions of dollars' worth of damage annually. These attacks usually come in the form of viruses, worms, denial of service attacks, and hacking." Whether it is gross incivility, harassment, fraud, theft, destruction, malfunctioning, surveillance, spying, hacktivism, terrorism, or deliberate misinformation—or any form of crime—violence and conflict is drawn to the Internet like a moth to flame. Understanding the risks to which the individual, the public and private organization, the state, and (more generally) society faces such threats enables us to act in informed ways. In order not to remain destitute and passive in the light of problems caused by cyber-attacks or the misuse of technology, political and economic stakeholders must take ownership of the fundamentals of cybersecurity necessary for the control of risks and the harmonious development of the digital ecosystem. Any pragmatic response to security, protection, disaster mitigation, and emergency response needs to be generated by the digital world. Our interactions and our dependence on information systems, cyberspace, and the Internet, need to be based on a strategic approach which sets the framework for taking action. This strategic vision is needed to govern, steer, and ensure the coherence and complementarity of strategic and operational measures. This also allows for efficiency and effectiveness (Emirates 24/7, 2014).

Examining the roles and risks of technology is prudent in every type of organization. Military, governmental, private, and nonprofit organizations use different forms of hardware; software; the Internet of Things (IoT); cloud data; and other technologies (Cavelty, 2014). According to Emirates (2014), security in the form of cybersecurity and physical security is required. As is supported by Brookes (2015), sensitive information is presented in different technological formats in the organizations—a fact which has always required an appropriate cybersecurity system. The emerging trends of cyber hacking may put organizations into a state of threat (Joiner, 2017). The discussion on the topic is essential for providing managerial-level implications and recommendations. The *desk research method* used in this chapter basically consists of collecting data from a variety of efficient resources. The secondary analysis can reinforce researchers' commitment to strengthening their knowledge base in given areas of research. Heaton (1998) stated, "Secondary analysis involves the utilization of existing data, collected for the purposes of a prior study, in order to pursue a research interest which is distinct from that of the original work."

Secondary research of the security issues of Bahraini organizations has been undertaken with respect to qualitative research. For this purpose, secondary data on the Bahraini security threats have been analyzed. The journal articles, magazines, Bahraini reports, and opinions of businesses on cybersecurity issues faced by Bahrain business organizations have analyzed. The objective of this chapter is to explore those cybersecurity issues and to suggest ways of securing and improving the existing security problems in Bahraini organizations.

LITERATURE REVIEW

Cybersecurity is not only important for businesses but also for business professionals. Advanced social engineering tactics are used to hack targeted individuals' information, including their bank accounts. The fact that now, cyber-attacks are automated and it is sometimes not possible to catch criminals is of major concern to businesses' cybersecurity departments. So, they have to fight with an unknown enemy. For the purpose of cybersecurity, business personnel are taught not to reply to unknown emails; for instance, even clicking a link claiming g to be a way to unsubscribe from receiving subsequent communications. They are also taught not to disclose any personal information 'required' by the email. These threats are more related to cybersecurity; but it is important that businesses invest in prevention on a timely basis in order to protect their data and profits from cyber attackers (Conklin & White, 2006).

Ensuring the cybersecurity of a country also means understanding the stakes and the impact of digital evolution in the military and defense sectors. Cyberspace is now considered the fifth battleground. It is a field of military operations the same as land, sea, air, and space. The civilian world and the military world are called upon to control cyber risks, whether for economic purposes; computer hardware companies in the United States (a store called Best Buy), once it is plugged into a computer, prompts the user to accept an agreement permitting all the data on the hard drive to be shared externally. Accepting this agreement is not necessary to actually use the drive, but not everyone might realize this. Moreover, it is alarming to think of how many busy professionals might not read the fine print. Imagine if sensitive business data were to be stored on this backup system,

or the fight against cybercrime; or for national security and defense purposes. Many factors contribute to the emergence of global and systemic approaches reflected in the notion of cybersecurity and cyber defense continuum. These include the *transversality* of the Internet; the importance of computer technologies; the skills needed to master digital infrastructures and their security; needs efficiency; and synergy. The international dimension of the Internet and of cybercrime, given that the world is globalized and interconnected, also constitutes new challenges to the control of cyber risks, which become more complex and global and whose cascading effects may have immediate or delayed impacts, sometimes far from their geographical origin. All these reasons increase the need for collaboration and cooperation at the national and international levels. Ideally, mastering cyber risks is not limited to setting up *technological patches* to temporarily mitigate the vulnerabilities of products designed with the fundamental flaw of having not taken into account the needs of security and data protection. Indeed, it is a question of being able to control all the dimensions of risk inherent to the extensive use of information and communication technologies in society. Effectively fighting cybercrime requires a preventive approach to make cyberspace less conducive to the expression of crime—and to reduce opportunities for criminals to exploit. It is necessary to raise the threshold of difficulty required to launch cyberattacks (Emirates 24/7, 2014). That is, it is advisable to increase their costs of doing so in terms of skills and resources needed by bad actors—thereby decreasing their expected profits (ibid.). It is also necessary to increase the risk of criminals being identified, located, and prosecuted (ibid.).

It is, therefore, necessary and urgent to contribute to:

- Reducing the number of technical, organizational, legal, and human vulnerabilities that could be exploited for malicious purposes;
- Increasing the robustness and resilience of IT infrastructures through security measures supported by coherent and complementary technological, procedural, and managerial initiatives;
- Developing a real ability to adapt cybersecurity and cyber defense resources to respond to a constantly changing situation; and
- Having means such as funding, introducing awareness programs, hiring skilled personnel, and training personnel to manage cyber crises and cybersecurity issues (please also refer to the recommendations proposed by Al-Bassam, 2018)

It also means that these actions must be part of a strong political will and states' commitment to making the fight against cybercrime and cybersecurity and cyber defense capacity building a priority. It is by acting on multiple factors in the political, socio-economic, legal, and technical fields that elements of response can be brought to bear on security needs. Respect for the fundamental rights of individuals (including respect for privacy, digital privacy, and freedom of expression) is a must. The security and defense measures adopted must be appropriate and proportionate to the actual threats and risks. Mobilizing federal resources; engaging various private and civil society actors in the fight against cybercrime; and building a trusted digital ecosystem is just as important as developing human competencies and capacities; putting awareness-raising initiatives in place; and training everyone in what to do and how to do it.

According to Al-Alawi (2005), banks have been providing electronic services to their customers for decades. Various models incorporate the principles governing *secure electronic transfers*—regardless of whether the amount happens to be small installments paid by small businesses, or enormous payments funded by corporate administrative frameworks. There are a number of scams and other cybercrimes found in the financial market—crimes similar to ATM scanners, cyber money laundering, and charge card frauds. In a few cases, the digital hoodlums use budgetary capabilities like a PIN; a secret key; endorsements; etc. to break into financial records and take a small amount of money. In other cases, they may take all the money and move the assets into anonymous accounts. At times, the goal of cybercriminals is to just cause mischief to damage the reputation of the bank. Along these lines, they hinder the bank servers, with their objective being denial of service—preventing clients from accessing their records.

The Need for Cybersecurity

Technological advancement is serving consumers in many ways. They are being given ways to operate seemingly everything remotely. Technological efficiency is making it easy for employees to do their work in a minimum number of hours. Furthermore, employees are placed at ease in that they are asked to expend less physical effort and are not supposed to perform redundant work (Cavelty, 2014). In the viewpoint of Brookes (2015), technological advancement is beneficial for businesses organizations; however, frauds and scams are very common nowadays. It has put the technology of multiple organizations at serious risk. It is very crucial for organizations today to secure their technology (whether that technology be hardware, software, the IoT, or cloud data) (Elmaghraby & Losavio, 2014). Furthermore, Al-Bassam stated that the experts of the Bahraini Information and e-Government Authority have also noted the scope of the cybersecurity tasks that need to be undertaken in the Kingdom soon.

Moreover, the Kingdom has already started a cybersecurity awareness campaign within the government as well as in private organizations designed to explain how cybersecurity is needed as a protection against any online risk or threats, and [to explain] about the need for the right infrastructure in order to protect the government and private organizations from data breaches (Al-Bassam 2018).

Moreover, Al-Bassam stated that

Bahrain is not prepared to overcome cyber-attacks and security, [only] 20% of companies in the country are[ ]prepared. However, the government is working hard to provide [forms of] protection[ ] against cybercrimes and attacks. Nevertheless, due to the increased number of cybercrimes in Bahrain, and the significant[ ] importance of this issue in the Kingdom, HM the King Hamad Bin Isa Al Khalifa[ ] issued [] Royal Decree No. 109/2011[ ] to develop a Cybercrime Directorate in Bahrain within the Ministry of [the] Interior. (Al-Bassam 2018)

The importance of the Cybersecurity and Awareness Program

According to the Economic Development Board of Bahrain (EDB) (n.d.), maintaining cybersecurity for corporations, governmental organizations, and other businesses is essential to Bahrain's economy. As IT security businesses drive to secure assets and data away from cybercriminals, assurance in the market strengthens. This, in turn, makes the Kingdom more attractive to investors and venture capitalists. It is necessary for more cybersecurity companies to invest in the Gulf Cooperation Council (GCC). Fulfilling that goal has never been challenging, since the need is great. For instance, only 37% of the MENA companies have inclusive training awareness programs, in comparison to 53% globally (ibid.). This need will put Bahrain into the best position for cybersecurity investment. Additionally, Bahrain has more than 400 banking and financial establishments (ibid.). Such an enormous number of organizations represents attacking such organizations represents a desirable objective of cyberattackers worldwide (ibid.). For example, the Shamoon malware 2012 attack on Saudi's Aramco was one of the most critical cyberattacks on the oil industry. Moreover, in 2012, the Qatari Natural Gas Company (Ras Gas) was also hit with a similar Saudi attack that shut down its website and email servers; and during 2013, UAE and Oman banks suffered a loss of more than $45 million from massive ATM cyber-thefts in the MENA region (Al-Bassam, 2018).

According to PricewaterhouseCoopers,

Cybersecurity is an area that we have to continually invest in. It used to be financial institutions that were the key drivers of it, but now people realize every business will need it. For the long term, that is going to be an area of growth. (Pricewaterhouse Coopers, 2016)

Al-Bassam (2018) investigated factors related to the adaptation of cybersecurity awareness in the banking sector in Bahrain and illustrated the gap in factors such as "top management commitment and support, budgeting, cybersecurity policy enforcement, and cybersecurity compliance and cybersecurity culture." To gauge the effectiveness of her study, she recommended that "cyber-attacks must be monitored after awareness and training." For future study, she stated that "further investigation of the same factors[,] and [measurement of] their impact on cybersecurity awareness in other sectors and countries, and more research [into] the different types of cybercrimes and [associated] risks[,] is required." Additionally, in 2017, the GCC started a cybersecurity lab in Bahrain. The idea of this lab is to expand awareness of cybersecurity and "to develop solutions in order to overcome the increasing rate of cyber-attacks that takes place in MENA regions." Furthermore, a 2016 study

[identifies] the areas which require attention. Factors such as knowledge, attitude and behavior affecting human awareness were identified and the Value-Focus-Thinking was used to identify Information Systems Security (ISS) focus-areas. The six ISS Focus-Areas were obtained such as commitment to ISS policy; effective use of passwords; safe usage of Internet and email; being aware of ISS threats; backing up the important files; and required updates for operating system and antivirus programs. (Al-Alawi, Al-Kandari, & Abdel-Razek, 2016)

Bahraini Proposal for a Unified GCC Center for Cybersecurity

In an August 2019 interview published in one of the local newspapers in Bahrain (Akhbar AlKhaleej, 2019), a number of Bahraini Parliamentary deputies proposed a desire to take necessary measures to establish a unified Gulf Center for Cybersecurity. They pointed out that with technological development and accelerated technological progress, wars have become cyber wars based on piracy, espionage, and cyber-attacks targeting various countries of the world, especially the Arab Gulf states. Electronic battalions have been recruited to serve the subversive objectives of terrorist groups. Means include piracy over the personal accounts of officials, companies, or government and military installations of countries. Goals include spying or sabotaging, in order to undermine the Gulf States. The explanatory memorandum of the proposal confirmed that this desire is shared by both the Speaker of the House of Representatives Fawzia Zainal and deputies Dr. Abdullah Al-Thawadi, Bassem Al-Malki, Abdullah Al-Dossari and Abdul Razzaq Hattab. The proposal is intended to take the necessary measures to establish a unified Gulf center to combat piracy and cyber terrorism. The goal is to do so through unifying efforts, coordination and cooperation among the Gulf States through the exchange of information and expertise and the use of experienced technicians to repel and prevent such systematic attacks at the level of the Arabian Gulf, and to train a new class of qualified youth in this area to be fully prepared and knowledgeable to stand against these attacks, in addition to working on the scientific research component of such an initiative.

Dr. Abdullah Al-Thawadi, confirmed the importance of establishing a unified coordination center for cybersecurity among the Gulf states in order to protect the Gulf Cooperation Council countries from being exposed to cyber-attacks and breaches, and to serve as a technical and strategic reference and avenue of cooperation in the exchange of information and experience in cybersecurity in order to deal with electronic incidents and prevent piracy at the level of the Gulf States. He pointed out that it has become necessary to have a unified entity for the Gulf Cooperation Council countries to face these threats in light of the increasing crimes of cyber terrorism—crimes that are targeting the countries of the region, adding that so-called *hackers* and cyber hackers have become one of the most important tools of terrorist organizations—targeting the economic institutions and services of countries in the region. Consideration of the parliamentary proposal to establish a Gulf center for cybersecurity as a protection for the national security of the Gulf States was urged. Al-Thawadi added that the major countries have become interested in this new challenge and that they can deal with it firmly—pointing out that the responsibility of the Gulf countries lies in the establishment of this unified coordinating center, and that the legislative councils in the Gulf States have the responsibility to provide the requisite legislative system, especially given the Bahrain Economic Vision 2030 plan that the Kingdom of Bahrain has in place. The comprehensive of Bahrain Economic Vision 2030 outlines the forthcoming footpath for the expansion of Bahraini economy. "It has been shared with a host of opinion leaders from the private sector, academia and development organizations, and the public sector. Their input has greatly added to the quality and significance of this document". This plan is divided into three sections such as

The Need for Coordinated Reforms: *National, regional and global developments compelling us to develop a coordinated Economic Vision.*

The Guiding Principles of our Economic Vision: *The principles embedded in our aspirations for the future: competitiveness, fairness and sustainability.*

Aspirations: *Bahrain's aspirations for the economy, government and society; and the actions required to attain them*

It is based on a free economy and digital transformation in the various economic, commercial, financial, and banking services, and even in the service sectors such as education, health, and others.

The head of the Parliamentary Committee on Human Rights pointed to the marked increase in cyber piracy operations of Gulf government and economic institutions. For the Middle East, it reports that "piracy groups have tracked and hacked 500 targets in the world, 44% of which are inside Saudi Arabia" (Akhbar AlKhaleej, 2019). There is no absolute protection from cyberattacks; and even developed countries are exposed to vital installations and attacks. Therefore, these attacks represent, in some respects, the development of the conflict between states and entities; and as there is a military, commercial or judicial conflict, there is also the struggle of cyber piracy. He added that the existence of a Gulf center for cybersecurity is important in that all measures need to be taken to protect against these attacks or at least to make the task difficult for hackers, and that these measures should be taken at the level of the Gulf States, institutions, individuals, and governments in order to carry out an assessment of the risk to potential targets such as sensitive information centers that may be under attack, leading to the prioritization of their protection.

DATA ANALYSIS AND INTERPRETATION

Global Spending on Cybersecurity

Security threats are continuing to rise. Alarmingly, the cost reached $280 billion in 2016. The most vulnerable element faced by businesses was the loss of reputation. This is so because company data have been at risk. For example, Bangladesh Bank was hacked by hackers using SWIFT—a consortium that can operate a trusted, closed network to help member banks communicate—to request transfers totaling nearly USD $1 billion to banks in the Philippines. This has resulted in a loss of USD $81 million and has also prevented the processing of USD $850 million in transactions (Vij, 2016; Al-Bassam, 2018). Aramco, the Saudi oil company, was faced with four different during the attack. First, a computer technician opened a scam email and clicked on a bad link. Secondly, screens flickered and files disappeared. Third, there was a computer shutdown by the virus. Finally, 35,000 computers were partially wiped or totally destroyed. This scenario temporarily stopped the selling of oil to domestic gas tank trucks. After 17 days, the corporation relented and started giving oil away for free to keep it flowing within Saudi Arabia. This incident resulted in over 55,000 Saudi Aramco workforce employees having to stay home (Al-Alawi & Al-Bassam, 2017; Al-Bassam, 2018; Al Amro, 2017; Easttom & Butler, 2019). As shown in Figure 1, the rate of reputation loss has been observed at about 29%;

and direct loss in the resulting turnover impacted about 7.4%. Cybercrime is in the process of dramatically disturbing international businesses. The entire amount of losses to industries has increased to over USD $280 billion, with reputation damage, workforce time, and consumer loss/churn being the crucial impacts of cyber-attacks. Exaction, too, is on the increase, with 95% of companies, still falling prey to weak training of staff and inadequate practices by staff (Consultancy United Kingdom, 2016). Now, the businesses that are in a good financial position or that have a strong profit margin are mostly the ones at risk of cyber-attacks. Due to globalization, individuals are aware of the financial position of a company; and by using advanced technologies, they can easily attack any business (Al-Alawi, 2014).

Figure 2 illustrates the global increase in cybersecurity spending from 2012 to 2026. With the increase in security threats, global spending on cybersecurity is gradually increasing. According to the Australian Cyber Security Growth Network (AustCyber, n.d.), global spending on cybersecurity has reached USD $131 billion—and this is expected to increase by 88% by 2026.

Figure 1. Business loss due to cybercrime
Source: Consultancy United Kingdom, 2016

The Motivation Behind Cybercrime

Passeri (2019) has identified several reasons for cyber-attacks. Among these, cybercrime is usually the purpose of the cybersecurity breach—accounting for approximately 88.5% of such breaches (as depicted by Figure 3). Cyber espionage accounts for 7.3%; hacktivism, 2.4%; and cyberwarfare, 1.8%.

The world is facing cybercrime challenges in the form of backdoors, exploits, miscellaneous Trojans, PWS and Monitoring Tools, Trojan downloaders and droppers, viruses, and worms. As shown in Figure 4, miscellaneous Trojans comprise a large portion of such challenges; and worms are also present in large numbers; this has placed organizations in the Middle East at risk of such attacks (Emirates 24/7, 2014).

According to Al-Mhiqani et al., (2018), prior incidents indicate that the cybersecurity threats which Bahraini businesses are most vulnerable to are cyberwarfare, cybercrime, hacktivism, and cyberespionage. Figure 5 shows that the most common cybersecurity threat that Bahraini businesses face is cyberwarfare. This indicates that company data may be destroyed. This underlies the category of cyberwarfare. Moreover, cybercrime is also very common in businesses because of the tough competition between industries (Emirates 24/7, 2014).

Figure 2. Global increase in cybersecurity spending from 2012 to 2026
Source: AustCyber, n.d.

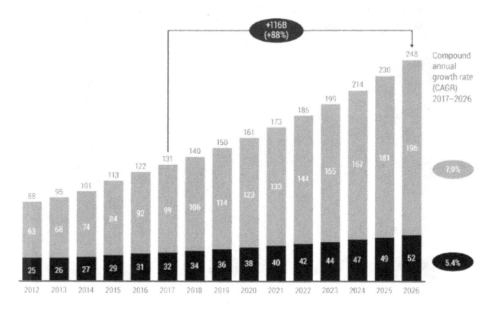

Figure 3. Reasons for cybercrime
Source: Passeri, 2019

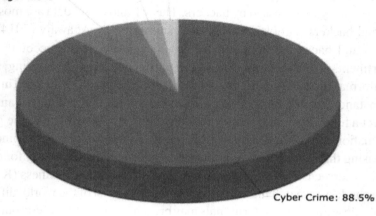

Figure 4. Risk of security threats in the Middle East
Source: Emirates 24/7, 2014

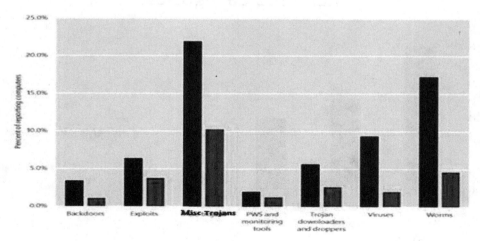

RESULTS AND DISCUSSION

The Cyber Threat to Bahraini Organizations

Businesses are finding that the security of their data is under threat. Unprotected data can easily be accessed by hackers. The IoT and cloud data are most at risk from external hackers (Brookes, 2015). It is supported by Abawajy (2014) that frauds, scams, and hacks are common for email, websites, bank accounts, the finance departments of organizations, and IT departments. Through hacking, a hacker may get information about a company—information that could be misused in several ways. For instance, the hacker may sell information to the competitors of an organization and get a huge amount of money in return. It is also possible that the government's information can be hacked by intelligence agencies. According to Joiner (2017), the increasing threats to sensitive information have made it necessary for organizations to use cybersecurity protections to avoid any loss to their business (Kshetri, 2013).

Secondary research indicates that similar to the rest of the world, different sectors of Bahrain are also at risk. Criminals may breach firewalls for several purposes. One of the reasons may be to provide important data to competitive companies or countries. Furthermore, the reason for a cybersecurity breach may be the goal of stealing a certain amount from the accounts of organizations (either a government organization

Figure 5. Cybercrime incidents categories
Source: Al-Mhiqani et al., 2018

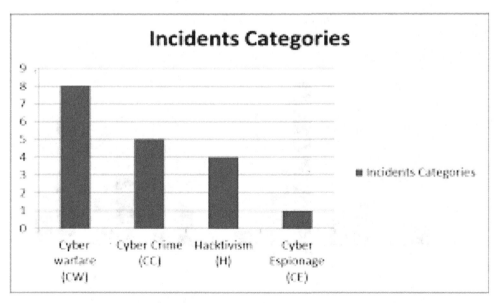

or one from the financial sector of Bahrain). As discussed above, analysis also indicates that Bahraini businesses commonly face cyberattacks. Moreover, hacking and malware are each affecting organizations on a small scale. Hence, it is can be observed from the kinds of threats note that competitors may use cybercrime and cyberwarfare as means to defeat rival businesses in Bahrain. The increasing global spending on cybersecurity has also put pressure on Bahraini businesses to launch an appropriately commensurate investment program in security in order to avoid any kind of comparative risk in future. Cybersecurity and cyber defense are not luxuries. They play a vital role in the capacity of countries to contribute to their economic and social development and their international recognition. To ensure their safety and economic well-being, all countries must strengthen their cybersecurity, anti-cybercrime, and cyber defense stance—and contribute individually and collectively to peace (which now also involves the construction of digital ecosystem confidence and mastery of security and defense issues in cyberspace) (Kshetri, 2013).

Nevertheless, through the Bahraini Parliament, it was proposed to take the necessary measures to establish a unified Gulf CyberSecurity Center to combat piracy and cyberterrorism, through unifying efforts, coordination and cooperation among the Gulf Cooperation Council countries as well as through conducting practical and academic research studies; training and developing youth in this field; and spreading cybersecurity knowledge and awareness.

CONCLUSION AND RECOMMENDATION

Introduction

The importance of cybersecurity for the businesses is important on a global scale. The major reason why businesses are concerned is that hackers not only hack profits but also the data related to the customers, and strategic plans. Businesses contain data of considerable importance; and that data not only includes customers' personal data but also sensitive information regarding employees and functions of the business. Sometimes, a business more concerned about profits and less about protecting the identity of its customers. Due to this, the leaking of business data is considered to be the major issue for many businesses regarding the threat of cybersecurity. For instance, if an insurance company were to hack the medical records of a hospital, they could save money by identifying preexisting conditions of potential clients who might not disclose that information willingly; and then deny coverage to those clients. Additionally, if the financial data of users were to be stolen, this would enable the thieves to perhaps withdraw an amount small enough that the bank would simply take the loss and replace the funds rather than inform the customer. In both cases, such a hack is less about the strategy of the business and more about exploiting other kinds of information. Furthermore, perhaps a biopharmaceutical company is in the process of developing and patenting a promising drug—and a rival company wants to steal the formula.

The other issue faced by the business in regard to cybersecurity is ransomware. This is described as a malware which encrypts the business data and then the businesses are bound to pay a large amount of money to unlock the data. This type of threat of cybersecurity only targets data saved on hardware. To resolve this problem, many businesses are now storing the data in the cloud. Many professionals believe that this is going to prevent any attack on the cybersecurity of the business, as the data will presumably be safer in the cloud than if it were to be stored on hardware.

CONCLUSION

This chapter addresses the many ways in which the cybersecurity of Bahraini organizations can be breached and are currently being breached. Secondary research was performed for the study according to the qualitative research method. Hence, information was gathered from journal articles, conference proceedings, magazines, a newspaper, and reports of Bahrain. Data analysis indicates that global spending on cybersecurity is continuously increasing and that it is expected to increase. This is because the global cyber threat faced by organizations is also expected to increase. It is observed that cyberwarfare is the most commonly used form of cyberattack in Bahrain. The research reveals that the most frequently occurring threats are cyberwarfare and cybercrime—and that this may affect large businesses, government organizations, and financial sectors for the sake of competition within the country.

Businesses are duty bound to urgently take appropriate measures and put measures in place to protect their business data and corporate information from these cyberattacks. Issues related to cybersecurity are growing with advances in technology. Businesses are required to have advanced technology and a skilled workforce which will help them survive cyberattacks. If such technology is used in an appropriate manner, then it can help a society to flourish; but the misuse of this technology is a threat not only to the business itself but also to society as a whole (Von Solms & Van Niekerk, 2013). Furthermore, data from different sectors are at risk because warfare is the purpose of those criminals whose objective is to cause a huge loss to the data of organizations, possibly by leaking data that can affect its reputation; as well as causing financial loss to Bahrain-based businesses. Whether governments, legislators, owners and operators of infrastructure, users, or providers of IT solutions, it is the duty of all stakeholders to contribute to securing cyberspace for the benefit of the community.

Hacking refers to any actions or activities that are carried out with the goal of compromising any digital devices connected to the Internet—devices such as, for instance, smartphones, laptops, desktops, tablet computers, all sizes of computers, smart TVs, ATMs, or even an entire organization's network. Hacking can be carried out by an individual or a group of people or even by institutions who may discover a vulnerability in an information technology system and then take advantage of that weakness. Hacks can be categorized according to what is exploited (Al-Alawi & Abdelgadir, 2006, Guru99, n.d., Malwarebytes, n.d.).

It is true that cybersecurity and cyber defense are sometimes presented as a luxury for developing countries and are not among the national priorities manifest in alternative initiatives such as the construction of clinics and hospitals; the training of health care staff; building classrooms; or creating jobs for young people; to name only a few examples. However, to limit oneself to such a vision would be to forget that behind each of these actions, there is now an information system to support them. It is the quality, security, and value of the information system that underpins, for example, the National Health Strategy, which drives the employment programs of young people, or those implemented in the management of public finances that depends on the functioning of society, the economy, and the state. In the 21st century, food-related data also pass through information systems (culture, resource management, access to water, energy, markets, import/export, and supply chains). What would happen to health or public finances if their associated information systems are processing data that is unavailable, unreliable, inaccurate, or untrustworthy? Several countries have experienced the unfortunate experience of having electoral lists that are not deemed trustworthy. Such instances are obvious examples of a failure to respect the principles of cybersecurity, including ensuring the accuracy of the data in the system, which is a problem of computer security. Furthermore, there have been some loopholes that have detected. The following are some of the major causes of weak cybersecurity and increased cybercrime:

- Weak protection/authentication,
- Ignorance of encryption,
- Insufficient knowledge and awareness of security standards,
- Delays in updates and security patches,
- Ineffective backup plans,
- Overconfidence in traditional and old practices, and
- IT administrators being mixed with security professionals.

RECOMMENDATIONS

The following are recommendations for businesses in Bahrain:

- They should increase the number and improve the quality of basic as well as advanced security systems in the organizations.
- They should train the staff to avoid any kind of risk from using cloud data, the IoT, hardware, and software in the organization.
- They should also train the staff of their organizations to maintain a strict monitoring of cybersecurity; and security systems should also be checked on a daily basis.

REFERENCES

Abawajy, J. (2014). User preference of cybersecurity awareness delivery methods. *Behaviour & Information Technology*, *33*(3), 237–248. doi:10.1080/014492 9X.2012.708787

Al-Alawi, A. I. (2005). Online banking: Security concerns and the acceptance of mature customers. In *3rd International Conference: Sciences of Electronic, Technologies of Information and Telecommunications* (pp. 27–31). Academic Press.

Al-Alawi, A. I. (2014). Cybercrimes, computer forensics and their impact in business climate: Bahrain status. *Research Journal of Business Management*, *8*(3), 139–156. doi:10.3923/rjbm.2014.139.156

Al-Alawi, A. I., & Abdelgadir, M. F. (2006). An empirical study of attitudes and opinions of computer crimes: A comparative study between UK and the Kingdom of Bahrain. *Journal of Computational Science*, *2*(3), 229–235. doi:10.3844/jcssp.2006.229.235

Al-Alawi, A. I., & Al-Bassam, S. A. (2017). Investigating the factors affecting cybersecurity awareness in [the] Bahrain banking sector. In *Cyber Security Symposium, Britain & Northern Ireland*. University of Manchester.

Al-Alawi, A. I., Al-Kandari, S. M., & Abdel-Razek, R. H. (2016). Evaluation of information systems security awareness in higher education: An empirical study of Kuwait University. *Journal of Innovation and Business Best Practice*. doi:10.5171/2016.329374

Al Amro, S. (2017). Cybercrime in Saudi Arabia: Fact or fiction? *International Journal of Computer Science Issues*, *14*(2), 36–42. doi:10.20943/01201702.3642

Al-Bassam, S. A. (2018). *Investigating the factors related to cybersecurity awareness in Bahraini banking sector* (Unpublished master's thesis). Arabian Gulf University.

Al-Mhiqani, M. N., Ahmad, R., Yassin, W., Hassan, A., Abidin, Z. Z., Ali, N. S., & Abdulkareem, K. H. (2018). Cyber-security incidents: A review cases in cyber-physical systems. *International Journal of Advanced Computer Science and Applications*, *9*, 499–508.

AlKhaleej. (2019, August 23). اقتراح نيابي بإنشاء مركز خليجي موحد للسيبراني السلمان [Parliamentary proposal to establish a unified Gulf Center for Cybersecurity]. Retrieved from http://www.akhbar-alkhaleej.com/news/article/1180085

AustCyber. (n.d.). *Australian Cyber Security Growth Network*. Australian Government—Department of Industry, Innovation and Science. Retrieved August 27, 2019 from https://www.austcyber.com/sites/default/files/inline-images/fig11.png

Brookes, C. (2015). *Cyber security: Time for an integrated whole-of-nation approach in Australia*. Centre for Defence and Strategic Studies. Retrieved August 27, 2019 from http://www.defence.gov.au/ADC/Publications/IndoPac/150327%20Brookes%20IPS%20paper%20-%20cyber%20(PDF%20final).pdf

Cavelty, M. D. (2014). Breaking the cyber-security dilemma: Aligning security needs and removing vulnerabilities. *Science and Engineering Ethics*, *20*(3), 701–715. doi:10.100711948-014-9551-y PMID:24781874

Conklin, A., & White, G. (2006). e-Government and cyber security: The role of cyber security exercises. *Proceedings of the 39th Annual Hawaii International Conference on System Sciences (HICSS'06)*. 10.1109/HICSS.2006.133

Consultancy United Kingdom. (2016). Costs of cybercrime have soared to $280 billion this year. *Consultancy United Kingdom*. Retrieved August 27, 2019 from https://www.consultancy.uk/news/12917/costs-of-cybercrime-have-soared-to-280-billion-this-year

Easttom, C., & Butler, W. (2019, January). A modified McCumber Cube as a basis for a taxonomy of cyber attacks. In *2019 IEEE 9th Annual Computing and Communication Workshop and Conference (CCWC)* (pp. 943-949). IEEE.

Economic Development Board (EDB). (n.d.). *Cybersecurity: Business opportunities: Information & communications technology.* Economic Development Board of Bahrain. Retrieved August 28, 2019, from https://bahrainedb.com/business-opportunities/information-communication-technology/cyber-security/

Elmaghraby, A. S., & Losavio, M. M. (2014). Cybersecurity challenges in smart cities: Safety, security and privacy. *Journal of Advanced Research, 5*(4), 491–497. doi:10.1016/j.jare.2014.02.006 PMID:25685517

Emirates 24/7. (2014). [The] majority [of] UAE users hit by cyber bugs [are] happily unaware. *Emirates.* Retrieved August 27, 2019 from https://www.emirates247.com/news/emirates/majority-uae-users-hit-by-cyber-bugs-happily-unaware-2014-06-10-1.552256

Guru99. (n.d.). *What is hacking? An introduction.* Retrieved August 30, 2019, from https://www.guru99.com/what-is-hacking-an-introduction.html

Heaton, J. (1998). Secondary analysis of qualitative data. *Social Research Update, 22.* Department of Sociology, University of Surrey, Guildford, UK. Retrieved August 27, 2019 from http://sru.soc.surrey.ac.uk/SRU22.html

Joiner, K. F. (2017). How Australia can catch up to US cyber resilience by understanding that cyber survivability test and evaluation drives defense investment. *Information Security Journal: A Global Perspective, 26*(2), 74–84.

Kshetri, N. (2013). Cybercrime and cybersecurity in the Middle East and North African economies. In *Cybercrime and Cybersecurity in the Global South* (pp. 119–134). London: Palgrave Macmillan. doi:10.1057/9781137021946_6

Malwarebytes. (n.d.). *What is hacking?* Retrieved August 30, 2019, from https://www.malwarebytes.com/hacker/

Passeri, P. (2019). *February 2019 cyber attacks[—]statistics. Hackmageddon.* Retrieved August 27, 2019 from https://www.hackmageddon.com/category/security/cyber-attacks-statistics/

PricewaterhouseCoopers (PwC). (2016). *CEO interview: Greg Becker* [Topic: Silicon Valley banking]. Formerly available from http://www.pwc.com/us/en/ceo-survey/ceo-interviews/greg-becker-silicon-valley-bank.html

Vij, A. (2016, June 02). *The threat is real: Battling cybercrime in banking.* Finextra. Retrieved from https://www.finextra.com/blogposting/12685/the-threat-is-real-battling-cybercrime-in-banking

Von Solms, R., & Van Niekerk, J. (2013). From information security to cyber security. *Computers & Security*, *38*, 97–102. doi:10.1016/j.cose.2013.04.004

Chapter 12

Building New Relationships:
Social Media Trustworthiness in Gulf Cooperation Countries

Afaf Mubarak Bugawa
Arabian Gulf University, Bahrain

Noora Abdulla Janahi
Arabian Gulf University, Bahrain

ABSTRACT

Given the current widespread popularity of social media, such as Twitter, Instagram, Snapchat, and many other applications, understanding users' attitudes and usage behavior of social media applications becomes a necessity in order to develop future placements of such technologies and increase the level of trust among the users. Therefore, the aim of this chapter is to shed light on the impact of trustworthiness of social media on the intention to use it. Data is gathered through a quantitative method, in which a questionnaire is used as a primary data. A convenient sampling is applied, in which the most easily accessible managers and employees in Ministry of Interior in Bahrain are chosen. The results demonstrate that there is a significant positive relationship between trustworthiness and intention to use social media. The study recommends future works to study the impact of security awareness on the usage of social media in public sector in Bahrain.

DOI: 10.4018/978-1-7998-2418-3.ch012

INTRODUCTION

The current trend of technology in the digital age extends the reach of communication media to all domains of social life in a network that is both global and local, generic and customized, and in a dynamic pattern. It is been argued that the Middle Eastern, in general, and the Countries Gulf Cooperation Countries (GCC), in particular, have heavy investments in their ICT infrastructure in order to develop Internet access through broadband along with 3G, 4G and 5G network services (Alqudsi-ghabra et al., 2011). In fact, the GCC economies in general has been leading the Middle East and North Africa (MENA) region's economic growth during 2018 and 2019 through large-scale infrastructure investment such as the Expo 2020 in the UAE (Selman & Faiq, 2018). They stated that the technology in the GCC has evolved from a highly fragmented market to an ecosystem of a wide variety of product and services.

The adoption of advanced technologies have been rapidly accelerated. In this regard, Chami (2019) recently declared that FinTech and blockchain have affected nearly all the industries located in the GCC and at different paces. In general, FinTech is playing a vital role in the future of financial services in both public and private sectors in the GCC and the UAE itself is embracing the potential of blockchain technology across industries through targeting to have all government documents on the blockchain by 2020 (Chami, 2019).

The telecommunication sector is a significant engine for economic growth, diversification and social cohesion in Bahrain. It is used to provide leading-edge services and respond to both consumers' and businesses' needs. It is crucial for improving productivity and enhancing the growth of new sectors such as energetic digital services sector. Therefore, a strong telecommunications platform as a part of a dynamic Information and Communications Technology (ICT) ecosystem will enable the government and citizens to achieve a range of enhancement in health care, education and communication with governmental bodies (TRA Annual Report, 2017).

Web 2.0 technology is found to provide an easy access to information, improve communication, ensure convenience in health, education, and other sectors, and it enhance both the efficiency and the productivity. However, internet users still hesitate to fully trust these social networks. Given the nature of social media platforms and the large number of users disseminating information, inaccurate or false information is considered as an inherent problem (Lindsay, 2011). It has been found that such mistaken and untruthful information has been spread through social media during disasters such as the Arab spring.

Previous literatures have identified social media as a significant vehicle in promoting social networking and connections in all fields. However, still there is a lack of addressing the impact of such connections in order to create trust in these fields. Therefore, this research aims to study the impact of trustworthiness of social media on the intention to use it among employees in the Ministry of Interior in Kingdom of Bahrain.

This chapter is organized as follows. First, the Web 2.0 technologies and social media evolution are highlighted. Then, a literature review on technology acceptance frameworks is outlined. In this context, a framework for users' trust is built to study the impact of trustworthiness of social media on the intention to use it among users. Finally, the case of Ministry of Interior in the Kingdom of Bahrain is discussed to link the conceptual framework developed in the preceding sections to practice. Conclusions and recommendations follow.

BACKGROUND – WEB 2.0 TECHNOLOGY AND SOCIAL MEDIA EVOLUTION

The term "Web 2.0" was officially coined in 2004 by Dale Dougherty (Tim, 2005). Web 2.0 is seen as a consequences of a more fully implemented Web. Whereas, Web is generally a set of technologies,

Web 2.0 is the attempt to conceptualize the significance of such set of outcomes that are enabled by Web technologies (Anderson, 2007). There are a number of Web-based services and applications that demonstrate the foundations of the Web 2.0 concept, including; blogs, wikis, multimedia sharing services, content syndication, podcasting and content tagging services (Anderson, 2007). One of the Web 2.0 characteristics is social participation, in which it provides users with the tools that allow them to engage in different activities such as Facebook, Twitter, and many other blogs (Merchant, 2009). It is apparent that Web 2.0 technologies enhance the experiences of various users. In this regard, Bugawa (2016) explained how the usage of Web 2.0 technologies could result in more interactive technologies among users.

The scale of Web impact has a vital role on the way the architectures of a given Web-based system are designed, especially for new technologies that are developed on the basis of Web 2.0 ideas (Anderson, 2007). The rise of social network sites is considered as a new socio-technical revolution, ranging from personal interaction to business, to culture, to social movements, to politics and so on. In fact, it can be noticed that currently the most important usage of the internet is the social networking. Social media has become the selected platform for different activities including; personal friendships, marketing, e-commerce, education, and entertainment (Manuel, 2013).

Users are experiencing new learning opportunities via social interaction (Merchant, 2009). Although the Middle East constitutes 3.2% of the worldwide internet users only, it has registered a remarkable growth in the internet usage 5,183% in the past 20 years compared with the rest of the world 1,114% (World Internet Usage Statistics News, 2010). As a result, this has attracted various online companies to conduct business in the Middle East and allowed many existing sectors such as education, health, airline and government to move their operations online (Aloul, 2010). Yet, the last few years have witnessed an increased number of cybercrime incidents (Aloul, 2010). Usage of advanced secure technologies in many organizations is forcing hackers to break into organizations with new and unusual technologies by targeting the weakest link (i.e., uneducated computer users) (Aloul, 2010). These technological changes have provided new ways of using the web that enhance users' behavior (Bugawa, 2016). There are various theories that explain users' behavior with respect to any given new technology. For instance, the Theory of Reasoned Action (TRA) proposed by Fishbein and Ajzen (1975) is generated from the field of social psychology that explains users' behavior through their intentions. This theory is then adopted by Davis (1986, 1989) who proposed the Technology Acceptance Model (TAM). Since then, TAM has been revised in various studies in order to fit a certain context of technology being examined, and the most recent one is by Rauniar, et al. (2014) who proposed a revised model of TAM to study the usage behavior of social media applications.

Greenwell (2011) reported five eras of information systems attacks. The first era, attacks were characterized as being primarily small scale and mostly harmless. The second era, attacks were characterized by their large scale and their different motivation for hacking. The third era witnessed the introduction of laws to protect information security. The forth era, hackers began targeting large corporations to obtain money and finally the fifth era hackers become motivated by politics.

Based on a survey distributed to both students and staff in the University of Bahrain, it was found that the majority of social media users had been exposed to the security threat of website failure, maintenance error, spamming, while few had dealt with unauthorized access to their account and data, faced malware and had their identities stolen (Zolait et al., 2014). In terms of user accountability, it was found that the majority of social media users believe that they should be responsible for protecting their own information and only few believed that it is the government's responsibility (Zolait et al., 2014).

In general, Gikas & Grant (2013) stated that Web 2.0 technologies are sometimes referred to as social media. Researchers are continuously intrigued by social media affordances and reach, supporting a wide range of interests and practices (Boyd & Ellison, 2008). Social network sites (SNSs) or social media in general is defined as *web-based services that allow individuals to construct a public or semi-public profile within bounded system, articulate a list of other users with whom they share a connection, and view and traverse their list of connections and those made by others within the system* (Boyd & Ellison, 2008). Lately, it is been observed that social media's popularity and the number of active participants are growing simultaneously (Bugawa, 2016).

The following section outlines conceptual frameworks for technology acceptance along with factors affecting users' attitude and usage behavior of a given technology.

The Problem of the Study

Theoretically, studies and research need to be re-evaluated to give a proper context and understanding of the widespread popularity of social media among its users. In this regard, Rauniar, et al. (2014) examined individual adoption behavior of Facebook as one of the popular social networking sites through revising TAM model and the results demonstrated that the revised model supported all the hypotheses of social media usage behavior. Since they focused only on Facebook, they claimed that future studies can include data analysis from other social media (Rauniar, et al., 2014).

Also Ghannam (2011) stated that there is an awakening of free expression in the Arab world which has helped break down the power of state in controlling media and information. The rise of an independent vibrant social media and citizen engagement on the internet is being increased, and is expected to attract 100 million Arab. Moreover, AL-Adawi, Yousafzai & Pallister (2005), claimed that trust can also influence behavioral intentions and attitude. Thus, it is important to detect what is arguably the most dramatic and unprecedented improvement in trustworthiness and access to information in order to peruse the Arab blogs, online videos, and other digital platforms (Ghannam, 2011).

Therefore, this study aims to address this knowledge gap in literature, in order to explain the users' behavior along with their trust of social media among employees in the Ministry of Interior in Kingdom of Bahrain through building on the revised TAM model by (Rauniar, et al., 2014).

CONCEPTUAL FRAMEWORKS FOR TECHNOLOGY ACCEPTANCE

Social media's widespread popularity is due to its acceptance and usage in the personal, social, and professional life of individual users (Rauniar, et al., 2014). Technology Acceptance Model (TAM) as proposed by Davis (1986, 1989) is one of the widely accepted theory on the actual usage behavior of a new technology, and it is derived from a popular theory called Theory of Reasoned Action (TRA) proposed earlier by Fishbein and Ajzen (1975) from the field of determinants of social psychology that explains a person's behavior through his/ her intentions. Specifically, TRA was theorized to explain general human behavior, while TAM was theorized to explain technology usage behavior (Davis. et al., 1989). Figure 1 and 2 below illustrate the TRA and TAM models respectively.

It is apparent that TAM breaks down the TRA's attitude construct into two constructs; perceived usefulness (PU) and perceived ease of use (EU) in order to explain technology usage behavior (Rauniar, et al., 2014). TAM has been revised in various studies in order to fit a certain context of technology being examined (Rauniar, et al., 2014) and one of the well-revised model of TAM is the inclusion of trustworthiness construct in predicting the usage behavior of a new technology by its users (Venktatesh & Davis, 2000), as shown in Figure 3.

Figure 1.

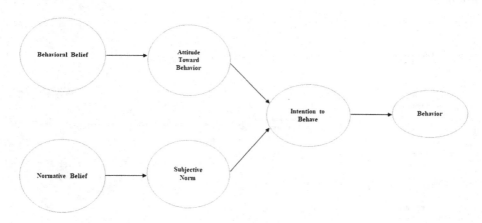

Figure 2.

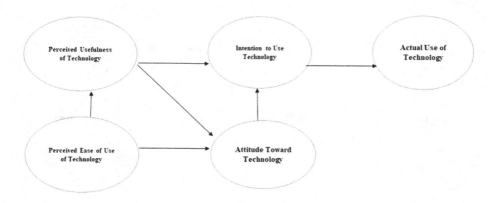

Research Framework

In this research, we built on the revised TAM model to study the impact of trustworthiness of social media on the intention to use it among employees in the Ministry of Interior in Bahrain, as it is shown in Figure 4 and this framework will be elaborated more upon in the text.

Table 1 summarizes the conceptual definition of each variable of this research as mentioned in the literature.

Figure 3.

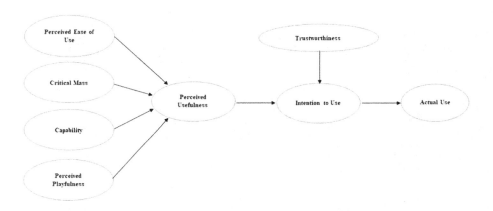

Figure 4.

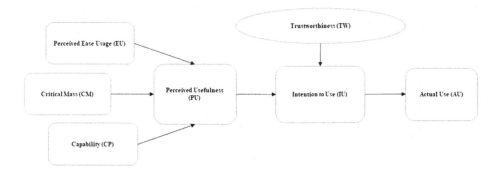

Perceived Ease Usage (EU) of Social Media

Venktatesh & Davis (2000) defined perceived ease usage as *the degree to which a person believes that using a particular system would be free of effort.*

It is been pointed out that the use of both Facebook and LinkedIn by adults has grown by 88% between 2009 and 2010 (Madden, 2010). This increasing diversity of users signing up with the social media is due to its relatively easy usage (Rauniar, et al., 2014). The concept of ease usage implies that users of social media will intend to use a given application that requires the least average effort, and they will be more appreciative of the minimum effort required to learn any specific feature such as uploading and sharing video or networking with their friends (Rauniar, et al., 2014).

The importance of perceived ease of use signifies the degree to which an innovation is perceived not to be difficult to, understand, learn, and use (Roger, 1962; Zeithmal, et al., 2002). It is clear that an easy to use application or site could enhance the user's experience. Thus, based on TAM, the following hypothesis is proposed:

Hypothesis One: There is a significant relationship between perceived easy usage and perceived usefulness of social media.

Table 1. Conceptual definitions of variables

Variable	Conceptual Definition	Source
Perceived Usefulness (PU)	The degree to which a person believes that using a particular system would enhance his/ her performance	Venktatesh & Davis (2000)
Perceived Ease Usage (EU)	The degree to which a person believes that using a particular system would be free of effort	
Critical Mass (CM)	The extent of the membership of people that matters most in a user's social media network	Cameron & Webster (2005)
Capability (CP)	Exchanges of diverse and rich media and the availability of applications enabling high levels of interactivity at social media	Daft & Lengel (1986)
Intention to Use (IU)	The voluntary and cognitive representation of the user's readiness to actually use the social media and it is determined by the user's perceived benefits from social media	Rauniar, et al. (2014)
Actual Use (AU)	The frequency of social media used by the user	
Trustworthiness (TW)	The extent to which a user is confident of the implicit contracts with the social media and other users and the user's confidence towards the websites concerning freedom from risk of danger or doubt during the e-service process	

Critical Mass (CM) of Social media

Cameron & Webster (2005) defined critical mass as *the extent of the membership of people that matters most in a user's social media network.*

TAM has become very popular due to its simplicity (i.e., parsimony), verifiability, and ability to predict acceptance and usage of new technologies in various fields (i.e., generalizability) (Lee. et al., 2003; Hoof et al., 2005). However, TAM assumed that information systems are used only inside organizations for workers' efficiency improvements and excluded the fact that information systems could also be used outside by individual users. Moreover, TAM theory does not explain the roles of other users in prompting an individual's usage behavior and attitude toward social media (Rauniar, et al., 2014).

From a psychological perspective, social impact is rooted from the assumption that a person's behavior is heavily influenced by the behavior of others (Rauniar, et al., 2014). Explicitly, the mass users networking in social media are considered as a critical component to explain the social media usage behavior (i.e. Critical Mass CM), and thus the following hypothesis is proposed:

Hypothesis Two: There is a significant relationship between critical mass and perceived usefulness of social media.

Capability (CP) of Social media

Daft & Lengel (1986) defined capability as *exchanges of diverse and rich media and the availability of applications enabling high levels of interactivity at social media.*

Various tools and applications are provided through social media which could boost the services provided to the users while they share and exchange information (Rauniar, et al., 2014). For instance, Snapchat allows users to communicate one-to-one with their followers, tell their stories in a unique way, save and share these stories on other platforms and they can view their story up to 24 hours before it is automatically deleted. Although it started just around 8 years ago in 2011, Snapchat is accessed by 150 million daily, and US advertisers spent around $50 million in 2015 (Meeker, 2014).

It is been argued that the vast growing usages of social media can also be attributed to the availability and effectiveness of tools and features in order to meet users' needs (i.e. Capability CP) (Rauniar, et al., 2014). Therefore, the following hypothesis is proposed:

Hypothesis Three: There is a significant relationship between capability and perceived usefulness of social media.

Perceived Usefulness (PU), Intention to Use (IU) and Actual Use (AU) of Social media

Venktatesh & Davis (2000) defined perceived usefulness as *the degree to which a person believes that using a particular system would enhance his/ her performance.* While Rauniar, et al. (2014) defined the intention to use as *the intended and cognitive representation of the user's readiness to actually use the social media and it is determined by the user's perceived benefits from social media* and the actual use as *the frequency of social media used by the user.*

Based on TAM, it is been assumed that attitudes about perceived usefulness could determine users' intention to use social media and accordingly their actual use (Davis, 1989; Venktatesh & Davis, 2000). Moreover, they argued that based on TRA, behaviors of social media users' is determined by their intentions and in turn, these intentions are a function of their perceived benefits from social media (i.e., Perceived Usefulness PU). In fact, there is extensive empirical evidence that has examined the belief-intention-behavior causality in the context of usage of various technologies (Davis et al., 1989; Davis, 1989 & Igbaria et al., 1996).

Social media intentions are the perceptive representation of a user's readiness in order to actually use the social media, and it is considered as the immediate antecedent of social media usage in TAM (Rauniar, et al., 2014). In this regard, TRA also recommends that the more favorable the attitude toward a behavior, the stronger the person's intention to perform such behavior. Thus the following hypotheses are proposed:

Hypothesis Four: There is a significant relationship between perceived usefulness and intention to use social media.

Hypothesis Five: There is a significant relationship between intention to use and actual use of social media.

Trustworthiness (TW) of Social media

Rauniar, et al. (2014) defined trustworthiness as *the extent to which a user is confident of the implicit contracts with the social media site and other users and the user's confidence towards the websites concerning freedom from risk of danger or doubt during the e-service process.*

The provenance, reputation, privacy and security of Web and email data are having a great deal of discussion. The material that people are posting to the public nowadays, would only have been seen by their close friends, and this in turn is changing the nature of privacy (George, 2006). Determining the accuracy of data from a given Web source becomes more difficult due to the large volume of information available (Anderson, 2007).

There is a concern with respect to some of the more doubtful aspects of search engine optimization, in which search engines are manipulated so that certain websites would appear higher in the rankings. This is for the purpose of having an excessively high score in search engine rankings and the potential for Semantic Web spam, which deliberately falsified published information (Mann, 2006). For this reason, trust is at the highest levels of the Semantic Web model (Matthews, 2005). For instance, there are large numbers of spam and email filters on the market, and they are still not regarded as fully adequate (Anderson, 2007). Brondsema & Schamp (2006) have been argued that such filters should make more use of trust ratings determined from social networks. Therefore, the following hypothesis is proposed:

Hypothesis Six: There is a significant relationship between trustworthiness and intention to use social media.

Based on the review of previous literature on social media and TAM model, few empirical studies have been conducted to scientifically evaluate and examine the usage behavior of social media (Rauniar, et al., 2014). In fact, a validated instrument of usage behavior of social media can provide usability experts and practitioners with a validated tool to assess social media acceptance and usage behavior. In this regard, Boyd and Ellison (2007) claimed that such instrument could gain a better understanding of "who is and who is not using social media, why and for what purposes". Figure 5 illustrate the research framework along with the proposed hypotheses based on the literature review.

Research Hypotheses

Hypothesis One: There is a significant relationship between perceived easy usage and perceived usefulness of social media.

Figure 5.

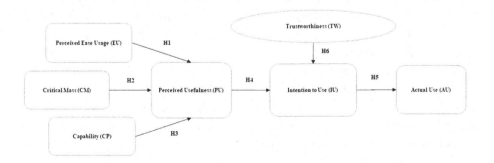

Hypothesis Two: There is a significant relationship between critical mass and perceived usefulness of social media.

Hypothesis Three: There is a significant relationship between capability and perceived usefulness of social media.

Hypothesis Four: There is a significant relationship between perceived usefulness and intention to use social media.

Hypothesis Five: There is a significant relationship between intention to use and actual use of social media.

Hypothesis Six: There is a significant relationship between trustworthiness and intention to use social media.

Methodology of The Study

Research Instrument and Tools

Data for this research was gathered through a quantitative method, in which a questionnaire was used as a primary data and the measurement of the variables is highlighted in Table 2. The questionnaire items were measured by means of five-point Likert scale from 1 to 5 rating from strongly disagree to strongly agree. The scales for these items were adapted from prior studies who have already established their reliability and validity, as it is illustrated in Table 2. However, the language of these items was modified to reflect the measurement of each variable for social media users. A Cronbach's Alpha test was re-conducted to test the reliability of the research instrument as it will be shown later in Table 4. Spearman's rank correlation was conducted to determine whether there is evidence of a linear relationship between the variables as per each hypothesis generated previously. All collected data were analyzed statistically using SPSS v25.0 software.

Operational Definitions of Variables

Operational definitions are used to define a given variable in terms of a process needed to determine its existence. The scale for this research variables are adapted from various literatures of which have already established their reliability and validity. For instance, the scale of perceived usefulness, perceived ease usage, intention to use and actual use were adapted from (Davis, 1986, 1989; Mathieson, 1991; Moore & Benbasat, 1991; Taylor & Todd, 1995; Venkatesh & Davis, 1996), critical mass was adapted from (Rouibah & Abbas, 2006), capability was (Rauniar et al. 2014), and trustworthiness was adapted from (Telzrow ey el. 2007; Fogels & Nehmad 2009).

In order to empirically examine the revised TAM model, a total of 25 items were generated. However, after conducting the reliability test using Cronbach Alpha, the initially adapted items were modified, dropped and re-worded for clarity and relevance for this research. The finalized items were 20, of which two items measure perceived usefulness, five items measure perceived ease usage, three items measure critical mass, two items measure capability, two items measure intention to use and two items measure actual use. The description of finalized items are illustrated in Table 2.

Research Sampling

A convenient sampling was applied, in which the most easily accessible managers and employees in MOI were chosen. This is due to time constraints and difficulty in reaching the entire population of MOI. The total sample size was 170, while the valid returned questionnaires were 165 and thus the response rate was 97%, as it is illustrated in Table 3.

DATA ANALYSIS

Demographic Profile of Respondents

First Dimension: Gender

Figure 6 below shows the respondents' gender, in which 58% of the respondents were male, while 42% were female of the total number of respondents. This implies that the sample size of this research is approximately mixed of both gender.

Second Dimension: Age

Figure 7 below shows the percentage of respondents' age. Based on the analysis, it was found that 59% of respondents were between 25 - 35 years old, followed by 21% for the age group between 36 - 45 years old. However, only 11% of respondents were less than 25 years old and 9% of respondents were 46 years and above. This implies that the majority of respondents are young adults. However, still the questionnaire is consisted of a mixed age groups, which indicates that the sample of this study is of a varied age groups. This in turn assures true interpretation of answers and prevents biases.

Table 2. Operational definitions of variables

Variables	Measurement	Source
Perceived Usefulness (PU)	1. Using social media makes it easier to stay in touch.	Davis, 1986, 1989; Mathieson, 1991; Moore & Benbasat, 1991; Taylor & Todd, 1995; Venkatesh & Davis, 1996
	2. Using social media makes it easier to stay informed with my friends and family.	
Perceived Ease Usage (EU)	1. Social media is flexible to interact with.	
	2. Interaction with social media is clear and understandable.	
	3. It is easy to become skilled at using social media.	
	4. I find it easy to get social media to do what I want to do.	
	5. I find social media easy to use.	
Critical Mass (CM)	1. Social media is popular among my friends.	Rouibah & Abbas (2006)
	2. Most of my friends are on social media.	
	3. Most of my colleagues are on social media.	
Capability (CP)	1. Social media provides clear instructions for posting.	Rauniar et al. (2014)
	2. Images and videos can easily be downloaded or uploaded on social media.	
Intention to Use (IU)	1. I intend to use social media for communicating with others.	Davis, 1986, 1989; Mathieson, 1991; Moore & Benbasat, 1991; Taylor & Todd, 1995; Venkatesh & Davis, 1996
	2. I will continue to use social media for my social networking.	
Actual Use (AU)	1. How often per day do you visit your social media accounts?	
	2. How many hours do you spend on your social media accounts per day?	
Trustworthiness (TW)	1. I trust social media for my personal information on my profile.	Telzrow ey el. (2007); Fogels & Nehmad (2009)
	2. Social media provides security for everything I post.	
	3. I feel safe in everything I post in social media.	

Third Dimension: Educational Level

Figure 8 below represents educational level of the respondents. Based on the analysis, it was found that 45% of the respondents have Bachelor's degree, while only 3% of total respondents have a PhD degree. This implies that the majority of the respondents have the required knowledge and understanding in order to fill the questionnaire. Moreover, their responses were consistent and accurate and only few clarifications were provided to some of them.

Table 3. Response rate

Description	No. of Questionnaires
No. of Questionnaires Distributed	170
No. of Questionnaires Retrieved	165
Response Rate	97%

Fourth Dimension: Occupational Level

Figure 9 below represents the occupational level of respondents. Based on the analysis, it was found that the respondents were approximately divided equally, in which 52% of them were of supervisory level, while 48% of them were of non-supervisory level. This implies that the sample of this study is of different occupational levels. This in turn assures true explanation of answers and prevents biases.

Figure 6.

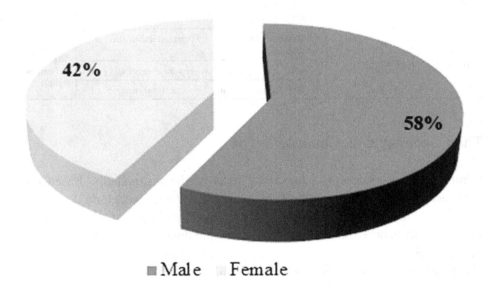

Gender Distribution of Respondents

42%

58%

■ Male ■ Female

Figure 7.

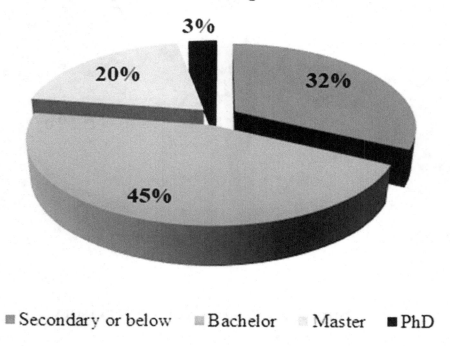

Educational Level of Respondents

■ Secondary or below ■ Bachelor ■ Master ■ PhD

Fifth Dimension: Years of Experience

Figure 10 below shows work experience of respondents in years. Based on the analysis, it is apparent that the majority of respondents have work experience between 5 to 10 years i.e., 41% and 25% have work experience between 11 to 15 years. However, those with work experience of 16 years and above constitute 16% of the total respondents. This implies that respondents have moderate work experience. They have been working within the Ministry for some time and their responses were based on what they have been experiencing at their work.

Scale Reliability Analysis

Cronbach's Alpha test was utilized in order to test the reliability of the research instrument. All returned questionnaires were included in the scale reliability. The overall scale reliability exceeded the minimum required Cronbach's alpha which

Figure 8.

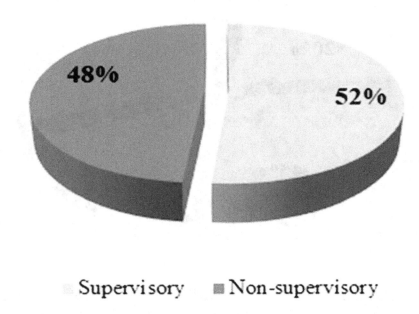

Occupational Level of Respondents

Supervisory   ■ Non-supervisory

is 0.70. This is an indication of a strong internal consistency among the variables' items. This implies that a respondent who intended to select a high score for one item of a variable also intended to select high scores for the others; similarly, a respondent who selected a low score for one item intended to select low scores for the other variable's items. Table 4 shows scale reliability analysis of the research instrument in this study:

Spearman's Correlation Analysis

Spearman's rank correlation coefficient is a nonparametric statistical measure of the strength of a relationship between paired data, in which the correlation ranges from -1 to 1 ($-1 \leq r_s \leq 1$).

Table 5 below represents the correlations among the variables as per the hypotheses. From the above table the following results are generated:

Figure 9.

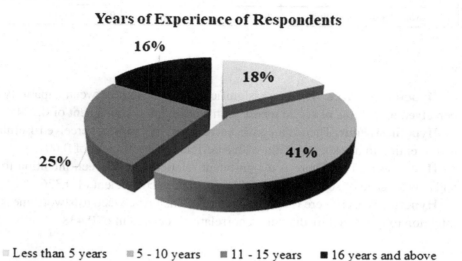

Years of Experience of Respondents

Less than 5 years   5 - 10 years   11 - 15 years   16 years and above

Hypothesis One: There is a significant relationship between perceived ease usage and Perceived Usefulness of social media with a correlation coefficient of 0.286.

Hypothesis Two: There is a significant relationship between critical mass and perceived usefulness of social media with a correlation coefficient of 0.334.

Figure 10.

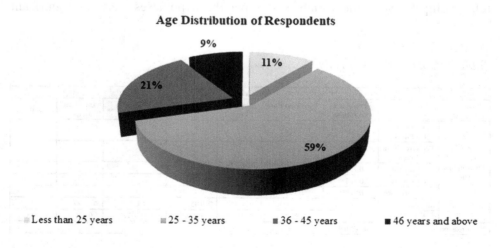

Age Distribution of Respondents

Less than 25 years   25 - 35 years   36 - 45 years   46 years and above

Table 4. Scale reliability analysis

	No. of Items	Cronbach's Alpha
Overall Scale Reliability	20	0.839

Hypothesis Three: There is a significant relationship between capability and perceived usefulness of social media with a correlation coefficient of 0.324.

Hypothesis Four: There is a significant relationship between perceived usefulness and intention to use social media with a correlation coefficient of 0.607.

Hypothesis Five: There is a significant relationship between intention to use and actual usage of social media with a correlation coefficient of 0.326.

Hypothesis Six: There is a significant relationship between trustworthiness and intention to use social media with a correlation coefficient of 0.438.

SOLUTIONS AND RECOMMENDATIONS

This study explained the impact of trustworthiness of social media on the intention to use it among employees in the Ministry of Interior, Kingdom of Bahrain, as a case study using the revised TAM model by (Rauniar, et al., 2014). For this purpose, the data was collected through questionnaires that were distributed to a convenient sample in the Ministry, in which the most easily accessible managers and employees were chosen. The research instrument was helpful to reach the objectives of the study and the results were accurate and provided proper understanding.

Based on the data collected through the questionnaire, it was found that the relationship between the variables - as per the hypotheses - are all significant

Table 5. Correlation analysis

		Correlations						
		Perceived Usefulness	Perceived Ease Usage	Critical Mass	Capability	Trustworthiness	Intention to Use	Actual Use
Spearman's rho	**Perceived Usefulness**	1.000						
	Perceived Ease Usage	0.286**	1.000					
	Critical Mass	0.334**	0.406**	1.000				
	Capability	0.324**	0.460**	0.413**	1.000			
	Trustworthiness	0.318**	0.181*	0.067	0.276**	1.000		
	Intention to Use	0.607**	0.404**	0.463**	0.453**	0.438**	1.000	
	Actual Use	0.247**	0.257**	0.201**	0.156*	0.183*	0.326**	1.000
** Correlation is significant at the level (2-tailed)								

positive relations. For instance, there is a significant positive relationship between trustworthiness and intention to use and between perceived usefulness and intention to use. This suggests that the higher the level of trust in social media, the higher will be the intentions to use it among employees in MOI. Similarly the higher the perceived usefulness of any given application, the higher will be the intentions to use it. Moreover, there is a significant positive relationship between perceived ease usage and perceived usefulness. With respect to the perceived ease usage, Bugawa & Mirzal (2017) have suggested that the Web 2.0 technologies offer a huge space for ease sharing experiences that could contribute to the reformation in the traditional learning concepts among users. Furthermore, critical mass is significantly related to perceived usefulness, in which MOI employees strongly believe that social media is popular among their friends and that most of their friends are using social media. This in turn makes it easier for them to stay in touch with their friends and family. In fact,

Rauniar, et al. (2014) have already mentioned that psychological concept of social influence is rooted from the assumption that a person's behavior is heavily influenced by the behavior and presence of others, and this what was founded among employees in MOI. Moreover, Bugawa (2016) demonstrated that the interactivity with peers through using Web 2.0 technologies is critical for promoting more engagement and communication and it is a powerful technological tool to enhance the user's learning experience. In fact, it is been stated that the use of social media amongst digital natives enhances a huge amount of informal learning to occur through the interaction with peers (Brown & Adler, 2008).

FUTURE RESEARCH DIRECTIONS

The study recommends the examination of the impact of security awareness on the usage of social media in public sector in Bahrain in future studies. In this study, the main challenge was the accessibility for data collection.

CONCLUSION

A case study was conducted in the Ministry of Interior, Kingdom of Bahrain to study the impact of trustworthiness of social media on the intention to use it among employees in the, using the revised TAM model by (Rauniar, et al., 2014). The study applied a quantitative method, in which the data was collected through questionnaires that were distributed to a convenient sample in the Ministry, thus the most easily accessible managers and employees were chosen. The research instrument was helpful to reach the objectives of the study and the results were accurate and provided proper understanding.

Through this study, it was found that the level of trust in the Ministry has a significant positive relation with the intention to use social media. Similarly, the intention to use social media and the actual usage were found to be significantly related.

In conclusion, it is apparent that the results of this study is well-matched with the previous literature including Rauniar, et al. (2014), which we have already adapted their model in this study. For instance, they have confirmed that in the context of social media, users may assess a given application or site based on its easiness and effectiveness in helping them accomplish their needs.

REFERENCES

Abbate, J. (1999). *Inventing the Internet (inside technology)*. Cambridge, MA: MIT Press.

Al-adawi, Z., Yousafzai, S., & Pallister, J. (2005, September). Conceptual model of citizen adoption of e-government. *The Second International Conference on Innovations in Information Technology*. 1-10.

Aloul, F. A. (2010). Information security awareness in UAE: A survey paper. In *2010 International Conference for Internet Technology and Secured Transactions* IEEE.

Alqudsi-ghabra, T. M., Al-Bannai, T., & Al-Bahrani, M. (2011). The Internet in the Arab Gulf Cooperation Council (AGCC): Vehicle of Change. *International Journal of Internet Science, 6*(1).

Anderson, C. (2006). *The Long Tail: How endless choice is creating unlimited demand*. London, UK: Random House Business Books.

Anderson, P. (2007). *What is Web 2.0? Ideas, technologies and implications for education*. Bristol: JISC.

Anhalt, K., Telzrow, C. F., & Brown, C. L. (2007). Maternal stress and emotional status during the perinatal period and childhood adjustment. *School Psychology Quarterly, 22*(1), 74–90. doi:10.1037/1045-3830.22.1.74

Bahrain ICT Shared Services. (2011). Retrieved from https://www.cisco.com/c/dam/en_us/about/ac79/docs/ps/Bahrain-Govt-SS_IBSG.pdf

Boyd, D. M., & Ellison, N. B. (2007). Social network sites: Definition, history, and scholarship. *Journal of Computer-Mediated Communication, 13*(1), 210–230. doi:10.1111/j.1083-6101.2007.00393.x

Brondsema, D., & Schamp, A. (2006). *Konfidi: trust networks using PGP and RDF*. Models of trust of the Web (MTW 06). WWW2006 Conference, Edinburgh, UK.

Bugawa, A. M., & Mirzal, A. (2017). The impact of the web 2.0 technologies on students' learning experience: Interactivity inside the classroom. *International Journal of Management and Applied Science., 3*(5), 46–50.

Bugawa, A. M., & Mirzal, A. (2018). The Impact of the Web 2.0 Technologies on the Learning Experience of Students in Higher Education: A Review. *International Journal of Management and Applied Science, 13*(3), 1–17.

Bugawa, A. M. M. (2016). *The impact of the interactivity of web 2.0 technologies on the learning experience of students in higher education* (Doctoral dissertation). Brunel University London.

Cameron, A. F., & Webster, J. (2005). Unintended consequences of emerging communication technologies: Instant messaging in the workplace. *Computers in Human Behavior, 21*(1), 85–103. doi:10.1016/j.chb.2003.12.001

Carlos Martins Rodrigues Pinho, J., & Soares, A. M. (2011). Examining the technology acceptance model in the adoption of social networks. *Journal of Research in Interactive Marketing, 5*(2/3), 116–129. doi:10.1108/17505931111187767

Chami, K. (2019). *FinTech in the Gulf Cooperation Council (GCC)*. Retrieved from https://gomedici.com/how-gulf-countries-are-embracing-fintech

Daft, R. L., & Lengel, R. H. (1986). Organizational information requirements, media richness and structural design. *Management Science, 32*(5), 554–571. doi:10.1287/mnsc.32.5.554

Davis, F. D. (1986). A technology acceptance model for empirically testing new end-user information systems. Cambridge, MA: Academic Press.

Davis, F. D. (1989). Perceived usefulness, perceived ease of use, and user acceptance of information technology. *Management Information Systems Quarterly, 13*(3), 319–340. doi:10.2307/249008

Davis, F. D., Bagozzi, R. P., & Warshaw, P. R. (1989). User acceptance of computer technology: A comparison of two theoretical models. *Management Science, 35*(8), 982–1003. doi:10.1287/mnsc.35.8.982

Fishbein, M., & Ajzen, I. (1975). *Belief, attitude, intention and behavior*. Academic Press.

Fogel, J., & Nehmad, E. (2009). Internet social network communities: Risk taking, trust, and privacy concerns. *Computers in Human Behavior*, *25*(1), 153–160. doi:10.1016/j.chb.2008.08.006

George, A. (2006). Things you wouldn't tell your mother. *New Scientist*, *191*(2569), 50–51. doi:10.1016/S0262-4079(06)60502-2

Ghannam, J. (2011). Social media in the Arab World: Leading up to the Uprisings of 2011. *Center for International Media Assistance, 3*(1), 1-44.

Gikas, J., & Grant, M. M. (2013). Mobile computing devices in higher education: Student perspectives on learning with cellphones, smartphones & social media. *The Internet and Higher Education*, *19*, 18–26. doi:10.1016/j.iheduc.2013.06.002

Igbaria, M., Parasuraman, S., & Baroudi, J. J. (1996). A motivational model of microcomputer usage. *Journal of Management Information Systems*, *13*(1), 127–143. doi:10.1080/07421222.1996.11518115

Klemperer, P. (2006). *Network Effects and Switching Costs: Two Short Essays for The New Palgrave. Working Paper Series*. Social Science Research Network.

Lee, Y., Kozar, K. A., & Larsen, K. R. (2003). The technology acceptance model: Past, present, and future. *Communications of the Association for Information Systems*, *12*(1), 50.

Liebowitz, S. J., & Margolis, S. (1994). Network Externality: An Uncommon Tragedy. *The Journal of Economic Perspectives*, *8*(2), 133–150. doi:10.1257/jep.8.2.133

Madden, M. (2010). Older adults and social media. *Pew Internet & American Life Project, 27*.

Mann, C. C. (2006). Spam+ Blogs= Trouble Splogs are the latest thing in online fraud-and they could smother the Net as we know it. *Wired, 14*(9), 104.

Manuel, C. (2013). *The Impact of the Internet on Society: A Global Perspective*. Retrieved from https://www.bbvaopenmind.com/en/articles/the-impact-of-the-internet-on-society-a-global-perspective/

Mathieson, K. (1991). Predicting user intentions: Comparing the technology acceptance model with the theory of planned behavior. *Information Systems Research*, *2*(3), 173–191. doi:10.1287/isre.2.3.173

Matthews, B. (2005). Semantic web technologies. *E-learning, 6*(6), 8.

Meeker, M. (2014). *Internet trends 2014-code conference.* Academic Press.

Merchant, G. (2009). Web 2.0, new literacies, and the idea of learning through participation. *English Teaching, 8*(3), 107–122.

Miniwatts Marketing Group. (2010). *World Internet Usage and Population Statistics.* Retrieved from https://www.internetworldstats.com/stats.htm

Moore, G. C., & Benbasat, I. (1991). Development of an instrument to measure the perceptions of adopting an information technology innovation. *Information Systems Research, 2*(3), 192–222. doi:10.1287/isre.2.3.192

Qasem, M., & Zolait, A. H. (2016). Determinants of Behavioral Intentions towards Using E-Government Services in the Kingdom of Bahrain. *International Journal of Computing and Digital Systems, 5*(04), 345–355. doi:10.12785/ijcds/050406

Rauniar, R., Rawski, G., Yang, J., & Johnson, B. (2014). Technology acceptance model (TAM) and Social media usage: An empirical study on Facebook. *Journal of Enterprise Information Management, 27*(1), 6–30. doi:10.1108/JEIM-04-2012-0011

Rogers, E. M. (1962). *Diffusion of Innovations.* New York, NY: Free Press.

Rouibah, K., & Abbas, H. (2006). A modified technology acceptance model for camera mobile phone adoption: development and validation. *ACIS 2006 Proceedings*, 13.

Seely Brown, J., & Adler, R. P. (2008). Open education, the long tail, and learning 2.0. *EDUCAUSE Review, 43*(1), 16–20.

Selman, Z., & Faiq, K. (2018). *Technology in the GCC.* Retrieved from https://www2.deloitte.com/eg/en/pages/about-deloitte/articles/transform-saudi-arabia/gcc-technology.html

Taylor, S., & Todd, P. A. (1995). Understanding information technology usage: A test of competing models. *Information Systems Research, 6*(2), 144–176. doi:10.1287/isre.6.2.144

Tim, O. (2005). *What is web 2.0? Design patterns and business models for the next generation of software.* Academic Press.

TRA Annual Report. (2017). Retrieved from http://www.tra.org.bh/media/document/TRA%20Annual%20Report%202017%20-%20English2.pdf

Van den Hooff, B., Groot, J., & de Jonge, S. (2005). Situational influences on the use of communication technologies: A meta-analysis and exploratory study. *The Journal of Business Communication, 42*(1), 4-27.

Venkatesh, V., & Davis, F. D. (1996). A model of the antecedents of perceived ease of use: Development and test. *Decision Sciences, 27*(3), 451–481. doi:10.1111/j.1540-5915.1996.tb01822.x

Venkatesh, V., & Davis, F. D. (2000). A theoretical extension of the technology acceptance model: Four longitudinal field studies. *Management Science, 46*(2), 186–204. doi:10.1287/mnsc.46.2.186.11926

Zolait, A. H. S., Al-Anizi, R. R., & Ababneh, S. (2014). User awareness of Social media security: The public sector framework. *International Journal of Business Information Systems, 17*(3), 261–282. doi:10.1504/IJBIS.2014.064973

Chapter 13
Cybersecurity:
Cybercrime Prevention in Higher Learning Institutions

Adel Ismail Al-Alawi
 https://orcid.org/0000-0003-0775-4406
University of Bahrain, Bahrain

Arpita A. Mehrotra
Royal University for Women, Bahrain

Sara Abdulrahman Al-Bassam
 https://orcid.org/0000-0003-0094-6149
The Social Development Office of His Highness the Kuwait Prime Minister's Diwan, Kuwait

ABSTRACT

The internet has revolutionized the way people communicate, how they manage their business, and even how they conduct their studies. Organizations can conduct meetings virtually and store all their data online. With this convenience, however, comes the risk of cybercrime (CC). Some of the world's most renowned organizations have found themselves having to incur huge recovery costs after falling prey to CC. Higher learning institutions' databases are increasingly falling victim to CCs, owing to the vast amounts of personal and research data they harbor. Despite this, the area of CCs in learning institutions remains understudied. This chapter seeks to identify how CC is manifested in such institutions and the specific cybersecurity measures that stakeholders could use to minimize their exposure to the same. The qualitative case study was designed to explore the research questions, and collected data through semistructured interviews. The findings showed hacking, phishing, and spoofing as the most common manifestations of cybercrime in higher learning institutions.

DOI: 10.4018/978-1-7998-2418-3.ch013

INTRODUCTION

The Internet is a part of daily living in the world today. Activities that traditionally required people to move physically across geographical areas are now conducted conveniently over the Internet. People can communicate easily and cheaply with relatives and friends miles away without the need to visit or travel physically. Similarly, banking activities, access to academic material, government services, and general data transfer have been made easier with the evolution of the Internet. The Internet has revolutionized the way things are done, opening up capabilities that would otherwise have never been realized. Unfortunately, these new capabilities have come at a cost; despite opening up opportunities for progress and prosperity, the Internet has brought new risks to nations, organizations, and individuals.

One of the prominent risks which are associated with Internet usage is cybercrime, namely crime executed with the help of electronic systems (Al-Alawi, 2014; Broadhurst, Grabsoky, Alazab, & Chon, 2014; Okeshola & Adeta, 2013). In order to protect themselves from cybercrime, nations, organizations, and individuals are pushed to put in place cybersecurity measures. This is mainly because, once a computer is connected to another device, it is described as "vulnerable" (Al-Alawi & Abdelgadir, 2006). Developing effective measures, however, requires a succinct understanding of the current landscape of cybercrime, including its nature, causes, and predisposing factors. This chapter focuses on cybercrime within higher learning institutions. It provides insight into the factors that predispose such institutions to cybercrime, the ways in which the same is manifested, and the measures that could be used to minimize the risk of exposure. For clarification purposes, the term "cybercrime" is integral to this text and will be taken to indicate the various efforts that institutions could use to secure their networks. Nevertheless, the precepts the authors present herein will provide guidance to policymakers in learning institutions on how to develop effective cybersecurity mechanisms to protect both data and students.

Problem Statement

Recent incidents depict higher learning institutions as attractive troves for cybercriminals. Several renowned institutions have fallen prey to cybercrime, in recent years, in the United States and beyond. In 2015, for instance, Penn State University fell victim to a data breach that affected the personal information of close to 18,000 students (Harris & Hammargren, 2016). In the same year, Harvard University had its systems in eight administrative offices and colleges compromised, although it is still not clear exactly what information the hackers were after. One of North Dakota University's databases was hacked, compromising the social security numbers and identities of over 300, 000 alumni. A similar breach was reported at the Indiana University in the same year, compromising the social security information, addresses, and names of close to 146,000 students. Maryland University also fell victim to a data breach in 2014, where the identification numbers, birth dates, and names of over 310,000 employees and students was compromised.

A report by the Ponemon Institute (2015) revealed that, in 2014, educational institutions in the U.S. incurred costs of close to $8 million in cybercrime-related incidents. Studies indicate that colleges and universities are attractive cybercrime targets, because they harbor huge amounts of sensitive student information, including health and financial data. Moreover, university databases harbor huge chunks of research data from which hackers could benefit by selling them (Okeshola & Adeta, 2013).

Despite the growing number of data breaches in higher learning institutions, the area remains severely understudied. Most studies have focused on cybercrime in general, creating a knowledge gap in the area of educational institutions. This chapter complements the existing literature by delving into the understudied area of cybercrime in higher learning institutions. It analyzes the nature of cybercrime in these institutions and the measures that could be taken to promote cybersecurity.

The research questions directing the chapter are:

1. What is the nature of cybercrime in higher learning institutions?
2. What cybersecurity measures can institutions put in place to reduce their exposure to cybercrime?

The chapter aims at realizing the following objectives:

1. Increasing knowledge on the ways in which cybercrime is manifested in higher learning institutions.
2. Investigating the security measures that institutions could use to reduce their exposure to the threat of cybercrime.

The chapter will be a source of insight for policymakers in higher learning institutions. Its findings will help reduce the prevalence of cybercrime and its associated costs in these institutions.

The chapter uses the qualitative case study approach. The authors propose the ABC University, which has been recently identified as home to the leading cybersecurity program in higher learning institutions, and the XYZ University as case studies. The researchers conducted a qualitative interview with the ABC's Network Services head to obtain insight into the ways in which cybercrime is manifested in the institution and the measures that the institution's management has put in place to safeguard against cybercrime. Also, the authors carried out document reviews, particularly in the cybersecurity program of XYZ University, as they were unable to physically visit the institution for data collection. They transcribed the answers they had obtained from the interview, analyzed them alongside those they had obtained from the review, and presented them in prose as the study findings.

LITERATURE REVIEW

This section reviews the literature in the area of cybercrime. Much has been studied and said about cybercrime. However, this review focuses on three areas that the authors deem most relevant to the chapter, namely the theoretical background of cybercrime, the drivers of cybercrime, and the types/tools of cybercrime. Literature focusing specifically on higher learning institutions is limited. Therefore, the review is not limited to articles touching on higher learning institutions.

The Theoretical Underpinning of Cybercrime

As the globe grows into digitization, it approaches more attacks. According to Fellows (2019), institutions of all size face day-to-day, if not every-minute, cyber interruptions, "as criminals, hacktivists, and hostile nations seek to profit from poor IT [information technology] security practices" Due to fast technology transformations, universities are accelerating their digital footsteps. Fellows indicated that a study by VMware and Dell EMC advises further work is needed, if higher educations are not going "to be easy ways to access national secrets." She added that 25% of top IT management who had studied at United Kingdom's higher education considered their security systems and defense study may have already been breached, and about 53% indicated that cyberattack on their university had managed "to research ending up in foreign hands" (par.). The targeted incidents in scientific (54%), medical (50%), economic (37%), and defense research (33%) were top of the list. About 50% of the respondents acknowledged that a lack investment in IT is pushing the necessity for more influential cybersecurity. Furthermore, the top IT management stated that cyberattack on their study data can cause critical financial damage for their university.

Gearhart, Abbiatti, and Miller's (2019) distributed questionnaires to the presidents of 150 higher education institutions in the USA to resolve the extent of top university management's participation in cybersecurity. The survey findings indicated that the board of cybersecurity strategy was mainly delivered to the top information systems or business managers, that main anxieties are "about the safety of data related to financial, student, faculty, and donor affairs," and about 50% of the higher education top management, and that about half of college leaders reveal cybersecurity correlated concerns two to six times a week. Besides, Gearhart et al. recommended research on how decisions are made about cybersecurity priorities, as well as how to best provide training for better cybersecurity decision-making.

Beyond the United States, in 2011, the Hawaii University incurred approximately $550,000 in restoration costs after a database was hacked, compromising the credit card details of over 90,000 students (Harris & Hammargren, 2016). An incident of similar magnitude was reported at the New England Elite University, in the UK, in 2015.

Chapman (2019) stated that, throughout 2018, over 1000 distributed denial of service (DDoS) attacks were identified, in contradiction of 241 different UK education and research institutions. Analyzing the timings of these attacks has indicated to assume that "many of them are 'insider' attacks launched by disgruntled students" or employees.

Raman, Kabir, Hejazi, and Aggarwal (2016) indicated that currently universities are reached at the top five industries to face unlimited numbers of cyberattacks, due to the huge amount of data of their repositories. Figure1 shows the significant rise in the number of cyberattacks on higher education institutions.

Figure 1 illustrates that the highest percentage of data breaches in universities is hacking and malware (36%), and unintended disclosure is the second to the highest (30%).

Raman et al. (2016) reported the cases of a few universities which had been hacked around the globe. The first case was King Saud University, in Saudi Arabia. In January 2012, an anonymous hacker attacked the university's official Web site, hacked 812 end-users' accounts, and dropped their contents (e.g., e-mail addresses, mobile phone

Figure 1. Data breaches in higher education institutions

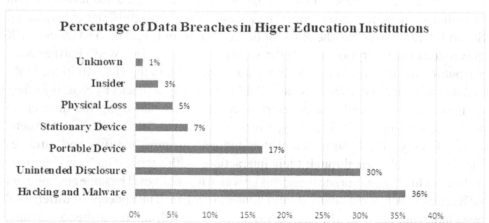

259

numbers, and passwords) on a file-sharing site. The second case was University of Delaware, in U.S. In July 2013, the cyberattack target was on the university's computer system. The hacker exploited a vulnerability in Web-based software Delaware University used, and stole and exposed the identities of more than 72,000 users (i.e., past and currents workers' names, address, and Social Security numbers. The third case was University of Maryland, U.S. In March 2014, the cyberattack aimed the network, compromising 287,580 data of the faculty members, students' records, university employees, and affiliated people. The database breach distracted all who had been issued a university ID cards between 1998 and February 2014, and the network was out of services for 3 days. The fourth case was Pennsylvania State University, U.S. In May 2015, two complicated cyberattacks (one of them was from foreign countries) aimed the Engineering College and threaten server holding data relating to 18,000 users that were undetected for someday. The fifth case included six Japanese universities. In July 2015, the networks of these Japanese universities originated a real-time cyberattack affecting 360 records, e-mail addresses, and ID numbers, which the hackers leaked from one university and linked to the Web site administrators of all other universities. The last case was Concordia University, in Canada. In March 2016, several library standing express workstations were breached by detecting Keylogger devices in the libraries. Keylogger devices can capture end-users data, such as login passwords and information. Furthermore, the access to the library's computers was obtainable for general public use for about 10 minutes a day.

Also, according to another source ("Yale University revealed," 2018), in June 2018, the IT team of Yale University, U.S., discovered a cyber breach of log during the regular servers security check. The hackers had been able to obtain access to the database to steal sensitive information. An article in *The Guardian* (Press Association, 2019) reported Lancaster University students' data and other records were stolen in cyberattacks, and retrieved student applicants for 2019-2020 and false bills sent in malicious hack to the students. The access consisted in phishing cyberattacks. Storm (2017) stated that the Russian hacker Rasputin breached 63 U.S. and UK universities before trying "to sell the stolen data on the dark web" Furthermore, Rasputin similarly attacked 35 universities, namely 24 in the U.S., 10 in the U.K., and one in India. The hacker conducted all of these cyberattacks by SQL injection.

Researchers contend that cybercrime can be explained using the differential association theory (Holt, Strumsky, Smirnova, & Kilger, 2012; Okeshola & Adeta, 2013). Cresey (1954) sustained that individuals acquire motives and attitudes for criminal behavior through their interactions with others. One's environment influences his/her culture and the norms by which he/she lives. The same environment influences which norms individuals choose to violate. The concept of differential association implies that, when an individual interacts with others and the community, he/she encounters elements that encourage him/her to violate the law and others that discourage him/her from doing so (Al-Alawi & Hafedh, 2006; Okeshola & Adeta, 2013). One is inclined to acquire criminal tendencies, if the elements that encourage criminality exceed those that discourage it (Okeshola & Adeta, 2013). This view supports Holt et al.'s (2012) idea that one is more likely to display criminal behavior, if his/her environment and social circle favor criminality, and if he/she perceives the gains of violation as exceeding those of compliance. Similarly, when one's legal (pro-social) influences exceed his/her criminal influences, he/she is less likely to display criminal behavior. The authors agree that differential association is more prevalent in socioeconomically disadvantaged areas, which tend to encourage resistance towards those in authority and, by extension, the law.

Okeshola and Adeta (2013) explained the mechanism by which an individual acquires these tendencies. According to these authors, the communication process forms the basis of behavioral acquisition. If an individual repeatedly watches as others in his/her social circle engage in criminal acts, he/she, in time, learns this criminal behavior. Individuals learn the drive, techniques, motives, and attitudes for committing crime. In the process, their ideas and opinions are rationalized such that they no longer perceive criminal actions as wrong.

Applying the differential association principle to cybercrime, the authors opine that cybercriminals learn their criminal acts from their environments and their daily interactions with others (Holt et al. 2012; Okeshola & Adeta, 2013). Cybercriminals are usually tech-savvy, knowledgeable, and very intelligent individuals. Their social circles are composed of individuals who share the same technological interests and who execute most of their interactions in the form of electronic communications. Initially, the individual may not have the inclination to engage in cybercrime as he/she perceives the same as an act of fraud. As he/she repeatedly sees others engage in the same, however, his/her opinions are rationalized and he/she is then influenced into performing acts of cybercrime.

Drivers of Cybercrime

Researchers have given diverse perspectives on the factors that drive individuals to engage in cybercrime. In the article *The Economics of Cybercrime,* Kshetri (2010) stated that people engage in cybercrime because of the economic attractiveness of the expected results. The author posited that economic disadvantages are a significant driver of cybercrime. Okeshola and Adeta (2013) held a similar view, expressing that economically disadvantaged people are more likely to engage in cybercrime, either because they perceive the laws as oppressive and blame the same for their poor conditions or because they view the target as being economically attractive. This explains why the rich are more likely than the poor to be victims of cybercrime. Indeed, Okeshola and Adeta (2013) conducted an empirical study on sampled perpetrators of cybercrime and showed poverty to be a crucial driver of cybercrime, with 86.5% of respondents identifying the factor as the leading motivator behind their engagement. However, the literature evidences that poverty is only a factor during the initial engagement. Once they have established themselves in the crime, cybercriminals live more flamboyant lifestyles and only engage in the crime to maintain their lavish lifestyles.

Researchers have faulted legislation for the high prevalence of cybercrime in the society today (Oh & Lee, 2014; Okeshola & Adeta, 2013). According to Oh and Lee (2014), when the legal framework is weak and does not advance punishment to cybercrime as it should, the propensity to engage in it is relatively high. The authors contended that countries need to make cybercrime more costly as a way of discouraging people from taking part in such acts. Seventy-four percent of the respondents in Okeshola and Adeta's (2013) study indicated that they perceived the law as being weak and unable to adequately punish cybercriminals. The society is also identified as a driver of cybercrime. Researchers opine that the society needs to stop idolizing cybercriminals. In most cases, cybercriminals are rated higher than other criminals and exalted, when they should be criminalized. Okeshola and Adeta suggest that societies increase the stigmatization levels of cybercriminals as a way of discouraging engagement.

In another attack to society, the above authors express that the tendency to celebrate wealth without questioning its source encourages individuals to engage in criminal activities, including cybercrime. This is a more prominent factor in developing economies, where a majority of the population is poor and the few rich individuals are idolized and portrayed as positive role models, without critically investigating the source of their wealth. The authors present the views of one respondent, who is also a cybercriminal, and who blames the tendency to celebrate wealth for his indulgent in cybercrime. In this respondent's view, politicians who misappropriate public funds are called upon to launch community projects and are held in high-esteem, and the society shows no intent of criminalizing them for their actions. Such attitudes portray the society as one which treats crime leniently for the wealthy. Individuals are thus inclined to engage in crime to amass wealth.

Peer pressure is another prominent driver of cybercrime, especially among younger criminals (Dashora, 2011). The famous Bal Bharati incident in Delhi, India, where a teenager was incarcerated for creating a pornographic Web site, offers a perfect example. Following intense interrogations, the court established that the delinquent had acted in response to constant harassment from his peers. Studies have further established that boys are more susceptible to this kind of influence than girls (Ang & Goh, 2010; den Hamer, & Konijn2015; Schneider, O'donnell, Stueve & Coulter, 2012)

Tools of Cybercrime

This subsection illustrates the technologies that criminals use to execute cybercrime. Four cybercrime tools are common across the literature: E-mail bombs, password crackers, and botnets (Goodman, 2015; Loundy, 2003; Snail, 2009).

E-Mail Bombs

E-mail bombs are identified as one of the most commonly used cybercrime tools. In this case, the perpetrator sends huge numbers of e-mails to his/her victim's mailbox to the extent that the capacity of the mailbox is exhausted. Consequently, the victim, who can either be an individual or an organization, is unable to access and read his/her/its legitimate e-mails. Serious e-mail bombing cases could paralyze an organization's entire system. The hackers' intention is to shut down the victim's Web site, network, or operating system (Snail, 2009).

As Loundy (2003) indicated, one of the most prominent incidents of e-mail bombing was that where the Tamil guerrilla group attacked the Sri Lankan Embassy's mailbox. Furthermore, they identified several indications of an e-mail flood: Syslog entries, service denial, connectivity losses, and network connection overloading and advises, which, in order to face this type of attack, the user could filter by spamming all e-mails coming from the attacker's IP address. This would address the problem, if the attacker employs a single IP address. Otherwise, the victim needs to use proxy servers, which identify malware and messages from IP addresses which are deemed suspicious and then filters the same by predetermined rules, before sending them to the clients' computers.

Password Crackers

Users who forget the passwords to their networks or computers can use password crackers to identify them (Vijayan, Joy, & Suchithra, 2014). Password crackers also present opportunities for people to gain unauthorized access to networks and computers that limit public access. Password crackers can either use dictionary searches or brute forces to identify unknown passwords (EC-Council, 2016). The dictionary search technique requires the password cracker to search the password dictionary word-by-word, in an attempt to identify the right password. Conversely, the brute force involves running through character combinations of a specified length until the right combination for the computer is identified. More advanced programs allow crackers to make searches for hybrids of both numbers and dictionary entries. Vijayan et al. (2014) posited that these programs can be helpful in networks that require users' passwords to combine numbers and letters.

In Okeshola and Adeta's (2013) study on sampled cybercriminals, 349 of the 400 respondents reported that they had used password crackers to gain unauthorized access to networks. These statistics supported Vijayan et al.'s position on the prominence of password cracking as a tool for executing cybercrime.

The literature identifies several measures that individuals and institutions could use to minimize the threat password crackers pose. Vijayan et al. suggested the use of complex passwords, perhaps containing both uppercase and lowercase letters, special symbols, and numbers. The authors further advised that network users make their passwords fairly long and change the same frequently (EC-Council, 2016; Vijayan et al., 2014). Alternatively, users could use Syskey to keep their networks secure.

Botnets

The term "botnet" is derived from the combination of two words, namely RobotNetwork. A botnet represents compromised computers in a network capable of being controlled remotely by a cybercriminal. The individual's compromised computers are referred to as drones or zombies. The attacker controls the zombies through Internet-sent commands. Communication between the attacker's computer and the zombies/bots is achieved through a command-and-control computer, communications channels, and a remote control (Wilson, 2008). DDos attacks and e-mail spamming are common forms of botnet attacks (Whitman & Mattors, 2010).

The literature identifies several security measures that organizations and individuals could use to protect themselves and their networks from botnet attacks. Whitman and Mattors (2010) suggested the use of updated antispyware and antivirus software. The authors advised users to make use of software that update themselves to remove viruses automatically. As a security measure, users need to set their operating systems in such a way that they can automatically download and install security updates (Al-Alawi,Al-Kandari & Abdel-Razek 2016; Wilson, 2008). Also, users need to keep their firewalls turned on as a way of denying hackers access. Firewalls increase network security by blocking communications from sources which are not authorized by the user. Whitman and Mattors (2010) stated that users of broadband need to particularly enable firewall activity. Users of MacOS and Windows do not have to install firewalls, as these operating systems have the same built-in. Users only need to ensure that the same is turned on.

Other proposed security measures include turning off one's computer when not in use and verifying the security of e-mail attachments before downloading them. Hackers cannot launch their attacks if their target victim is not online. Users are advised to only download files from trusted sites that have been declared safe to use and visit (Al-Alawi & Hafedh 2006; Whitman & Mattors, 2010). Programs such as SiteAdvisor allow users to verify the status of sites before downloading files.

This review shows that cybercrime is a richly studied area. There are studies focusing on the causes and types of cybercrime, as well as the cybersecurity measures that victims could put in place to minimize the inherent risk. However, most of these studies have taken a general approach, with very little focus on specific organizations. Studies focusing on cybercrime, particularly in higher learning institutions, are almost nonexistent. This chapter addresses this knowledge gap. The research intent is comparing the general precepts the authors presented in this review with the data they collected on the ground to determine how the two compare. More specifically, the aim is to identify the differences and similarities between the general population's cybercrime and cybersecurity measures and those higher learning institutions use.

METHODOLOGY

This section covers the research procedures the authors used in seeking answers to the research questions. It provides details on the research design, sampling techniques, the research instrument, data collection techniques, and data analysis procedures. The authors determined the research questions directing the chapter as:

1. What is the nature of cybercrime in higher learning institutions?
2. What cybersecurity measures can institutions put in place to reduce their exposure to cybercrime?

Research Procedures

The researchers visited ABC University for the interview with the head of the Networking Department. They had been sought permission to conduct the interview through written correspondence three weeks before its date and had made follow-ups a week before the scheduled date to confirm the respondent's availability. They conducted the interview at the respondent's office within the university, based on an interview guide (Table 1).

The authors selected ABC University as the reference point for this chapter, owing to its high-standing reputation in cybersecurity.

The researchers conducted a review on XYZ University's cybersecurity program. These materials were largely available online. The search criteria the authors used to identify relevant materials was "XYZ University cybersecurity program." They compiled relevant materials from sites they deemed credible. The decision to use document review was driven by resource limitations that made it impossible for the researchers to visit both institutions for interviews.

Table 1. Study interview guide

Demographic Information
 1. What is your networking background?
 2. How long have you served as a network administrator at the University?
 3. What would you identify as your success factors given the University's high ranking in the area of cybersecurity?
Information Related to the Research Questions
 1. What definition do you think best describes:
   a. Cybercrime?
   b. Cybersecurity?
 2. What cybercrime threats have you encountered working in the networking department at the University?
 3. What recovery and preventive measures did you take afterward?
 4. What measures do you take to safeguard your networks and databases from cybercrime?
 5. What structural frameworks do you have in place in terms of cybersecurity?
 6. How many times have you encountered internal cybercrime threats since you started working at the University?
 7. How many times have you encountered external threats?
 8. How did you manage these threats?
 9. How much does the University generally spend on cybersecurity every year?
 10. What areas do you think educational institutions need to improve on when it comes to cybersecurity?
 11. What factors do you regard as being significant drivers of cybercrime in the society today?
 12. What criteria would you use to assess the eligibility of a suspicious e-mail?
 13. Do you think cybercrime is as significant an issue in higher learning institutions as the literature and media portray?
 14. How do you protect your system and network from virus attacks?
 15. How does your department protect itself from botnet attacks?
 16. Do you have any measures in place to control the strength of users' passwords within your network?
 17. What factors do you think make it easy or difficult to crack someone's password?
 18. As the head of one of the nation's most successful cybersecurity programs; what advice would you give to other universities whose run has not been as successful?

In this chapter the authors adopted a qualitative approach for two fundamental reasons. First, qualitative approaches bring out the hidden meanings that people attach to events and experiences that they encounter in life (Bogdan & Biklen, 2003). Such techniques help to uncover the hidden meanings that individuals attach to phenomena and are thus preferred in studies that are of an exploratory nature. The open-ended nature of the research questions guiding this chapter supported the choice of qualitative techniques. According to Creswell and Creswell (2017), open-ended research questions begin with "what" or "how" and are best tackled using qualitative techniques that do not restrict respondents' answers to specific predetermined categories.

Secondly, qualitative techniques allow for the extraction of thought processes and feelings that may not be uncovered using conventional approaches (Strauss & Corbin, 1998). This chapter sought to obtain the lived experiences and perceptions of university staff who are tasked with reducing the risk of cybercrime. Limiting questionnaires would not effectively bring out the participants' perceptions and attitudes.

Research Instrument

The authors used qualitative case studies to gain an understanding of the phenomenon under investigation. They selected the two universities, namely the XYZ University and the ABC University, as case studies owing to their high-ranking reputations in the area of cybersecurity and based on their potential to contribute to the realization of the study objectives (Maxwell, 2005).

The interview guide in Table 1 was the primary data collection instrument for the chapter. The guide was composed of open-ended questions touching on the respondents' demographic details and their experiences with cybercrime incidents and cybersecurity measures at the institution. The open-ended questions sought to give respondents the opportunity to give open responses to the interviewer's questions (Merriam, 2002).

Sample Size

The sample consisted of two universities. The small sample size was informed by time constraints as well as resource limitations, which made it difficult to visit the data collection points. The small sample may not adequately represent the population of number of universities and colleges. All the same, it suffices because the chapter's aim is not to make generalizations about the population, but to increase the audience's understanding of the phenomenon under study.

Data Collection

The authors collected data through semistructured interviews and document reviews. Resource limitations impeded to physically conduct interviews in both universities. ABC University document used to obtain data from the XYZ University. The authors obtained the documents they reviewed from the universities' databases and Web site.

Two reasons supported the authors to use interviews. First, interviews present an opportunity to understand what is in the respondents' mind (Merriam, 2002). They help the researchers form an opinion from those things that they cannot observe. In this case, obtaining the interviewees' hidden attitudes towards cybercrime was crucial, as it helped to build a case for which there is need to address this issue. Secondly, interviews allow for data triangulation–the verification of data obtained from other sources—and this increases the study's credibility (Merriam, 2002).

For this chapter, the researchers interviewed only one participant, namely the ABC's Network Support Department head. This could be identified as a key informant, given his knowledge and vast experience at the university, spanning over 10 years. The interview was conducted at the participant's office within the university.

The participant allowed to audio-record the interview as a way of increasing accuracy during the transcription process (Merriam, 2002). In line with Merriam's (2002) suggestions, it was keen to explain the aim of the research, the expected benefits, and the element of voluntary participation to the interviewee, at the very onset.

Data Analysis

The researchers used Creswell and Creswell's (2017) six-step framework to analyze the gathered data. In the first step, they transcribed and stored electronically the data which were stored in the audio-recorder and the notes from the reviewed documents. The second step involved familiarizing with the data by reading through to obtain a general perspective of the ideas and opinions therein. In the third step, they organzed the data into categories based on similarities in the ideas being conveyed. They grouped together, in the same category in preparation for coding, sentences or paragraphs advancing the same idea. The fourth step consisted in assigning codes to these categories and using the assigned codes to identify consistent themes. The researchers organized the themes into a general description. In the fifth step, they put the themes together into a qualitative narrative, in such a way that the findings flowed in a logical sequence. The final step involved interpreting the data to make meaning and draw inferences. at the authors analyzed the data from a theoretical perspective, as Creswell and Creswell (2017) advised. Thus, the interpretation of the data was informed by the researchers' understanding of the topic following the literature review that they had conducted in the early stages of the research.

Limitations and Delimitations

The main limitation of the study is that the authors were able to collect interview data, which was the main basis for the developed findings, only from a single departmental head and could not consider insight from other relevant personnel, such as junior network operators, who deal with cybercrime issues first-hand, on a daily basis. The departmental head's role is more supervisory than practical, and there is the risk that the related findings may not be applicable to similar contexts. Secondly, since the data the researchers obtained from the interview were dependent primarily on the interviewee, the information may be limited to his or her own experiences and perceptions, which may be different from those of other personnel.

A core weakness of the study was its limited scope to only two case studies. It is not possible to speculate, therefore, that the findings would be similar to universities in other localities. Future studies could replicate this research with a larger sample size and more participants to see whether the findings would be consistent.

RESULTS AND DISCUSSION

RQ1: What Is the Nature of Cybercrime in Higher Learning Institutions?

The study found hacking, phishing, and spoofing to be the most prevalent manifestations of cybercrime in higher learning institutions. Hacking is the unauthorized break-in into a protected network or system with the aim of installing malware, or destroying, changing or stealing information (EC-Council, 2016). Hackers are skilled and knowledgeable about operating systems and can gain access to their target system in several ways, including using password crackers, network sniffers, through virus dissemination, and social engineering. Password cracking involves using brainstorming (brute force) or password dictionaries to identify unknown passwords, and thereby gain unauthorized access to an institution's database.

Also, commonplace is the strategy of disseminating a virus, usually Trojan Horse, to the target computer network. Trojan Horse works by recording all of the victim's keystrokes on his/her computer, network or database. Through Trojan, a hacker illegally obtains and records crucial information about the victim, including his/her credit card numbers and account passwords. Hacking through social engineering also came out as a common manifestation of cybercrime in educational institutions. This form involves contacting unsuspecting employees within the institution and tricking them to divulge crucial information. Finally, hackers can make use of packet sniffers, which allow for the interception of logging traffic as it moves across the network.

Phishing is another way through which cybercrime is manifested in higher learning institutes. It involves using e-mail to trick one's victim to provide his/her personal details. The spoofing technique is also common. In this case, the attacker imitates one of his/her clients' e-mail headers to make them believe that it came from a different person and duping them to provide sensitive. Many phishing incidents have been reported, so the significance of user awareness, technical measurements, laws, and legislation has been portrayed in governments (Al-Alawi, 2014; Al-Alawi et al., 2016).

Other cybercrime acts, such as cyber defamation, cyberstalking, cyber defamation, cyber identity theft, software piracy, and credit card fraud, though common in the case of the general population, are not common in learning institutions. Administrators and institution heads need to target their cybersecurity efforts towards those forms of cybercrime that are relevant to learning institutions. Targeted approaches are deemed to work more effectively than umbrella cybersecurity solutions.

RQ2: What Cybersecurity Measures Can Institutions Put in Place to Reduce Their Exposure to Cybercrime?

The two institutions the authors investigated in this study propose the best practice of targeting different forms of cybercrime uniquely, rather than devising an umbrella solution without first understanding which of the various forms of cybercrime are prevalent in one's institution. In order to safeguard their networks against hacking, institutions can take several measures. First, they could adopt the use of Syskey, which is a feature on Windows that provide encryption to a field. Syskey secures data stored in files, making it impossible for attackers to copy the information therein.

The researchers found ABC University offers its staff training opportunities on password development and maintenance. Other institutions could take up this strategy. In order to make users' passwords more secure, the ABC required all its network users to have passwords that incorporate the letters of the alphabet (both uppercase and lowercase), special symbols, and numbers. Moreover, passwords need to be kept fairly long changed regularly, and must not be constructed using the subject's identifying elements, such as their age, names, or telephone numbers.

In order to minimize the effect of viruses and dangerous malware, both the ABC and XYZ Universities offer regular trainings to students and staff on how to enable firewalls and other security measures, and how to verify the safety of Web sites before downloading files using software. Staff and students also receive regular trainings on how to detect cyber-attacks through common indicators, such as digital signature and malicious Web sites. The institutions further implement conveniently designed reporting mechanisms, in addition to educating individual members on how to use proxy servers and intrusion detection systems to block IP addresses that look suspicious.

Institutions need to put up effective structural mechanisms for dealing with cybercrime threats. However, this alone is not sufficient. Equal importance needs to be placed on the aspect of training and continuous education to ensure that members remain up-to-date in the wake of changing threats.

CONCLUSION AND RECOMMENDATIONS

As the popularity and usage of the Internet increases, the risk of cybercrime also rises. Some of the world's greatest companies have found themselves falling prey to cybercrime and losing millions in recovery costs. One area that has suffered greatly as a consequence of the increasing prominence of cybercrime is that of higher education. Higher education institutions have been victims of cybercrime and continue to be attractive targets, owing to the large quantities of research and personal data they handle. Despite this, the area of cybercrime in these institutions remains severely understudied. This study sought to identify the ways in which cybercrime manifests itself in higher learning institutions and specific cybersecurity strategies that institutions could use to counter it. Guided by the literature review and findings from the two case studies, the authors make the following recommendations:

1. That higher learning institutions conduct needs assessments to identify the cyber threats that pose the greatest challenges to their institutions. This will help them develop target-based as opposed to umbrella interventions for minimizing their exposure to cybercrime.
2. Both institutions put in place adequate structural mechanisms, such as antivirus software, firewalls, and verification software such as Site Advisor, which help users verify the safety of Web sites and downloaded files.
3. Institutions complement structural programs with trainings and continuous education on how to identify a cyber-attack, develop a strong password, and how to use the available mechanisms to respond to the same.
4. Institutions design their networks in a way that compels them to have strong passwords, perhaps combining numbers, special symbols, and letters to make cracking difficult. Systems could also be designed to issue regular prompts (e.g., once every month) that encourage users to change their passwords for security purposes.
5. Institutions could have the screensavers on their computers advocating for cybersecurity and educating users on the strategies cybercriminals use as well as measures that they (i.e., users) could take to safeguard themselves and the larger network from the same.
6. Higher learning institutions have to carry out continuous awareness campaigns to update and educate employees about the importance of cybersecurity (Al-Alawi et al., 2016).

REFERENCES

Al-Alawi, A. I. (2014). Cybercrimes, computer forensics, and their impact on business climate: Bahrain status. *Journal of Business and Management*, 8(3), 139–156.

Al-Alawi, A. I., & Abdelgadir, M. (2006). An empirical study of attitudes and opinions of computer crimes: A comparative study between U.K. and the Kingdom of Bahrain. *Journal of Computational Science, 2*(3), 229–235. doi:10.3844/jcssp.2006.229.235

Al-Alawi, A. I., Al-Kandari, S. M. H., & Abdel-Razek, R. H. (2016). Evaluation of information systems security awareness in higher education: An empirical study of Kuwait University. *Journal of Innovation & Business Best Practice.* doi:10.5171/2016.329374

Al-Alawi, A. I., & Hafedh, E. A. (2006). Auditing of information privacy. *Journal of Information Technology, 5*(1), 177–182. doi:10.3923/itj.2006.177.182

Ang, R. P., & Goh, D. H. (2010). Cyberbullying among adolescents: The role of affective and cognitive empathy, and gender. *Child Psychiatry and Human Development, 41*(4), 387–397. doi:10.100710578-010-0176-3 PMID:20238160

Bogdan, R. C., & Biklen, S. K. (2003). *Qualitative research for education: An introduction to theories and management* (4th ed.). New York, NY: Pearson Education Group.

Broadhurst, R., Grabsoky, P., Alazab, M., & Chon, S. (2014). Organizations and cybercrime: An analysis of the nature of groups engaged in cybercrime. *International Journal of Cyber Criminology, 8*(1), 1–20.

Chapman, J. (2019, April 4). *How safe is your data? Cyber-security in higher education.* Retrieved from https://www.hepi.ac.uk/2019/04/04/how-safe-is-your-data-cyber-security-in-higher-education/

Cresey, D. R. (1954). Differential association theory and compulsive crimes. *Journal of Criminal Law and Criminology, 45*(1), 29–40. doi:10.2307/1139301

Creswell, J. W., & Creswell, J. D. (2017). *Research design: Qualitative, quantitative, and mixed methods approach.* Los Angeles, CA: Sage Publications.

Dashora, K. (2011). Cybercrime in the society: Problems and prevention. *Journal of Alternative Perspectives in the Social Sciences, 3*(1), 24–59.

den Hamer, A. H., & Konijn, E. A. (2015). Adolescents' media exposure may increase their cyberbullying behavior: A longitudinal study. *The Journal of Adolescent Health, 56*(2), 203–208. doi:10.1016/j.jadohealth.2014.09.016 PMID:25620303

EC-Council. (2016). *Computer forensics. Investigating file and operating systems: Wireless network and storage (CHFI).* Boston, MA: Cengage Learning.

Fellows, L. (2019, May 31). *A daily threat – Universities, cyber-attacks and national security in the UK*. Retrieved from https://blogs.vmware.com/emea/en/2019/05/a-daily-threat-universities-cyber-attacks-and-national-security-in-the-uk/

Gearhart, G. D., Abbiatti, M. D., & Miller, M. T. (2019). Higher education's cyber security: Leadership issues, challenges and the future. *International Journal on New Trends in Education & Their Implications, 10*(2), 11-16.

Goodman, M. (2015). *Future crimes: Everything is connected, everyone is vulnerable and what we can do about it* (1st ed.). New York: Anchor, Penguin Random House LLC.

Harris, C. E., & Lammargren, R. (2016). *Higher education vulnerability to cyber-attacks*. University Business. Retrieved from https://universitybusiness.com/higher-educations-vulnerability-to-cyber-attacks/

Holt, T. J., Strumsky, D., Smirnova, O., & Kilger, M. (2012). Examining the social networks of malware writers and hackers. *International Journal of Cyber Criminology, 6*(1), 891.

Kshetri, N. (2010). *The global cybercrime industry*. Berlin: Springer. doi:10.1007/978-3-642-11522-6

Loundy, D. J. (2003). *Computer crime, information warfare & economic espionage*. Durham, NC: Carolina Academic Press.

Maxwell, J. A. (2005). *Qualitative research design: An interactive approach*. Thousand Oaks, CA: Sage.

Merriam, S. B. (2002). *Qualitative research in practice: Examples for discussion and analysis*. San Francisco, CA: Josey-Bass.

Oh, S., & Lee, K. (2014). The need for specific penalties for hacking in criminal law. *The Scientific World Journal, 16*(1), 73–78. PMID:25032236

Okeshola, F. B., & Adeta, A. K. (2013). The nature, causes and cons of cybercrime in tertiary institutions in Zaria-Danuna, Nigeria. *American International Journal of Contemporary Research, 3*(9), 98–114.

Ponemon Institute. (2015, May 23). *2015 cost of data breach study: Global analysis*. Ponemon Institute Research Report. Retrieved from http://public.dhe.ibm.com/common/ssi/ecm/se/en/sew03053wwen/SEW03053W WEN.PDF

Press Association. (2019, July 23). Lancaster University students' data stolen in cyber-attack. *The Guardian*. Retrieved from https://www.theguardian.com/technology/2019/jul/23/lancaster-university-students-data-stolen-cyber-attack

Raman, A., Kabir, F., Hejazi, S., & Aggarwal, K. (2016, August 25). *Cybersecurity in higher education: The changing threat landscape*. Retrieved from https://consulting.ey.com/cybersecurity-in-higher-education-the-changing-threat-landscape/

Schneider, S. K., O'donnell, L., Stueve, A., & Coulter, R. W. (2012). Cyberbullying, school bullying, and psychological distress: A regional census of high school students. *American Journal of Public Health*, *102*(1), 171–177. doi:10.2105/AJPH.2011.300308 PMID:22095343

Snail, S. (2009). Cybercrime in South Africa – Hacking, crack, and other unlawful online activities. *Journal of Information. Law and Technology*, *10*(1), 1–13.

Storm, D. (2017, February 15). *Hacker breached 63 universities and government agencies*. Retrieved from https://www.computerworld.com/article/3170724/hacker-breached-63-universities-and-government-agencies.html

Strauss, A., & Corbin, J. (1998). Basics of qualitative research: Techniques and procedures for developing grounded theory (2nd ed.). Thousand Oaks, CA: Academic Press.

Vijayan, V., Joy, J. P., & Suchithra, M. S. (2014). A review on password cracking strategies. *International Journal of Research in Computer and Communication Technology*, *1*(1), 8–15.

Whitman, M. E., & Mattors, H. J. (2010). *Readings and cases in information security: Law & ethics*. Boston, MA: Cengage Learning.

Wilson, C. (2008). *Botnets, cybercrime, and cyberterrorism: Vulnerabilities and policy issues for Congress*. Washington, DC: Congressional Research Service, the Library of Congress. Retrieved from https://apps.dtic.mil/dtic/tr/fulltext/u2/a477642.pdf

Yale University revealed a data breach which happened a decade ago. (2018, August 5). Retrieved from https://securereading.com/yale-university-revealed-a-data-breach-which-happened-a-decade-ago/

Chapter 14
Cyber Security, IT Governance, and Performance:
A Review of the Current Literature

Abdalmuttaleb M. A. Musleh Al-Sartawi
https://orcid.org/0000-0001-9755-5106
Ahlia University, Bahrain

Anjum Razzaque
Ahlia University, Bahrain

ABSTRACT

Cybersecurity is an emerging field with a growing body of literature and publications. It is fundamentally based in computer science and computer engineering but has recently gained popularity in business management. Despite the explosion of cybersecurity, there is a scarcity of literature on the definition of the term 'Cybers Security' and how it is situated within different contexts. Henceforth, this chapter presents a review of the work related to cybersecurity, within different contexts, mainly IT governance and firm performance context. The work reviewed is separated into four main categories: the importance of cybersecurity and how it is measured, corporate governance and IT governance, IT governance mechanisms, and financial performance measures.

INTRODUCTION

The Internet is regarded as the fastest growing technical infrastructure within two decades, where it started from an innovation to an indispensable entity with

DOI: 10.4018/978-1-7998-2418-3.ch014

2.5 billion users, that is one-third of the world's population, connected to it at all times (World Economic Forum, 2019). In the business environment context, many disruptive technologies like cloud computing, social computing and next generation mobile computing are continuously changing how information technology is used by organizations to share and conduct information. Nowadays, around 70% of transactions are done online which increase the need for highly secured systems to ensure transparent and best transactions (PayTabs, 2018). The terminology used to describe the security aspect of digital devices and information included "Computer Security", "IT Security", and "Information Security". However, recently, new terminology has started to become more popular: "Cyber Security".

According to Schatz et al., (2017), researchers claim that cyber security represents a superset of security practices such as information security, IT security and other related practices Therefore, the scope of Cyber Security does not include the security of IT systems within the enterprise only but also cover the cyber space itself and its critical infrastructure. Cyber security has a great role in the development information technology and Internet services. Nation's security and economic wellbeing is so crucial; hence, cyber security enhancement and critical information infrastructure protection is so vital (ITU, 2018). There is a scarcity of literature on what the term 'Cybers Security' actually means and how it is situated within various contexts. The absence of a universally acceptable definition that captures the different dimensions of cybersecurity hinders technological and scientific advances by reinforcing the predominantly technical view of cybersecurity while separating disciplines that should be acting in concert to resolve complex cybersecurity challenges (Craigen et al., 2014; Al-Sartawi, 2019b).

For the purposes of this book chapter, we look at cyber security from an industrial perspective. ISACA (2014) takes states that cyber security emerges within the fields of information security and traditional security. Business should therefore distinguish between standard information security and cyber security. The difference is in the scope, motive, opportunity and method of the attack (Schatz et al., 2014). Chang (2012), explains the interdisciplinary nature of cybersecurity as a science of which offers several opportunities for advances based on a multidisciplinary approach, because it is based in adversarial engagement. Humans must defend machines that are attacked by other humans using machines. So, in addition to the traditional fields of computer science, perspectives from other fields are needed.

Nonetheless, it is agreed that most business activities are dependent on cyber systems like finance, commerce, communication, national defense, health care, energy, entertainment and communication. Research showed that the public awareness regarding the privacy of personal information has increased since 2006, particularly when social networking platforms started making headlines as a social and a technological phenomenon (Cavoukian, 2009). Due to privacy threats and breaches, Internet users are concerned about how much personal information they share.

Understanding the importance of cyber security may help to improve our thinking in four different ways. First, we may gain a clearer understanding of the value and limitations of the concepts we have mapped form other domains into the cyber system. Second, trying out less common and new metaphors may feed the imagination of researchers and policy developers. Third, metaphors that work well will be developed into a whole new model to approach the cyber security system. Fourth, metaphors serve to bring a clear understanding of cyber security field concepts so that non specialist will be more familiar (Karas, Moore, & Parrott, 2008). Cyber security depends on the decision people make and the care people take while setting up, maintaining and using computers and the internet. It ensures full physical protection of all personal information including hardware and software and all technology resources from all illegal accesses (Federal Commnuications Commission, 2013).

The problems are created by the users' mistakes, and such problems cannot be solved by adding more technology, it must be solved with the combined efforts of Information Technology community as well as the general business community with the support of top management. Many organizations hesitate adopting cloud computing services die to the risks associated with its privacy and security (Khan et al., 2013). Security, as well as privacy, are two concerns that are hindering the of real-time businesses related to cloud computing (Sankareswari & Hemanth, 2014). Both academic and industry thinkers need to formulate new means of services and technologies which can provide a securer. Cloud computing services range from authentication, audit and authorization. Cloud security is fundamental for the successful adoption of such services concerning confidentiality, availability and integrity. While network security improves data confidentiality while the integrity should assure that the information received is like what was intended by the sender. And, the availability assures the reliability and stability of the networks and its systems to guarantee and secure channel for accessing information (Krutz, 2010; Khan et al., 2013).

Threats

Two major threated are recognized to affect the cyber security. First one is the cyber-attacks which are intended to destroy the cyber systems and the second one is the cyber exploitation that intend to exploit the cyber infrastructure for harmful purpose without damaging that infrastructure. Cyber exploitation uses the internet and other cyber systems to steal and violate copyright and other rules with limitation of information distribution and to convey some controversial messages. Following are some new threats to cyberspace.

Smart Phones Pose Security Challenges

Smart phones and cloud computing means that we are seeing a new set of different problems that are related to interconnection and it requires new regulation and thinking. Smart phones users are connecting mobile devices together many are in developing countries. The sheer number are likely to have social impact like flash mobs. A lot of politics are now migrating to the cyber space field.

Cloud Computing

It has been 40 years with the outsourcing the filling of data. The new thing is the wide spread of the storage. Cloud computing is defined by The National Institute of Standards and Technology as a rapid, on demand network to a shared pool of computing resources. Outsourcing means cost saving and it is used widely by companies for computation and data storage. The big names such as Amazon, eBay, Google and Facebook are all outsourcing computation to cloud. Among other raised issues is the cost of process power and connectivity and net neutrality. The problem of security and jurisdiction has been raised with the new storage facilities.

Current Cyber-Security Measures

The internet is highly secured currently through different private regulatory activities and many defensive products and strategies, international cooperation and regulation and many defensive strategies and products.

Private Measures

Non-governmental entities play major roles in the cyber security arena. Technical standards for the Internet (including current and next-generation versions of the Internet Protocol) are developed and proposed by the privately controlled Internet Engineering Task Force (IETF); the Web Consortium, housed at the Massachusetts Institute of Technology, defines technical standards for the Web. Other privately controlled entities that play significant operational roles on aspects of cyber security include the major telecommunications carriers, Internet Service Providers (ISPs), and many other organizations, including: The Forum of Incident Response and Security Teams (FIRST), which attempts to coordinate the activities of both government and private Computer Emergency Response Teams (CERTs) and is also working on cyber security standards; The Institute of Electrical and Electronics Engineers (IEEE), which develops technical standards through its Standards Association and in conjunction with the U.S. National Institute of Standards and Technology (NIST);

The Internet Corporation for Assigned Names and Numbers (ICANN), which operates pursuant to a contract with the U.S. Department of Commerce (September 2009) transferring to ICAAN the technical management of the Domain Name System.

National Measures

Many national governments have adopted laws aimed at punishing and thereby deterring specific forms of cyber-attacks or exploitation. The U.S., for example, has adopted laws making criminal various forms of conduct, including improper intrusion into and deliberate damage of computer systems. These laws have little or no effect, however, on individuals, groups, or governments over whom the U.S. lacks or is unable to secure regulatory or criminal jurisdiction.US national security experts almost exclusively emphasize the need for national measures for enhancing cyber security. They recommend national laws to protect the sharing of information about threats and attacks; methods for government bodies, such as the NSA, to cooperate with private entities in evaluating the source and nature of cyber-attacks; and more effective defenses and responses to cyber-attacks and exploitation developed through government-sponsored research and coordination pursuant to cyber security plans. The GAO's July 2010 report details the specific roles being played by many U.S. agencies in efforts to enhance ——global cybersecurity‖, but ultimately concludes that these efforts are not part of a coherent strategy likely to advance U.S. interests.

International Measures

National governments often cooperate with each other informally by exchanging information, investigating attacks or crimes, preventing or stopping harmful conduct, providing evidence, and even arranging for the rendition of individuals to a requesting state. States have also made formal, international agreements that bear directly or indirectly on cyber security. The international agreements apply to the criminal activities specified, including situations in which the alleged criminals have used cyber systems in those activities. International agreements that potentially bear upon cyber-security activities also include treaties(the UN Charter and Geneva Conventions) and universally accepted rules of conduct (customary law).International law also provides rules related to the use of force during armed conflict that presumably apply to cyber-attacks, including for example requirements that noncombatants and civilian institutions such as hospitals not be deliberately attacked, and that uses of force be restricted to measures that are necessary and proportionate.

Necessity of Cyber Security

Information is the most valuable asset with respect to an individual, cooperate sector, state and country. With respect to an individual the concerned areas are: (1) protecting unauthorized access, disclosure, modification of the resources of the system, (2) security during on-line transactions regarding shopping, banking, railway reservations and share markets, (3) security of accounts while using social-networking sites against hijacking, (4) one key to improved cyber security is a better understanding of the threat and of the vectors used by the attacker to circumvent cyber defenses, (5) the need of separate unit handling security of the organization, (6) the different organizations or missions attract different types of adversaries, with different goals, and thus need different levels of preparedness, and (7) in identifying the nature of the cyber threat an organization or mission faces, the interplay of an adversary's capabilities, intentions and targeting activities must be considered.

Corporate Governance and IT Governance

In order to understand the concept of IT governance a detailed insight into the principles of corporate governance and its constituents is needed. In their publications on measuring the performance of corporate boards, M.J. Epstein and M.J. Roy state that "governance concerns relate to practices of both corporate boards and senior managers" and "the question being asked is whether the decision-making process and the decisions themselves are made in the interest of shareholders, employees, and other stakeholders or whether they are primarily in the interests of the executives (Al-Sartawi, 2016)

The corporate governance framework is there to encourage the efficient use of resources and equally to require accountability for the stewardship of those resources. The aim is to align as nearly as possible the interests of individuals, corporations and society (Al-Sartawi and Sanad, 2015). IT governance is a set of economized in three categories: structure of decision making (specify decisional rights and responsibilities relative to using IT in a firm), relational mechanisms (to promote synergic communication between employees) and processes (approaches that guide decision making, monitoring, and control of IT) (Peterson, 2004; Al-Sartawi, 2017a). IT governance is applicable for cultivating a favorable atmosphere for organizations to perform more efficiently, and this has been the stance by several scholars in recent studies; e.g., (Weill & Ross, 2004; Pang, 2014). IT governance is a subset of corporate governance (Lunardi et al., 2014; Al-Sartawi, 2017b), and it is the responsibility of executives of an organization so that IT governance can aid firms to manage risks from technological losses (Mohamed & Gian Singh, 2012).

Scholars report that there is an increasing reliance on IT by firms, a global phenomenon, as IT is a major and a vital facilitator for the betterment of firm performance. (Wilkin & Chenhall, 2010; Al-Sartawi et al. 2017). IT governance aids in managing investments related to IT, and this is why firms are increasingly gaining interest in IT governance: as it facilitates them to monitor and control IT effectiveness and IT related investments (Bradley et al., 2012; Al-Sartawi, 2018a). The reason why IT governance becomes vital is because IT is due to the interconnectedness of the various complex components of IT systems and their relative infrastructure and architecture. Such interconnectedness is overwhelming when one takes under consideration the constant threats and regulations faced outside of an organization, and in relation with IT.

Further, IT internal controls (i.e., the safeguarding of management, firm's operations, and technical affairs to maintain and sustain confidentiality, availability, and integrity of information) also needs to be implemented in order to moderate the external risks (National Institute of Standards and Technology, 2006). Recent literature has expressed a concern over IT governance pertaining to IT controls, i.e., though IT controls are growing in importance; establishing a business case for management to focus on IT controls is still a challenge, as there are multiple perspectives to identify and manage risks (Power, 2009). As a result the aim of this study is to cultivate the awareness that the weakness of IT controls is a firm's liability, thus an empirical investigation into understanding the effect of IT governance on firm's performance is vital. However, on the other hand, literature in the field of Computer Science assessed the technical aspects of IT security and standards (e.g., Siponen & Iivari, 2006) while other research focused on the economics of IT controls, but still remaining scarce (Kannan & Telang, 2005; Gordon & Loeb, 2002). Such scholars tend to guesstimate the economic cost of ineffective IT security controls with mixed results (Cavusoglu et al., 2004; Al-Sartawi, 2015; Sanad and Al-Sartawi, 2016).

IT governance concerns relate to IT practices of boards and senior managers. The question is whether IT structures, processes, relational mechanisms and IT decisions are made in the interest of shareholders and other stakeholders, or primarily in the executives' interests. IT governance closely relates to corporate governance, the structure of the IT organization and its objectives and alignment to the business objectives. IT Governance is the process for controlling an organization's IT resources, including information and communication systems and technology. According to the IT Governance Institute, IT governance is the responsibility of executives and board of directors, and consists of leadership, organizational structures and processes that ensure that enterprise's IT sustain and extends the organization's strategies and objectives. It is an integral part of enterprise governance and consists of the leadership and organizational structures and processes that ensure that the organization's IT sustains and extends the organization's strategies and objectives.

Figure 1 depicts a clear difference between IT governance and IT management. While IT management is mainly focused on the daily effective and efficient supply of IT services and IT operations, IT governance is much broader concept which focuses on performing and transforming IT to meet present and future demands of business and the business' customers. This means that executive management members and corporate governance organizations bodies need to take responsibility for governing IT, which makes IT Governance a key executive function.

IT GOVERNANCE MECHANISMS

IT governance has primarily been driven by the need for the transparency of enterprise risks and the protection of shareholder value. The overall objective of IT governance is to understand the issues and the strategic importance of IT, so that the firm can maintain its operations and implement strategies to enable the company to better compete now and in the future.

IT governance thus enables the enterprise to take full advantage of its information, thereby maximizing benefits, capitalizing on opportunities and gaining competitive advantage. Key IT governance mechanisms are: Business/IT strategic alignment, Value creation and delivery, Risk management (value preservation), Resource management and IS auditing and performance measurement. Primarily of interest to business and technology management are the management guidelines tools and

Figure 1.

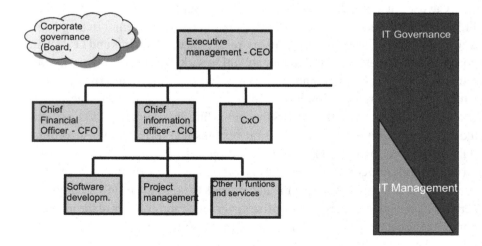

mechanisms to help assign responsibility, measure performance, and benchmark and address gaps between actual and desired capability. The guidelines help provide answers to typical management questions (Al-Sartawi, 2018b).

Financial Performance in Companies

Financial performance is a term that describes how well a company can use assets from its main mode of business and generate profits. It is also used as a wider measure of a company's overall financial strength within a specific period of time, and can be used in comparing similar firms within the same industry or sectors. The corporation itself as well as involved groups such as managers, shareholders, creditors, tax authorities and others seeks answers to important questions. These questions can be answered using the financial analysis of a firm. It includes financial statements which is a structured collection of information according to rational and reliable accounting measures (Al-Sartawi, 2019a). The purpose behind it is to spread a good understanding of some financial characteristics of a business firm. It may focus on Balance Sheet in some circumstances, or may disclose a series of accomplishments over a specific period of time which refers to Income Statement. Therefore, the term "financial statements" usually refers to two important statements which are: The Balance Sheet and the Income Statement.

- The Balance Sheet displays the financial position of the company at a certain point of time. It provides a snapshot and may be observed as a static image. BS is a summary of a company's financial condition on a specified date that shows total assets = total liabilities + owner's equity.
- The income statement indicates the performance of the corporation over a period. Income statement is a summary of two main parts which are revenues and expenses over a specific period, in conclusion it shows two results either net income or loss.
- Cash Flow Statement The cash flow statement includes both the IS income statement and BS balance sheet. For some forecasters, this statement is the most significant financial statement since it provides a settlement between net income and cash flow. This is where forecasters can see how much the company is paying on dividends, stock repurchases and capital expenditures. It also offers the source and usages of cash flow from processes, capitalizing and financing.

The main objective of recording, keeping and analyzing financial statements is to make an improved business decision. Recognizing emerging issues and starting timely corrective act, as well as recognizing probable chances for better profit, are some of the clear benefits. Hopefully, continues analysis will assist the manager find previous errors and learn from them. The data taken from these three financial statements also can be used to make extra financial methods that disclose the strong points and weak points of the firm. These additional financial measures can be used to make some evaluations and comparisons (Al-Sartawi and Sanad, 2019).

Financial Performance Measures

The Firm Financial Values Assembly developed the (Financial Guidelines for Agricultural Producers), a set of suggested consistent financial aspects, measures and recording formats that can be used to improved understanding of business. The suggested procedures for financial analysis are gathered into five broad classes: solvency, liquidity, financial efficiency, profitability and repayment capability. These typical performance measures, occasionally mentioned to as the "sweet 16", historical and current financial information are not the only reasons affecting financial performance. Keep in mind that checking the "sweet 16" measures as a set is more significant than concentrating on only one or two measures (Al-Sartawi, 2018c).

RECOMMENDATIONS AND FUTURE RESEARCH DIRECTIONS

The lack of collaboration across disciplines such as computer science and business management highlight the need for more comprehensive standard terminology for both cyber security and broader cyber research. To guarantee that firms are working efficiently with improved financial performance level, they must first understand the term and scope of cyber security system, since it provides a higher stage of security for both users and workers. Training employees is one of the most important aspects that increase their knowledge about day to day enhancement. On the other hand, IT governance is a must, because as we wish to get a higher security level, we would definitely need members in the board of directors and also workers with IT background to take the right decisions. Neglecting these two variables could negatively affect in the performance of firms (Al-Sartawi, 2018d).

For the future, researchers can conduct an empirical research, to build on the knowledge that is accounting the IT background by adding more elements and variables such as: training, for more in-depth sectors this topic will be significant reference to firms and individuals who seek for innovation and creativity.

REFERENCES

Al-Sartawi, A. (2015). The effect of corporate governance on the performance of the listed companies in the Gulf cooperation council countries. *Jordan Journal of Business Administration, 11*(3), 705–725.

Al-Sartawi, A. (2016). Measuring the level of online financial disclosure in the Gulf Cooperation Council Countries. *Corporate Ownership and Control, 14*(1), 547–558. doi:10.22495/cocv14i1c4art1

Al-Sartawi, A. (2017a). The Effect of the Electronic Financial Reporting on the Market Value Added of the Islamic banks in Gulf Cooperation Council Countries. In *8th Global Islamic Marketing Conference.* International Islamic Marketing Association.

Al-Sartawi, A. (2017b). The Level of Disclosing Intellectual Capital in the Gulf Cooperation Council Countries. *International Research Journal of Finance and Economics,* (159), 1-10.

Al-Sartawi, A. (2018a). Institutional ownership, social responsibility, corporate governance and online financial disclosure. *International Journal of Critical Accounting, 10*(3/4), 241–255. doi:10.1504/IJCA.2018.10014001

Al-Sartawi, A. (2018b). Corporate governance and intellectual capital: Evidence from Gulf Cooperation council countries. *Academy of Accounting and Financial Studies Journal, 22*(1), 1–12.

Al-Sartawi, A. (2018c). Does Institutional Ownership Affect the Level of Online Financial Disclosure? *Academy of Accounting and Financial Studies Journal, 22*(2), 1–10.

Al-Sartawi, A. (2018d). Ownership structure and intellectual capital: evidence from the GCC countries. *International Journal of Learning and Intellectual Capital, 15*(3), 277-291.

Al-Sartawi, A. (2019a). Board independence, frequency of meetings and performance. *Journal of Islamic Marketing, 10*(1), 290–303. doi:10.1108/JIMA-01-2018-0017

Al-Sartawi, A. (2019b). Information Technology Governance and Cybersecurity at the Board Level. *International Journal of Critical Infrastructures.* (accepted for publication)

Al-Sartawi, A., Alrawahi, F., & Sanad, Z. (2017). Board characteristics and the level of compliance with IAS 1 in Bahrain. *International Journal of Managerial and Financial Accounting, 9*(4), 303–321. doi:10.1504/IJMFA.2017.10009970

Al-Sartawi, A., & Sanad, Z. (2015). The effect of corporate governance on stock performance: Evidence from Bahrain. In *6th Global Islamic Marketing Conference*. International Islamic Marketing Association.

Al-Sartawi, A., & Sanad, Z. (2019). Institutional ownership and corporate governance: Evidence from Bahrain. *Afro-Asian Journal of Finance and Accounting*, *9*(1), 101–115. doi:10.1504/AAJFA.2019.10017933

Bradley, R., Byrd, T. A., Pridmore, J. L., Trasher, E., Pratt, R. M., & Mbarika, V. W. (2012). An empirical examination of antecedents and consequences of IT governance in US hospitals. *Journal of Information Technology*, *27*(2), 156–177. doi:10.1057/jit.2012.3

Cavoukian, A. (2009, March). *Online Privacy: Make Youth Awareness and Education a Priority*. Toronto, Ontorio, Canada: Information and Privacy Commissioner of Ontario. Retrieved July 26, 2019, from https://www.ipc.on.ca/wp-content/uploads/resources/youthonline.pdf

Cavusoglu, H., Mishra, B., & Raghunathan, S. (2004). The effects of internet security breach announcements on market value: Capital market reactions for breached firms and internet security developers. *International Journal of Electronic Commerce*, *9*(1), 69–104. doi:10.1080/10864415.2004.11044320

Chang, F. R. (2012). Guest Editor's Column. *The Next Wave*, *19*(4), 1–2.

Colorado Technical University. (2019). *The History of Cybersecurity Worms. Viruses. Trojan horses. Logic bombs*. Spyware.

Craigen, D., Diakun-Thibault, N., & Purse, R. (2014). Defining cybersecurity. *Technology Innovation Management Review, 4*(10).

Federal Commnuications Commission. (2013). *Cyber Security Planning Guide*. Retrieved July 26, 2019, from https://transition.fcc.gov/cyber/cyberplanner.pdf

Gelnaw, A. (2018). *Creating a Cybersecurity Awareness Culture at Financial Institutions*. Retrieved July 26, 2019, from https://www.bitsight.com/blog/creating-a-cybersecurity-awareness-culture-at-financial-institutions ges/European-CybersecurityImplementation-Series.aspx

Gordon, L., & Loeb, M. (2002). The economics of information security investment. *ACM Transactions on Information and System Security*, *5*(4), 438–457. doi:10.1145/581271.581274

Investopedia. (2019). *Financial Performance*. Retrieved July 26, 2019, from https://www.investopedia.com/terms/f/financialperformance.asp

ISACA. (2014). *European Cybersecurity Implementation: Overview.* Retrieved on 10 October 2019 from http://www.isaca.org/KnowledgeCenter/Research/ ResearchDeliverables/Pa

ITU. (2018). *Critical Information Infrastructure Protection Role of CIRTs and Cooperation at National Level.* Retrieved July 26, 2019, from Global Cybersecurity AgendaITU: https://www.energypact.org/wp-content/uploads/2018/03/Maloor_ Day2_Critical-Information-Infrastructure-Protection.pdf

Kannan, K., & Telang, R. (2005). Market for software vulnerabilities? Think again. *Management Science, 51*(5), 726–740. doi:10.1287/mnsc.1040.0357

Karas, T. H., Moore, J. H., & Parrott, L. K. (2008, Aug). *Metaphors for Cyber Security.* Sandia Report. Retrieved July 26, 2019, from https://evolutionofcomputing. org/Cyberfest%20Report.pdf

Khan, N. A., Kiah, M. M., & Khan, S. U. (2013). Towards secure mobile cloud computing; A survey. *Future Generation Computer Systems, 29*(5), 1278–1299. doi:10.1016/j.future.2012.08.003

Krutz, R. L. (2010). *Cloud security: a comprehensive guide to secure cloud computing.* Wiley.

Lunardi, G., Becker, J. L., Maçada, A. C. G., & Dolci, P. C. (2014). The impact of adopting IT governance on financial performance: An empirical analysis among Brazilian companies. *International Journal of Accounting Information Systems, 15*(1), 66–81. doi:10.1016/j.accinf.2013.02.001

Mohamed, N., & Gian Singh, J. K. (2012). A conceptual framework for information technology governance effectiveness in private organizations. *Information Management & Computer Security, 20*(2), 88–106. doi:10.1108/09685221211235616

nibusinessinfo.co.uk. (2019). *Measure your financial performance.* Retrieved July 26, 2019, from https://www.nibusinessinfo.co.uk/content/measure-your-financial-performance

PayTabs. (2018, July 3). *7 Tips for Safe Online Transactions.* Retrieved July 26, 2019, from PayTabs Blog: https://www.paytabs.com/en/7-tips-for-safe-online-transactions/

Peterson, R. (2004). Crafting Information Technology Governance. *Information Systems Management, 21*(4), 7–23. doi:10.1201/1078/44705.21.4.20040901/84183.2

Power, M. (2009). The risk management of nothing. *Accounting, Organizations and Society, 34*(6/7), 849–855. doi:10.1016/j.aos.2009.06.001

Sanad, Z., & Al-Sartawi, A. (2016). Investigating the relationship between corporate governance and internet financial reporting (IFR): Evidence from Bahrain bourse. *Jordan Journal of Business Administration*, *12*(1), 239–269. doi:10.12816/0030063

Sankareswari, S., & Hemanth, S. (2014). Attribute Based Encryption with Privacy Preserving using Asymmetric Key in Cloud Computing. *International Journal of Computer Science and Information Technologies*, *5*(5), 6792–6795.

Schatz, D., Bashroush, R., & Wall, J. (2017). Towards a more representative definition of cyber security. Journal of Digital Forensics. *Security and Law*, *12*(2), 8.

Siponen, M., & Iivari, J. (2006). IS security design theory framework and six approaches to the application of IS security policies and guidelines. *Journal of the Association for Information Systems*, *7*(7), 445–472. doi:10.17705/1jais.00095

Weill, P., & Ross, J. (2004). *IT Governance: How top performer manage IT decision rights for superior results*. Boston, MA: Harvard Business School Press.

Wilkin, C. L., & Chenhall, R. H. (2010). A review of IT governance: A taxonomy to inform accounting information systems. *Journal of Information Systems*, *14*(2), 107–146. doi:10.2308/jis.2010.24.2.107

World Economic Forum. (2019). *1. Introduction: The Digital Infrastructure Imperative*. Retrieved July 26, 2019, from World Economic Forum: http://reports.weforum.org/delivering-digital-infrastructure/introduction-the-digital-infrastructure-imperative/

Compilation of References

Abawajy, J. (2014). User preference of cybersecurity awareness delivery methods. *Behaviour & Information Technology*, *33*(3), 237–248. doi:10.1080/0144929X.2012.708787

Abbate, J. (1999). *Inventing the Internet (inside technology)*. Cambridge, MA: MIT Press.

Abdelzaher, T., Han, J., Faloutsos, C., & Eliassi-Rad, T. (2018). *Robustness Analysis and Anomaly Detection of Interdependent Physical and Social Networks*. University of Illinois at Urbana Champaign Urbana United States.

Abdolahnezhad, M., & Banirostam, T. (2016). Hybrid Email Spam Detection Method Using Negative Selection and Genetic Algorithms. *IJARCCE*, *5*(4), 1–5. doi:10.17148/IJARCCE.2016.5401

Abdulhamid, Shuaib, Osho, Ismaila, & Alhassan. (2018). Comparative Analysis of Classification Algorithms for Email Spam Detection. *International Journal of Computer Network and Information Security*, *10*(1), 60–67. doi:10.5815/ijcnis.2018.01.07

Abou Daya, A. (2019). *BotChase: Graph-Based Bot Detection Using Machine Learning*. University of Waterloo.

ACL Wiki. (2006). *Spam filtering datasets*. Available: https://aclweb.org/aclwiki/Spam_filtering_datasets

Aghdam, M. (2009). Combination of Ant Colony Optimization and Bayesian Classification for Feature Selection in a Bioinformatics Dataset. *Journal of Computer Science and Systems Biology*, *2*(3), 186–199. doi:10.4172/jcsb.1000031

Agyapong, K., Hayfron-Acqua, D., & Asante, D. (2016). An Overview of Data Mining Models (Descriptive and Predictive). *International Journal of Software & Hardware Research in Engineering*, *4*(5), 53–60.

Ahmed, H., & Glasgow, J. (2012). *Swarm Intelligence: Concepts, Models and Applications*. Technical Report 585. School of Computing. Queen's University Kingston, Ontario, Canada.

Akoglu, L., & Faloutsos, C. (2013, February). Anomaly, event, and fraud detection in large network datasets. In *Proceedings of the sixth ACM international conference on Web search and data mining* (pp. 773-774). ACM. 10.1145/2433396.2433496

Akoglu, L., Tong, H., & Koutra, D. (2015). Graph based anomaly detection and description: A survey. *Data Mining and Knowledge Discovery, 29*(3), 626–688. doi:10.100710618-014-0365-y

Akula, R. K. (2018). *Botnet Detection Using Graph Based Feature Clustering.* Mississippi State University.

Al Amro, S. (2017). Cybercrime in Saudi Arabia: Fact or fiction? *International Journal of Computer Science Issues, 14*(2), 36–42. doi:10.20943/01201702.3642

Al-adawi, Z., Yousafzai, S., & Pallister, J. (2005, September). Conceptual model of citizen adoption of e-government. *The Second International Conference on Innovations in Information Technology.* 1-10.

Al-Alawi, A. I. (2005). Online banking: Security concerns and the acceptance of mature customers. In *3rd International Conference: Sciences of Electronic, Technologies of Information and Telecommunications* (pp. 27–31). Academic Press.

Al-Alawi, A. I., & Al-Bassam, S. A. (2017). Investigating the factors affecting cybersecurity awareness in [the] Bahrain banking sector. In *Cyber Security Symposium, Britain & Northern Ireland.* University of Manchester.

Al-Alawi, A. I., Al-Kandari, S. M., & Abdel-Razek, R. H. (2016). Evaluation of information systems security awareness in higher education: An empirical study of Kuwait University. *Journal of Innovation and Business Best Practice.* doi:10.5171/2016.329374

Al-Alawi, A. I. (2014). Cybercrimes, computer forensics and their impact in business climate: Bahrain status. *Research Journal of Business Management, 8*(3), 139–156. doi:10.3923/rjbm.2014.139.156

Al-Alawi, A. I. (2014). Cybercrimes, computer forensics, and their impact on business climate: Bahrain status. *Journal of Business and Management, 8*(3), 139–156.

Al-Alawi, A. I., & Abdelgadir, M. F. (2006). An empirical study of attitudes and opinions of computer crimes: A comparative study between UK and the Kingdom of Bahrain. *Journal of Computational Science, 2*(3), 229–235. doi:10.3844/jcssp.2006.229.235

Al-Alawi, A. I., & Hafedh, E. A. (2006). Auditing of information privacy. *Journal of Information Technology, 5*(1), 177–182. doi:10.3923/itj.2006.177.182

Al-Ali, M., & AlMogren, A., (2017). Fuzzy logic methodology for cyber security risk mitigation approach. *Journal of Networking Technology, 8*(3).

Al-Bassam, S. A. (2018). *Investigating the factors related to cybersecurity awareness in Bahraini banking sector* (Unpublished master's thesis). Arabian Gulf University.

Albastaki, Y. (2009). An Artificial Neural Networks-Based On-Line Monitoring Odor Sensing System. *Journal of Computational Science,* 878–882.

Albastaki, Y., & Albalooshi, F. (Eds.). (2018). *Electronic Noses and Technologies and Advances in Machine Olfaction.* IGI Global. doi:10.4018/978-1-5225-3862-2

Albastaki, Y., & Almutawa, K. (2013). *ANN Based Approach to Integrate Smell Sense in Multimedia Systems, Technology Diffusion and Adoption: Global Complexity, Global Innovation: Global Complexity, Global Innovation.* IGI Global.

Al-Fahed Nuseirat, A. M., & Zitar, R. A. (2001). A neural network approach to _rm grip in the presence of small slips. *International Journal of Robotic Systems, 18*(6), 305–315. doi:10.1002/rob.1025

Al-jarrah, O., Khater, I., & Al-duwairi, B. (2012). Identifying potentially useful email header features for email spam filtering. *The Sixth International Conference on Digital Society,* 140–145.

AlKhaleej. (2019, August 23). اقتراح برلماني بإنشاء مركز خليجي موحد للأمن السيبراني [Parliamentary proposal to establish a unified Gulf Center for Cybersecurity]. Retrieved from http://www.akhbar-alkhaleej.com/news/article/1180085

Al-Mhiqani, M. N., Ahmad, R., Yassin, W., Hassan, A., Abidin, Z. Z., Ali, N. S., & Abdulkareem, K. H. (2018). Cyber-security incidents: A review cases in cyber-physical systems. *International Journal of Advanced Computer Science and Applications, 9,* 499–508.

Al-Muhammed & Zitar. (2019). Mesh-Based Encryption Technique Augmented with Effective Masking and Distortion Operations. *Proceedings of the computing conference 2019.*

Al-Muhammed, M. J., & Abuzitar, R. (2017). Dynamic Text Encryption. *International Journal of Security and its Applications, 11*(11), 13-30.

Al-Muhammed, M. J., & Abuzitar, R. (2017). K-Lookback Random-Based Text Encryption Technique. *Journal of King Saud University-Computer and Information Sciences, 2019*(31), 92–104.

Aloul, F. A. (2010). Information security awareness in UAE: A survey paper. In *2010 International Conference for Internet Technology and Secured Transactions* IEEE.

Alqudsi-ghabra, T. M., Al-Bannai, T., & Al-Bahrani, M. (2011). The Internet in the Arab Gulf Cooperation Council (AGCC): Vehicle of Change. *International Journal of Internet Science, 6*(1).

Al-Sartawi, A. (2017b). The Level of Disclosing Intellectual Capital in the Gulf Cooperation Council Countries. *International Research Journal of Finance and Economics,* (159), 1-10.

Al-Sartawi, A. (2018d). Ownership structure and intellectual capital: evidence from the GCC countries. *International Journal of Learning and Intellectual Capital, 15*(3), 277-291.

Al-Sartawi, A. (2019b). Information Technology Governance and Cybersecurity at the Board Level. *International Journal of Critical Infrastructures.* (accepted for publication)

Al-Sartawi, A. (2015). The effect of corporate governance on the performance of the listed companies in the Gulf cooperation council countries. *Jordan Journal of Business Administration*, *11*(3), 705–725.

Al-Sartawi, A. (2016). Measuring the level of online financial disclosure in the Gulf Cooperation Council Countries. *Corporate Ownership and Control*, *14*(1), 547–558. doi:10.22495/cocv14i1c4art1

Al-Sartawi, A. (2017a). The Effect of the Electronic Financial Reporting on the Market Value Added of the Islamic banks in Gulf Cooperation Council Countries. In *8th Global Islamic Marketing Conference*. International Islamic Marketing Association.

Al-Sartawi, A. (2018a). Institutional ownership, social responsibility, corporate governance and online financial disclosure. *International Journal of Critical Accounting*, *10*(3/4), 241–255. doi:10.1504/IJCA.2018.10014001

Al-Sartawi, A. (2018b). Corporate governance and intellectual capital: Evidence from Gulf Cooperation council countries. *Academy of Accounting and Financial Studies Journal*, *22*(1), 1–12.

Al-Sartawi, A. (2018c). Does Institutional Ownership Affect the Level of Online Financial Disclosure? *Academy of Accounting and Financial Studies Journal*, *22*(2), 1–10.

Al-Sartawi, A. (2019a). Board independence, frequency of meetings and performance. *Journal of Islamic Marketing*, *10*(1), 290–303. doi:10.1108/JIMA-01-2018-0017

Al-Sartawi, A., Alrawahi, F., & Sanad, Z. (2017). Board characteristics and the level of compliance with IAS 1 in Bahrain. *International Journal of Managerial and Financial Accounting*, *9*(4), 303–321. doi:10.1504/IJMFA.2017.10009970

Al-Sartawi, A., & Sanad, Z. (2015). The effect of corporate governance on stock performance: Evidence from Bahrain. In *6th Global Islamic Marketing Conference*. International Islamic Marketing Association.

Al-Sartawi, A., & Sanad, Z. (2019). Institutional ownership and corporate governance: Evidence from Bahrain. *Afro-Asian Journal of Finance and Accounting*, *9*(1), 101–115. doi:10.1504/AAJFA.2019.10017933

Alsmadi, I., & Alhami, I. (2015). Clustering and classification of email contents. *Journal of King Saud University - Computer and Information Sciences*, *27*(1), 46–57. doi:10.1016/j.jksuci.2014.03.014

Al-Tahrawi, M. M., & Zitar, R. A. (2008). Polynomial networks versus other techniques in text categorization. *International Journal of Pattern Recognition and Artificial Intelligence*, *22*(2), 295–322. doi:10.1142/S0218001408006247

Amiel, F. (2007). *Passive and active combined attacks: Combining fault attacks and side channel analysis. In FDTC* (pp. 92–102). IEEE.

Amro, S., Elizondo, D., Solanas, A., & Martinez-Balleste, A. (2012). Evolutionary Computation in Computer Security and Forensics: An Overview. In Computational Intelligence for Privacy and Security, SCI 394, (pp. 25–34). Springer-Verlag Berlin Heidelberg.

Amudha, P., & Abdulrauf, H. (2012). *A Study on Swarm Intelligence Techniques in Intrusion Detection. IJCA.*

Anderson, P. (2007). *What is Web 2.0? Ideas, technologies and implications for education.* Bristol: JISC.

Anderson, R., Biham, E., & Knudsen, L. (2018). *Serpent: A Pro-posal for the Advanced Encryption Standard.* Retrieved from http://www.cl.cam.ac.uk/ rja14/Papers/serpent.pdf

Anderson, C. (2006). *The Long Tail: How endless choice is creating unlimited demand.* London, UK: Random House Business Books.

Ang, R. P., & Goh, D. H. (2010). Cyberbullying among adolescents: The role of affective and cognitive empathy, and gender. *Child Psychiatry and Human Development, 41*(4), 387–397. doi:10.100710578-010-0176-3 PMID:20238160

Anhalt, K., Telzrow, C. F., & Brown, C. L. (2007). Maternal stress and emotional status during the perinatal period and childhood adjustment. *School Psychology Quarterly, 22*(1), 74–90. doi:10.1037/1045-3830.22.1.74

Asar, A. O., & Arıkan, A. (2012). *Sayılar Teorisi.* Ankara: Gazi Kitabevi.

Aski, A., & Sourati, N. (2016). Proposed efficient algorithm to filter spam using machine learning techniques, Pacific Science Review A. *Natural Science and Engineering, 18*(2), 145–149.

AustCyber. (n.d.). *Australian Cyber Security Growth Network.* Australian Government—Department of Industry, Innovation and Science. Retrieved August 27, 2019 from https://www.austcyber.com/sites/default/files/inline-images/fig11.png

Awad, W. A. (2011). Machine Learning Methods for Spam E-Mail Classification. *International Journal of Computer Science & Information Technology, 3*(1), 12. doi:10.5121/ijcsit.2011.3112

Bachwani, R., Crameri, O., & Bianchini, R. (2012). *Mojave: A recommendation system for software upgrades.* Academic Press.

Bahrain ICT Shared Services. (2011). Retrieved from https://www.cisco.com/c/dam/en_us/about/ac79/docs/ps/Bahrain-Govt-SS_IBSG.pdf

Balakumar, C., & Ganeshkumar, D. (2015). A Data Mining Approach on Various Classifiers in Email Spam Filtering. *International Journal for Research in Applied Science and Engineering Technology, 3*(1), 8–14.

Balamurugan, S., Rajaram, D., Athiappan, G., & Muthupandian, M. (2007). Data Mining Techniques for Suspicious Email Detection: A Comparative Study. *IADIS European Conference Data Ming 2007,* 213-217.

Barenghi. (2012). Fault injection attacks on cryptographic devices:theory, practice and countermeasures. *Proceedings of IEEE, 100*(11).

Bassiouni, M., Ali, M., & El-Dahshan, E. A. (2018). Ham and Spam E-Mails Classification Using Machine Learning Techniques. *Journal of Applied Security Research. Taylor & Francis, 13*(3), 315–331. doi:10.1080/19361610.2018.1463136

Batina, L., Gierlichs, B., Prouff, E., Rivain, M., Standaert, F.-X., & Veyrat-Charvillon, N. (2011). VeyratCharvillon, N.: Mutual Information Analysis: a Comprehensive Study. *Journal of Cryptology, 24*(2), 269–291. doi:10.100700145-010-9084-8

Bauer, A. (2013). *Horizontal and Vertical Side-Channel Attacks Against Secure RSA Implementations – Extended Version*. Cryptology ePrint Archive.

Bayati, M., & Jabbar, S. (2015). Developing a Spam Email Detector. *International Journal of Engineering and Innovative Technology, 5*(2), 16–21.

Beni, G., & Wang, J. (1989). *Swarm intelligence in cellular robotic systems*. NATO.

Bezdek, J. (1994). *What is Computational Intelligence? Computational Intelligence Imitating Life*. IEEE Press.

Bhattacharyya, D., Ranjan, R., Alisherov, F. A., & Choi, M. (2009). Biometric Authentication: A Review. International Journal of u- and e- Service. *Science and Technology, 2*(3), 13–27.

Bhuiyan, H. (2018). 'A Survey of Existing E-Mail Spam Filtering Methods Considering Machine Learning Techniques,' Global. *Journal of Computer Science and Technology, 18*(2), 21–29.

Biham, E. (1997). Differential Fault analysis of secret key cryptosystems. *Proceedings CRYPTO,* 1294, 513-525. 10.1007/BFb0052259

Biham, E., & Shamir, A. (1991). Differential Cryptanalysis of DES-like Cryptosystems. *Journal of Cryptology, 4*(1), 3–72. doi:10.1007/BF00630563

Biham, E., & Shamir, A. (1993). *Differential Cryptanalysis of the Data Encryption Standard*. Springer-Verlag. doi:10.1007/978-1-4613-9314-6

Bluszcz, Fitisova, Hamann, & Trifonov. (2019). *Application of Support Vector Machine Algorithm in E-Mail Spam Filtering*. Academic Press.

Bogdanov, A., Mendel, F., Regazzoni, F., & Rijmen, V. (2014). ALE: AES-Based Lightweight Authenticated Encryption. In S. Moriai (Ed.), Lecture Notes in Computer Science: Vol. 8424. *Fast Software Encryption. FSE 2013*. Berlin: Springer.

Bogdanov, A., Mendel, F., Regazzoni, F., Rijmen, V., & Tischhauser, E. (2014). ALE: AES-Based Lightweight Authenticated Encryption. In S. Moriai (Ed.), *FSE 2013. LNCS* (Vol. 8424, pp. 447–466). Heidelberg, Germany: Springer.

Bogdan, R. C., & Biklen, S. K. (2003). *Qualitative research for education: An introduction to theories and management* (4th ed.). New York, NY: Pearson Education Group.

Bollobas, B. (2012). *Graph theory: an introductory course* (Vol. 63). Springer Science & Business Media.

Bourkache, G., Mezghiche, M., & Tamine, K. (2011). A Distributed Intrusion Detection Model Based on a Society of Intelligent Mobile Agents for Ad Hoc Network. In *Proceedings of the IEEE 2011 Sixth International Conference on Availability, Reliability and Security (ARES)* (pp. 569-572). Vienna: IEEE. 10.1109/ARES.2011.131

Boyd, D. M., & Ellison, N. B. (2007). Social network sites: Definition, history, and scholarship. *Journal of Computer-Mediated Communication, 13*(1), 210–230. doi:10.1111/j.1083-6101.2007.00393.x

Bradley, R., Byrd, T. A., Pridmore, J. L., Trasher, E., Pratt, R. M., & Mbarika, V. W. (2012). An empirical examination of antecedents and consequences of IT governance in US hospitals. *Journal of Information Technology, 27*(2), 156–177. doi:10.1057/jit.2012.3

Breitman, K., Casanova, M. A., & Truszkowski, W. (2007). Software Agents. In *Semantic Web: Concepts, Technologies and Applications. NASA Monographs in Systems and Software Engineering* (pp. 219–228). London, UK: Springer.

Brier, E., Clavier, C., & Olivier, F. (2004). Correlation Power Analysis with a Leakage Model. In M. Joye & J. J. Quisquater (Eds.), Lecture Notes in Computer Science: Vol. 3156. *Cryptographic Hardware and Embedded Systems - CHES 2004. CHES 2004*. Berlin: Springer. doi:10.1007/978-3-540-28632-5_2

Brin, S., & Page, L. (1998). The anatomy of a large-scale hypertextual web search engine. *Computer Networks and ISDN Systems, 30*(1-7), 107-117.

Broadhurst, R., Grabsoky, P., Alazab, M., & Chon, S. (2014). Organizations and cybercrime: An analysis of the nature of groups engaged in cybercrime. *International Journal of Cyber Criminology, 8*(1), 1–20.

Brondsema, D., & Schamp, A. (2006). *Konfidi: trust networks using PGP and RDF*. Models of trust of the Web (MTW 06). WWW2006 Conference, Edinburgh, UK.

Brookes, C. (2015). *Cyber security: Time for an integrated whole-of-nation approach in Australia*. Centre for Defence and Strategic Studies. Retrieved August 27, 2019 from http://www.defence.gov.au/ADC/Publications/IndoPac/150327%20Brookes%20IPS%20paper%20-%20cyber%20(PDF%20final).pdf

Brownlee, J. (2019). *What is Data Mining and KDD*. Available: https://machinelearningmastery.com/what-is-data-mining-and-kdd/

Bugawa, A. M. M. (2016). *The impact of the interactivity of web 2.0 technologies on the learning experience of students in higher education* (Doctoral dissertation). Brunel University London.

Bugawa, A. M., & Mirzal, A. (2017). The impact of the web 2.0 technologies on students' learning experience: Interactivity inside the classroom. *International Journal of Management and Applied Science., 3*(5), 46–50.

Bugawa, A. M., & Mirzal, A. (2018). The Impact of the Web 2.0 Technologies on the Learning Experience of Students in Higher Education: A Review. *International Journal of Management and Applied Science, 13*(3), 1–17.

Burnet, F. M. (1959). *The clonal selection theory of acquired immunity.* Cambridge University Press.

Burwick, C., Coppersmith, D., D'Avignon, E., Gennaro, R., Halevi, S., Jutla, C., & Zunic, N. (1999). *The MARS Encryption Algorithm.* IBM.

Byrski, A., & Carvalho, M. (2008). Agent-Based Immunological Intrusion Detection System for Mobile Ad-Hoc Networks. In *Proceedings of the International Conference on Computational Science* (584-593). Kraków, Poland: LNCS. 10.1007/978-3-540-69389-5_66

Calder, A. (2018). *NIST Cybersecurity Framework – A pocket guide.* IT Governance Publishing. doi:10.2307/j.ctv4cbhfx

Cameron, A. F., & Webster, J. (2005). Unintended consequences of emerging communication technologies: Instant messaging in the workplace. *Computers in Human Behavior, 21*(1), 85–103. doi:10.1016/j.chb.2003.12.001

Cao, B., Mao, M., Viidu, S., & Philip, S. Y. (2017, November). HitFraud: A Broad Learning Approach for Collective Fraud Detection in Heterogeneous Information Networks. In *2017 IEEE International Conference on Data Mining (ICDM)* (pp. 769-774). IEEE. 10.1109/ICDM.2017.90

Carlos Martins Rodrigues Pinho, J., & Soares, A. M. (2011). Examining the technology acceptance model in the adoption of social networks. *Journal of Research in Interactive Marketing, 5*(2/3), 116–129. doi:10.1108/17505931111187767

Cavelty, M. D. (2014). Breaking the cyber-security dilemma: Aligning security needs and removing vulnerabilities. *Science and Engineering Ethics, 20*(3), 701–715. doi:10.100711948-014-9551-y PMID:24781874

Cavoukian, A. (2009, March). *Online Privacy: Make Youth Awareness and Education a Priority.* Toronto, Ontorio, Canada: Information and Privacy Commissioner of Ontario. Retrieved July 26, 2019, from https://www.ipc.on.ca/wp-content/uploads/resources/youthonline.pdf

Cavusoglu, H., Mishra, B., & Raghunathan, S. (2004). The effects of internet security breach announcements on market value: Capital market reactions for breached firms and internet security developers. *International Journal of Electronic Commerce, 9*(1), 69–104. doi:10.1080/108644 15.2004.11044320

Cesar, J. (2004). Evolutionary Computation in Computer Security and Cryptography. *New Generation Computing, 23*, 193–199.

Chadli, S., Saber, M., Emharraf, M., & Ziyyat, A. (2016). Implementation an Intelligent Architecture of Intrusion Detection System for MANETs. In *Proceedings of the Mediterranean Conference on Information & Communication Technologies. Lecture Notes in Electrical Engineering* (*vol. 381*, pp.479-487). Saidia, MA: Springer. 10.1007/978-3-319-30298-0_49

Chakrabarti, S. (2007, May). Dynamic personalized pagerank in entity-relation graphs. In *Proceedings of the 16th international conference on World Wide Web* (pp. 571-580). ACM. 10.1145/1242572.1242650

Chalapathy, R., & Chawla, S. (2019). *Deep learning for anomaly detection: A survey.* arXiv preprint arXiv:1901.03407

Chami, K. (2019). *FinTech in the Gulf Cooperation Council (GCC).* Retrieved from https://gomedici.com/how-gulf-countries-are-embracing-fintech

Chang, F. R. (2012). Guest Editor's Column. *The Next Wave, 19*(4), 1–2.

Chang, K., & Shin, K. G. (2010). Application-Layer Intrusion Detection in MANETs. In *Proceedings of the 43rd Hawaii International Conference on System Sciences* (1-10). Honolulu, HI: IEEE.

Chapman, J. (2019, April 4). *How safe is your data? Cyber-security in higher education.* Retrieved from https://www.hepi.ac.uk/2019/04/04/how-safe-is-your-data-cyber-security-in-higher-education/

Cheng, B., & Tseng, R. (2011). A context adaptive intrusion detection system for MANET. *Computer Communications, 34*(3), 310–318. doi:10.1016/j.comcom.2010.06.015

Chen, H. H., & Giles, C. L. (2013, August). ASCOS: an asymmetric network structure context similarity measure. In *2013 IEEE/ACM International Conference on Advances in Social Networks Analysis and Mining (ASONAM 2013)* (pp. 442-449). IEEE. 10.1145/2492517.2492539

Choudhary, M., & Dhaka, V. (2015). Automatic e-mails Classification Using genetic Algorithm. *International Journal of Computer Science and Information Technologies, 6*(6), 5097–5103.

Chowdhary, M., & Dhaka, V. (2015). E-mail Spam Filtering Using Genetic Algorithm: A Deeper Analysis. *International Journal of Computer Science and Information Technologies, 6*(3), 2272–2276.

Chowdhury, S., Khanzadeh, M., Akula, R., Zhang, F., Zhang, S., Medal, H., ... Bian, L. (2017). Botnet detection using graph-based feature clustering. *Journal of Big Data, 4*(1), 14. doi:10.118640537-017-0074-7

Cilio, W. (2013). *Mitigating power and timing based side channel attacks using dual spacer dual rail delay insensitive asynchronous logic," in journal of microelectronics.* Elsevier. doi:10.1016/j.mejo.2012.12.001

CISCO. (2019). *Email and Spam Data || Cisco Talos Intelligence Group - Comprehensive Threat Intelligence.* Available: https://www.talosintelligence.com/reputation_center/email_rep

COBIT. (2019). *COBIT's.* Retrieved from http://www.cobitonline.isaca.org

Colorado Technical University. (2019). *The History of Cybersecurity Worms. Viruses. Trojan horses. Logic bombs.* Spyware.

Conklin, A., & White, G. (2006). e-Government and cyber security: The role of cyber security exercises. *Proceedings of the 39th Annual Hawaii International Conference on System Sciences (HICSS'06)*. 10.1109/HICSS.2006.133

Consultancy United Kingdom. (2016). Costs of cybercrime have soared to $280 billion this year. *Consultancy United Kingdom*. Retrieved August 27, 2019 from https://www.consultancy. uk/news/12917/costs-of-cybercrime-have-soared-to-280-billion-this-year

Cooper, G. F. (1990). The computational complexity of probabilistic inference using Bayesian belief networks. *Artificial Intelligence, 42*(2-3), 393–405. doi:10.1016/0004-3702(90)90060-D

Courrège, J.-C., Feix, B., & Roussellet, M. (2010). Simple Power Analysis on Exponentiation Revisited. *9th IFIP WG 8.8/11.2 International Conference on Smart Card Research and Advanced Applications (CARDIS)*, 65-79. .ffhal01056099f10.1007/978-3-642-12510-2_6ff

Craigen, D., Diakun-Thibault, N., & Purse, R. (2014). Defining cybersecurity. *Technology Innovation Management Review, 4*(10).

Cresey, D. R. (1954). Differential association theory and compulsive crimes. *Journal of Criminal Law and Criminology, 45*(1), 29–40. doi:10.2307/1139301

Creswell, J. W., & Creswell, J. D. (2017). *Research design: Qualitative, quantitative, and mixed methods approach*. Los Angeles, CA: Sage Publications.

CSC. (2019). *Critical Security Controls*. Retrieved from https://www.cisecurity.org/about-us/

da Cunha Neto, R. P., Zair, A., Fernandes, V. P. M., & Froz, B. R. (2013). Intrusion Detection System for Botnet Attacks in Wireless Networks Using Hybrid Detection Method Based on DNS. In T. Sobh & K. Elleithy (Eds.), Emerging Trends in Computing, Informatics, Systems Sciences, and Engineering, Lecture Notes in Electrical Engineering 151 (pp. 689-702). Springer. doi:10.1007/978-1-4614-3558-7_59

Daemen, J., & Rijmen, V. (2002). *The Design of RIJNDAEL: AESThe Advanced Encryption Standard. Springer*. Berlin: German. doi:10.1007/978-3-662-04722-4

Daft, R. L., & Lengel, R. H. (1986). Organizational information requirements, media richness and structural design. *Management Science, 32*(5), 554–571. doi:10.1287/mnsc.32.5.554

Dasgupta, S., & Hsu, D. (2008, July). Hierarchical sampling for active learning. In *Proceedings of the 25th international conference on Machine learning* (pp. 208-215). ACM.

Dashora, K. (2011). Cybercrime in the society: Problems and prevention. *Journal of Alternative Perspectives in the Social Sciences, 3*(1), 24–59.

Daudi, J. (2015). An Overview of Application of Artificial Immune System in Swarm Robotic Systems. Automation. *Control and Intelligent Systems, 3*(2), 11–18. doi:10.11648/j. acis.20150302.11

David, N., & Lucia, S. & Bindura. (2013). Hidden Markov Models And Artificial Neural Networks For Spam Detection. *International Journal of Engineering Research & Technology*, *2*(2), 1–5. doi:10.1177/2393957514555052

Davis, F. D. (1986). A technology acceptance model for empirically testing new end-user information systems. Cambridge, MA: Academic Press.

Davis, F. D. (1989). Perceived usefulness, perceived ease of use, and user acceptance of information technology. *Management Information Systems Quarterly*, *13*(3), 319–340. doi:10.2307/249008

Davis, F. D., Bagozzi, R. P., & Warshaw, P. R. (1989). User acceptance of computer technology: A comparison of two theoretical models. *Management Science*, *35*(8), 982–1003. doi:10.1287/mnsc.35.8.982

Davis, M., Liu, W., Miller, P., & Redpath, G. (2011, October). Detecting anomalies in graphs with numeric labels. In *Proceedings of the 20th ACM international conference on Information and knowledge management* (pp. 1197-1202). ACM. 10.1145/2063576.2063749

Deepika & Rani. (2017). Performance of Machine Learning Techniques for Email Spam Filtering. *International Journal of Recent Trends in Engineering & Research*, 245-248.

Delona, C., J., Haripriya, P., V., & Anju, J., S. (2017). Negative Selection Algorithm: A Survey. *International Journal of Science, Engineering and Technology Research, 6*(4).

den Hamer, A. H., & Konijn, E. A. (2015). Adolescents' media exposure may increase their cyberbullying behavior: A longitudinal study. *The Journal of Adolescent Health*, *56*(2), 203–208. doi:10.1016/j.jadohealth.2014.09.016 PMID:25620303

Deveci, Ö., Karaduman, E., & Sağlam, G. (2016). The Jacobsthal sequences in finite groups. *Bulletin of the Iranian Mathematical Society*, *42*(1), 79–89.

Devi, K., Supriya, N., & Alekya, P. (2017). Overview of Content- based spam filters Techniques and Similarity hashing Algorithms. *International Journal of Innovations & Advancement in Computer Science*, *6*(11), 265–271.

Devi, V. A., & Bhuvaneswaran, R. S. (2011). Agent Based Cross Layer Intrusion Detection System for MANET. In *CNSA 2011, CCIS 196* (pp. 427–440). Springer Verlag-Berlin.

Ding, K., Li, J., Bhanushali, R., & Liu, H. (2019, May). Deep Anomaly Detection on Attributed Networks. In *Proceedings of the 2019 SIAM International Conference on Data Mining* (pp. 594-602). Society for Industrial and Applied Mathematics. 10.1137/1.9781611975673.67

Dong, S., Liu, D., Ouyang, R., Zhu, Y., Li, L., Li, T., & Liu, J. (2019). Second-Order Markov Assumption Based Bayes Classifier for Networked Data With Heterophily. *IEEE Access: Practical Innovations, Open Solutions*, *7*, 34153–34161. doi:10.1109/ACCESS.2019.2892757

Dong, Y., Zhang, J., Tang, J., Chawla, N. V., & Wang, B. (2015, August). Coupledlp: Link prediction in coupled networks. In *Proceedings of the 21th ACM SIGKDD International Conference on Knowledge Discovery and Data Mining* (pp. 199-208). ACM. 10.1145/2783258.2783329

Dorigo, M. (1992). *Optimization, learning and natural algorithms* (Ph.D. Thesis). Dipartimento diElettronica, Politecnico di Milano, Italy.

Easttom, C., & Butler, W. (2019, January). A modified McCumber Cube as a basis for a taxonomy of cyber attacks. In *2019 IEEE 9th Annual Computing and Communication Workshop and Conference (CCWC)* (pp. 943-949). IEEE.

Eberhart, R., & Shi, Y. (2007). *Computational Intelligence: Concepts to Implementations.* Elsevier. doi:10.1016/B978-155860759-0/50002-0

Eberle, W., & Holder, L. (2007, October). Discovering structural anomalies in graph-based data. In *Seventh IEEE International Conference on Data Mining Workshops (ICDMW 2007)* (pp. 393-398). IEEE. 10.1109/ICDMW.2007.91

EC-Council. (2016). *Computer forensics. Investigating file and operating systems: Wireless network and storage (CHFI).* Boston, MA: Cengage Learning.

Economic Development Board (EDB). (n.d.). *Cybersecurity: Business opportunities: Information & communications technology.* Economic Development Board of Bahrain. Retrieved August 28, 2019, from https://bahrainedb.com/business-opportunities/information-communication-technology/cyber-security/

Eiben, A. E., & Schoenauer, M. (2002). Evolutionary computing. *Information Processing Letters, 82*(1), 1–6. doi:10.1016/S0020-0190(02)00204-1

Eiben, A. E., & Smith, J. E. (2015). *Introduction to Evolutionary Computing* (2nd ed.). Springer-Verlag Berlin Heidelberg. doi:10.1007/978-3-662-44874-8

ElGamal, T. (1985). A public key cryptosystem and a signature scheme based on discrete logarithms. *IEEE Transactions on Information Theory, 31*(4), 469–472. doi:10.1109/TIT.1985.1057074

Elmaghraby, A. S., & Losavio, M. M. (2014). Cybersecurity challenges in smart cities: Safety, security and privacy. *Journal of Advanced Research, 5*(4), 491–497. doi:10.1016/j.jare.2014.02.006 PMID:25685517

Emirates 24/7. (2014). [The] majority [of] UAE users hit by cyber bugs [are] happily unaware. *Emirates.* Retrieved August 27, 2019 from https://www.emirates247.com/news/emirates/majority-uae-users-hit-by-cyber-bugs-happily-unaware-2014-06-10-1.552256

Esmaeili, M., Arjomandzadeh, A., Shams, R., & Zahedi, M. (2017). An Anti-Spam System using Naive Bayes Method and Feature Selection Methods. *International Journal of Computers and Applications, 165*(4), 1–5. doi:10.5120/ijca2017913842

Farhan, A. F., Zulkhairi, D., & Hatim, M. T. (2008). Mobile Agent Intrusion Detection System for Mobile Ad Hoc Networks: A Non-overlapping Zone Approach. In *Proceedings of the 4th IEEE/IFIP International Conference on Internet* (pp. 1-5). Tashkent: IEEE. 10.1109/CANET.2008.4655310

Farhan, A.F., & Dahalin, Z. M., & Jusoh, S. (2010). Distributed and cooperative hierarchical intrusion detection on MANETs. *International Journal of Computers and Applications*, *12*(1), 32–40.

Farmer, J. D., Packard, N. H., & Perelson, A. S. (1986). The immune system, adaptation, and machine learning. *Physica*, *22*, 187–204.

Federal Commnuications Commission. (2013). *Cyber Security Planning Guide*. Retrieved July 26, 2019, from https://transition.fcc.gov/cyber/cyberplanner.pdf

Fellows, L. (2019, May 31). *A daily threat – Universities, cyber-attacks and national security in the UK*. Retrieved from https://blogs.vmware.com/emea/en/2019/05/a-daily-threat-universities-cyber-attacks-and-national-security-in-the-uk/

Fishbein, M., & Ajzen, I. (1975). *Belief, attitude, intention and behavior*. Academic Press.

Fogel, B. (Ed.). (1998). *Evolutionary Computation: The Fossil Record*. Piscataway, NJ: IEEE Press. doi:10.1109/9780470544600

Fogel, J., & Nehmad, E. (2009). Internet social network communities: Risk taking, trust, and privacy concerns. *Computers in Human Behavior*, *25*(1), 153–160. doi:10.1016/j.chb.2008.08.006

Fogel, L., Owens, A., & Walsh, M. (1966). *Artificial Intelligence through Simulated Evolution*. Chichester, UK: Wiley.

Galluccio, L., Michel, O., Comon, P., & Hero, A. O. III. (2012). Graph based k-means clustering. *Signal Processing*, *92*(9), 1970–1984. doi:10.1016/j.sigpro.2011.12.009

Gao, J., Liang, F., Fan, W., Wang, C., Sun, Y., & Han, J. (2010, July). On community outliers and their efficient detection in information networks. In *Proceedings of the 16th ACM SIGKDD international conference on Knowledge discovery and data mining* (pp. 813-822). ACM. 10.1145/1835804.1835907

Garcia-Teodoro, P., Diaz-Verdejo, J., Maciá-Fernández, G., & Vázquez, E. (2009). Anomaly-based network intrusion detection: Techniques, systems and challenges. *Computers & Security*, *28*(1), 18–28. doi:10.1016/j.cose.2008.08.003

Gayathri, G. (2018). A Comparative Study of Classification Algorithms on Spam Detection. *International Journal for Research in Applied Science and Engineering Technology*, *6*(4), 4791–4795. doi:10.22214/ijraset.2018.4785

Gearhart, G. D., Abbiatti, M. D., & Miller, M. T. (2019). Higher education's cyber security: Leadership issues, challenges and the future. *International Journal on New Trends in Education & Their Implications*, *10*(2), 11-16.

Gelnaw, A. (2018). *Creating a Cybersecurity Awareness Culture at Financial Institutions*. Retrieved July 26, 2019, from https://www.bitsight.com/blog/creating-a-cybersecurity-awareness-culture-at-financial-institutions ges/European-CybersecurityImplementation-Series.aspx

George, A. (2006). Things you wouldn't tell your mother. *New Scientist, 191*(2569), 50–51. doi:10.1016/S0262-4079(06)60502-2

Getoor, L., Friedman, N., Koller, D., & Pfeffer, A. (2001). Learning probabilistic relational models. In *Relational data mining* (pp. 307–335). Berlin: Springer. doi:10.1007/978-3-662-04599-2_13

Ghannam, J. (2011). Social media in the Arab World: Leading up to the Uprisings of 2011. *Center for International Media Assistance, 3*(1), 1-44.

Gharib, M., Moradlou, Z., Doostari, M. A., & Movaghar, A. (2017). Fully distributed ECC-based key management for mobile ad hoc networks. *Computer Networks, 113*(1), 269–283. doi:10.1016/j.comnet.2016.12.017

Gierlichs, B. (2008). *Mutual Information Analysis. In Lecture notes CHES* (Vol. 5154, pp. 426–442). Springer.

Gikas, J., & Grant, M. M. (2013). Mobile computing devices in higher education: Student perspectives on learning with cellphones, smartphones & social media. *The Internet and Higher Education, 19*, 18–26. doi:10.1016/j.iheduc.2013.06.002

Giraud, C. (2006, September). An RSA Implementation Resistant to Fault Attacks and to Simple Power Analysis. *IEEE Transactions on Computers, 55*(9), 1116–1120. doi:10.1109/TC.2006.135

Gomathi, K., Parvathavarthini, B., & Saravanakumar, C. (2017). An Efficient Secure Group Communication in MANET Using Fuzzy Trust Based Clustering and Hierarchical Distributed Group Key Management. *Wireless Personal Communications, 94*(4), 2149–2162. doi:10.100711277-016-3366-x

Goodman, E., Ingram, J., Martin, S., & Grunwald, D. (2015, December). Using bipartite anomaly features for cyber security applications. In *2015 IEEE 14th International Conference on Machine Learning and Applications (ICMLA)* (pp. 301-306). IEEE. 10.1109/ICMLA.2015.69

Goodman, M. (2015). *Future crimes: Everything is connected, everyone is vulnerable and what we can do about it* (1st ed.). New York: Anchor, Penguin Random House LLC.

Gordon, L., & Loeb, M. (2002). The economics of information security investment. *ACM Transactions on Information and System Security, 5*(4), 438–457. doi:10.1145/581271.581274

Goweder, A. M., Rashed, T., Elbekaie, A., & Alhammi, H. A. (2008). An Anti-Spam System Using Artificial Neural Networks and Genetic Algorithms. *Proceedings of the 2008 International Arab Conference on Information Technology.*

Goyal, P., Kamra, N., He, X., & Liu, Y. (2018). *Dyngem: Deep embedding method for dynamic graphs.* arXiv preprint arXiv:1805.11273

Guo, J., & Zhu, W. (2018, April). Partial multi-view outlier detection based on collective learning. *Thirty-Second AAAI Conference on Artificial Intelligence.*

Gupta, D. K., & Goyal, S. (2018). *Email Classification into Relevant Category Using Neural Networks.* Available at http://arxiv.org/abs/1802.03971

Gupte, M., & Eliassi-Rad, T. (2012, June). Measuring tie strength in implicit social networks. In *Proceedings of the 4th Annual ACM Web Science Conference* (pp. 109-118). ACM. 10.1145/2380718.2380734

Guru99. (n.d.). *What is hacking? An introduction.* Retrieved August 30, 2019, from https://www.guru99.com/what-is-hacking-an-introduction.html

Hamerdheidari, S., & Rafeh, R. (2013). A Novel Agent-Based Approach to Detect Sinkhole Attacks in Wireless Sensor Networks. *Computers & Security, 37*(1), 1–14. doi:10.1016/j.cose.2013.04.002

Han, J., Kamber, M., & Pei, J. (2011). *Data mining.* Amsterdam: Elsevier/Morgan Kaufmann.

Harmer, P., Williams, P., Gunsch, G., & Lamont, G. (2002). An Artificial Immune System Architecture for Computer Security Applications. *Transactions on Evolutionary Computation, 6*(6).

Harmer, G. (2014). *Governance of Enterprise IT based on COBIT®5: A Management Guide.* IT Governance Publishing.

Harris, C. E., & Lammargren, R. (2016). *Higher education vulnerability to cyber-attacks.* University Business. Retrieved from https://universitybusiness.com/higher-educations-vulnerability-to-cyber-attacks/

Hasib, S., Motwani, M., & Saxena, A. (2012). Anti-Spam Methodologies: A Comparative Study. *International Journal of Computer Science and Information Technologies, 3*(6), 5341–5345.

Haveliwala, T. H. (2003). Topic-sensitive pagerank: A context-sensitive ranking algorithm for web search. *IEEE Transactions on Knowledge and Data Engineering, 15*(4), 784–796. doi:10.1109/TKDE.2003.1208999

Heaton, J. (1998). Secondary analysis of qualitative data. *Social Research Update, 22.* Department of Sociology, University of Surrey, Guildford, UK. Retrieved August 27, 2019 from http://sru.soc.surrey.ac.uk/SRU22.html

Hecht-Nielsen, R. (1987). *Kolmogorov's Mapping Neural Network Existence Theorem.* Hecht-Nielsen Neurocomputer Corporation.

Henderson, K., Eliassi-Rad, T., Faloutsos, C., Akoglu, L., Li, L., Maruhashi, K., & Tong, H. (2010, July). Metric forensics: a multi-level approach for mining volatile graphs. In *Proceedings of the 16th ACM SIGKDD international conference on Knowledge discovery and data mining* (pp. 163-172). ACM. 10.1145/1835804.1835828

Henderson, K., Gallagher, B., Li, L., Akoglu, L., Eliassi-Rad, T., Tong, H., & Faloutsos, C. (2011, August). It's who you know: graph mining using recursive structural features. In *Proceedings of the 17th ACM SIGKDD international conference on Knowledge discovery and data mining* (pp. 663-671). ACM. 10.1145/2020408.2020512

Holland, J. (1973). Genetic algorithms and the optimal allocation of trials. *SIAM Journal on Computing*, *2*, 88–105.

Holt, T. J., Strumsky, D., Smirnova, O., & Kilger, M. (2012). Examining the social networks of malware writers and hackers. *International Journal of Cyber Criminology*, *6*(1), 891.

Hong-Song, C., Jianyu, Z., & Lee, H. W. J. (2008). A novel NP-based security scheme for AODV routing protocol. *Journal of Discrete Mathematical Sciences and Cryptography*, *11*(2), 131–145. doi:10.1080/09720529.2008.10698172

Hong-song, C., Zhenzhou, J., Mingzeng, H., Zhongchuan, F., & Ruixiang, J. (2007). Design and performance evaluation of a multi-agent-based dynamic lifetime security scheme for AODV routing protocol. *Elsevier Journal of Network and Computer Applications*, *30*(1), 145–166. doi:10.1016/j.jnca.2005.09.006

Hota, H. S., Shrivas, A. K., & Singhai, S. K. (2013). Artificial Neural Network, Decision Tree and Statistical Techniques Applied for Designing and Developing E-mail Classifier. *International Journal of Recent Technology and Engineering*, (16), 2277–3878.

Hsieh, W., & Tang, B. (1998). Applying Neural Network Models to Prediction and Data Analysis in Meteorology and Oceanography. *Bulletin of the American Meteorological Society*, *79*(9), 1855–1870. doi:10.1175/1520-0477(1998)079<1855:ANNMTP>2.0.CO;2

Huang, Q., Singh, V. K., & Atrey, P. K. (2018). On cyberbullying incidents and underlying online social relationships. *Journal of Computational Social Science*, *1*(2), 241–260. doi:10.100742001-018-0026-9

Hung-Jen, L., Chun-Hung, R. L., Ying-Chih, L., & Kuang-Yuan, T. (2013). Intrusion detection system: A comprehensive review. *Elsevier Journal of Network and Computer Applications*, *36*(1), 16–24. doi:10.1016/j.jnca.2012.09.004

Hu, Y.-C., Johnson, D. B., & Perrig, A. (2003). SEAD: Secure efficient distance vector routing for mobile wireless ad hoc networks. *Ad Hoc Networks*, *1*(1), 175–192. doi:10.1016/S1570-8705(03)00019-2

Hwang, M. S., Chang, C. C., & Hwang, K. F. (2002). An ElGamal-like cryptosystem for enciphering large messages. *IEEE Transactions on Knowledge and Data Engineering*, *14*(2), 445–446. doi:10.1109/69.991728

IBM. (2017). *IBM X-Force Threat Intelligence Index 2017*. Available: https://www-01.ibm.com/common/ssi/cgi-bin/ssialias?htmlfid=WGL03140USEN&

Ide, J., & Renault, M. S. (2012). Power Fibonacci Sequences. *The Fibonacci Quarterly*, *50*(2), 175–180.

Idris, I., & Selamat, A. (2015). A Swarm Negative Selection Algorithm for Email Spam Detection. *Journal of Computer Engineering & Information Technology*, *4*(1).

IEEE CIS. (2019). *What is Computational Intelligence?* Retrieved from: https://cis.ieee.org/about/what-is-ci

Igbaria, M., Parasuraman, S., & Baroudi, J. J. (1996). A motivational model of microcomputer usage. *Journal of Management Information Systems*, *13*(1), 127–143. doi:10.1080/07421222.1996.11518115

Igor, H., Bohuslava, J., Martin, J., & Martin, N. (2013). Application of Neural Networks in Computer Security. In *24th DAAAM International Symposium on Intelligent Manufacturing and Automation*. Elsevier Ltd.

Inbavalli, P., & Nandhini, G. (2014). Body Odor as a Biometric Authentication. *International Journal of Computer Science and Information Technologies*, *5*(5), 6270–6274.

Investopedia. (2019). *Financial Performance*. Retrieved July 26, 2019, from https://www.investopedia.com/terms/f/financialperformance.asp

Iqbal, M., Abid, M. M., Ahmad, M., & Khurshid, F. (2016). Study on the Effectiveness of Spam Detection Technologies. *International Journal of Information Technology and Computer Science*, *8*(1), 11–21. doi:10.5815/ijitcs.2016.01.02

ISACA. (2014). *European Cybersecurity Implementation: Overview*. Retrieved on 10 October 2019 from http://www.isaca.org/KnowledgeCenter/Research/ResearchDeliverables/Pa

Isenburg, M., & Snoeyink, J. (2003). Binary Compression Rates for ASCII Formats. *Proceedings of Web3D Symposium'03*, 173-178. 10.1145/636593.636619

Ishida, Y. (1990). Fully distributed diagnosis by PDP learning algorithm: towards immune network PDP model. *IEEE International Joint Conference on Neural Networks*. 10.1109/IJCNN.1990.137663

ISO/IEC 27001:2013. (2019, June 3). Retrieved from https://www.iso.org/standard/54534.html

ITU. (2018). *Critical Information Infrastructure Protection Role of CIRTs and Cooperation at National Level*. Retrieved July 26, 2019, from Global Cybersecurity AgendaITU: https://www.energypact.org/wp-content/uploads/2018/03/Maloor_Day2_Critical-Information-Infrastructure-Protection.pdf

Jain, C. (Ed.). (1999). *Intelligent Biometric Techniques in Fingerprint and Face Recognition*. Boca Raton, FL: CRC Press.

Jain, C., & Lazzerini, B. (Eds.). (1999). *Knowledge-Based Intelligent Techniques in Character Recognition*. Boca Raton, FL: CRC Press.

Jameel, N. G. M. (2013). Detection of Phishing Emails using Feed Forward Neural Network. *International Journal of Computers and Applications*, *77*(7), 10–15. doi:10.5120/13405-1057

Janaki Meena, K., Chandran, K. R., Karthik, A., & Vijay Samuel, A. (2012). An enhanced ACO algorithm to select features for text categorization and its parallelization. *Expert Systems with Applications, 39*(5), 5861–5871. doi:10.1016/j.eswa.2011.11.081

Jasper, S. (2017). *Strategic Cyber Deterrence: The Active Cyber Defense Option.* Rowman & Lttlefield.

Javed, A., & Pandey, M. K., (2014). Advance Cyber Security System using fuzzy logic. *Journal of Management and IT, 10*(1).

Jawale, D., Mahajan, A., Shinkar, K., & Katdare, V. (2018). Hybrid spam detection using machine learning, International Journal of Advance Research. *Ideas and Innovations in Technology, 4*(2), 2828–2832.

Jayanthi, S. K., & Subhashini, V. (2016). *Efficient Spam Detection using Single Hidden Layer Feed Forward Neural Network. International Research Journal of Engineering and Technology,* 690–696.

Jensen, D., Neville, J., & Gallagher, B. (2004, August). Why collective inference improves relational classification. In *Proceedings of the tenth ACM SIGKDD international conference on Knowledge discovery and data mining* (pp. 593-598). ACM.

Jeswani, D., & Kale, S. (2015). The Particle Swarm Optimization Based Linear Cryptanalysis of Advanced Encryption Standard Algorithm. *International Journal on Recent and Innovation Trends in Computing and Communication, 3*(4).

Jin, X., Liang, J., Tong, W., Lu, L., & Li, Z. (2017). Multi-agent trust-based intrusion detection scheme for wireless sensor networks. *Computers & Electrical Engineering, 59*(1), 262–273. doi:10.1016/j.compeleceng.2017.04.013

John, S. P., & Samuel, P. (2015). Self-organized key management with trusted certificate exchange in MANET. *Ain Shams Engineering Journal, 6*(1), 161–170. doi:10.1016/j.asej.2014.09.011

Joiner, K. F. (2017). How Australia can catch up to US cyber resilience by understanding that cyber survivability test and evaluation drives defense investment. *Information Security Journal: A Global Perspective, 26*(2), 74–84.

Jones, G. A., & Jones, J. M. (1998). *Elementary number theory.* Springer Science & Business Media. doi:10.1007/978-1-4471-0613-5

Joseph, R. (2018). *Grid Search for model tuning.* Available at: https://towardsdatascience.com/grid-search-for-model-tuning-3319b259367e

Jukic, S., Azemovic, J., Keco, D., & Kevric, J. (2015). Comparison of Machine Learning Techniques in Spam E-Mail Classification. *Southeast Europe Journal of Soft Computing, 4*(1), 32–36. doi:10.21533cjournal.v4i1.88

Kahraman, C., Ihsan Kaya, I., & Didem, C. (2010). Computational Intelligence: Past, Today, and Future. In D. Ruan (Ed.), *Computational Intelligence in Complex Decision Systems.* doi:10.2991/978-94-91216-29-9_1

Kalaibar, S., & Razavi, S. (2014). Spam filtering by using Genetic based Feature Selection. *International Journal of Computer Applications Technology and Research, 3*(12), 839–843. doi:10.7753/IJCATR0312.1018

Kang, U., Chau, D. H., & Faloutsos, C. (2011, April). Mining large graphs: Algorithms, inference, and discoveries. In *2011 IEEE 27th International Conference on Data Engineering* (pp. 243-254). IEEE.

Kannan, K., & Telang, R. (2005). Market for software vulnerabilities? Think again. *Management Science, 51*(5), 726–740. doi:10.1287/mnsc.1040.0357

Karaboga, D. (2005). *An Idea Based On Honey Bee Swarm for Numerical Optimization.* Academic Press.

Karaklajic. (2013). Hardware designers guide to fault attacks. *IEEE Transactions on Very Large Scale Integration (VLSI) Systems, 21*(12).

Karas, T. H., Moore, J. H., & Parrott, L. K. (2008, Aug). *Metaphors for Cyber Security.* Sandia Report. Retrieved July 26, 2019, from https://evolutionofcomputing.org/Cyberfest%20Report.pdf

Karlik, B. & Albastaki, Y. (2005). Bad breath diagnosis system using OMX-GR sensor and Neural Network for telemedicine, Computer Medicine '2005, Scientific-practical Conference [eHealth]. *ElectronicHealthcare,* 23–25.

Kaspersky. (2019). *Types of spam.* Available: https://encyclopedia.kaspersky.com/knowledge/types-of-spam/

Kaur, H., & Sharma, A. (2016). Novel Email Spam Classification using Integrated Particle Swarm Optimization and J48. *International Journal of Computers and Applications, 149*(7), 23–27. doi:10.5120/ijca2016911466

Kennedy, J., & Eberhart, R. (1995). Particle Swarm Optimization. *Proceedings of IEEE International Conference on Neural Networks,* 1942–1948.

Khan, N. A., Kiah, M. M., & Khan, S. U. (2013). Towards secure mobile cloud computing; A survey. *Future Generation Computer Systems, 29*(5), 1278–1299. doi:10.1016/j.future.2012.08.003

Klemperer, P. (2006). *Network Effects and Switching Costs: Two Short Essays for The New Palgrave. Working Paper Series.* Social Science Research Network.

Knuden, L. R. (2015). Dynamic Encryption. *Journal of Cyber Security and Mobility, 3*(4), 357–370. doi:10.13052/jcsm2245-1439.341

Kocher, P.C. (1998). Introduction to Differential Power Analysis. *Journal of Cryptographic Engineering, 1*(1), 5–27.

Komal, T., Ashutosh, R., Roshan, R., & Nalawade. S.M. (2015). Encryption and Decryption using Artificial Neural Network. *International Advanced Research Journal in Science, Engineering and Technology, 2*(4).

Konar, A. (2005). *Computational Intelligence-Principles, techniques and Applications.* Springer-Verlag Berlin.

Krishnan, D. (2014). Article. In *Proceedings of International Conference on Information and Communication Technologies* (*vol. 46*, pp. 1203-1208). Elsevier.

Krutz, R. L. (2010). *Cloud security: a comprehensive guide to secure cloud computing.* Wiley.

Kshetri, N. (2010). *The global cybercrime industry.* Berlin: Springer. doi:10.1007/978-3-642-11522-6

Kshetri, N. (2013). Cybercrime and cybersecurity in the Middle East and North African economies. In *Cybercrime and Cybersecurity in the Global South* (pp. 119–134). London: Palgrave Macmillan. doi:10.1057/9781137021946_6

Kulikowski, K. J. (2006). DPA on faulty cryptographic hardware and countermeasures. FDTC, 211–222.

Kumar, P., & Reddy, K. (2014). An Agent based Intrusion detection system for wireless network with Artificial Immune System (AIS) and Negative Clone Selection. In *Proceedings of the International Conference on Electronic Systems, Signal Processing and Computing Technologies* (pp. 429-433). IEEE. 10.1109/ICESC.2014.73

Kumar, S., & Arumugam, S. (2015). A Probabilistic Neural Network Based Classification of Spam Mails Using Particle Swarm Optimization Feature Selection. *Middle East Journal of Scientific Research, 23*(5), 874–879.

Lakshmi, R., & Radha, N. (2010). Spam classification using supervised learning techniques. *Proceedings of the 1st Amrita ACM-W Celebration on Women in Computing in India - A2CWiC '10.* 10.1145/1858378.1858444

Lamba, H., Hooi, B., Shin, K., Faloutsos, C., & Pfeffer, J. (2017, September). zooRank: Ranking suspicious entities in time-evolving tensors. In *Joint European Conference on Machine Learning and Knowledge Discovery in Databases* (pp. 68-84). Springer. 10.1007/978-3-319-71249-9_5

Lee, Y., Kozar, K. A., & Larsen, K. R. (2003). The technology acceptance model: Past, present, and future. *Communications of the Association for Information Systems, 12*(1), 50.

Li, Y., Huang, X., Li, J., Du, M., & Zou, N. (2019). *SpecAE: Spectral AutoEncoder for Anomaly Detection in Attributed Networks.* arXiv preprint arXiv:1908.03849

Liben-Nowell, D., & Kleinberg, J. (2007). The link-prediction problem for social networks. *Journal of the American Society for Information Science and Technology, 58*(7), 1019–1031. doi:10.1002/asi.20591

Liebowitz, S. J., & Margolis, S. (1994). Network Externality: An Uncommon Tragedy. *The Journal of Economic Perspectives*, *8*(2), 133–150. doi:10.1257/jep.8.2.133

Liu, C., Yan, X., Yu, H., Han, J., & Yu, P. S. (2005, April). Mining behavior graphs for "backtrace" of noncrashing bugs. In *Proceedings of the 2005 SIAM International Conference on Data Mining* (pp. 286-297). Society for Industrial and Applied Mathematics. 10.1137/1.9781611972757.26

Li, W., Tug, S., Meng, W., & Wang, Y. (2019). Designing collaborative blockchained signature-based intrusion detection in IoT environments. *Future Generation Computer Systems*, *96*(1), 481–489. doi:10.1016/j.future.2019.02.064

Li, Y., & Qian, Z. (2010). Mobile agents-based intrusion detection system for mobile ad hoc networks. In *Proceedings of the International Conference on Innovative Computing and Communication and 2010 Asia-Pacific Conference on Information Technology and Ocean Engineering* (pp. 145-148). Macao, China: IEEE. 10.1109/CICC-ITOE.2010.45

Løken, E. (2016). *Graph Classification via Neural Networks* (Master's thesis).

Loundy, D. J. (2003). *Computer crime, information warfare & economic espionage*. Durham, NC: Carolina Academic Press.

Lugo, A. (2017). *Coevolutionary Genetic Algorithms for Proactive Computer Network Defences* (Master's thesis). MIT.

Lumbiarres, R. (2016). *A new countermeasure against side channel attacks based on hardware software co-design," in journal of microelectronics*. Elsevier.

Lunardi, G., Becker, J. L., Maçada, A. C. G., & Dolci, P. C. (2014). The impact of adopting IT governance on financial performance: An empirical analysis among Brazilian companies. *International Journal of Accounting Information Systems*, *15*(1), 66–81. doi:10.1016/j.accinf.2013.02.001

Madden, M. (2010). Older adults and social media. *Pew Internet & American Life Project, 27*.

Malwarebytes. (n.d.). *What is hacking?* Retrieved August 30, 2019, from https://www.malwarebytes.com/hacker/

Manikandan, D. R. S. (2018). Machine Learning Algorithms for Classification. *International Journal of Academic Research and Development*, 384–389. doi:10.13140/RG.2.1.2044.4003

Mann, C. C. (2006). Spam+ Blogs= Trouble Splogs are the latest thing in online fraud-and they could smother the Net as we know it. *Wired*, *14*(9), 104.

Manuel, C. (2013). *The Impact of the Internet on Society: A Global Perspective*. Retrieved from https://www.bbvaopenmind.com/en/articles/the-impact-of-the-internet-on-society-a-global-perspective/

Marchang, N., & Datta, R. (2008). Collaborative techniques for intrusion detection in mobile ad-hoc networks. *Ad Hoc Networks*, *6*(4), 508–523. doi:10.1016/j.adhoc.2007.04.003

Mark, B., & Perrault, R. C. (2005). *Enron email dataset*. Retrieved from http://www-2.cs.cmu. edu/~enron/

Mathieson, K. (1991). Predicting user intentions: Comparing the technology acceptance model with the theory of planned behavior. *Information Systems Research, 2*(3), 173–191. doi:10.1287/ isre.2.3.173

Mathur, N., & Bansode, R. (2016). AES Based Text Encryption using 12 Rounds with Dynamic Key Selection. *Procedia Computer Science, 79*, 1036–1043. doi:10.1016/j.procs.2016.03.131

Matsui, M. (1994). Linear Cryptanalysis Method for DES Cipher. Lecture Notes in Computer Science, 765, 386-397. doi:10.1007/3-540-48285-7_33

Matthews, B. (2005). Semantic web technologies. *E-learning, 6*(6), 8.

Maxwell, J. A. (2005). *Qualitative research design: An interactive approach*. Thousand Oaks, CA: Sage.

Meeker, M. (2014). *Internet trends 2014-code conference*. Academic Press.

Mendel, J. (1995). Fuzzy logic systems for engineering: A tutorial. *Proceedings of the IEEE, 83*(3), 345–377. doi:10.1109/5.364485

Merchant, G. (2009). Web 2.0, new literacies, and the idea of learning through participation. *English Teaching, 8*(3), 107–122.

Merkow, M. S., & Breithaupt, J. (2014). *Information Security: Principles and Practices*. Pearson.

Merriam, S. B. (2002). *Qualitative research in practice: Examples for discussion and analysis*. San Francisco, CA: Josey-Bass.

Metsis, V. I. A., & G. P. (2006). *Enron Dataset*. Available at: http://www2.aueb.gr/users/ion/ data/enron-spam/

Michelakos, I., Mallios, N., Papageorgiou, E., & Vassilakopoulos, M. (2011). Ant Colony Optimization and Data Mining. In N. Bessis & F. Xhafa (Eds.), *Next Generation Data Technologies for Collective Computational Intelligence. Studies in Computational Intelligence* (Vol. 352, pp. 31–60). Berlin: Springer.

Miniwatts Marketing Group. (2010). *World Internet Usage and Population Statistics*. Retrieved from https://www.internetworldstats.com/stats.htm

Mishra, S. (Ed.). (2018). *Artificial Intelligence and Natural Language Processing*. Newcastle upon Tyne, UK: Cambridge Scholars Publishing.

Mitchell, M. (1997). *Machine Learning*. New York: McGraw-Hill.

Mohamed, N., & Gian Singh, J. K. (2012). A conceptual framework for information technology governance effectiveness in private organizations. *Information Management & Computer Security, 20*(2), 88–106. doi:10.1108/09685221211235616

Moore, G. C., & Benbasat, I. (1991). Development of an instrument to measure the perceptions of adopting an information technology innovation. *Information Systems Research*, 2(3), 192–222. doi:10.1287/isre.2.3.192

Müller, E., Sánchez, P. I., Mülle, Y., & Böhm, K. (2013, April). Ranking outlier nodes in subspaces of attributed graphs. In *2013 IEEE 29th International Conference on Data Engineering Workshops (ICDEW)* (pp. 216-222). IEEE. 10.1109/ICDEW.2013.6547453

Nadeem, A., & Howarth, M. P. (2014). An Intrusion Detection and Adaptive Response Mechanism for MANETs. *Ad Hoc Networks*, *13*(1), 368–380. doi:10.1016/j.adhoc.2013.08.017

Nancy, Y. L. (2012). *Bio-Privacy: Privacy Regulations and Challenge of Biometrics*. Academic Press.

Naser, M. A., & Mohammed, A. H. (2014). Emails classification by data mining techniques. *Journal of Babylon University*, *14*(2), 634–640.

Natale, D. C., Macagnano, A., Martinelli, E., Paolesse, R., D'Arcangelo, G., Roscioni, C., & D'Amico, A. (2003). Lung cancer identification by the analysis of breath by means of an array of non-selective gas sensors. *Biosensors & Bioelectronics*, *18*(10), 1209–1218. doi:10.1016/S0956-5663(03)00086-1 PMID:12835038

National Institute of Standards and Technology (NIST). (n.d.). Retrieved from https://www.nist.gov

Ndumiyana, D., Magomelo, M., & Sakala, L. (2013). Spam Detection using a Neural Network Classifier. *Online Journal of Physical and Environmental Science Research*, *2*(2), 28–37.

Neville, J., & Jensen, D. (2000, July). Iterative classification in relational data. In *Proc. AAAI-2000 Workshop on Learning Statistical Models from Relational Data* (pp. 13-20). Academic Press.

Neville, J., & Jensen, D. (2003). Collective classification with relational dependency networks. In *Workshop on Multi-Relational Data Mining (MRDM-2003)* (p. 77). Academic Press.

nibusinessinfo.co.uk. (2019). *Measure your financial performance*. Retrieved July 26, 2019, from https://www.nibusinessinfo.co.uk/content/measure-your-financial-performance

Nie, T., & Zhang, T. (2009). A Study of DES and Blowsh Encryption Algorithm. *Proc. of IEEE Region 10th Conference.*

NIST Special Publication 800-67 Recommendation for the Triple Data Encryption Algorithm (TDEA) Block Cipher Revision 1. (2012). Gaithersburg, MD: NIST.

Niven, I., Zuckerman, H. S., & Montgomery, H. L. (1991). *An introduction to the theory of numbers*. John Wiley & Sons.

Noble, C. C., & Cook, D. J. (2003, August). Graph-based anomaly detection. In *Proceedings of the ninth ACM SIGKDD international conference on Knowledge discovery and data mining* (pp. 631-636). ACM. 10.1145/956750.956831

Nuseirat, A. F., & Zitar, R. A. (2003). Trajectory path planning using hybrid reinforcement and back propagation through time training. *International Journal of Cybernetics and Systems, 34*(8).

Odesile, A., & Thamilarasu, G. (2017). Distributed Intrusion Detection Using Mobile Agents in Wireless Body Area Networks. In *Proceedings of the International Conference on Emerging Security Technologies* (vol. 7, pp. 144-149). Canterbury, UK: IEEE. 10.1109/EST.2017.8090414

Oduguwa, V., Tiwari, A., & Roy, R. (2004). Evolutionary computing in manufacturing industry: An overview of recent applications. *Applied Soft Computing, 5*(3), 281–299. doi:10.1016/j.asoc.2004.08.003

Oh, S., & Lee, K. (2014). The need for specific penalties for hacking in criminal law. *The Scientific World Journal, 16*(1), 73–78. PMID:25032236

Okeshola, F. B., & Adeta, A. K. (2013). The nature, causes and cons of cybercrime in tertiary institutions in Zaria-Danuna, Nigeria. *American International Journal of Contemporary Research, 3*(9), 98–114.

Omar, R. (2018). *A Comparison of Machine Learning Techniques: E-Mail Spam Filtering From Combined Swahili and English Email Messages* (Thesis). Institut teknologi Sepuluh Nopember Surabaya.

Ott, M., Choi, Y., Cardie, C., & Hancock, J. T. (2011). Finding deceptive opinion spam by any stretch of the imagination. *Proceedings of the 49th Annual Meeting of the Association for Computational Linguistics (ACL)*, 309–319.

Oyeleye, C. A., Fagbola, T. M., Babatunde, R. S., & Adigun, A. A. (2012). An Exploratory Study of Odor Biometrics Modality For Human Recognition. *International Journal of Engineering Research & Technology, 1*(9).

Ozarkar, P., & Patwardhan, D. (2013). Efficient Spam Classification by Appropriate Feature Selection. *Global Journal of Computer Science and Technology Software & Data Engineering, 13*(5), 49–57.

Ozyilmaz, C. & Nalli, A. (2019). Restructuring Of Discrete Logarithm Problem And Elgamal Cryptosystem By Using The Power Fibonacci Sequence Module M. *Journal of Science and Arts Quarterly*, (1), 61-70.

Page, L., Brin, S., Motwani, R., & Winograd, T. (1999). *The PageRank citation ranking: Bringing order to the web*. Stanford InfoLab.

Pandhre, S., & Balasubramanian, V. N. (2018). *Understanding Graph Data Through Deep Learning Lens* (Doctoral dissertation). Indian Institute of Technology Hyderabad.

Pareja, A., Domeniconi, G., Chen, J., Ma, T., Suzumura, T., Kanezashi, H., . . . Leisersen, C. E. (2019). *Evolvegcn: Evolving graph convolutional networks for dynamic graphs*. arXiv preprint arXiv:1902.10191

Parveen J., R., (2017). Neural Networks in Cyber Security. *International Research Journal of Computer Science, 9*(4).

Parveen, P., & Halse, G. (2016). Spam Mail Detection using Classification. *International Journal of Advanced Research in Computer and Communication Engineering, 5*(6), 347–349.

Passeri, P. (2019). *February 2019 cyber attacks[—]statistics. Hackmageddon.* Retrieved August 27, 2019 from https://www.hackmageddon.com/category/security/cyber-attacks-statistics/

Patil, P., Narayankar, P., Narayan, D. G., & Meena, S. M. (2016). A Comprehensive Evaluation of Cryptographic Algorithms: DES, 3DES, AES, RSA and Blow sh. *Procedia Computer Science, 78*, 617–624. doi:10.1016/j.procs.2016.02.108

Pattanayak, B. K., & Rath, M. (2014). A Mobile Agent Based Intrusion Detection System Architecture for Mobile Ad Hoc Networks. *Journal of Computational Science, 10*(6), 970–975. doi:10.3844/jcssp.2014.970.975

PayTabs. (2018, July 3). *7 Tips for Safe Online Transactions.* Retrieved July 26, 2019, from Pay Tabs Blog: https://www.paytabs.com/en/7-tips-for-safe-online-transactions/

Pearce, T. C. (1997). Computational parallels between the biological olfactory pathway and its analogue. The Electronic Nose ': Part II. Sensor-based machine olfaction. *Bio Systems, 41*(2), 69–90. doi:10.1016/S0303-2647(96)01660-7 PMID:9043677

Peterson, R. (2004). Crafting Information Technology Governance. *Information Systems Management, 21*(4), 7–23. doi:10.1201/1078/44705.21.4.20040901/84183.2

Ping, Y., Futai, Z., Xinghao, J., & Jianhua, L. (2007). Multi-agent cooperative intrusion response in mobile adhoc networks. *Elsevier Journal of Systems Engineering and Electronics, 18*(4), 785–794. doi:10.1016/S1004-4132(08)60021-3

Pires, H., Abdelouahab, Z., Lopes, D., & Santos, M. (2017). A Framework for Agent-based Intrusion Detection in Wireless Sensor Networks. In *Proceedings of the Second International Conference on Internet of Things, Data and Cloud Computing* (vol. 2, pp. 1-7). Cambridge, UK: ACM. 10.1145/3018896.3056805

Ponemon Institute. (2015, May 23). *2015 cost of data breach study: Global analysis.* Ponemon Institute Research Report. Retrieved from http://public.dhe.ibm.com/common/ssi/ecm/se/en/sew03053wwen/SEW03053W WEN.PDF

Power, M. (2009). The risk management of nothing. *Accounting, Organizations and Society, 34*(6/7), 849–855. doi:10.1016/j.aos.2009.06.001

Press Association. (2019, July 23). Lancaster University students' data stolen in cyber-attack. *The Guardian.* Retrieved from https://www.theguardian.com/technology/2019/jul/23/lancaster-university-students-data-stolen-cyber-attack

PricewaterhouseCoopers (PwC). (2016). *CEO interview: Greg Becker* [Topic: Silicon Valley banking]. Formerly available from http://www.pwc.com/us/en/ceo-survey/ceo-interviews/greg-becker-silicon-valley-bank.html

Python Software Foundation. (2019). *Pickle — Python object serialization.* Available at: https://docs.python.org/3/library/pickle.html

Qasem, M., & Zolait, A. H. (2016). Determinants of Behavioral Intentions towards Using E-Government Services in the Kingdom of Bahrain. *International Journal of Computing and Digital Systems, 5*(04), 345–355. doi:10.12785/ijcds/050406

Rajan, R., Fakhuruddin, N., Hassan, N., & Nasimul Islam, M. (2014). Chemical Fingerprinting of Human Body Odor: An Overview of Previous Studies. *Malaysian Journal of Forensic Sciences, 4*(1), 33–38.

Ramachandran, C., Misra, S., & Obaidat, M. S. (2008). A novel two-pronged strategy for an agent-based intrusion detection scheme in ad-hoc networks. *Elsevier Comput. Commun, 31*(16), 3855–3869. doi:10.1016/j.comcom.2008.04.012

Raman, A., Kabir, F., Hejazi, S., & Aggarwal, K. (2016, August 25). *Cybersecurity in higher education: The changing threat landscape.* Retrieved from https://consulting.ey.com/cybersecurity-in-higher-education-the-changing-threat-landscape/

Rankl, W., & Effing, W. (1997). *Smart card handbook.* John Wiley & Sons.

Rashmi, S., & Neha, S. (2017). Knowledge Representation in Artificial Intelligence using Domain Knowledge and Reasoning Mechanism. *International Journal of Scientific Engineering and Research, 5*(3), 17–20.

Rastgarpour, M., & Shanbehzadeh, J. (2011). Application of AI Techniques in Medical Image Segmentation and Novel Categorization of Available Methods and Tools. *Proceeding of the International Multi Conference of Engineers and Computer Scientists.*

Rathee, N., Sachdeva, R., Dalel, V., & Jaie, Y. (2016, August). A Novel Approach for Cryptography Using Artificial Neural Networks. *International Journal of Innovative Research in Computer and Communication Engineering, 4*, 4.

Rathi, M., & Pareek, V. (2013). Spam Mail Detection through Data Mining – A Comparative Performance Analysis. *International Journal of Modern Education and Computer Science, 5*(12), 31–39. doi:10.5815/ijmecs.2013.12.05

Rauniar, R., Rawski, G., Yang, J., & Johnson, B. (2014). Technology acceptance model (TAM) and Social media usage: An empirical study on Facebook. *Journal of Enterprise Information Management, 27*(1), 6–30. doi:10.1108/JEIM-04-2012-0011

Ravi, S. P. (2015). Delay Insensitive Ternary CMOS Logic for Secure Hardware. *Journal of Low Power Electron. Appl., 5*(3), 183–215. doi:10.3390/jlpea5030183

Razi, Z., & Asghari, S. (2017). Providing An Improved Feature Extraction Method For Spam Detection Based On Genetic Algorithm In An Immune System. *Journal of Knowledge-Based Engineering and Innovation*, 4(8), 569–605.

Renuka, K. D. (2015). A Hybrid ACO Based Feature Selection Method for Email Spam Classification. *WSEAS Transactions on Computers*, 14, 171–177.

Richardson, M., & Domingos, P. (2006). Markov logic networks. *Machine Learning*, 62(1-2), 107–136. doi:10.100710994-006-5833-1

Riecker, M., Biedermann, S., El Bansarkhani, R., & Hollick, M. (2015). Lightweight energy consumption-based intrusion detection system for wireless sensor networks. *International Journal of Information Security*, 14(2), 155–167. doi:10.100710207-014-0241-1

Rivest, R. L., Shamir, A., & Adleman, L. (1978). A method for obtaining digital signatures and public-key cryptosystems. *Communications of the ACM*, 21(2), 120–126. doi:10.1145/359340.359342

Rogers, E. M. (1962). *Diffusion of Innovations*. New York, NY: Free Press.

Rouibah, K., & Abbas, H. (2006). A modified technology acceptance model for camera mobile phone adoption: development and validation. *ACIS 2006 Proceedings*, 13.

Roy, D. B., & Chaki, R. (2011). MABHIDS: A New Mobile Agent Based Black Hole Intrusion Detection System. In N. Chaki & A. Cortesi (Eds.), *CISIM 2011, CCIS 245* (pp. 85–94). Springer Verlag-Berlin. doi:10.1007/978-3-642-27245-5_12

Roy, S., & Viswanatham, V. (2016). Classifying Spam Emails Using Artificial Intelligent Techniques. *International Journal of Engineering Research in Africa*, 22, 152–161. doi:10.4028/www.scientific.net/JERA.22.152

Rukhin, A., Soto, J., Nechvatal, J., Smid, M., Barker, E., Leigh, S., ... Vo, S. (2001). *A Statistical Test Suite for Random and Pseudorandom Number Generators for Cryptographic Applications*. Academic Press.

Rusland, N., Wahid, N., Kasim, S., & Hafit, H. (2017). Analysis of Naïve Bayes Algorithm for Email Spam Filtering across Multiple Datasets. *IOP Conference Series. Materials Science and Engineering*, 226, 012091. doi:10.1088/1757-899X/226/1/012091

Saad, Y. (2018). Dimension Reduction Techniques for Document Categorization with Back Propagation Neural Network. *Journal of Engineering and Applied Sciences (Asian Research Publishing Network)*, 1304–1309.

Sanad, Z., & Al-Sartawi, A. (2016). Investigating the relationship between corporate governance and internet financial reporting (IFR): Evidence from Bahrain bourse. *Jordan Journal of Business Administration*, 12(1), 239–269. doi:10.12816/0030063

Sankareswari, S., & Hemanth, S. (2014). Attribute Based Encryption with Privacy Preserving using Asymmetric Key in Cloud Computing. *International Journal of Computer Science and Information Technologies*, 5(5), 6792–6795.

Santos, O. (2019). *Developing Cybersecurity Programs and Policies*. Pearson Education.

Sanzgiri, K., LaFlamme, D., Dahill, B., Levine, B. N., Shields, C., & Royer, E. (2005). Authenticated routing for ad hoc networks. *IEEE Journal on Selected Areas in Communications, 23*(3), 598–610. doi:10.1109/JSAC.2004.842547

Saswati, M., Matangini, C., Samiran, C., & Pragma, K. (2018). EAER-AODV: Enhanced Trust Model Based on Average Encounter Rate for Secure Routing in MANET. In C. Rituparna, C. Agostino, S. Khalid, & C. Nabendu (Eds.), *Advanced Computing and Systems for Security (6)* (pp. 135–151). Singapore: Springer.

Savage, D., Zhang, X., Yu, X., Chou, P., & Wang, Q. (2014). Anomaly detection in online social networks. *Social Networks, 39*, 62–70. doi:10.1016/j.socnet.2014.05.002

Schatz, D., Bashroush, R., & Wall, J. (2017). Towards a more representative definition of cyber security. Journal of Digital Forensics. *Security and Law, 12*(2), 8.

Schmidt. (2008). A Practical Fault Attack on Square and Multiply. *5th Workshop on Fault Diagnosis and Tolerance in Cryptography*, 53-58.

Schneider, S. K., O'donnell, L., Stueve, A., & Coulter, R. W. (2012). Cyberbullying, school bullying, and psychological distress: A regional census of high school students. *American Journal of Public Health, 102*(1), 171–177. doi:10.2105/AJPH.2011.300308 PMID:22095343

Schwefel, H. (1995). *Evolution and Optimum Seeking*. New York: Wiley.

Sciket learns. (2019). *Mutual Information*. Available at: https://scikit-learn.org/stable/modules/generated/sklearn.feature_selection.mutual_info_classif.html

Scikit-learn developers. (2019a). *Grid Search*. Available at: https://scikit-learn.org/stable/modules/generated/sklearn.model_selection.GridSearchCV.html

Scikit-learn developers. (2019b). *Scikit learn Classifiers*. Available at: https://scikit-learn.org/stable/supervised_learning.html

Seely Brown, J., & Adler, R. P. (2008). Open education, the long tail, and learning 2.0. *EDUCAUSE Review, 43*(1), 16–20.

Selman, Z., & Faiq, K. (2018). *Technology in the GCC*. Retrieved from https://www2.deloitte.com/eg/en/pages/about-deloitte/articles/transform-saudi-arabia/gcc-technology.html

Sen, J. (2010). An Intrusion Detection Architecture for Clustered Wireless Ad Hoc Networks. In *Proceedings of the Second International Conference on Computational Intelligence, Communication Systems and Networks* (pp. 202-207). Liverpool, UK: IEEE. 10.1109/CICSyN.2010.51

Sen, P., Namata, G., Bilgic, M., Getoor, L., Galligher, B., & Eliassi-Rad, T. (2008). Collective classification in network data. *AI Magazine, 29*(3), 93–93. doi:10.1609/aimag.v29i3.2157

Servin, A., & Kudenko, D. (2008). Multi-agent Reinforcement Learning for Intrusion Detection. In *Adaptive Agents and Multi Agent Systems III: Adaptation and Multi Agent Learning* (pp. 211–223). Springer-Verlag Berlin Heidelberg. doi:10.1007/978-3-540-77949-0_15

Sethuraman, P., & Kannan, N. (2017). Refined Trust Energy-Ad hoc on Demand Distance Vector (ReTE-AODV) routing algorithm for secured routing in MANET. *Wireless Networks*, 23(7), 2227–2237. doi:10.100711276-016-1284-1

Shahi, T. B., & Yadav, A. (2014). Mobile SMS Spam Filtering for Nepali Text Using Naïve Bayesian and Support Vector Machine. *International Journal of Intelligence Science*, 4(01), 24–28. doi:10.4236/ijis.2014.41004

Shai, S., & Shai, B. (2014). *Understanding Machine Learning: From Theory to Algorithms.* New York: Cambridge University Press.

Shama, N. T. (2017). Neural Network Model for Email-Spam Detection. *International Journal of Multi-Disciplinary*, 2(1), 1–4.

Shapiro, S. (2010). Knowledge Representation and Reasoning Logics for Artificial Intelligence. University at Buffalo, The State University of New York Buffalo.

Sharaff, A., Nagwani, N., & Dhadse, A. (2016). *Comparative Study of Classification Algorithms for Spam Email Detection. In Emerging Research in Computing, Information, Communication and Applications* (pp. 237–244). New Delhi: Springer. doi:10.1007/978-81-322-2553-9_23

Sharma, A. A. (2014). SMS Spam Detection Using Neural Network Classifier. *International Journal of Advanced Research in Computer Science and Software Engineering*, 4(6), 2277–128. Available at: http://ijarcsse.com/Before_August_2017/docs/papers/Volume_4/6_June2014/V4I6-0151.pdf

Sharma, U., & Khurana, S. S. (2017, June). SHED: Spam Ham Email Dataset. *International Journal on Recent and Innovation Trends in Computing and Communication*, 1078–1082.

Sheu, J., Chu, K., Li, N., & Lee, C. (2017). An efficient incremental learning mechanism for tracking concept drift in spam filtering. *PLoS One*, 12(2), e0171518. doi:10.1371/journal.pone.0171518 PMID:28182691

Shrivastava, S., & Anju, R. (2017). Spam mail detection through data mining techniques. *International Conference on Intelligent Communication and Computational Techniques*, 61-64.

Shrivastava, J., & Bindu, M. (2014). E-mail Spam Filtering Using Adaptive Genetic Algorithm. *International Journal of Intelligent Systems and Applications*, 6(2), 54–60. doi:10.5815/ijisa.2014.02.07

Sichu, L. (2009). *Overview of Odor Detection Instrumentation and the Potential for Human Odor Detection in Air Matrices.* MITRE Nano systems Group, MITRE Innovation Program and U.S. Government Nano-enabled Technology Initiative, Project No. 07MSR216 and 15095320, Dept. E552.

Singh, D., & Bedi, S. S. (2016). Multiclass ELM Based Smart Trustworthy IDS for MANETs. *Arabian Journal for Science and Engineering, 41*(8), 3127–3137. doi:10.100713369-016-2112-8

Siponen, M., & Iivari, J. (2006). IS security design theory framework and six approaches to the application of IS security policies and guidelines. *Journal of the Association for Information Systems, 7*(7), 445–472. doi:10.17705/1jais.00095

Snail, S. (2009). Cybercrime in South Africa – Hacking, crack, and other unlawful online activities. *Journal of Information. Law and Technology, 10*(1), 1–13.

Sonakshi V., Amita, J., Devendra, T., & Oscar, C. (2018). An Analytical Insight to Investigate the Research Patterns in the Realm of Type-2 Fuzzy Logic. *Journal of Automation, Mobile Robotics & Intelligent Systems, 12*(2).

Soto, J. (1999). *Randomness Testing of the Advanced Encryption Standard Candidate Algorithms.* NIST IR 6390.

Soto, J. J. (2018). *Randomness Testing of the AES Candidate Algorithms.* Retrieved from http://csrc.nist.gov/archive/aes/round1/r1-rand.pdf

Stafrace, S. K., & Antonopoulos, N. (2010). Military tactics in agent-based sinkhole attack detection for wireless ad hoc networks. *Elsevier Comput. Commun., 33*(5), 619–638. doi:10.1016/j.comcom.2009.11.006

Stallings, W. (2016). *Cryptography and Network Security: Principles and Practice* (7th ed.). Pearson.

Stephen, M. (2019). *Biometrics Updates.* Retrieved from https://www.biometricupdate.com

Stinson, D. R. (2002). *Cryptography Theory and Practice.* New York: Chapman & Hall / CRC.

Stockham, R.A., Slavin, D.L., & Kift, W. (2004). Specialized Use of Human Scent in Criminal Investigations. *Forensic Sciences Communications*, 1-12.

Storm, D. (2017, February 15). *Hacker breached 63 universities and government agencies.* Retrieved from https://www.computerworld.com/article/3170724/hacker-breached-63-universities-and-government-agencies.html

Strauss, A., & Corbin, J. (1998). Basics of qualitative research: Techniques and procedures for developing grounded theory (2nd ed.). Thousand Oaks, CA: Academic Press.

Suhail Najam, S., & Hashim AL-Saedi, K. (2018). Spam classification by using association rule algorithm based on segmentation. *IACSIT International Journal of Engineering and Technology, 7*(4), 2760–2765. doi:10.14419/ijet.v7i4.18486

Sun, J., Qu, H., Chakrabarti, D., & Faloutsos, C. (2005, November). Neighborhood formation and anomaly detection in bipartite graphs. In *Fifth IEEE International Conference on Data Mining (ICDM'05).* IEEE.

Symantec. (2017). Email Threats 2017 An ISTR Special Report Analyst: Ben Nahorney Internet Security Threat Report. *Symantec Security.* Available at: https://www.symantec.com/content/dam/symantec/docs/security-center/white-papers/istr-email-threats-2017-en.pdf

Taggu, A., & Taggu, A. (2011). TraceGray: An Application-layer Scheme for Intrusion Detection in MANET using Mobile Agents. In *Proceedings of the IEEE 3rd International Conference on Communication Systems and Networks (COMSNETS)* (pp. 1-4). Bangalore: IEEE. 10.1109/COMSNETS.2011.5716475

Taylor, S., & Todd, P. A. (1995). Understanding information technology usage: A test of competing models. *Information Systems Research, 6*(2), 144–176. doi:10.1287/isre.6.2.144

Tebrich, S. (1993). *Human Scent and Its Detection.* Retrieved from: https://www.cia.gov/library/center-forthe- study-of-intelligence/kentcsi/ vol5no2/html/v05i2a04p_0001.htm

Thamilarasu, G., & Ma, Z. (2015). Autonomous Mobile Agent based Intrusion Detection Framework in Wireless Body Area Networks. In *Proceedings of the IEEE 16th International Symposium on a World of Wireless, Mobile and Multimedia Networks* (vol. 16, pp. 1-3). Boston, MA: IEEE. 10.1109/WoWMoM.2015.7158178

Tim, O. (2005). *What is web 2.0? Design patterns and business models for the next generation of software.* Academic Press.

Torres, A., Torres, M. D., & de León, E. P. (2016, October). Automated analog synthesis with an estimation of the distribution algorithm. In *Mexican International Conference on Artificial Intelligence* (pp. 173-184). Springer.

TRA Annual Report. (2017). Retrieved from http://www.tra.org.bh/media/document/TRA%20Annual%20Report%202017%20-%20English2.pdf

Trivedi, R., Farajtabar, M., Biswal, P., & Zha, H. (2018). *Dyrep: Learning representations over dynamic graphs.* Academic Press.

Trivedi, P., & Singh, S. (2015). A Score Point based Email Spam Filtering Genetic Algorithm, International Journal. *Computer Technology and Application, 6*(6), 955–960.

Turcotte, M., Moore, J., Heard, N., & McPhall, A. (2016, September). Poisson factorization for peer-based anomaly detection. In *2016 IEEE Conference on Intelligence and Security Informatics (ISI)* (pp. 208-210). IEEE. 10.1109/ISI.2016.7745472

Vairagade, R. S. (2017). Survey Paper on User Defined Spam Boxes using Email Filtering. *International Journal of Computers and Applications, 157*(6), 3.

Van den Hooff, B., Groot, J., & de Jonge, S. (2005). Situational influences on the use of communication technologies: A meta-analysis and exploratory study. *The Journal of Business Communication, 42*(1), 4-27.

Varghese & Jacob. (2015). Finding Template Mails from Spam Corpus Using Genetic Algorithm and K-Means Algorithm. *International Journal of Computer Science and Information Technologies*, *6*(4), 3548–3551.

Venkatesh, V., & Davis, F. D. (1996). A model of the antecedents of perceived ease of use: Development and test. *Decision Sciences*, *27*(3), 451–481. doi:10.1111/j.1540-5915.1996. tb01822.x

Venkatesh, V., & Davis, F. D. (2000). A theoretical extension of the technology acceptance model: Four longitudinal field studies. *Management Science*, *46*(2), 186–204. doi:10.1287/ mnsc.46.2.186.11926

Verma, T. (2017). E-Mail Spam Detection and Classification Using SVM and Feature Extraction, International Journal of Advance Research. *Ideas and Innovations in Technology*, *3*(3), 1491–1495.

Vij, A. (2016, June 02). *The threat is real: Battling cybercrime in banking.* Finextra. Retrieved from https://www.finextra.com/blogposting/12685/the-threat-is-real-battling-cybercrime-in-banking

Vijayan, P., Chandak, Y., Khapra, M. M., Parthasarathy, S., & Ravindran, B. (2018). *Fusion graph convolutional networks.* arXiv preprint arXiv:1805.12528

Vijayan, V., Joy, J. P., & Suchithra, M. S. (2014). A review on password cracking strategies. *International Journal of Research in Computer and Communication Technology*, *1*(1), 8–15.

Virtue, T., & Rainey, I. (2015). *HCISPP Study Guide. Syngress.* Elsevier.

Von Solms, R., & Van Niekerk, J. (2013). From information security to cyber security. *Computers & Security*, *38*, 97–102. doi:10.1016/j.cose.2013.04.004

Wang, B., Phillips, J. M., Schreiber, R., Wilkinson, D., Mishra, N., & Tarjan, R. (2008, April). Spatial scan statistics for graph clustering. In *Proceedings of the 2008 SIAM International Conference on Data Mining* (pp. 727-738). Society for Industrial and Applied Mathematics. 10.1137/1.9781611972788.66

Wang, W., Wang, H., Wang, B., Wang, Y., & Wang, J. (2013). Energy-aware and self-adaptive anomaly detection scheme based on network tomography in mobile ad hoc networks. *Elsevier Information Sciences*, *220*(20), 580–602. doi:10.1016/j.ins.2012.07.036

Wang, X., Govindan, K., & Mohapatra, P. (2010). Provenance-based information trustworthiness evaluation in multi-hop networks. In *Proceedings of 2010 IEEE Global Telecommunications Conference GLOBECOM* (pp. 1-5). 10.1109/GLOCOM.2010.5684158

Weill, P., & Ross, J. (2004). *IT Governance: How top performer manage IT decision rights for superior results.* Boston, MA: Harvard Business School Press.

Wei, T. E., Lee, H. M., Jeng, A. B., Lamba, H., & Faloutsos, C. (2019). WebHound: A data-driven intrusion detection from real-world web access logs. *Soft Computing*, 1–19.

Whitman, M., & Mattord, J. H. (2017). Principles of Information Security. Cengage Learning.

Whitman, M. E., & Mattors, H. J. (2010). *Readings and cases in information security: Law & ethics.* Boston, MA: Cengage Learning.

Wilkin, C. L., & Chenhall, R. H. (2010). A review of IT governance: A taxonomy to inform accounting information systems. *Journal of Information Systems, 14*(2), 107–146. doi:10.2308/jis.2010.24.2.107

Wilson, A., & Baietto, M. (2009). Applications and Advances in Electronic-Nose technologies. *Sensors (Basel), 9*(7), 5099–5148. doi:10.339090705099 PMID:22346690

Wilson, C. (2008). *Botnets, cybercrime, and cyberterrorism: Vulnerabilities and policy issues for Congress.* Washington, DC: Congressional Research Service, the Library of Congress. Retrieved from https://apps.dtic.mil/dtic/tr/fulltext/u2/a477642.pdf

World Economic Forum. (2019). *1. Introduction: The Digital Infrastructure Imperative.* Retrieved July 26, 2019, from World Economic Forum: http://reports.weforum.org/delivering-digital-infrastructure/introduction-the-digital-infrastructure-imperative/

Xu, X., Yuruk, N., Feng, Z., & Schweiger, T. A. (2007, August). Scan: a structural clustering algorithm for networks. In *Proceedings of the 13th ACM SIGKDD international conference on Knowledge discovery and data mining* (pp. 824-833). ACM. 10.1145/1281192.1281280

Yale University revealed a data breach which happened a decade ago. (2018, August 5). Retrieved from https://securereading.com/yale-university-revealed-a-data-breach-which-happened-a-decade-ago/

Yang, H., Li, T., Hu, X., Wang, F., & Zou, Y. (2014). A Survey of Artificial Immune System Based Intrusion Detection. The Scientific World Journal. doi:10.1155/2014/156790

Yasir, M. A., & Azween, B. A. (2009). Biologically Inspired Model for Securing Hybrid Mobile Ad hoc Networks. In *Proceedings of the International Symposium on High Capacity Optical Networks and Enabling Technologies* (187-191). Penang: IEEE.

Yeşilot, G., & Özavşar, M. (2013). *Soyut Cebir Çözümlü Problemleri.* Ankara: Nobel Akademi.

Ye, X., & Li, J. (2010). A Security Architecture Based on Immune Agents for MANET. In *Proceedings of the International Conference on Wireless Communication and Sensor Computing* (pp. 1-5). Chennai: IEEE.

Youn, S., & McLeod, D. (2007). A Comparative Study for Email Classification. In K. Elleithy (Ed.), *Advances and Innovations in Systems, Computing Sciences and Software Engineering* (pp. 387–391). Dordrecht: Springer. doi:10.1007/978-1-4020-6264-3_67

Yu, R., Qiu, H., Wen, Z., Lin, C., & Liu, Y. (2016). A survey on social media anomaly detection. *ACM SIGKDD Explorations Newsletter, 18*(1), 1–14. doi:10.1145/2980765.2980767

Yu, W., Cheng, W., Aggarwal, C. C., Zhang, K., Chen, H., & Wang, W. (2018, July). Netwalk: A flexible deep embedding approach for anomaly detection in dynamic networks. In *Proceedings of the 24th ACM SIGKDD International Conference on Knowledge Discovery & Data Mining* (pp. 2672-2681). ACM. 10.1145/3219819.3220024

Yu-Wei, C. (2015). *Machine Learning with R Cookbook*. Birmingham, UK: Packt Publishing Ltd.

Zadeh, L. A. (1965). Fuzzy Sets. *Information and Control, 8*(3), 338–353. doi:10.1016/S0019-9958(65)90241-X

Zavvar, M., Rezaei, M., & Garavand, S. (2016). Email Spam Detection Using Combination of Particle Swarm Optimization and Artificial Neural Network and Support Vector Machine. *International Journal of Modern Education and Computer Science, 7*, 68–74. doi:10.5815/ijmecs.2016.07.08

Zhang, X., Liu, J., Zhang, Y., & Wang, C. (2006). Spam behavior recognition based on session layer data mining. *Proceedings of third international conference on fuzzy systems and knowledge discovery*, 1289-1298. 10.1007/11881599_160

Zhanna, K. (2005). Biometric Person Authentication: Odor. *Techylib*. Retrieved from https://www.techylib.com/en/view/nauseatingcynical/biometric_person_authentication_odor_2

Zhiwei, M., Singh, M., & Zaaba, Z. (2017). Email spam detection: A method of metaclassifiers stacking. *Proceedings of the 6th International Conference on Computing and Informatics*, 750-757.

Zhu, H. (2001). *Survey of Computational Assumptions Used in Cryptography Broken or Not by Shor's Algoritm* (Master Thesis). McGill University School of Computer Science, Montreal, Canada.

Zitar & Al-Jabali. (2005). Towards general neural network model for glucose/insulin in diabetics-II. *Informatica: An International Journal of Computing and Informatics, 29*.

Zitar. (2004). Optimum gripper using ant colony intelligence. *Industrial Robot Journal, 23*(1).

Zitar, R. A., & Al-Fahed Nuseirat, A. M. (2001). A theoretical approach of an intelligent robot gripper to grasp polygon shaped object. *International Journal of Intelligent and Robotic Systems, 31*(4), 397–422. doi:10.1023/A:1012094400369

Zitar, R. A., & Hamdan, A. (2011). Spam detection using genetic based artificial immune system: A review and a model. *Artificial Intelligence Review*.

Zitar, R. A., & Hassoun, M. H. (1995). Neurocontrollers trained with rule extracted by a genetic assisted reinforcement learning system. *IEEE Transactions on Neural Networks, 6*(4), 859–879. doi:10.1109/72.392249 PMID:18263375

Zolait, A. H. S., Al-Anizi, R. R., & Ababneh, S. (2014). User awareness of Social media security: The public sector framework. *International Journal of Business Information Systems, 17*(3), 261–282. doi:10.1504/IJBIS.2014.064973

About the Contributors

Yousif Abdullatif Albastaki received a BSc. degree from University of Bahrain, Msc from University of Leeds, UK and a PhD degree from University of Nottingham, UK. Recently he has been appointed as an IT advisor at the Deputy Prime Minster at the Kingdom of Bahrain and previously worked as the Dean of College of IT at the University of Bahrain. Currently he is an associate professor at Ahlia University, Kingdom of Bahrain. His research interests are Neural Networks, genetic algorithms E-Learning, Distance Education and e-government strategies and implementation.

Wasan Awad is an associate professor of Computer Science, College of Information Technology, Ahlia University, Bahrain. Her research areas include information security, computational intelligence, and coding theory. She published a number of papers in computational intelligence, information security, and block codes in a number of international journals and conferences.

* * *

Raed Abu Zitar, B.S. Electrical Engineering, University of Jordan, 1988. M.S. Computer Engineering, North Carolina A&T State University, 1989, Ph.D. Computer Engineering, Wayne State University, Michigan, 1993. Winner of many awards including Hisham Al-Hijjawi Regional Award on IT sector for the year 2008 and Al-Hussien Fund for Excellence award for Computer Science for the year 2003, in addition to several grants for research funding. More than 25 years of experience in teaching, research, and administration. Held many administrative positions as dean and chairperson in Jordan. Authored and co-authored more than 70 papers in journals and conferences. Supervised many graduate students. Conducted many training workshops and chaired many committees. Helped in organizing many conferences. Participated in many Ministry of Higher Education Accreditation committees. Member of the Editorial board of many International Journals. Member of the IEEE CS society. Active in community service for fighting computer illiteracy. Research interests include Artificial Intelligence, Pattern Recognition, Data Mining, and Robotics. Currently, he is a faculty member at the department of computer engineering at Ajman University, UAE.

Adel Ismail Al-Alawi earned his BSc. in Business Information Systems (BIS) from Husson University, USA and MBA in Information Systems from Thomas College, USA and holds a Ph.D. in Management Information Systems (MIS) from University of Leeds, UK and is a Full Professor of Management & Information Systems at University of Bahrain (UOB). Previously, in his sabbatical leave, he was Head of Business Department at Royal University for Woman in Bahrain, Dean of School of Business at University College of Bahrain. Prof. Al-Alawi is the founder of Business Information Systems Department (BIS) and was a Chairperson of BIS department at the College of Business in UOB and also the founders of College of Information Technology, and Head of BIS Department, where he served UOB for more than 30 years. His research in MIS and management has been published in several Scopus indexed journals such as Journal of International Women's Studies, Research Journal of Information Technology, Research Journal of Business Management, Issues in Information Systems, Information Technology Journal, Journal of Computer Science, Journal of Knowledge Management, Electronic Government: An International Journal (refer https://www.researchgate.net/profile/Adel_Al-Alawi). Adel received many awards such as the award in BIS from the Late Amir of Bahrain, HRH Sheikh Isa Bin Salman Al-Khalifa presented the Award on National Education day (1985); Excellence in MIS, award of the Husson University Alumni Association – Maine, US (1993); award in MIS from the late Amir of Bahrain- HRH Sheikh Isa Bin Salman Al-Khalifa presented the Award on National Education Day (1993); Judge Award in Bahrain Website Competition – the award presented by the King's son Sh. Khalifa bin Hamad Al-Khalifa (2006); award of Appreciation from Bahrain Information Technology Society (BITS) in its 25th Anniversary for providing Leadership and Excellent Services to BITS in furtherance of its objectives (2008); eGovernment Excellence Award - the Award presented by Sh. Ahmed Bin Ateyat Allah Al-Khalifa Minister of Cabinet Affairs (2010); TechNo Disabilities Award for the Recognition of Outstanding Contribution and Academic Advisor -The award was presented by HRH Sh. Khalid bin Hamad Al-Khalifa the King's son (2017). Adel is also one of the founders and board members for Information Systems Audit & Control Association (ISACA, Bahrain Chapter), Bahrain Information Technology Society; Bahrain Academic Society and he is the past President of ISACA, Bahrain Chapter and chapter awarded the best innovative chapter in the world (2018). Adel is considered as an MIS Authority in the Kingdom of Bahrain. Major areas: Innovation, Management, Information Systems, Cybersecurity, Knowledge Management, Information Technology, and HRM.

Hesham Al-Ammal is the Dean of the College of Information Technology at the University of Bahrain. He received his PhD from the University of Warwick (Coventry, UK) in Computer Science and MSc from Louisiana State University (Baton Rouge, USA) and BSc from KFUPM (Dhahran, Saudi Arabia). His main research interests are in the analysis of algorithms, data mining, big data, and computer security. He is head of the Applied Data Analytics Group at the College of IT, University of Bahrain. Currently, Dr. Al-Ammal is a Senior Member of the Association for Computing Machinery (ACM). He has extensive experience with ABET accreditation, quality assurance reviews is a certified EFQM reviewer, and worked as a consultant with the Bahrain Center for Excellence. Dr. Al-Ammal was responsible for establishing the Quality Assurance and Accreditation Center at the University of Bahrain in 2009 and was part of the working groups that established the Bahraini National Qualifications Framework policies and standards.

Sara AbdulRahman Al-Bassam holds a BSc. in Management Information (MIS) from Gulf University for Science and Technology, Kuwait, MSc. in Innovation and Information Systems from Arabian Gulf University in the Kingdom of Bahrain her thesis titled "Investigating the Factors Related to Cybersecurity Awareness in the Bahraini Banking Sector" and Sara is a candidate for a Ph.D. in Innovation and Information Systems. Sara Carries many years of experience in Management Information Systems in Kuwaiti banks and government. Sara is a very active member of many professional associations such as ISACA Bahrain Chapter. Sara's current research area is in Cybersecurity in Banking and Financial Sector and currently published a paper in International Journal of Business Information Systems, Sara is also coauthor of a book published by IGA 2019 with Dr. Yousif Al-Basstaki and Prof. Adel Al-Alawi in Knowledge Management.

Abdalmuttaleb M. A. Musleh Al-Sartawi is the Chairperson of the Accounting and Economics department, Editor-in-Chief of the International Journal of Electronic Banking (IJEBank). He received his PhD in Accounting, from UBFS. He has presented and published many papers in regional and international conferences and journals. He has chaired as well as served as a member in various editorial boards and technical committees in international refereed journals and conferences. He is a member of several international organizations and associations such as the European Accountants Association (EAA), the Bahrain Management Society, the Middle East Economic Association (MEEA), the International Islamic Marketing Association (IIMA), the Arab Academy for Banking and Financial Sciences, the Palestinian Accounting Association, and the Palestinian Farmers Association.

Mohamed Ali Madan Maki is currently pursuing Master of Information Technology at Ahlia University. His research interests are Machine Learning, Security and Database Maintenance.

Afaf Buqawa is an Assistant professor in the Technology Management and Innovation Program, Arabian Gulf University, holds a doctorate in Information and Communications Technology from Brunel University - United Kingdom in 2015. She holds Master's degree in Technology Management from the Arabian Gulf University in 2004 and a BSc. in Computer Science from the University of Bahrain in 1995. Additionally, she also hold an accredited degree in Teaching and Learning from Brunel Centre for academic Excellence. Moreover, Dr. Afaf had an extensive experience extends to 19 years in the field of education and scientific research, where she worked as a lecturer at the University of Bahrain and in the College of Health Sciences before its joint the Arabian Gulf University in 2008. She has several positions in the academic and administrative field and presided over a number of administrative committees in College of Health Sciences. Dr. Afaf is the coordinator with the Quality Excellence center in AGU and with the industrial and government sector. Dr. Afaf participated in local, regional and international conferences; it also has attended several specialized workshops on leadership skills, RefWork, Nvivo program, Structural Equation Modeling (SEM). She organized a series of workshops and seminars on topics related to methods of scientific research, quantitative analysis and qualitative analysis, as well as Science, Technology and Innovation. She participated in organizing a number of events including the 'e-Learning 2.0' conference at Brunel University - United Kingdom. It is worth mentioning that Dr. Afaf is the only woman, Arab academy for winning a fellowship from Japanese Embassy and Japan Foundation in 2008, to study "The impact of ICT on Gender". Dr. Afaf have different research interests in Information and Technology areas including Web 2.0 Technologies and Learning, Social Media, Web 3.0, Cloud Computing, e commerce, e government, Innovation, e Learning 2.0.

Talal Mohammed Delaim is a senior information security specialist in the Information and eGovernment Authority (IGA). He has more than 10 years of IT experience. He has worked in a variety of roles, including network engineering, collaboration administration and security engineering. Talal holds a bachelor's degree in Business Information Systems from the University of Bahrain.

Fatiha Djemili received a Ph.D. degree in computer Science from the University Franche Comte of Besançon, France in 2007. She is currently an associate professor at UBMA and a member of the LRS research Laboratory. Her research interests include: Wireless networks, QoS support and energy control in adhoc and sensor networks.

Salim Ghanemi earned a PhD from Loughborough University, England in 1987, Parallel and Distributed Processing, Master Of Science with thesis from Aston University in Birmingham, England, BSc in Computer Science from Constantine University, Algeria, Currently, working as an Associate Professor at Badji-Mokhtar University, Annaba, Algeria, Previously, he worked as an Associate Professor abroad in Philadelphia University in Amman, Jordan and King Saud University, Riyadh, Saudi Arabia Kingdom.

Noora Janahi is an Accredited ISO9001:2018 Quality Management and Financial Auditor in Bahrain Ministry of Interior (MOI). She is an experienced audit professional serving in roles such as risk assessment, financial analysis and quality management. She has had success in managing internal audit projects along with strategic modelling and process re-engineering. She has been enrolled in several proficiency-training programs in the Ministry of Finance, National Audit Office and the Bahrain Institute of Banking and Finance. She is passionate about investigating and gathering clues related to certain work issues in order to convince employees at various levels to re-design their procedures accordingly. Maintaining high-audit quality and restoring trust in the audit function is a priority for Noora in order to build confidence and trust in the financial reports prepared by the Ministry. She has a Bachelor degree in Accounting and an MBA from Business Administration College in University of Bahrain, which is accredited by the Association to Advance Collegiate Schools of Business. Currently, she is preparing for a PhD degree in Innovation Management in the Arabian Gulf University. In her spare time she likes reading books and novels and doing exercises for nurturing both her mind and body.

Harsimranjit Kaur, PhD. (Electronics & Communication), M.Tech (Electronics & Communication), B. Tech (Electronics & Communication), teaching experience of more than 14 years, more than 30 publications in refereed journals and two patents in credit. Consultancy Area:Communication link designs, Circuit design and analysis, Control system design and analysis, Sensor design, Photonic Devices, Nano Photonics, Plasmonics, OFDM and Fiber-Optic Transmission Systems. Field of Specialization:Nano-Photonics and Integrated Optics, Plasmonics, Photonic Crystal cavities, Opto-Electronic Devices, Photonic Devices, Optical Communication Systems, Development and Performance analysis of Adaptive Optical Systems and Networks (Linear and Non-linear), Radio-over-Fiber links, Modulation formats, Optical Orthogonal Frequency Division Multiplexing, Wireless communications:

Digital Signal Processing for Wireless Channel Estimation, Equalization, Cognitive radio, Error control coding.

Leila Mechtri received her Ph.D degree in Computer Sciences from the University of Badji Mokhtar, Annaba, Algeria in 2018. Her research interests include: Wireless networks, Security, and intrusion detection and response.

Arpita Anshu Mehrotra earned her Bachelor and Master degrees in Commerce (India) and holds a Ph.D. in Commerce from Lucknow University, India. She is an Assistant Professor of Accounting, Finance, and Management at the Royal University For Women (RUW), Kingdom of Bahrain. Dr. Arpita is the Head of Banking & Finance Department at the College of Business & Financial Sciences, RUW. She is also the chairperson of the RUW Alumnae Committee and the co-chairperson of the Teaching and Learning committee at RUW. In her 15 years of experience, she has also served as the Director of Marketing and Academics in Mumbai School of Business, India. Dr. Arpita has been a leading academician with in-depth teaching experience in Financial Management, Accounting and Marketing both at the undergraduate and postgraduate levels. Further, she led a team that organized a national level seminar on "The Emerging Economies and their rising Global Influence" in India. The seminar witnessed the participation of professors, corporate dignitaries, and university level students. Dr. Arpita has also presented several research papers in Banking & Finance in International Conferences, wherein two of them she received the "best paper" award.

Ayşe Nalli is a professor and supervisor of doctoral and master students in the Department of Mathematics, Karabük University, Karabük, Turkey. She received her B.Sc, M. Sc and Ph. D in Mathematics from Selçuk University, Konya, Turkey. Her research interests cryptography, algebra, Diophantine equation and number theory.

Çağla Özyılmaz is a research assistant and a Ph. D student in the Department of Mathematics, 19 Mayıs University, Samsun, Turkey. She received her B.Sc and M. Sc in Mathematics from Uludağ University and Karabük University from Turkey, respectively. Her research interests cryptography, coding theory and number theory.

Wafa Mohamed Rafiq received her MSc in Information Technology and Computer Science from Ahlia University-Bahrain in 2019. She currently works as a Cyber Threat Analyst at CTM360.

Suresh Subramanian is Assistant Professor of Computer Science at Ahlia University Kingdom of Bahrain. His research interests are in the areas of Machine learning including the area of sentiment analysis, email security and deep learning techniques for analyzing the English and Arabic text. Published research papers in the renowned journals and the peer reviewer for international journals. Professional software developer using Microsoft technology such as .Net and Sql Server. Microsoft Certified Professional Developer (MCPD) in ASP .Net and Sharepoint and recently completed the Amazon Web Services (AWS) Certified Cloud Practitioner certification. Ardent toastmaster and social worker.

Index

A

Actual Usage 234, 248, 250
Ad-hoc On-demand Distance Vector (AODV) 112, 125, 129
Anomaly Detection 13, 99, 102, 109, 112-114, 116-117, 128, 146-151, 153, 155-158, 160-162
Ant Colony Optimization 10, 67, 70, 102
Artificial Neural Networks 1, 5-6, 41, 69, 84-86, 94-95, 131, 143
Asymmetric Cryptography 98, 163-164, 166
Attitude 216, 234-235, 238-239, 252
Authentication 10, 73, 75-79, 82, 84, 91-92, 95-97, 225, 277

B

Backpropagation Neural Network 131
Behavior 72, 150, 155, 160, 183-184, 200, 216, 230, 233-235, 238-240, 249, 251-252, 260-261, 272
Biometrics 73-75, 78-84, 95-96
Blackhole 46, 105, 112, 129
Botnets 153, 255, 263-264, 274

C

Ciphertext 163-165, 170, 176-177
Classification 6, 12, 45, 48-49, 54, 56, 60-62, 66-72, 75, 86, 91, 112, 129, 133, 139, 141-144, 155-156, 159-161, 183, 185

Combined

Combined Implementation 187, 192
Composite Number 167-168, 172, 178, 181
Corporate Governance 275, 280-282, 285-286, 288
Correlation Power Analysis 187, 190, 194
Critical Security Controls 196, 199-200, 209
Cryptography 11-12, 19, 41, 98, 125, 163-166, 168, 178-181, 195
Cyber Security 6, 16-19, 21, 40, 159, 196, 200, 219, 226-227, 229, 273, 275-280, 284, 286-288
Cyberattack 210, 224, 258, 260
Cybercrime 17, 210-211, 213-215, 219-225, 227-229, 233, 255-258, 260-269, 271-274
Cybercrime, Tools of 258, 263
Cybercriminals 44, 214-215, 255-256, 261-262, 264, 271
Cybersecurity 9, 146-147, 153, 207, 209-220, 222-228, 255-259, 265, 267, 270-271, 274-276, 279, 285-287
CyberTrust 196, 198, 201, 208
Cyberwarfare 210, 220, 223-224

D

Data Mining 43-45, 47-50, 54, 56, 66-72, 106, 147, 157-162
Differential Power Analysis 187-188, 190, 195
Drivers of Cybercrime 255, 258, 261
Dynamic Source Routing (DSR) 112, 129

E

Economics 261, 281, 285-286
Education 46, 70, 145, 206, 209, 218, 227, 231-233, 250-253, 258-259, 270-274, 286
E-Mail Bombs 263
E-Mail Spam 17, 41, 43-48, 50, 54-62, 65-72, 131-134, 136, 141-145, 160, 240, 252
Encryption 11-12, 21, 23-27, 29-32, 34-36, 38-41, 110, 116, 122, 164-165, 168, 173, 181-182, 193, 225, 270, 288
Evolutionary Computation 1, 5, 7-9, 19-20

F

False Negatives 43-45, 64, 129
False Positives 43-45, 47, 64, 114, 129
Fibonacci Sequence 163, 166-168, 170, 172, 179-181
Filter 43-45, 47, 56, 66, 68, 115, 131, 134, 263
Fraud 14, 132, 146-147, 149, 154, 157, 211, 261, 269
Fuzzy Systems 1, 3-5, 15-16, 18, 72

G

Generator 30-34, 38, 165-167, 172, 177
Genetic Algorithms 7-9, 20-21, 43, 67, 69
Government 16, 95, 196, 198, 200-209, 215-218, 222, 224, 227, 231, 233, 256, 274, 278-279
Graph Algorithms 146-147, 149
Grayhole 111, 129
Gulf Cooperation Council (GCC) 215-216, 231, 251, 253, 285

H

Hacking 6, 210-212, 222-223, 225, 228, 233, 255, 259, 269-270, 273-274
Hidden Weights 23

I

Information Systems 2, 199-200, 211, 216, 225, 227, 233, 238, 251-254, 258, 272, 287-288
Intention to Use 230, 232, 236, 239-242, 248-250
Internet Of Things (IoT) 126, 183, 193, 211, 214, 222, 226
Intrusion 6, 10-11, 13-15, 19, 22, 97-100, 102-110, 112-114, 116-117, 121-130, 146, 153, 162, 270, 279
Intrusion Detection 6, 10-11, 13-15, 19, 22, 97-100, 102-110, 112-114, 116-117, 121-130, 146, 153, 162, 270
Intrusion Detection System 6, 10, 100, 102-103, 109, 112, 114, 124-127, 130
IT Governance 199, 209, 275, 280-282, 284, 286-288

J

Jacobsthal Sequence 170-173, 176, 179

M

Machine Learning 1-2, 14, 20-22, 43, 47, 68-70, 132, 134, 143-144, 146-148, 150, 153-161
Misuse Detection 99, 114
Mobile Ad-Hoc Networks (MANET) 99, 103-107, 110-112, 114, 116-117, 120-130
Multi-agent System 101, 104, 113
Mutual Information Analysis 187, 191, 194-195

N

Naïve Bayes 71, 131, 137, 144, 155
Neural Network 5-7, 13, 20, 23-26, 35, 38-41, 70, 73, 76, 84, 86, 88, 91-95, 132, 138, 144-145, 148, 156

O

Odor 73, 75-79, 84-89, 91-96
Odor Sensing 73, 76, 84-86, 92, 94
One Way Function 165, 181

P

Particle Swarm Optimization 10-12, 21, 69-70, 145
Password Crackers 263-264, 269
Performance 4, 9-10, 18, 26, 59, 61, 68, 70, 102-103, 112, 116, 122-123, 125, 131-134, 138-139, 142-143, 156, 207, 210-211, 239, 275, 280-287
Phishing 17, 46, 131, 144, 255, 260, 269
Plaintext 30, 163-165, 167, 170, 177-179
Power Analysis Techniques 187, 193
Power Attacks 182, 185, 192-193
Power Fibonacci Sequence 163, 166-168, 170, 172, 179-180
Primitive Eleman 177
Private Key 165-167, 172, 177-179, 181
Public Key 164-167, 172, 177, 180-181
Public Key Cryptosystem 180-181

R

Receiver 24-25, 35, 44, 165, 177
Risk 9, 12, 16-17, 19, 115, 210, 213-215, 218-224, 226, 239, 252, 255-256, 265-266, 268, 270, 282, 287
Risk Factors 17

S

Security Framework 196, 198, 203, 208
Security Maturity Level 207
Security Risks 199, 201

Security Threats 17, 97, 121, 130, 132, 205, 210, 212, 218-219, 221
Sender 44, 46, 177-178, 277
Side Channel Attacks 182-183, 185, 192-195
Simple Power Analysis 187-188, 195
Software Agents 97, 99-100, 102, 105, 120, 123-124, 129
Spoofing 255, 269
Support Vector Machine (SVM) 71, 133, 136-137, 139-141, 143
Swarm Intelligence 1, 3-4, 10-11, 18-19, 117

T

Technology Acceptance Model (TAM) 230, 233-241, 248-249, 253
Theory of Reasoned Action (TRA) 230-231, 233-235, 239, 253
Trapdoor 165, 181
True Negatives 61, 130
True Positives 61, 130
Trustworthiness 112, 128, 230-232, 234-236, 239-241, 248-249

U

Universities 257-260, 267, 269-270, 273-274

W

Web 2.0 Technologies 230, 232-233, 249, 251
Wireless Networks 97-99, 114, 122, 124, 127

Ensure Quality Research is Introduced to the Academic Community

Become an IGI Global Reviewer for Authored Book Projects

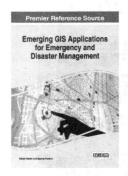

The overall success of an authored book project is dependent on quality and timely reviews.

In this competitive age of scholarly publishing, constructive and timely feedback significantly expedites the turnaround time of manuscripts from submission to acceptance, allowing the publication and discovery of forward-thinking research at a much more expeditious rate. Several IGI Global authored book projects are currently seeking highly-qualified experts in the field to fill vacancies on their respective editorial review boards:

Applications and Inquiries may be sent to:
development@igi-global.com

Applicants must have a doctorate (or an equivalent degree) as well as publishing and reviewing experience. Reviewers are asked to complete the open-ended evaluation questions with as much detail as possible in a timely, collegial, and constructive manner. All reviewers' tenures run for one-year terms on the editorial review boards and are expected to complete at least three reviews per term. Upon successful completion of this term, reviewers can be considered for an additional term.

If you have a colleague that may be interested in this opportunity, we encourage you to share this information with them.

IGI Global Proudly Partners With eContent Pro International

Receive a 25% Discount on all Editorial Services

Editorial Services

IGI Global expects all final manuscripts submitted for publication to be in their final form. This means they must be reviewed, revised, and professionally copy edited prior to their final submission. Not only does this support with accelerating the publication process, but it also ensures that the highest quality scholarly work can be disseminated.

English Language Copy Editing

Let eContent Pro International's expert copy editors perform edits on your manuscript to resolve spelling, punctuaion, grammar, syntax, flow, formatting issues and more.

Scientific and Scholarly Editing

Allow colleagues in your research area to examine the content of your manuscript and provide you with valuable feedback and suggestions before submission.

Figure, Table, Chart & Equation Conversions

Do you have poor quality figures? Do you need visual elements in your manuscript created or converted? A design expert can help!

Translation

Need your documjent translated into English? eContent Pro International's expert translators are fluent in English and more than 40 different languages.

Email: customerservice@econtentpro.com   **www.igi-global.com/editorial-service-partners**

Printed in the United States
By Bookmasters